PIETY PROMOTED,

IN A COLLECTION OF DYING SAYINGS

OF MANY OF THE PEOPLE CALLED

QUAKERS.

WITH AN APPENDIX.

PIETY PROMOTED,

IN A

COLLECTION OF DYING SAYINGS

OF MANY OF

THE PEOPLE CALLED QUAKERS:

WITH

A BRIEF ACCOUNT OF SOME OF THEIR LABOURS IN THE GOSPEL, AND SUFFERINGS FOR THE SAME.

A NEW AND COMPLETE EDITION,

COMPRISING THE ELEVEN PARTS HERETOFORE SEPARATELY PUBLISHED.

EDITED BY

WILLIAM EVANS AND THOMAS EVANS.

IN FOUR VOLUMES.

VOLUME FIRST.

PHILADELPHIA:

FOR SALE AT FRIENDS' BOOK STORE,

No. 84 ARCH STREET.

1854.

INDEX

TO

THE FIRST VOLUME.

INTRODUCTION

TO THE

AMERICAN EDITION.

THE present edition of Piety Promoted is believed to be the only one extant which contains all the parts of this interesting and valuable collection. Its contents extend over a period of more than one hundred and seventy years, and embrace concise accounts of the godly lives and peaceful deaths of above six hundred persons. Among these is to be found a great variety in age, condition in life, station in the Church, and growth in religious knowledge and experience; but they all agree in a concurrent testimony to the blessed effects of a religious life, and to the consolation and support it furnishes on a dying bed. They form but a small portion of the cloud of witnesses who have lived and died in the Christian principles and practices of the religious Society of Friends, and who have proved by happy experience their value and excellence, both as a rule for the government of conduct through life, and as a foundation on which they could safely rest their hopes for eternity, in the hours of sickness and of death.

A distinguishing trait in the character of the primitive Friends was the earnestness with which they enforced, both by example and precept, the indispensable obligation of a life of holiness in the fear of God. Many of them had been educated after the strictest manner, among the different religious societies then existing in Great Britain, and were esteemed for their piety before they joined in profession with Friends. When they left the societies with which they had been in communion, although they objected to the notion of three distinct and separate Persons in the Deity, to the use of the word Trinity as unscriptural, and some other of the school terms; yet it was not from any dissatisfaction or disunity with the scripture doctrine of the Holy Three that bear record in heaven, the eternal divinity of the Lord Jesus, his propitiatory sacrifice on the Cross, as the one universal offering for the sins of the whole world, or any of his offices for man's salvation. They declared their full faith in all these, and that they were seeking to attain to a more full and practical experience of the heart-changing efficacy of vital religion, free from those outward rites and impositions of men, on which they believed themselves, as well as others, to have been improperly relying, instead of pressing after the living virtue and power of the gospel, to redeem the soul from the pollution of sin, and to enable it to walk in newness of life.

While they felt the necessity of having a sound and firm belief in all the doctrines of the Christian religion, as set forth in the Holy Scriptures, they were also convinced that, unless this belief was carried out in the daily walk and conversation, and accompanied by those fruits of the Spirit which are the evidence of true faith, as well as the ornament of the Christian, it would be of little avail. Recognizing in its full extent the declaration, "Except a man be born again, he cannot see the kingdom of God," and the test laid down by the Saviour of men, "By their fruits shall ye know them," as well as his solemn words, "Not every one that saith unto me, Lord, Lord, shall enter into the kingdom of heaven, but he that doeth the will of my Father which is in heaven;" they were concerned to warn all against the delusive notion that men might live in sin, and in the indulgence of their carnal wills and appetites, and yet be saved by a professed dependence on what the Lord Jesus Christ has graciously done in his flesh for the redemption of mankind.

They were plain, practical, self-denying men and women, deeply and earnestly engaged to live and walk in the obedience of faith to all the requirements of the Divine law; and their minds being enlightened from on high to see the true nature and effects of the religion of the gospel, they apprehended that many of its professors were resting their hopes of salvation in a mere assent of the understanding to the truths recorded in the Scriptures, without bringing forth those "good works which were before ordained that we should walk in them." The inward life of righteousness in the daily fear of God being the great object of their earnest concern and engagement, both for themselves and others, they called on their hearers to come home into their own hearts, and examine, in the light which Christ gives, whether they were clean and pure, or defiled and unholy.

With no less earnestness they pressed upon all, the necessity of a close attention and obedience to the teachings of the Spirit of Truth in the heart, as the great enlightener and sanctifier of man, his guide in things pertaining to salvation, by which every one might come to see his own state, as seen by the Searcher of hearts, and be shown the way to come out of the thraldom of sin, into the glorious liberty of the children of God.

They invited men to come to and believe in Christ Jesus the Lord, not only as testified of in the Bible as the Redeemer, Propitiation, Mediator, and Intercessor with the Father for lost, fallen man; but also as he reveals himself in the heart by his Spirit, showing man his undone condition in the fall, and the only means by which he can be brought out of it, and be born again of the Spirit, and also as a swift witness against evil, and a comforter for well-doing. Esteeming this knowledge as the very essence of true religion, they dwelt much upon it in their ministry and writings, and, even in their dying sayings, enjoined it on their hearers as of the first importance to all who hoped for salvation.

The views we have here portrayed sometimes led the opponents of the early Friends to charge them with slighting or undervaluing, and with saying but little about, the work of the Lord Jesus Christ in his outward appearance for man's sake, and with depending for salvation on their own good works. Such charges they steadfastly denied, declaring that they had living faith in Him as the only Saviour and Redeemer, a reverent esteem for all his holy offices, and that they looked and hoped for salvation only in and through Him. That such was their religious belief is abundantly evident by their approved writings, a few extracts from which are here inserted.

George Fox, in a letter to the Governor and Council of Barbadoes, makes the following declaration of faith, viz.:

"Whereas, many scandalous lies and slanders have been cast upon us, to render us odious; as that we deny God, Christ Jesus, and the Scriptures of truth, &c.; this is to inform you, that all our books and declarations, which for these many years have been published to the world, clearly testify the contrary. Yet for your satisfaction, we now plainly and sincerely declare:

"That we own and believe in the Only, Wise, Omnipotent, and Everlasting God, the Creator of all things in Heaven and earth, and the Preserver of all that he hath made; who is God over all blessed for ever, to whom be all honour, glory, dominion, praise, and thanksgiving, both now and for evermore!

"And we own and believe in Jesus Christ, his beloved and only begotten Son, in whom he is well pleased, who was conceived by the Holy Ghost and born of the Virgin Mary; in whom we have redemption through his blood, even the forgiveness of sins; who is the express image of the invisible God, the First Born of every creature; by whom were all things created that are in Heaven and in earth, visible and invisible, whether they be thrones, dominions, principalities, or powers, all things were created by Him.

"And we own and believe, that he was made a sacrifice for sin, who knew no sin; neither was guile found in his mouth; that he was crucified for us, in the flesh, without the gates of Jerusalem; and that he was buried and rose again the third day, by the power of his Father, for our justification, and that he ascended up into Heaven, and now sitteth at the right hand of God.

"This Jesus, who was the foundation of the holy prophets and apostles, is our foundation; and we believe there is no other foundation to be laid, but that which is laid, even Christ Jesus, who tasted death for every man, shed his blood for all men; is the propitiation for our sins, and not for ours only, but also for the sins of the whole world: according as John the Baptist testified of him, when he said, 'Behold the Lamb of God that taketh away the sins of the world.' John i. 29.

"We believe that He alone is our Redeemer and Saviour, the Captain of our Salvation, who saves us from sin, as well as from Hell and the wrath to come, and destroys the devil and his works; He is the seed of the woman, that bruises the serpent's head, viz. Christ Jesus, the Alpha and Omega, the first and the last. He is, as the Scriptures of truth say of him, our wisdom, righteousness, justification and redemption; neither is there salvation in any other, for there is no other name under heaven, given among men, whereby we may be saved. He alone is the Shepherd and Bishop of our souls: He is our Prophet whom Moses long since testified of, saying, 'A Prophet shall the Lord your God raise up unto you, of your brethren like unto me; Him shall ye hear in all things, whatsoever He shall say unto you: and it shall come to pass that every soul that will not hear that Prophet, shall be destroyed from among the people.' Acts ii. 22, 23.

"He is now come in Spirit, 'and hath given us an understanding that we know him that is true.' He rules in our hearts by his law of love and life, and makes us free from the law of sin and death. We have no life but by him, for he is the quickening Spirit, the second Adam, the Lord from Heaven, by whose blood we are cleansed and our consciences sprinkled from dead works to serve the living God. He is our Mediator, who makes peace and reconciliation between God offended, and us offending. He being the Oath of God, the new covenant of light, life, grace and peace, the author and finisher of our faith. This Lord Jesus Christ, the Heavenly Man, the Immanuel, God with us, we all own and believe in; He whom the High Priest raged against, and said he had spoken blasphemy; whom the priests and elders of the Jews took counsel together against, and put to death; the same whom Judas betrayed for thirty pieces of silver, which the priests gave him, as a reward for his treason; who also gave large money to the soldiers, to broach a horrible lie, namely, that his disciples came and stole him away by night, whilst they slept. After he was risen from the dead, the history of the Acts of the Apostles sets forth, how the chief priests and elders persecuted the disciples of this Jesus, for preaching Christ and his resurrection. This, we say, is that Lord Jesus Christ, whom we own to be our life and salvation."

In his Answer to all such as falsely say the Quakers are no Christians, he says, viz.:

"We own the Father, the Son and the Holy Ghost, as the Apostles have declared.

"And it is the Spirit that beareth witness, because the Spirit is truth; for there are Three that bear record in Heaven, the Father, the Word, and the Holy Ghost, and these Three are one; and there are Three which bear record in earth, &c., *which we own*, 1 John, v. 6, 7. And now let none be offended, because we do not call them by those unscriptural names of Trinity, and Three Persons, which are not Scripture words; and so do falsely say, that we deny the Father, the Word, and the Holy Ghost, which Three are one that bear record in Heaven, &c., which Three we own with all our hearts, as the Apostle John did, and as all true Christians ever did, and now do; and if you say we are not Christians, because we do not call the Father, Son, and Holy Ghost, the Trinity, distinct and separate persons, then you may as well conclude that John was no Christian, who did not give the Father, Word, and Holy Ghost, these names.

"We believe concerning God the Father, Son, and Spirit, according to the testimony of the Holy Scripture, which we receive and embrace as the most authentic and perfect declaration of Christian faith, being indited by the Holy Spirit of God, that never errs: 1st, That there is one God and Father, of whom are all things; 2dly, That there is one Lord Jesus Christ, by whom all things were made, John i. and xvii. and Rom ix., who was glorified with the Father before the world began, who is God over all, blessed for ever, John xiv. That there is one Holy Spirit, the promise of the Father and the Son, and leader, and sanctifier, and comforter of his people, 1 John v. And we further believe, as the Holy Scriptures soundly and sufficiently express, that these Three are one, even the Father, the Word, and Spirit."

Robert Barclay in his Apology for the true Christian divinity, has these words, viz.:

"First then, as by the explanation of the former thesis appears, we renounce all natural power and ability in ourselves, in order to bring us out of our lost and fallen condition, and first nature; and confess, that as of ourselves we are able to do nothing that is good, so neither can we procure remission of sins or justification by any act of our own, so as to merit it, or draw it as a debt from God due unto us, but we acknowledge all to be of and from his love, which is the original and fundamental cause of our acceptance.

"Secondly: — God manifested this love towards us in the sending of his beloved Son, the Lord Jesus Christ, into the world; who gave himself for us, an offering and a sacrifice to God, for a sweet smelling savour; and having made peace through the blood of his cross, that he might reconcile us unto himself, and by the Eternal Spirit, offered himself without spot unto God, and suffered for our sins, the just for the unjust, that he might bring us unto God.

"Thirdly then, Forasmuch as all men who have come to man's estate, (the man Jesus only excepted,) have sinned, therefore all have need of this Saviour, to remove the wrath of God from them, due to their offences: in this respect he is truly said to have borne the iniquities of us all, in his body on the tree, and therefore is the only Mediator, having qualified the wrath of God towards us; so that our former sins stand not in our way, being, by virtue of his most satisfactory sacrifice, removed and pardoned. Neither do we think that remission of sins is to be expected, sought, or obtained, any other way, or by any works or sacrifice whatsoever, though, as has been said formerly, they may come to partake of this remission, that are ignorant of the history."

William Penn, in his Primitive Christianity Revived, has the following, viz.:

"We do believe, that Jesus Christ was our holy sacrifice,

atonement and propitiation; that he bore our iniquities, and that by his stripes we were healed of the wounds Adam gave us in his fall; and that God is just in forgiving true penitents upon the credit of that holy offering, Christ made of himself to God for us, and that what he did and suffered, satisfied and pleased God, and was for the sake of fallen man, that had displeased God: and that through the offering up of himself once for all, through the Eternal Spirit, he hath for ever perfected those, in all times, that were sanctified, who walked not after the flesh, but after the Spirit. Rom. viii. 1. Mark that.

"In short, justification consists of two parts, or hath a twofold consideration, viz., justification from the guilt of sin, and justification from the power and pollution of sin; and in this sense, justification gives a man a full and clear acceptance before God. For want of this latter part it is, that so many souls, religiously inclined, are often under doubts, scruples, and despondencies, notwithstanding all that their teachers tell them of the extent and efficacy of the first part of justification. And it is too general an unhappiness among the professors of Christianity, that they are apt to cloak their own active and passive disobedience, with the active and passive obedience of Christ. The first part of justification, we do reverently and humbly acknowledge, is only for the sake of the death and sufferings of Christ: nothing we can do, though by the operation of the Holy Spirit, being able to cancel old debts, or wipe out old scores: it is the power and efficacy of that propitiatory offering, upon faith and repentance, that justifies us from the sins that are past; and it is the power of Christ's spirit in our hearts, that purifies and makes us acceptable before God. For till the heart of man is purged from sin, God will never accept of it."

George Whitehead, writing in the name of the Society, makes the following declarations, viz.:

"The Holy Scripture Trinity, or Three thereby meant, we never questioned, but believed; as also the unity of Essence; that they are one substance, one Divine infinite Being, and also we question not, but sincerely believe, the relative properties of Father, Son, and Holy Ghost, according to Holy Scripture testimony, Matt. xxviii. 19, and that these Three are One. 1 John v. 7."

"We sincerely profess and declare in the sight of God and men, that we do faithfully believe and profess the divinity and humanity, or manhood, of our blessed Lord and Saviour Jesus Christ, the eternal Word of God: and that in the fulness of time he took flesh, being miraculously conceived by the Holy Ghost and born of the Virgin Mary, and suffered the cruel death of the cross, as an universal offering and sacrifice, both in his body and blood shed thereon, for the sins of the whole world; and was buried and rose again the third day, and visibly ascended (was seen in his ascending) and passed into heaven and glory; and that he ascended far above all heavens, that he might fill all things; and that by his suffering and sacrifice he hath obtained eternal redemption for us, which, through faith in his name and power, true repentance and conversion, we livingly receive and effectually partake of.

"That we are not pardoned, justified, redeemed or saved by our own righteousness, works, merits or deservings; but by the righteousness, merits and works of this our blessed Lord and Saviour Jesus Christ, being both imparted and imputed to us, as He is of God made unto us, wisdom, righteousness, sanctification and redemption. Our reconciliation, redemption, pardon, sanctification and justification, having respect both to his suffering death, and blood, upon the cross, as the one peace-offering and sacrifice, and as our High Priest; thereby making atonement and reconciliation for us, and giving himself a ransom for all mankind: and also to the effectual saving work of his grace and good Spirit within us, bringing us to experience true repentance, regeneration and the new birth, wherein we partake of the fellowship of Christ's sufferings and power of his resurrection. In which grace we ought to persevere in newness of life and faithful obedience unto him, unto the end, that we may be heirs of the eternal salvation, which Christ is the author of.

"We sincerely believe also, that the man Christ Jesus, is the only Mediator between God and men, our Intercessor and Advocate with the Father; and that he exerciseth his kingly office, and his priestly and prophetical office in his kingdom and church here on earth, wherein he governs, and plentifully affords both immediate inspiration and instruction to his faithful followers who walk in his light, to guide them into all truth; and he that hath not the Spirit of Christ is none of his.

"And that this same Lord Jesus Christ, who died for all men, enlightens every man coming into the world, and was and is the light of the world, the Way, the Truth, and the Life: and that the same Christ that was crucified and put to death as concerning the flesh, and quickened by the Spirit and power of the Father, he is inwardly revealed and spiritually in the hearts of true and spiritual believers by his holy Spirit, light, life and grace. And that therefore his coming and appearing outwardly in the flesh and inwardly in the Spirit, cannot render him two Christs, but one and the same very Christ of God, blessed for evermore."

Richard Claridge, in stating the belief of the Society of Friends on the doctrine of justification, uses the following language, viz.:

"In a word, if justification be considered in its full and just latitude, neither Christ's work without us, in the prepared body, nor his work within us, by his Holy Spirit, is to be excluded; for both have their place and service in our complete and absolute justification.

"By the propitiatory sacrifice of Christ without us, we, truly repenting and believing, are, through the mercy of God, justified from the imputations of sins and transgressions that are past, as though they had never been committed; and by the mighty work of Christ within us, the power, nature, and habits of sin are destroyed, that as sin once reigned unto death, even so now grace reigneth, through righteousness, unto eternal life, by Jesus Christ our Lord. And all this is effected, not by a bare or naked act of faith, separate from obedience; but in the obedience of faith, Christ being the author of eternal salvation to none but those that obey him."

In a pamphlet declaratory of the faith of the religious

Society of Friends, drawn up in the form of question and answer for the information of the Parliament of Great Britain, and published in the year 1689, we find the following, viz.:

"Question. What's your belief concerning the blessed Trinity, as our term is?

"Answer. Our belief is, that in the unity of the Godhead there is Father, Son, and Holy Ghost, being those Three Divine Witnesses that bear record in Heaven, the Father, the Word, and the Holy Spirit, and that these Three are one, according to Holy Scripture testimony."

"Question. Do you believe the divinity and humanity of Jesus Christ, the eternal Son of God, or that Jesus Christ is truly God and man?

"Answer. Yes, we verily believe that Jesus Christ is truly God and man, according as Holy Scripture testifies of Him; God over all, blessed for ever, the true God and eternal life; the one Mediator between God and men, even the Man Christ Jesus.

"Question. Do you believe and expect salvation and justification by the righteousness and merits of Jesus Christ, or by your own righteousness or works?

"Answer. By Jesus Christ, his righteousness, merits, and works, and not by our own: God is not indebted to us for our deservings, but we to him for his free grace in Christ Jesus, whereby we are saved through faith in him, not of ourselves, and by his grace enabled truly and acceptably to serve and follow him as he requires. He is our all in all, who worketh all in us that is well pleasing to God.

"Question. Do you believe remission of sins and redemption, through the sufferings, death, and blood of Christ?

"Answer. Yes; through faith in him, as he suffered and died for all men, gave himself a ransom for all; and his blood being shed for the remission of sins, so all they who sincerely believe and obey him, receive the benefits and blessed effects of his suffering and dying for them: they, by faith in his name, receive and partake of that eternal redemption which he hath obtained for us, who gave himself for us that he might redeem us from all iniquity: He died for our sins, and rose again for our justification; and if we walk in the light as he is in the light, we have fellowship one with another, and the blood of Jesus Christ his Son cleanseth us from all sin."

Another declaration of faith, dated in 1693, contains the following, viz.:

"We sincerely profess faith in God by his only begotten Son Jesus Christ, as being our light and life, our only way to the Father, and also our only Mediator and Advocate with the Father.

"That God created all things, he made the worlds, by his Son Jesus Christ, he being that powerful and living Word of God by whom all things were made; and that the Father, the Word, and Holy Spirit are one, in Divine Being inseparable; one true, living and eternal God, blessed for ever."

"Yet that this Word, or Son of God, in the fulness of time, took flesh, became perfect man, according to the flesh descended and came of the seed of Abraham and David, but was miraculously conceived by the Holy Ghost, and born of the Virgin Mary. And also further declared powerfully to be the Son of God, according to the Spirit of sanctification, by the resurrection from the dead.

"That in the Word, or Son of God, was life, and the same life was the light of men; and that he was that true light which enlightens every man coming into the world; and therefore that men are to believe in the light, that they may become the children of the light; hereby we believe in Christ the Son of God, as he is the light and life within us; and wherein we must needs have sincere respect and honour to, and belief in, Christ, as in his own unapproachable and incomprehensible glory and fulness; as he is the fountain of life and light, and giver thereof unto us; Christ, as in himself, and as in us, being not divided. And that as man, Christ died for our sins, rose again, and was received up into glory in the heavens. He having, in his dying for all, been that one great universal offering, and sacrifice for peace, atonement, and reconciliation between God and man; and he is the propitiation not for our sins only, but for the sins of the whole world. We were reconciled by his death, but saved by his life.

"That Jesus Christ, who sitteth at the right hand of the throne of the Majesty in the heavens, yet he is our King, High Priest, and Prophet, in his church, a Minister of the sanctuary, and of the true tabernacle which the Lord pitched, and not man. He is Intercessor and Advocate with the Father in heaven, and there appearing in the presence of God for us, being touched with the feeling of our infirmities, sufferings and sorrows. And also by his Spirit in our hearts, he maketh intercession according to the will of God, crying, Abba, Father."

"That divine honour and worship is due to the Son of God; and that he is in true faith to be prayed unto, and the name of the Lord Jesus Christ called upon, as the primitive Christians did, because of the glorious union or oneness of the Father and the Son; and that we cannot acceptably offer up prayers and praises to God, nor receive a gracious answer or blessing from God, but in and through his dear Son, Christ."

An opponent having charged the Society with being Socinians, and denying the divinity of Christ, &c., the following declaration of faith was drawn up, signed by thirty-two Friends, and presented to Parliament in 1693, viz.:

"1. That we sincerely believe and confess that Jesus of Nazareth, who was born of the Virgin Mary, is the true Messiah, the very Christ, the Son of the living God, to whom all the prophets gave witness. And we do highly value his death, sufferings, works, offices, and merits, for the redemption and salvation of mankind, together with his laws, doctrines, and ministry.

"2. That this very Christ of God, was and is the Lamb of God, that takes away the sins of the world, who was slain, was dead, and is alive, and lives for evermore, in his divine, eternal glory, dominion, and power, with the Father.

"3. That the Holy Scriptures of the Old and New Testament, are of divine authority, as being given by inspiration from God.

"4. And that magistracy or civil government, is God's ordinance, the good ends thereof being for the punishment of evil doers, and praise of them that do well.

"And we know of no other doctrine or principle, preached, maintained, or ever received among or by us, since we were a people, contrary to these before mentioned."

The doctrines set forth in the foregoing extracts, have been steadfastly maintained by the religious Society of Friends, down to the present day. In perusing the following pages the reader is requested to bear in mind the preceding observations and testimonies, and to remember that those pious persons whose dying sayings are there recorded, were firm believers in the Lord Jesus, both as he appeared at Jerusalem, and as he reveals himself in the heart by the Holy Spirit; and having through Him experienced redemption from sin, the great barrier between the soul and God, they dwelt chiefly on the necessity of regeneration and sanctification, knowing it was the thing most needed among the professors of the name of Christ; his divinity, and his offices in the work of salvation, being then seldom denied or called in question. Notwithstanding all they said of that freedom from sin and obedience unto righteousness, to which the Holy Scriptures bear such ample testimony, and of which they were made joyful partakers through submission to the power of the Holy Spirit working in them; still their dependence was on the Lord Jesus Christ, their Redeemer, Sanctifier, propitiation, and complete Saviour.

In putting forth a new edition of Piety Promoted, it is the desire of the publishers that the serious perusal of its instructive contents may incite the reader to follow the bright examples there exhibited of humble, self-denying, and consistent walking with God, that being found in the footsteps of Christ's companions, he also may receive the end of his faith, even the salvation of the soul.

William Evans.
Thomas Evans.

Philadelphia, 1st Month, 1854.

PIETY PROMOTED,

IN A COLLECTION OF DYING SAYINGS

OF MANY OF THE PEOPLE CALLED

QUAKERS;

WITH A BRIEF ACCOUNT OF SOME OF THEIR LABORS IN THE GOSPEL, AND SUFFERINGS FOR THE SAME.

THE FIRST PART.

BY JOHN TOMKINS.

"These all having obtained a good report, through faith.—Rest from their labors, and their works follow them.—Receiving the end of their faith, the salvation of their souls."—HEB. xi. 39. REV. xiv. 13. 1 PET. i. 9.

"Say to the righteous, that it shall be well with them, for they shall eat the fruit of their doings."—ISA. iii. 10.

TO THE READER.

I HERE present thee with a collection of the Dying Sayings of many persons who lived and died in faith and communion with the people called Quakers, some of whom it pleased God eminently to make use of, for the gathering of that people into a distinct fellowship and society from other professions in religion. And as God was pleased to call them forth into that work, so he supported them in it, and crowned their labours with success, and gave them not only peace in their own souls, but also full assurance of eternal life in the world to come.

And inasmuch as the Lord delivered these from evil works, and has preserved them unto his heavenly kingdom, and their names are written in his book, so with us they ought to be had in remembrance. And some "are worthy of double honour, especially they who laboured in the word and doctrine," for the service they have done in their generation, who "followed the Lord Jesus Christ, denied themselves, and took up their cross, despising the friendship and glory of this world." For what things were gain to them before, those they counted loss for Christ's sake, for whom they suffered the loss of all things, and counted them but dung that they might win Christ, and be found in him. Christ Jesus was the object of their faith, however the world, who were unworthy of them, represented and slandered them. It was in the name of Jesus Christ that they preached salvation, faith, and remission of sins; "for there is no other name under heaven given among men whereby we must be saved." This name, which they preached to others, their faith was in, and that gave them victory over the world, so that they became more than conquerors through Him that loved them. Great was their faith, zeal, and labour in the gospel, speaking in this name of the things of the kingdom of God, and spreading the same abroad throughout the nations, notwithstanding they were persecuted for their faithful testimony. For they made the like choice with Peter and John, to "hearken unto God rather than men," when they were commanded not to speak at all, nor teach in the name of Jesus; for they could not but speak the things which they had seen and heard.

Manifold were their sufferings for the same, as cutting off of ears, whipping and beating till their flesh was like a jelly, knocking down, and sore abuses in public places of worship, and in markets and streets; and many other evil intreatings, which but briefly to mention would make a large volume; besides long imprisonments under premunire, and otherwise, in nasty jails and dungeons, and holes, whereby many lost their lives.

Others were openly executed in New England, for no other offence than being Quakers, and preaching in the name of Jesus, contrary to the command of men. Yet they steadfastly kept the faith, like those faithful soldiers recorded in the 11th chapter of the Hebrews, who, though they were tortured, refused deliverance, it being not offered them upon terms agreeable to the will of God. God was with them, and bore up their spirits over all the wrath and cruelty of men, yea, and over death itself, and filled their souls so much with the joy of the Holy Ghost, that they declared, as they were led to the gallows, that it was the greatest joy and honour that they could enjoy in this world: farther saying, no eye could see, no ear could hear, no tongue could speak, nor heart could understand, the sweet incomes and refreshings of the Spirit of the Lord, which they at that time enjoyed. They also declared, that they suffered not as evil-doers, but as those who had testified and manifested the truth; putting the people in mind of the day of their visitation, and exhorting them to mind the light that was in them, which is the light of Christ; which they testified of, and were then going to seal [their testimony] with their blood; committing their cause to God, and their souls to the

Lord Jesus Christ; praying at the hour of death, in the words of the martyr Stephen, "Lord Jesus receive my soul."

So that it hath pleased God, not only to give some of his despised people, called Quakers, faith to believe in Christ Jesus, who is the "true light which lighteth every man that cometh into the world," but also hath given them power and ability to suffer for that blessed testimony which he hath again raised up in this latter age, and also to seal the same with their blood. This testimony is the same with John's testimony, who was sent from God, and did "bear witness of the light, that all men through him might believe. He was not that light, but was sent to bear witness of that light. That was the true light, which lighteth every man that cometh into the world."

It was the work of the primitive preachers "to turn people from darkness unto light, that they might receive the forgiveness of their sins, and an inheritance among them which are sanctified by faith which is in Christ." And it is the same doctrine which the great Lord of all, Jesus Christ himself, preached in the days of his flesh — "I am the light of the world: he that followeth me shall not walk in darkness, but shall have the light of life." And again — "While ye have the light, believe in the light, that ye may be the children of the light." This way the prophet Isaiah exhorted the house of Jacob to walk in, after he had foretold the peaceable effects that the word of the Lord should bring to pass in the nations in the latter days; "O, house of Jacob, come ye, and let us walk in the light of the Lord." To this agreeth the testimony of John the divine, "that the nations of them that are saved shall walk in the light of God and the Lamb:" and those who walk in the light, "the blood of Jesus Christ our Lord cleanseth them from all sin."

Reader, dost thou desire to die the death of the righteous, and have thy last end like unto his? Take then heed to this light that shineth in thy heart. "For God, who commanded light to shine out of darkness, hath shined in our hearts, to give the light of the knowledge of the glory of God, in the face of Jesus Christ." Here the apostle asserts, that the great love of God in Christ Jesus is manifested in man. Therefore, thou who desires to have peace with God on a dying bed, "believe in the light, so thou wilt become a child of the light," and wilt do the truth. He who doth truth, cometh to the light; he loves it, and desires to be tried by it; for, as our Lord said, he bringeth his deeds to the light, that his deeds may be manifest that they are wrought in God.

It was this experience that those of our friends, mentioned in the ensuing collection, attained unto. They believed in the light, they walked in the light, and, according to their several measures, they knew the blood of Jesus to cleanse their souls, and to "sprinkle their hearts from an evil conscience, and their bodies [to be] washed with pure water;" and when they came to die, they could declare their experience of the work of Christ in their souls, and that God had forgiven them their sins, for Christ's sake. They could say that there was no cloud in the way, God having fulfilled his promise of the latter days upon them, saying, "I will forgive their iniquity, and I will remember their sin no more. Their hearts did not condemn them, but their conscience did bear them witness, and their thoughts excused them." Blessed are they who arrive at this experience: they can say with the prophet, "The work of righteousness is peace, and the effect of righteousness, quietness and assurance for ever;" and with the apostle, "Glory, honour, and peace to every man that worketh good."

So that the terms on which we must inherit eternal life, are faith and obedience; and to that end the apostle declared, that "the mystery which was kept secret since the world began, is now made known to all nations for the obedience of faith." The same apostle saith, that "God will give to them, who by patient continuance in well-doing, seek for glory, honour, and immortality, eternal life: but unto them who obey not the truth, but obey unrighteousness, indignation and wrath." Therefore is Christ called the "Author of eternal salvation to all them that obey him."

Wouldst thou not be afraid to die? come then unto Christ,

believe in him, and obey him, and he will bring forth the work of righteousness in thee, the fruit whereof shall be peace and assurance for ever: Thus it is well with the righteous, even here, as the promise is, "It shall be well with him hereafter."

Help is laid upon Christ, and he is mighty to save. Receive him in the "manifestation of his holy Spirit, light and grace in thy heart," where thou wilt receive power to overcome sin in the bud, or first appearance of it; for our Lord has taught us that "out of the heart proceed evil thoughts, before they come into action, as murder, adultery, fornication, &c." So that if we keep to the cross of Christ, that will crucify the "flesh with the affections and lusts," and we shall be preserved from the consent to sin, and so from the guilt and wrath to come. This will make a sick-bed easy to us, death will be no terror to these. The sting thereof, which is sin, being taken away, it will be embraced as the door of entrance into eternal rest, as one of our friends said, viz. Judith Fell, being as it were her last words, 'This is the way to rest, this is the way to rest for ever.' And indeed many are the living testimonies which they have left behind, of the certainty of their knowledge that their Redeemer lived, and that there was a crown of life which God, the righteous judge, would give unto them, and they desired to be dissolved, that they might inherit the same, having already "their inheritance sealed unto them by the Spirit of God."

Some said as followeth, viz.:

Richard Hubberthorn: 'I know the ground of my salvation, and am satisfied for ever in my peace with the Lord God.'

Thomas Loe: 'I am near leaving you, I think; but as well in my spirit as I can desire. I bless the Lord, I never saw more of the glory of God than I have done this day;' and he sang, 'Glory, glory to the Lord for ever.'

Richard Farnsworth: 'I am filled with the love of God more than I can express; and God has really appeared for us. If God himself had come down and spoken as a man, he could not have spoken more clearly to us than he hath done, by many testimonies from heaven in his people.'

Josiah Coale: 'For my part, I have walked in faithfulness with the Lord, and I have thus far finished my testimony, and have peace with the Lord, and his majesty is with me, and his crown of life is upon me.'

Francis Howgill: 'As for me, I am well content to die; and if any enquire after my latter end, let them know that I die in the faith in which I lived and suffered for.'

William Bayley: 'Tell my friends, I go to my Father and to their Father, to my God and to their God; and let not my wife mourn in sorrow, for it is well with me.'

Sarah Beck: 'I feel sweet peace and great joy. O the joy that is laid up for the righteous: who would not fear the Lord! who would not be faithful!'

Yea, we find children crying Hosannah upon their dying beds. A young maid of sixteen or seventeen years old, viz. Elizabeth Braithwait, who was in prison for the truth, said, 'I had rather die here than in any other place. — I believe God will shortly set me free from these and all other bonds, over all their heads; and in his peace, in true patience I possess my soul, and am contented, if it be his will, to be dissolved.'

A child of nine years old, viz. Sarah Camm, said, 'My sins are forgiven me, and I shall have a resting-place in heaven. — The Lord hath redeemed my soul to praise his name on high for ever. Oh, praises, praises to the Lord, bless his holy name, O my soul.—It will be well with me and all that fear the Lord, for we shall have everlasting joy in heaven.'

One about twelve years old, viz. Mary Samm, said, 'I cannot but praise the name of the Lord whilst I have being. I do not know how to praise him enough. I shall die to-day, and my soul shall go to heavenly joy, and everlasting peace forevermore.'

A friend said, viz. Stephen Crisp: 'I have a full assurance of my peace with God in Christ Jesus; my integrity and uprightness of heart is known to the Lord, and I have peace and justification in Christ Jesus.'

I shall not insert more of this kind in the preface, for thou wilt find great plenty of such like testimonies behind; only to show how well it goes with the righteous here, and how desirable their latter end is, and what blessed fruits righteousness brings, and what assurance it giveth of everlasting life. Oh! that I could, by these good examples, prevail upon some to be wise and understand this, to consider their latter end; and that those who are young in years might not put off this consideration till old age, seeing that here are many instances of young persons, who, if they had forgotten the Lord in their early days, he would not have spoken peace to them therein.

This may be observed in the instance of Mary Harris, who, for a time, withstood the visitation of the Lord, and hardened her heart against his reproofs; though upon her sincere repentance and deep humiliation she was pulled as a brand out of the burning, and God showed mercy to her soul. But what said she, as a warning to others who lived in pleasures? 'See here, the Lord hath made these bones bare for my rebellion. Because I would not submit to his precious truth, he hath brought me to the dust, and I must lay down this body. Oh! do not you stand out; it will cost you dear if ever you find mercy.'

Let these things prevail upon some, to be warned by others' harms: did she repent upon a death-bed, and obtain mercy? Do not thou, therefore, presume to go on in sin, because grace has abounded unto her. God forbid: if thou put it off, thou dost not know but it may be too late. For thus, indeed, our Lord said, "Are there not twelve hours in the day?" And we read of many called at several hours, as the "third, fifth, ninth, and eleventh hour," but do not read of any called after the eleventh hour. It is dangerous standing idle till the last extremity, lest the long-suffering and forbearance of God should come to an end, and he should say of thee, as he said of Ephraim of old, who was joined to idols, "Let him alone."

Therefore, thou who hast not made thy peace with God, turn unto him with all thy heart, and meet him in the way of repentance; for, as the Psalmist saith, "The Lord is good, and ready to forgive, and plenteous in mercy unto all them that call upon him." But if thou choose thy own ways, and say,

'It is time enough;' remember what our Lord hath left for a caution to thee, concerning an evil servant who said in his heart, "My Lord delayeth his coming," so took liberty, fell to eating and drinking with the drunken, &c. "The Lord of that servant shall come in a day when he looketh not for him, and in an hour that he is not aware of, and shall cut him asunder, and appoint him his portion with the hypocrites: there shall be weeping and gnashing of teeth."

To prevent this, let none harden their hearts, but embrace the offers of grace in the present time, for the Lord will not always strive with men. Wherefore the Holy Ghost hath said, "To-day, if you will hear his voice, harden not your hearts, as in the provocation, in the day of temptation in the wilderness, when your fathers tempted God. Wherefore God was grieved with that generation, and said, They do always err in their hearts: so he sware in his wrath, they shall not enter into his rest." Read the third and fourth chapters to the Hebrews, and observe with what fervency that author labours with them to embrace the present visitation of God's love: for he saith, chap. iv, ver. 7, that God limiteth a certain day. Take heed, therefore, lest there be in any an evil heart of unbelief, in departing from the living God. "But," said he, "with whom was God grieved? Was it not with them that did sin? To whom sware he, that they should not enter into his rest, but to them that believed not?"

Oh! that the youth among us would lay these things to heart, and embrace the visitation of God to them, that they may not sin against God, and grieve him; nor, through unbelief, provoke him to exclude them from that rest which he hath prepared for his people. Those who are the offspring of believing parents have not those difficulties to pass through that their parents formerly had, in respect of making a profession of the blessed truth, as believed in by the people of God called Quakers. It is not now as it was in the days of Jael, when the highways were unoccupied, and the travellers walked in by-ways; but our fathers have gone before us through the gates, and "have prepared the way of the people: they have cast up the highway, and gathered (in a great measure) the stones out of it, and lifted up a standard for the people." These privileges have they procured for us, with the hazard of their lives, like the mighty men of old, who broke through the host of the Philistines, to fetch water for David out of the well of Bethlehem.

We have great cause to be careful, having reaped such benefits through their zeal and faithfulness, not to sit down at ease under the profession of the truth only, and content ourselves in that, but we must enter into the sheepfold by the Lord Jesus, who is the Shepherd of the sheep; and himself hath said, "I am the door; by me, if any man enter in, he shall be saved." When he putteth forth his own sheep, he goeth before them, and the sheep follow him. This is the right way to take up a profession of the true religion, to know the Lord to lead us forth, and in all things to practise from true conviction, and not from imitation or example only. It was this door that our fathers, and those who were in Christ before us, entered, and made a good confession before men, and were not ashamed of the cross of Christ, nor to bear his reproach, esteeming it greater riches than all the glory of the world.

Neither the frowns nor the flatteries of men could prevail upon them to sell the truth; no, it had cost them dear, even the loss of all; and they looked for nothing in this world to recompense them, but the "Peace of God, which passeth all understanding," and was the legacy our Lord left his disciples. And in Mat. xix. 29, it is called the "hundred-fold," which our Lord promised they should receive, who had forsaken anything for his name-sake, besides the inheritance of everlasting life. This reward was that which those our dear friends had in their prospect, which made many of them so cheerfully run through such great difficulties, and when the time came that their end was near, they did sing for joy.

This is also a confirmation to those who are yet behind, that these our friends, who worshipped God after the way that men call heresy, were accepted of him; and that the "anointing" (or grace of God) which we have received of Christ, and "abideth in us, teaching us of all things, is truth and is no lie," or delusion of the devil. It is that grace of God that bringeth salvation, spoken of in the second of Titus, which hath appeared to all men, and hath "taught them to deny ungodliness and worldly lusts, to live soberly, righteously and godly in this present world; looking for the blessed hope and glorious appearing of the great God, and our Saviour Jesus Christ, who gave himself for us, that he might redeem us from all iniquity, and purify to himself a peculiar people, zealous of good works.

These, I say, are a cloud of witnesses to the sufficiency of this holy anointing, and grace of God (which brings salvation to them who follow the teachings thereof), not only in their holy living, but patient sufferings, and joyful deaths. It has been a great strength and confirmation to me, to continue in the way of truth, as professed by the people called Quakers, to observe the hope that the righteous have in their latter end, both from what I have been an eye and ear witness of, as well as from the credible accounts I have seen of the peaceable and happy end of those, against whom the hatred of our adversaries hath been mostly bent, and against whom they have spoken all manner of evil. I have observed, that the Lord upheld them in their service, through all opposition, and stood by them to the end; as one of them declared, viz., Edward Burrough, even at the point of death, that the presence of the Lord was with him, and his life he felt to justify him: so that I have desired to follow their faith, "considering" (as the apostle saith) "the end of their conversation" which was peace with God through Jesus Christ; and that the Lord owned them, even to the last, though they were hated and persecuted of men. The experience of the prophet was their experience, who said, "For the Lord God will help me, therefore shall not I be confounded: therefore have I set my face as a flint, and I shall not be ashamed; he is near that justifieth me, who will contend with me?" And the Apostle saith, "Who shall lay anything to the charge of God's elect? It is God that justifieth." And if this light, spirit, grace, and anointing, be sufficient to lead some, it is able to lead all men, if they will follow the teachings thereof, into all truth.

The blessed hope of life and immortality, which is brought to light through the gospel, hath been the consolation of the children of God. For if their hope in Christ had been in this life only, they had been the most miserable, considering the many tribulations and persecutions that they have met with in this world. But we look for a better resurrection, when the hour shall come, "in the which, all that are in their graves shall hear his voice, and shall come forth; they that have done good, unto the resurrection of life; and they that have done evil, unto the resurrection of damnation." For we believe, that the dead shall be raised incorruptible, and we shall be changed: "So when this corruptible shall have put on incorruption, and this mortal shall have put on immortality, then shall be brought to pass the saying that is written, Death is swallowed up in victory." But we are cautious, and desire not to pry into those secret things which God hath seen meet, in his divine Wisdom, to reserve unto himself, remembering the reproof of the apostle to some in his day, who were questioning, "How are the dead raised, and with what bodies do they come?" Leaving it to the All-wise God to give us a body as it pleaseth him; since we are told, that "God will change our vile or low body, that it may be fashioned like unto Christ's glorious body, according to the working whereby he was able, even to subdue all things unto himself."

The design of the publication of this collection is, that godliness and righteousness may increase and prevail amongst men, that they may have "Fruit unto holiness, that their end may be everlasting life." Having in the course of my reading, met with many excellent sayings of our dying friends, that afforded me much satisfaction of mind, as aforesaid, I have collected some of them together for the benefit of others; knowing, that usually the words of dying persons make deeper impression on the minds of men, than words spoken at other times. I have contented myself, for the most part, with what I have by me, except the sayings of two or three, which I have inserted at the desire of their relations; for if I had collected all that I know of this kind, it would make a large volume: but here are witnesses enough to establish the truth, for I intend brevity. Some account I was obliged to give, concerning some of our dear friends' sufferings and labours in the gospel, the better to let the reader understand the weight, and indeed meaning, of some of their expressions, not with purpose to exalt men, but to exalt the great God, and his grace in Christ Jesus, by which they were what they were. The Lord give them that read, a heart to understand the things which belong to their peace; and if these shall be a means to stir up any to more faithfulness and diligence, in making their calling and election sure, my design is answered and God shall have the praise of all, who is worthy for ever.

JOHN TOMKINS.

LONDON the 28th of the Eleventh Month, 1701.

PIETY PROMOTED.

THE FIRST PART.

JAMES PARNELL, born at Retford, in Nottinghamshire, was a young man who received the blessed truth early. About the year 1654, he visited George Fox, who was at that time a prisoner in Carlisle, where he disputed with, and confuted, divers priests and others; and afterwards travelled southward, preaching truth, and disputing with its opposers in Huntingtonshire, the Isle of Ely, and some parts in Cambridgeshire, being then in the eighteenth year of his age.

He was the first called a Quaker who preached the gospel in the county of Essex, viz. at Stebbing, Felsted, Witham, Coggeshall, Halsted, &c., by whose ministry many thousands were turned to the Lord Jesus Christ.

About the middle of summer, 1655, he came to Colchester, and on the next day, being the first-day of the week, he preached the gospel to thousands of people in that town, first at his lodging, then at the public parish place of worship, and then in a great meeting appointed on purpose. After that he disputed with the town-lecturer, and with another priest in the French school. All this was in one day; in which the wisdom and patience of Christ appeared very gloriously, for the convincing of many who believed; and he put to silence, by his sound doctrine, the gainsayers. But some hardened their hearts, others beat him with their fists and staves, as particularly one, who struck him with a great staff as he came out of a steeple-house, and said, 'There, take that for Christ Jesus's sake:' to which he returned this answer, 'Friend, I do receive it for Jesus Christ his sake.' And many other intolerable affronts they offered him.

After he had laboured in Colchester, he went back to Coggeshall, where the professors had appointed a fast. From thence he was committed to Colchester Castle, and then had in irons to Chelmsford assizes, and there was fined forty pounds, and committed back again to Colchester. Here they suffered none to come to him but such as came to scorn, abuse, and beat him; not allowing him at some times to have food brought to him, and at other times took the food away when it was brought to him; and forced him to lie on the stones, which in wet seasons would run down with water. Then they put him into a hole in the wall, high from the ground, where the ladder was too short by six feet, not permitting his victuals to be brought to him, nor he to draw it up with a basket and a cord, which his friends had provided, but he must either come down by a rope, or famish in the hole.

After long suffering in this hole, it having no place either for the air or smoke to pass out, his limbs were so much benumbed, that one day climbing up to the top of the ladder, and catching at the rope with his other hand, he missed it, and fell from a very great height down upon the stones, whereby he was exceedingly wounded in his head and body, and taken up for dead. After that they put him into another little hole called the Oven (some ovens more broad), where they would not suffer him to have charcoal, neither would they accept of bail, nor body for body, which his friends offered, that he might recover of his hurts. One day, the door being open, he did but once get out of that nasty close hole, and walk for a little air into a stinking yard before the door, when the jailor came in a rage and locked up the hole, and shut him out in the yard all night, being in the coldest time in all the winter. By these cruelties he grew weaker and weaker, finding no mercy at the hands of his enemies. Near his departure he said (being all along borne up in much patience), 'Here I die innocently:'

and further said, 'Now I must go:' and turned his head, and said, 'This death I must die:' 'I have seen glorious things;' and to his friends about him, 'Will you hold me?' One of them said, 'Dear heart, we will not hold thee.' Then he said, 'Now I will go:' and stretching himself out, fell into a sweet sleep for about an hour (as he often had said, one hour's sleep would cure him of all), and so drew breath no more.

He died about the nineteenth year of his age, in the year 1656.

JOHN CAMM, born at Cam's-gill, within the barony of Kendal, in the county of Westmoreland, was a man inclined to religion of the strictest sort, from his childhood. He, with many more, who sought after the best things, separated themselves from the national worship of those times, and met apart at a place called Firbank chapel, and other places, among which people he was sometimes a preacher. But in the year 1652, he was (with many hundreds of the congregation, among whom were John Audland, Francis Howgill, Edward Burrough, and Richard Hubberthorn) convinced of the truth, by the preaching of that servant of the Lord, George Fox. He submitted to the mighty power of the Lord, and the operation of his blessed Spirit in his heart, and was made willing to take up the cross, and forsake the glory and friendship of the world; and after a day of great trouble, through the spirit of judgment and burning, wherein he found the old heavens and earth to pass away; even as a prepared vessel, the Lord filled him with his power, and put his word into his mouth, and sent him forth to publish the same; and he was obedient and travelled into all the northern counties, to the borders of Scotland, and from thence to London, in company with Francis Howgill, with a message from the Lord to Oliver Cromwell, then protector.

After his return from London into the north he, with John Audland, Francis Howgill, Edward Burrough, and Richard Hubberthorn, went southward; John Camm and Edward Burrough travelling through the middle of the nation, the others through other parts, and they met together at London, with several other of their brethren.

After some time, John Camm and John Audland were called towards Bristol, where an effectual door was opened to them, and many hundreds were, by their word and testimony which they published, turned to God.

John Camm was naturally of a weak constitution of body, and by the daily travels that he underwent, spent his strength exceedingly, and had a violent cough a considerable time before his death. He was a man richly furnished with the gifts of the Holy Spirit, patient in exercises, grave in behaviour, profound in judgment, quick in discerning, and a sharp reprover of wickedness, hypocrisy, and of disorderly walkers in the profession of truth. Unity of brethren was his soul's delight; his ministry weighty and deep, not pleasant to itching ears, but reached the witness of God; careful not to make the gospel chargeable, having an estate of his own; and often suffered the spoiling of his goods joyfully, in a faithful testimony against tithes.

He would often call his children together, and exhort them to fear the Lord; and would wonderfully praise God for his goodness, counting his bodily weakness an happiness, being sanctified unto him by that word which had sanctified his soul; under the sense of which he would say, 'How great a benefit do I enjoy beyond many. I have such a large time of preparation for death, being daily dying, that I may live forever with my God in that kingdom that is unspeakably full of glory. My outward man daily wastes and moulders down, and draws towards its place and centre; but my inward man revives and mounts upwards towards its place and habitation in the heavens.'

The morning he departed this life, he called his wife, children and family, and gave them seasonable instruction to love the Lord, and his way, and truth, and to walk in the same, saying, his glass was run; the time of his departure was come; he was to enter into everlasting ease, joy and rest; charging them all to be patient and content in parting with him. So, presently fainting, he passed quietly away as into a sweet sleep, whereupon some about him did weep aloud; at which he was awakened as out of a sleep, and desired to be helped a little upon his bed, saying, 'My dear hearts you have wronged me, and disturbed me, for I was at sweet rest. You should not passionately sorrow for my departure. This house of clay must go to its place, but this soul and spirit is to be gathered up to the Lord, to live with him for ever, where we shall meet with everlasting joy.' So, again taking his leave of every one of them, charging them to be content with his departure, he lay down, and in a little time departed this life.

He was convinced in 1652, and died in 1656, being aged about fifty-two years.

WILLIAM ROBINSON, of London, merchant, and Marmaduke Stevenson, of Yorkshire, husbandman, both suffered martyrdom for their obedience to God, in bearing their testimony to his blessed truth in New England, on the 27th of the Eighth month, 1659.

When they were brought before the court of Boston in New England, on the 20th of the said month, the governor said to them, 'We have made laws, and endeavoured several ways to keep you from us, and neither whipping, nor imprisonments, nor cutting off ears, nor banishment upon pain of death, will keep you from among us. Give ear, and hearken to your sentence: You shall go to the place from whence you came, and from thence to the gallows, and be hanged till you are dead.'

Accordingly the said William Robinson and Marmaduke Stevenson, with Mary Dyer, were taken out of prison; who having parted with their friends in prison, full of the joy of the Lord, who had counted them worthy to suffer for his name, and having embraced each other with fervency of love and gladness of heart, in peace with God, were led to the place of execution the back way, lest their innocent sufferings should too much affect the people; and when they attempted to speak, their cruel persecutors caused the drums to be beaten to drown their voice.

One of their chief preachers, meeting the said sufferers going to be executed, said tauntingly, and shaking his head in a scoffing manner, 'Shall such jacks as you come in before authority, with your hats on?' To which William Robinson said to the people, 'Mind you, it is for not putting off our hats that we are put to death.' When he was upon the ladder, he spoke to the people thus; that they suffered not as evil-doers, but as those who testified and manifested the truth, and that this was the day of their visitation; and therefore desired them to mind the light that was in them, which was the Light of Christ; of which they testified, and were now going to seal it with their blood. So the executioner put William Robinson to death, and afterwards Marmaduke Stevenson, who both of them died full of the joy of the Lord, and stood fast in him, sealing their testimony with their blood, their countenances not changing when the halters were about their necks.

Their enemies not permitting their bodies to be taken down, cut them down, and the fall broke the skull of William Robinson; and with their knives they ripped off their shirts, and dragged their naked bodies into a hole, not suffering their friends to take them away and bury them; and afterwards when a friend brought pales to inclose the ground, that the brute beasts might not prey on their bodies, it was denied him; and their bodies were left in a pit in the open field, which was soon covered with water.

Here follows a copy of William Robinson's paper, offered to the court, before he was sentenced to death, concerning their coming into those parts, for which they were put to death; which was denied by the governor to be read.

'On the 8th day of the Eighth month, 1659, in the after part of the day, in travelling betwixt Newport in Rhode Island and Daniel Gould's house, with my dear brother Christopher Holder, the Word of the Lord came expressly to me, which did fill me immediately with life and power, and heavenly love, by which he constrained me, and commanded me to pass to the town of Boston, my life to lay down in his will, for the accomplishing of his service, that he had there to perform at the day appointed. To which heavenly voice I presently yielded obedience, not questioning the Lord how he would bring the thing to pass, being I was a child, and obedience was demanded of me by the Lord, who filled me with living strength and power from his heavenly presence, which at that time did mightily overshadow me, and my life at that time did say amen to what the Lord required of me, and had commanded me to do, and willingly I was given up from that time to this day, the will of the Lord to do and perform, whatever became of my body.

'For the Lord had said unto me, My soul shall live in everlasting peace, and my life shall enter into rest, for being obedient to the God of my life. I being a child, durst not question the Lord in the least, but rather willing to lay down my life than to bring dishonour to the Lord. And as the Lord made me willing, dealing gently and kindly with me, as a tender father by a faithful child whom he tenderly loves, so the Lord did deal with me, in ministering his life unto me, which gave and gives me strength to perform what the Lord required of me. And still as I did and do stand in need, he ministered and ministereth more strength and virtue, and heavenly power and wisdom, whereby I was and am made strong in God, not fearing what man shall be suffered to do unto me, being filled with heavenly courage, which is meekness and innocence, for the cause is the Lord's that we go in, and the battle is the Lord's; and thus saith the Lord of Hosts, the mighty and the terrible God, "Not by strength, nor by might, nor by power of man, but by my Spirit," saith the Lord of Hosts. I will perform what my mouth hath spoken, through my servants, whom I have chosen; mine elect, in whom my soul delighteth."

'Friends, the God of my life, and the God of the whole earth, did lay this thing upon me, for which I now suffer bonds near unto death. He, by his Almighty power, and everlasting love, constrained me, and laid this thing upon me, and truly I could not deny the Lord, much less resist the Holy One of Israel. Therefore all who are ignorant of the motion of the Lord in the inward parts, be not hasty in judging in this matter, lest ye speak evil of the thing ye know not. Of a truth, the Lord God of heaven and earth commanded me by his spirit, and spake unto me by his Son, whom he hath made heir of all things, and in his life I live, and in it I shall depart this earthly tabernacle, if unmerciful men be suffered to take it from me.

'Herein I rejoice, that the Lord is with me, the Ancient of Days, the Life of the suffering Seed, for which I am freely given up, and singly do I stand in the will of God; for to me to live is Christ, and to die is gain. Truly I have great desire and will herein, knowing that the Lord is with me, whatever ignorant men shall be able to say against me; for the witness of the spirit I have received, and the presence of the Lord and his heavenly life accompany me, so that I can say in truth, and from an upright heart, Blessed be the Lord God of my life, who hath counted me worthy, and called me hereunto, to bear my testimony against ungodly and unrighteous men, who seek to take away the life of the righteous without a cause; as the rulers of Massachusetts Bay do intend, if the Lord stop them not from their intent.

'Oh! hear ye rulers, and give ear and listen, all ye that have any hand herein to put the innocent to death, for in the name, and fear, and dread of the Lord God, I here declare the cause of my staying here amongst you, and continuing in the jurisdiction after there was a sentence of banishment upon pain of death, as ye said, pronounced against me without a just cause; as ye all know that we that were banished committed nothing worthy of banishment, nor of any punishment, much less banishment upon pain of death. And now, ye rulers, ye do intend to put me to death, and my companion, unto whom the word of the Lord came, saying, Go to Boston with thy brother William Robinson. Unto which command he was obedient, who had said unto him, he had a great work for him to do.

'This thing is now seen, and the Lord is now doing it; and it is in obedience to the Lord, the God of the whole earth, that we continued amongst you, and that we came to the town of Boston again, in obedience to the Lord, the Creator of heaven and earth, in whose hand your breath is. Will ye put us to death for obeying the Lord, the God of the whole earth? Well, if ye do this act, and put us to death, know this, and be it known unto you all, ye rulers and people within this jurisdiction, that whosoever hath an hand therein will be guilty of innocent blood. Not only upon yourselves will ye bring innocent blood, but upon the town, and the inhabitants thereof, and everywhere within this jurisdiction, that had the least hand therein. Therefore be instructed, ye rulers of this land, and take warning betimes, and learn wisdom, before it be hid from your eyes.

'Written in the common jail the 19th of the Eighth month, 1659, in Boston, by one who feareth the Lord, who is by ignorant people called a Quaker, and unto such am I only known by the name of William Robinson, yet a new name have I received, which such know not.'

Here followeth a copy of Marmaduke Stevenson's paper of his call to the work and service of the Lord, given forth by him a little before he was put to death, and after he had received his sentence.

'In the beginning of the year 1655, I was at the plough in the east parts of Yorkshire, in old England, near the place where my outward being was. And as I walked after the plough, I was filled with the love and presence of the living God, which did ravish my heart when I felt it; for it did increase and abound in me like a living stream, so did the life and love of God run through me like a precious ointment giving a pleasant smell, which made me to stand still. As I stood a little still, with my heart and mind stayed upon the Lord, the word of the Lord came to me in a still small voice, which I did hear perfectly, saying to me, in the secret of my heart and conscience, I have ordained thee a prophet unto the nations. At the hearing of the word of the Lord I was put to a stand, seeing that I was but a child for such a weighty matter.

So, at the time appointed, Barbadoes was set before me, unto which I was required of the Lord to go, and leave my dear and loving wife, and tender children; for the Lord said unto me, immediately by his Spirit, that he would be as an husband to my wife, and as a father to my children, and they should not want in my absence, for he would provide for them when I was gone. I believed the Lord would perform what he had spoken, because I was made willing to give up myself to his work and service, to leave all and follow him, whose presence and life is with me, where I rest in peace and quietness of spirit, with my dear brother, under the shadow of His wings, who hath made us willing to lay down our lives for his name's sake, if unmerciful men be suffered to take them from us; and if they do, we know we shall have peace and rest with the Lord for ever in his holy habitation, when they shall have torment night and day.

'In obedience to the living God, I made preparation to pass to Barbadoes in the Fourth month, 1658. After some time that I had been on the said island in the service of God, I heard that New England had made a law to put the servants of the living God to death, if they returned after they were sentenced away, which did come near me at that time; and as I considered the thing, and pondered it in my heart, immediately came the word of the Lord unto me, saying, 'Thou knowest not but thou mayst go thither.' I kept this word in my heart, and did not declare it to any until the time appointed. So after that, a vessel was got ready for Rhode Island, which I passed in.

'After a little time that I had been there, visiting the seed which the Lord had blessed, the word of the Lord came to me, saying, 'Go to Boston with thy brother William Robinson;' and at his command I was obedient, and gave up to his will, that so his work and service may be accomplished: for he had said unto me, that he had a great work for me to do, which is now come to pass. For yielding obedience to, and for obeying the voice and command of the Everlasting God, which created heaven and earth, and the fountains of waters, do I, with my dear brother, suffer outward bonds, near unto death.

And this is given forth to be upon record, that all people may know who hear it, that we came not in our own wills, but in the will of God.

'Given forth by me, who am known to men by the name of Marmaduke Stevenson; but have a new name given me, which the world knows not of, written in the Book of Life.'

Written in Boston Prison, in the Eighth Month, 1659.

MARY DYER, a faithful woman, fearing God, the wife of an husband of good estate in Rhode Island, and mother of several children, was also condemned to death at the same time with William Robinson and Marmaduke Stevenson. When she received the sentence, that she should be hanged at the place of execution till she was dead, she replied, 'The will of the Lord be done.' Then the governor saying take her away, she answered, 'Yea, joyfully shall I go;' and was led to the place of execution between her two fellow-sufferers, William Robinson and Marmaduke Stevenson. One of her enemies upbraiding her therewith, she replied, 'It is the greatest joy and honour I can enjoy in this world;' adding these words, 'No eye can see, no ear can hear, no tongue can speak, no heart can understand, the sweet incomes and refreshings of the spirit of the Lord which I now enjoy.' Having seen her two friends die before her face, and giving herself up to die also, her hands and feet being tied, and her face covered, with the halter about her neck, she was even with the Lord in joy and peace, an order came for her reprieve, upon the petition of her son; which being read, and the halter taken off, and she loosed, was desired to come down; but she tarrying to wait upon the Lord to know his mind, they pulled her down with the ladder, and had her to prison, and next morning she was carried out of the country towards Rhode Island. And as a lively testimony of the virtue of truth, which can look death in the face, and to be a record to future generations, how truth hath conquered in a woman, is here inserted Mary Dyer's letter, which she wrote the day after her reprieve, as followeth:

'The 28th of the Eighth Month, 1659.

'Once more to the general court assembled in Boston, speaks Mary Dyer, even as before. My life is not accepted, neither availeth me, in comparison of the lives and liberty of the truth and servants of the living God, for which, in the bowels of love and meekness I sought you; yet, nevertheless, with wicked hands have you put two of them to death, which makes me to feel, that the mercies of the wicked are cruelty. I rather choose to die than to live, as from you, as guilty of their innocent blood.

'Therefore, seeing my request is hindered, I leave you to the righteous Judge and searcher of all hearts, who with the pure measure of light he hath given every man to profit withal, will in his due time let you see whose servants you are, and of whom you have taken counsel, which I desire you to search into. But all his counsel hath been slighted, and you would none of his reproofs. Read your portion; for verily the night cometh on apace, wherein no man can work, in which you shall assuredly fall to your own master. In obedience to the Lord, whom I serve with my spirit, and in pity to your souls, which you neither know nor pity, I can do no less than once more warn you to put away the evil of your doings, and kiss the Son, the light in you, before his wrath be kindled in you. For where it is, nothing without you can help or deliver you out of his hand at all, and if these things be not so, then say, there hath been no prophet from the Lord amongst you: though we be nothing, yet it is his pleasure, by things that are not, to bring to nought things that are.

'When I heard your last order read, it was a disturbance to me, that was so freely offering up my life to him that gave it me, and sent me hither so to do. This obedience being his own work, he gloriously accompanied with his presence, and peace, and love in me, in which I rested from my labour, till by your order and the people I was so far disturbed, that I could not retain any more of the words thereof, than that I should return to prison and there remain forty and eight hours, to which I submitted, finding nothing from the Lord to the contrary, that I may know what his pleasure and counsel is concerning me, on whom I wait therefor; for he is my life, and length of my days; and as I said before, I came at his command, and go at his command. MARY DYER.'

Mary Dyer being thus freed as aforesaid, returned to Rhode Island, where her husband and children dwelt, and after some stay with them, she went towards Long Island, and was at Shelter Island, and had good service for the Lord; where she thought she might pass home to Rhode Island: but she was moved of the Lord to return to Boston again, and she came thither on the 21st of the Third month, 1660. On the 31st of the same she was sent for to the general court, where the governor said to her, 'Are you the same Mary Dyer that was here the last general sessions?'

M. Dyer. I am the same Mary Dyer.

Governor. You will own yourself a Quaker, will you not?

M. Dyer. I own myself to be so reproachfully called.

Governor. The sentence was passed upon you the last general court, and now likewise; you must return to the prison from whence you came, and there remain till to-morrow at nine o'clock, then from thence you must go to the gallows, and there be hanged till you are dead.

M. Dyer. This is no more than what thou saidst before.

Governor. And now it is to be executed; therefore prepare yourself to-morrow at nine o'clock.

M. Dyer. I came in obedience to the will of God to the last general court, desiring you to repeal your unrighteous laws of banishment upon pain of death, and that same is my work now, and earnest request, because you refused before to grant me my request; although I told you, that if you refused to repeal them, the Lord would send other of his servants to witness against them.

Governor. Are you a prophet?

4*

M. Dyer. I spoke the words that the Lord spake in me.

And beginning to speak of the call of the Lord to her, the governor said, 'Away with her, away with her.' So she was had to prison, and kept close till the next day at the ninth hour, when the marshal called hastily for her; to whom she mildly replied, 'Stay a little; I shall be ready presently.' But he cruelly replied, he could not wait upon her. So he had her away with a company of soldiers, beating a drum before and behind, that they might not hear her speak; and being upon the ladder at the place of execution, some said to her, if she would return, she might save herself.

M. Dyer. Nay, I cannot; for in obedience to the will of the Lord God I came, and in his will I abide faithful unto death.

A priest called out to her, 'Mary Dyer, O repent, repent.'

M. Dyer. Nay, man; I am not now to repent.

One said that she should say that she had been in paradise.

M. Dyer. Yes, I have been in paradise several days.

And more she spoke concerning her eternal happiness. So, sweetly and cheerfully in the Lord she finished her testimony, and died a faithful martyr of Jesus Christ, the 1st of the Fourth month, 1660.*

Here followeth the copy of a letter that Mary Dyer sent to the rulers of Boston, after she had received sentence of death.

'To the General Court in Boston.

'Whereas I am by many charged with guiltiness of my own blood: if you mean in my coming to Boston, I am therein clear, and justified by the Lord, in whose will I came, who will require my blood of you be sure, who have made a law to take away the lives of the innocent servants of God, if they come among you, who are called by you cursed Quakers; although I say, and am a living witness for them and the Lord, that he hath blessed them, and sent them unto you. Therefore be not found fighters against God, but let my counsel and request be accepted with you, to repeal all such laws, that the truth and

* See New England Judged; containing an account of the persecutions and martyrdom of the people called Quakers.

servants of the Lord may have free passage amongst you, and you be kept from shedding innocent blood, which I know there are many among you would not do, if they knew it so to be. Nor can the enemy, that stirreth you up thus to destroy this holy seed, in any measure countervail the great damage that you will by thus doing procure.

'Therefore, seeing the Lord hath not hid it from me, it lieth upon me, in love to your souls, thus to persuade you. I have no self-ends, the Lord knoweth, for if my life were freely granted by you, it would not avail me, nor could I expect it of you, so long as I should daily hear or see the sufferings of these people, my dear brethren, with whom my life is bound up, as I have done these two years; and now it is like to increase even unto death, for no evil doing, but coming among you. Were ever the like laws heard of among a people that profess Christ come in the flesh? Have such no other weapons but such laws to fight with against spiritual wickedness, as you call it? Woe is me for you! Of whom take you counsel? Search with the light of Christ in you, and it will show you of whom, as it hath done me, and many more, who have been disobedient and deceived, as now you are. As you come into this light, and obey what is made manifest to you therein, you will not repent that you were kept from shedding blood, though by a woman.

'It is not mine own life I seek (for I choose rather to suffer with the people of God, than to enjoy the pleasures of Egypt), but the life of the seed, which I know the Lord hath blessed; and therefore the enemy thus vehemently seeks to destroy the life thereof, as in all ages he ever did. Oh! hearken not unto him, I beseech you, for the seed's sake, which is one in all, and is dear in the sight of God, which they that touch, touch the apple of his eye, and cannot escape his wrath; whereof I having felt, cannot but persuade all men that I have to do withal; especially you, who name the name of Christ, to depart from such iniquity as shedding blood, even of the saints of the Most High.

'Let my request have as much acceptance with you, if you be Christians, as Esther's had with Ahasuerus, whose relation is short of that which is between Christians, and my request is the same that her's was; and he said not that he had made a law, and it would be dishonourable for him to revoke it; but when he understood that these people were so prized by her (as in truth these are to me) you may see what he did for her. Therefore I leave these lines with you, appealing to the faithful and true witness of God, which is one in all consciences, before whom we must all appear, with whom I shall eternally rest, in everlasting joy and peace, whether you will hear or forbear: with him is my reward, with whom to live is my joy, and to die is my gain, though I had not had your forty-eight hours' warning, for the preparation to the death of Mary Dyer.

'And know this also, that if through the enmity, you shall declare yourself worse than Ahasuerus, and confirm your law, though it be but the taking away the life of one of us, that the Lord will overthrow both your law and you by his righteous judgments and plagues poured justly upon you, who now, whilst you are warned thereof, and tenderly sought unto, may avoid the one by removing the other.

'If you neither hear nor obey the Lord nor his servants, yet will he send more of his servants among you, so that your ends shall be frustrated, that think to restrain them you call cursed Quakers, from coming among you, by any thing you can do to them. Yea, verily, he hath a seed here among you, from whom we have suffered all this while, and yet suffer, whom the Lord of the harvest will send forth more labourers to gather out of the mouths of the devourers of all sorts, into his fold, where he will lead them into fresh pastures, even the paths of righteousness, for his name's sake. Oh! let none of you put this day far from you, which, verily, in the light of the Lord, I see approaching, even to many in and about Boston, which is the bitterest and darkest professing place, and so to continue so long as you have done, that ever I heard of. Let the time past therefore suffice for such a profession as brings forth such fruits as these laws are.

In love and in the spirit of meekness, I again beseech you, for I have no enmity to the persons of any; but you shall know that God will not be mocked, but what you sow, that shall you reap from him, that will render to every one according to the deeds done in the body, whether good or evil; even so be it, saith Mary Dyer.'

WILLIAM LEDDRA, an inhabitant of the island of Barbadoes, who came also into the jurisdiction of bloody Boston in New England, to visit his friends who lay under great sufferings in prison, was himself cast into prison, and locked in chains, with a log of wood tied to him, lying down and rising up with the same, during a miserably cold winter, in an open prison, till the First month, 1661, when he was brought to the court at Boston with his chains and log at his heels. The court told him that he was found guilty, and was to die.

W. Leddra asked what evil he had done.

The court replied that his own confession was as good as a thousand witnesses.

W. Leddra. What was that?

The court answered, that he had owned, that those who were put to death, viz. William Robinson, Marmaduke Stevenson, and Mary Dyer, were innocent [of that] for which they died; and that he would not put off his hat in court, and that he would say thee and thou to the magistrates.

W. Leddra. Then you put me to death for speaking English, and for not putting off my clothes.

After some more words they pronounced sentence of death upon him, and on the 14th of the First month, 1661, they knocked off his chains, and he took his leave of his fellow-prisoners in most tender love, led as a sheep to the slaughter, in the meekness of the spirit of Jesus, resigned up in the will of God to seal the truth of the testimony he had borne, with his blood. Being encompassed with the guards, and as he was about to ascend the ladder, he said, 'All that will be Christ's disciples must take up the cross.' And standing where the guards ordered him, with an exceedingly fresh living countenance he spoke to the people, and said, 'For bearing my testimony for the Lord against deceit, and the deceived, am I brought here to suffer:' which much affected the people. And as the executioner was putting the halter about his neck, in the meekness and sense of Christ Jesus he said, 'I commit my cause to thee, O God.' And just at turning off the ladder he called out, 'Lord Jesus receive my spirit.'

An Epistle of William Leddra, to Friends, written by him the day before he was put to death.

'To the society of the little flock of Christ, grace and peace be multiplied.

'Most dear and inwardly beloved!

'The sweet influences of the morning star, like a flood, distilling into my innocent habitation, have so filled me with the joy of the Lord in the beauty of holiness, that my spirit is as if it did not inhabit a tabernacle of clay, but is wholly swallowed up in the bosom of eternity, from whence it had its being.

'Alas! alas! what can the wrath and spirit of man that lusteth to envy, aggravated by the heat and strength of the king of the locusts, which came out of the pit, do unto one that is hid in the secret places of the Almighty? or unto them that are gathered under the healing wings of the prince of peace? Under his armour of light they shall be able to stand in the day of trial, having on the breast-plate of righteousness, and the sword of the spirit, which is their weapon of war against spiritual wickedness, principalities and powers, and the rulers of the darkness of this world, both within and without.

'O my beloved, I have waited like a dove at the windows of the ark, and have stood still in that watch, which the Master, without whom I could do nothing, did at his coming reward with the fulness of his love, wherein my heart did rejoice, that I might in the love and life of God speak a few words to you, sealed with the spirit of promise, that the taste thereof might be a savour of life to your life, and a testimony in you of my innocent death. And if I had been altogether silent, and the Lord had not opened my mouth unto you, yet he would have opened your hearts, and there have sealed my innocence with the streams of life, by which we are all baptized into that body which is of God, with whom and in whose presence there is life, in which, as you abide, you stand upon the pillar and ground of truth. For the life being the truth and the way, go not one step without it, lest you should compass a mountain in the wilderness; for unto every thing there is a season.

'As the flowing of the ocean doth fill every creek and branch thereof, and then retires again towards its own being and fulness, and leaves a savour behind it, so doth the life and virtue of God flow into every one of your hearts, whom he hath made partakers of his divine nature; and when it withdraws but a little, it leaves a sweet savour behind it, that many can say, they are made clean through the word that he hath spoken to them; in which innocent condition you may see what you are in the presence of God, and what you are without him.

'Therefore, my dear hearts, let the enjoyment of the life alone be your hope, your joy and consolation, and let the man of God flee those things that would lead the mind out of the cross, for then the savour of life will be buried. And though some may speak of things that they received in the life, as experiences, yet the life being veiled, and the savour that it left behind being washed away by the fresh flood of temptation, the condition that they did enjoy in the life, boasted of by the airy mind, will be like the manna that was gathered yesterday, without any good scent or savour. For it was only well with the man while he was in the life of innocency, but being driven from the presence of the Lord into the earth, what can he boast of?

'Although you know these things, and many of you much more than I can say, yet for the love and zeal I bear to the truth and honour of God, and tender desire of my soul to those that are young, that they may read me in that from which I write, to strengthen them against the wiles of the subtle serpent that beguiled Eve; I say, stand in the watch within, in the fear of the Lord, which is the very entrance of wisdom, and the state wherein you are ready to receive the secrets of the Lord. Hunger and thirst patiently, be not weary, neither doubt. Stand still, and cease from thine own working, and in due time thou shalt enter into the rest, and thy eyes shall behold his salvation, whose testimonies are sure, and righteous altogether. Let them be as a seal upon thine arm, and as jewels about thy neck, that others may see what the Lord has done for your souls. Confess him before men, yea, before his greatest enemies; fear not what they can do unto you: greater is he that is in you, than he that is in the world. He will clothe you with humility, and in the power of his meekness, you shall reign over all the rage of your enemies in the favour of God, wherein, as you stand in faith, ye are the salt of the earth; for many seeing your good works, may glorify God in the day of their visitation.

'Take heed of receiving that which you see not in the light, lest you give ear to the enemy. Bring all things to the light, that they may be proved whether they are wrought in God. The love of the world, the lust of the flesh, and the lust of the eye, are without the light, in the world. Therefore possess your vessels in all sanctification and honour, and let your eye look at the mark. He that hath called you is holy: and if there be an eye that offends, pluck it out, and cast it from you. Let not a temptation take hold, for if you do, it will keep you from the favour of God, and that will be a sad state; for without grace possessed, there is no assurance of salvation. By grace ye are saved, and the witnessing of it is sufficient for you, to which I commend you all, my dear friends, and in it remain your brother,

'William Leddra.

'Boston jail, 13th of First Month, 1660–1.'

THOMAS FORSTER, of London, was convinced about the year 1658, and thereupon forsook much of this world's gain and preferment for the sake of Christ, (he then belonging to the civil law) and was in his life-time freely given up to serve the Lord with body, soul and whole substance, that he might run the race and keep the truth; which made him willing to deny himself, and take up the daily cross for Christ's sake, that he might be truly wise. He foresaw, several years before it happened, that the city of London should be destroyed; and his wife and family, at his admonition, removed into the out parts, and by that means escaped the judgment which afterwards came to pass upon the city, when it was burned by fire in the year 1666. He also foretold the sufferings which God's people have since been tried with, saying, 'The holy city will be besieged; but blessed are they who keep in the faith, for the time of deliverance will assuredly come,' &c. And a little before his departure out of this world, he said, 'Ah! friends, abide in God's pure holy truth all the day long, and you shall see the rising of his glory.'

So he finished his course, and fell asleep, in the year 1660.

RICHARD HUBBERTHORN was born in the north part of Lancashire; his father was a yeoman of the county, and of good repute. Richard was his only son, inclinable from his youth to religion, fearing the Lord, and was faithful in all things according to the light and knowledge received. His natural disposition was meek and lowly, and he loved peace among men, and he sometimes preached among his sober and sincere companions.

When it pleased God to raise up his people in the north parts of England, this same person was one among the first whose heart the Lord touched with the sense of his power, and he went through great afflictions, through the dispensation of the grace and spirit of Christ Jesus, until such time as the same power that killed did make alive; it wounded, and also healed. Being raised up by the holy spirit of the Lord, he was made a minister of the everlasting gospel, and accordingly went forth in the name and power of the Lord Jesus Christ, and travelled to and fro in the nation for the space of nine years; and thousands were as seals to the power and verity of his ministry, and of his faithfulness among the churches of Christ.

He was a man of small stature, of a weak constitution of body, and though slow of speech, yet he was very wise, and knew his season when to speak, and when to be silent. When he spoke, it was with such discretion and plainness of words, that reached perfectly the matter intended; and his speech being with grace, and his ministry savoury, God made him and his service a blessing to many. He was not easily moved into grief by adversity, or into joy by prosperity; a faithful contender for the living faith once delivered to the saints, which stands in the power of God, and worketh by love.

He was, with many others of the people called Quakers, taken from the Bull and Mouth meeting-house in London, and had before Sir Richard Brown, who with his own hands did violence to him, and then committed him to Newgate, where being thronged up in a nasty prison, he was taken sick, and in a few days grew weaker and weaker.

About two days before his decease, some of his dearest friends visiting him, asked if any thing was on his mind; his answer was, that there was no need to dispute matters, he knew the ground of his salvation, and was satisfied for ever in his peace with the Lord; and we know, said he, one another well, and what each of us can say about these things. During his sickness he expressed much love to friends; and his mind was redeemed out of all visible things; and several times he would say, 'The word of the Lord is with me.' And farther, 'That faith which hath wrought my salvation I well know, and have grounded satisfaction in it.'

In the time of his sickness, he was kept feeding in retiredness within, so that one might feel his strength in the Spirit, that kept him so still, that it was not remembered that he groaned all the time of his sickness. On the seventh day in the morning he asked for the mistress of the house, and said, 'This night, or to-morrow, I shall depart hence.' The next morning he said to one sitting by him, 'Do not seek to hold me, for it is too strait for me; and out of this straitness I must go, for I am wound into largeness, and am to be lifted up on high, far above all:' so in the evening, being the first day of the week, and the 17th of the Sixth month, 1662, he finished his course, according to his own words, and was gathered up to his Father.

He wrote many treatises, which are collected together in print.

EDWARD BURROUGH, born in the county of Westmoreland, about the year 1635, of honest parents, was in his childhood ripe in knowledge, and did far excel many of his years. Grey hairs were upon him when but a youth, and he was inclinable to the best things and the nearest way of worship according to the scriptures, accompanying the best men. His natural disposition was bold and manly, dexterous and fervent, and what he took in hand, he did with his might. Loving, courteous, merciful, and easy to be entreated; he delighted in conference, and reading of the holy scriptures.

When it pleased God to visit his people in the north of England, this servant of Christ was early called, viz., in the year 1652, when about seventeen years of age. He was sent forth by the Spirit of the Lord to preach the everlasting gospel, repentance, conversion, salvation, and remission of sins, in the name and power of the Lord Jesus Christ, the saviour of mankind; and was an able minister of the glad tidings of salvation. In most parts of England, and through Ireland several times, and in Scotland and Flanders, his ministry was made effectual by the mighty power of God, in turning many thousands from darkness to light; for as he began early, so he laboured much in the heat of the day, breaking up rough places, and untilled ground, and often walked as it were among briars and thorns, which scratched, pricked, and tore with great opposition. But he broke through them all, not regarding the opposition, and the sufferings that he met with, for the good of souls.

His industry in the Lord's work was very great, he seldom having many hours repose, making the Lord's work his whole business, not taking so much liberty as to spend one week to himself, about any outward occasion, in ten years; and it was his grief if any opportunity was missed in doing good. He was a man of no great learning, which men so much admire, yet he had the tongue of the learned, having had experience of the work of God in many conditions, so that he could speak a word, in due season, to the understandings and consciences of all men with whom he had converse, for his words administered grace to the hearer.

At the age of nineteen, in the year 1654, he came up to London, and was one of the first who preached in that city, and great opposition he met with there; but God made his ministry effectual to the conversion of hundreds. He continued about London very much, at times, between eight and nine years, speaking of the things of the kingdom of God. His heart was much drawn towards London, and he often said, when sufferings came for the gospel's sake, 'I can freely go to that city, (i. e. London,) and lay down my life for a testimony of that truth which I have declared through the power and spirit of God.'

In the year 1662, visiting friends in the city of Bristol, he took his leave, and said to many, 'I am going up to the city of London, to suffer among friends in that place.' A little after his return to the said city, he was taken from a meeting of the people called Quakers, at the Bull and Mouth meeting-house, by soldiers under the command of Sir Richard Brown, mayor, and committed to Newgate by the said mayor, not for evil doing, but for testifying to the name of the Lord Jesus, and for the worship of God. There he lay in prison with six or seven score friends more, upon the same account, many of them being shut up among felons in nasty places; and for want of prison-room they grew weak, sickened, and died, among whom this young man was one; his sickness increasing upon him daily, though in much patience he was carried through all.

He was in prayer often, both day and night, saying at one time, 'I have had a testimony of the Lord's love to me from my youth, and my heart hath been given up to do his will. I have preached the gospel freely in this city, and have often given up my life for the gospel's sake. Lord, rip open my heart, and see if it be not right before thee.' Another time he said, 'There lies no iniquity at my door; but the presence of the Lord is with me, and his life I feel justifies me.' Afterwards he said to the Lord, 'Thou hast loved me when I was in the womb, and I have loved thee from my cradle, and from my youth unto this day, and have served thee faithfully in my generation.'

He spoke to friends that were about him to live in love and peace, and love one another; and said, 'The Lord takes the righteous from the evil to come:' and prayed for his enemies and persecutors, and said, 'Lord, forgive Richard Brown who imprisoned me.' Again he said, 'Though this body of clay must turn to dust, yet I have this testimony, that I have served God in my generation; and that spirit which hath lived, and acted, and ruled in me, shall yet break forth in thousands.' In the morning before he departed, being sensible of his death, he said, 'Now my soul and spirit is centred in its own being with God, and this form of person must return from whence it was taken.' And after a little season, he gave up the ghost, as a martyr for the word of God, and testimony of Jesus.

He was born in 1635, began to preach 1652, and died 1662, of whose written labours there is a volume printed, containing almost nine hundred pages in folio.

HUMPHREY SMITH, of Little Cowrne, in the county of Hereford, formerly a public preacher, was convinced of truth about the year 1655, and came to be an able minister of the gospel of Christ, which he freely preached, and turned many to righteousness, and gave forth many warnings and exhortations to the people, as may be seen at large in the printed collection of his works. The Lord showed him in a vision, in the fifth month, 1660, the destruction of the city of London by fire, which was six years before it came to pass; and which vision he published before-hand, as a warning to the people to repent; part whereof is as follows:

Part of the vision of Humphrey Smith, which he saw concerning the burning of the city of London, in the fifth month, 1660, which was three years before his decease, and six years before it was fulfilled.

'As for the city herself, and her suburbs, and all that belonged to her [I beheld] a fire was kindled therein, but she knew not how, even in her goodly palaces, and the kindling of it was in the foundation of her buildings. There was none could quench it, neither was there any able; and the burning thereof was exceedingly great, and burned inward in an hidden manner, which cannot be expressed. The fire consumed foundations which the city stood upon, and the tall buildings fell, and it consumed all the lofty things therein, and the fire searched out all the hidden places, and burned most in secret places, but the consumption was exceedingly great wherewith it was consumed.

'And as I passed through her streets, I beheld her state to be very miserable, and very few were those that were left in her, who were but here and there one, and they feared not the fire, neither did the burnings hurt them; but they were (and walked) as mournful people, and the fire burned every where, so that there was no escaping of it. And thus she became a desolation, and as an astonishment; for the burning was suffered of God for her chastisement, and could not be quenched nor overcome. There was none could stop the flaming; and the fire consumed all things, both stone and timber; and burned under all things, and under all foundations; and that which was lifted up above it fell down, and the fire consumed it. The flaming continued, though the foundation was burnt up, and all the lofty part brought down by the fire; yet there was much old stuff, and part of broken desolate walls and buildings in the midst, which the fire continued burning against; and that which was taken, as to make use of, which yet escaped the fire, became useless in men's hands, as a thing of naught. And the vision thereof remained in me, as a thing that was secretly showed me of the Lord.

'And now let her wise men find out the matter, and her prudent men read, and her divines, so called, interpret the vision, and let every one look to their own ways.'

This, with much more that Humphrey Smith saw, was printed and published in the year 1660, as a warning whereby people might stand in the day of trial, and endure the hour of trouble. See it at large in his printed vision in the year 1660.

Besides other things which the Lord revealed to him, he had also a clear sight of his own sufferings, and death thereby. For about the year 1662, travelling among friends about London, he told some of them that he had a narrow path to pass through; and said several times, before he was taken up, he saw he should be imprisoned, and that it might cost him his life. Taking leave of his friends, he set forward, in the will of God, westward; and being in a meeting of the people called Quakers, at Alton in Hampshire, he was taken from thence, and had before the two lieutenants of the county, who committed him to the stinking close prison of Winchester, where, after a whole year's imprisonment, he fell sick.

In the time of his sickness he spoke many precious words to friends about him, signifying that he was given up to the will of God, either in life or death. And as he lay under great illness, he said, 'My heart is filled with the power of God;' and, 'It is good for a man, at such a time as this, to have the Lord to be his friend.' Another time he said, 'Lord, thou hast sent me forth to do thy will, and I have been faithful unto thee in my small measure, which thou hast committed unto me; but if thou wilt yet try me further, thy will be done.' Also he said, 'I am the Lord's; let him do what he will.' And near the time of his departure, he prayed earnestly, saying, 'O Lord, hear the inward sighs and groans of thine oppressed, and deliver my soul from the oppressor: hear me, O Lord, uphold and preserve me. I know that my Redeemer liveth: thou art strong and mighty, O Lord.' He prayed that the Lord would deliver his people from their cruel oppressors; and for those who had been convinced by him, that the Lord would be their teacher.

He lay quiet and still, sensible to the last moment, and died a prisoner for the truth, in the common jail of Winchester, on the 4th of the Eighth month, in the year 1663.

JOHN AUDLAND was born in the county of Westmoreland, near Cam's-gill, and when a child, he was ripe and quick of understanding. About the eighteenth year of his age, the Lord inclined his heart towards himself, and he delighted in reading the scriptures; and having a large knowledge and memory, could discourse of things relating to religion, and became an eminent preacher, not only amongst the most strict sort of professors, but sometimes also at chapels, and public parish-places of worship, where great multitudes of people would flock after him.

About the twentieth year of his age he married Anne Newby, of Kendal, belonging to the same religious meeting, afterwards the wife of Thomas Camm, of Cam's-gill in Westmoreland. This John Audland was one of those before mentioned, who was convinced the first time that he heard George Fox at Firbank chapel, and received him into his house. Seeing the emptiness of his own high-flown notions and profession in religion, he sat down in silence and astonishment, like Job, for many days; and great was the work of the Lord upon him, being stripped of his earthly wisdom, and in that state he mourned and wept bitterly, for he saw where he had been, and that it was the Lord alone that could help him.

In great compassion the Lord revealed his saving health and arm of power, by which he raised him up, and filled him with wisdom and strength for the performance of that work [in which] he would concern him, in gathering home the outcasts of Israel, and the dispersed of Jacob; and sent him forth to preach redemption, in the name of the Lord Jesus Christ, to the poor, and deliverance to the captive, and the day of vengeance upon the wicked. Leaving all his outward concerns, he went forth, and the dread, wisdom, and majesty of the Lord was with him, and many hundreds were turned to the Lord through him, as an instrument in God's hand. Bristol, and several counties in the west of England, were witnesses of the power and efficacy of his ministry, who with John Camm, was of the first of those called Quakers who went to that city, preaching Christ Jesus the light of the world. He was often concerned in disputations, and the Lord furnished him with matter, so that he stopped the mouths of gainsayers; his testimony was large and free, affecting almost to all sorts of people, and he had a word in season to all conditions; but notwithstanding he was young and strong, yet that service much spent him several years before he died.

He had been several times in prison for his testimony's sake, as at Newcastle, and at Bristol; and often in great perils, sore beatings, and cruel mockings, both of the rabble, and also of the bitter spirited professors, but through all, the Lord preserved him faithful. He growing weak by a lingering distemper of a cough and consumption, would often say in his sickness, 'Ah! those great meetings in the orchard at Bristol, I may not forget. I would so gladly have spread my net over all, and have gathered all, that I forgot myself, never considering the inability of my body. But it is well, my reward is with me, and I am content to give up and be with the Lord, for that my soul values above all things.'

Near his death, friends visiting him, the Lord did wonderfully open his mouth in exhortation, to their great refreshment and joy, as if he had been without sense of sickness. He had a tender regard to his dear wife; 'But in this,' said he, 'my will is in true subjection, submitting to the will of the Lord, whether life or death.' He desired his wife to give him up freely to the disposing hand of the Lord; and the Lord strengthened her freely to recommend him into his hands, which made him easy.

He was often, in the time of his sickness, exceedingly filled with the high praises of God, being overcome in the sense of God's love, joy, and everlasting peace. When he grew weaker, he would be helped up upon his knees, and upon his bed fervently supplicated the Lord, in the behalf of his whole heritage, that they might be preserved in the truth, out of the evil of the world; and that his gospel might spread, and be published, to the gathering of all that appertain to Israel. So was he sweetly taken away in the joy of the Lord, on the 22d of the First month, in the year 1664.

He was convinced in 1652, and died 1664, being aged about thirty-four years.

RICHARD FARNSWORTH, of Balby, in Yorkshire, was also one of those whom the Lord raised up early in the work of the ministry. He suffered about twelve months' imprisonment at Banbury, in Oxfordshire, in the year 1655, and many were turned to God by him. He was mighty in discourses, and disputes with priests and professors, and after much labour in the work of the ministry, and great sufferings and persecutions, he at last finished his testimony in London.

A little space before his departure out of this life, sitting up in his bed, he spoke in as much power and strength of spirit as he had ever done at any time in his health, these words following: 'Friends, God hath been mightily with me, and hath stood by me at this time, and his power and presence have encompassed me all along. God hath appeared for the owning of my testimony, and hath broken in upon me as a flood, and I am filled with his love more than I am able to express; and God has really appeared for us. If God himself had come down, and spoken as a man, he could not have spoken more clearly to us than he hath done, by the many testimonies from heaven in his people. Therefore I beseech you, friends, here of this city of London, whether I live or die, be you faithful to your testimony God hath committed to you.'

He died in the city of London, in the year 1666.

MARY HARRIS, of London, a maid young and beautiful, went often with her relations to the meetings of the people called Quakers, and had a love raised in her to the blessed truth, and to them who held it in a pure conscience; yet still lived in the customs and fashions of this evil world. But the same love of God that had begotten tenderness in her heart, and love to truth, followed her, and would not suffer her to sit down in the world without trouble. The Lord visited her with great weakness, so that she grew ill, and fell into a consumption for about three years; and being often visited by Josiah Coale, and put in mind to consider, whether the hand of the

Lord was not upon her for her unfaithfulness and disobedience, she did consider the matter, and the Lord set it home upon her heart, and she cried to him for mercy; and applied her heart to the Lord, and his faithful messengers, saying, 'I have hardened my heart at many precious meetings, when the Lord hath smitten me; and I have seen plainly, that the Lord would have gathered me; but I said in my heart, if I receive this, if I give up to this, I must be a Quaker, and I cannot be a Quaker. Then would I take my heart from attending upon the ministration of truth, and then my heart became more hard. What shall I do,' said she, 'that now I may receive the faithful sayings of the servants of the Lord? Oh! that my heart were open; but it is shut and hard: when shall I find mercy in this state?'

She remained so for some time, and grew weaker and weaker in body; and on the first day she took her bed she was much under the righteous judgments of the Lord, and felt his word in her heart as fire. But the Lord in judgment remembered mercy, and having brought her very low, he showed her the child's state, which she with great delight desired; and indeed she became as a little child, fit for the kingdom of heaven. Then did the Lord rend the veil, and showed her his glory, and the preciousness of his pure truth, and the light shined out of darkness, and in it she saw light, and received the knowledge of God; and her heart was filled with joy and praises to the Lord, saying, 'I am well; I feel no pain. I am full; my cup runs over. I am filled as it were with marrow and fatness. I have seen his glory, and tasted his precious truth. How pure is God's everlasting truth? Nothing so pure; and they who indeed receive it, are made pure by it. Praised be the Lord who hath made me partaker of it, and placed me among his people. Oh! blessed God, who hath given me cause to sing aloud of thy praise.' Many precious words she spoke to several persons who came to visit her, to their several conditions, showing to some, who lived in pleasure, her hands, saying, 'See here, the Lord hath made these bones bare for my rebellion; because I would not submit to his precious truth. He hath brought me to the dust, and I must lay down this body as a sacrifice. Oh! do not you stand out, it will cost you dear, if ever you find mercy.' Then she would sing praises to the Lord, and exhorted all speedily to embrace truth, and warned others professing truth, from following the fashions of the world, crying to the Lord to wash her thoroughly. Some would say to her, 'It may be thou mayest recover.' 'No, no,' she replied, 'I must lay down this body for my rebellion. In my vain life, if any had said I should recover, it would for a little time seem to refresh me; and if they had said surely I could not live long, it would cast me down; but now I long for death. I must lay down this body; for,' said she, 'when I received God's everlasting truth, I received the sentence of death:' and this she was positive in all along.

More sensible expressions she uttered, which I omit for brevity. About half an hour before her departure, she was taken with a very great trembling, and seemed to be somewhat troubled; when one near her said, 'What is the matter? art thou in any doubt concerning the truth of which thou art made partaker?' She replied, 'No, no; that is God's pure everlasting truth, which the people of God, called Quakers, are made partakers of, and for which they suffer; that is everlasting, that is the true spirit, and their God is my God; and although I see it not now as I have seen it, yet I bring in my testimony, that is the truth that shall abide for ever; that is pure, and nothing that is defiled shall be sheltered under it. That is the truth which enlighteneth every man coming into the world: the little seed in me is become great, great, great! Blessed be God who hath placed me among his people, and I possess what they possess; and when the faithful die as I die, my portion will be their portion; and my cup is full, it runs over and over.' Then she breathed a little thicker for about the space of a quarter of an hour; and so without groan or sigh, or the least motion, she shut her eyes and slept. Glory to God for ever.

She died at the widow Mary Forster's, in that called St. John's street, near Smithfield, London, in the year 1668

JOSIAH COALE, born of a family of good repute among men, near the city of Bristol, was convinced of God's everlasting truth, through the powerful ministry of that servant of God, John Audland, about the year 1655. The word of life pierced Josiah to the heart, and wrought effectually to his salvation and redemption. He walked for a time under deep judgment, and mournfully, so that he became a gazing stock and wonder to his former acquaintance. But God's arm was strong, and plucked up every evil plant, and purified him, and made him fit for the Lord's use, and an able minister of the everlasting gospel of Christ Jesus; an incessant labourer, few more spent in God's service. His soul seemed wholly bent to the renowning the name of Christ; and the enemies of truth he ever accounted his enemies.

His declaration was to the ungodly like an axe, or hammer, and a sword sharp and piercing, being mostly attended with an eminent appearance of the dreadful power of the Lord, to the cutting down many tall cedars, and making the strong oaks to bow; but to the faithful and diligent, who minded the things of Christ more than their own, oh! how soft and pleasant were the streams of immortal life that ran through him, to the refreshing of those! It was his life and joy to be speaking the word of the Lord, and not his own words; and many thousands were living witnesses to the power, virtue and efficacy of his ministry; but above all, he was terrible to the sowers of strife, secret backbiters, and such as rend the holy body, and separated from the life, love, and fellowship of the blessed truth; who, in their own selfish spirits, set themselves over their brethren, by feignedness and deceitful appearances, to the destroying the simple-hearted.

In his conversation, his kindness was so mixed with seriousness, and his familiarity with a staid and exemplary behaviour, that he was an honour to the truth, and therein a confirmer of his holy testimony and weaker brethren.

He was hardy, valiant, and fixed; not of those who shun the cross, or sell their birth-right for a mess of pottage. He baulked no danger for the sake of his blessed testimony, which he bore faithfully in England, Holland, the Low Countries, and Barbadoes; and had also sore travels among the heathen in America, as in Maryland, Virginia, and New England, preaching the gospel of Christ among them. He travelled on foot through the wilderness, from Virginia to New England, in danger of wild beasts and venomous creatures, [enduring] much hunger and cold, and weariness, and through bogs and waters, often obliged to eat chesnuts for food when hungry, as appears at large in the record of New England's persecution.

He was a good example, as well for his liberality as faithfulness; for as the prosperity of God's truth was above all things most in his eye, so he was always cautious of making the gospel chargeable to any; for, having some estate of his own, he freely employed it in the Lord's service, counting nothing too dear for the name and service of the Lord.

Thus having laboured his natural strength away in this heavenly warfare, for the promotion of the glorious truth of the Lord, and for the advancement of its interest and dominion in the world, for above twelve years together, he did, with perfect understanding, and in an extraordinary enjoyment of the Lord's life, majesty, and presence, to the refreshment of the beholders, cheerfully lay down his mortal body.

George Fox, visiting him upon his sick-bed, queried whether he had any thing upon his mind to write to friends in England, or beyond sea. He said that he was clear of writing to them; and that as the Lord by his power had carried him through England and other nations, so he had nothing to write; but he desired his love to all friends. One thing, he said, did lie upon him, in that he understood Lodowick Muggleton (a most blasphemous ranter) and his company would boast against him; and understanding George Fox was preparing a book in answer to the said Muggleton, desired he might put in a few words as his last testimony against Muggleton; which George Fox desired him to prepare, and he would call for it as he came back. He spake them forth in the power of the Lord, as fresh as if he had ailed nothing, and a friend took it in writing, which is as followeth:

'Forasmuch as I have been informed, that Lodowick Muggleton hath vaunted concerning my departure out of the body, because of his pretended sentence of damnation given against me; I am moved to leave this testimony concerning him, behind me, viz. That he is a son of darkness, and a co-worker with the prince of the bottomless pit, in which his inheritance shall be for ever. The judgment that I then declared against him, stands sealed by the Spirit of the Lord, by which I then declared unto him, That in the name of that God that spanneth the heavens with his span, and measureth the waters in the hollow of his hand, I bind thee here on earth, and thou art bound in heaven; and in the chain under darkness, to the judgment of the great day thou shalt be reserved; and thy faith and strength thou boasted of I defy and trample under foot. I do hereby further declare the said Lodowick Muggleton to be a false prophet, in what he said to me at that time, viz. That from henceforth I should always be in fear of damnation, which should be a sign to me that I was damned; which fear I never was in since; so that his sign given by himself did not follow his prophecy, which sufficiently declares him to be a false prophet.'

George Fox, when he came back again, found Josiah sitting by the fire-side, filled with the power of the Lord, and speaking to friends about him as followeth: 'Well, friends, be faithful to God, and seek nothing for self, or your own glory; and if any thing wrong arise, judge it down by the power of the Lord God, that so you may be clear in his sight, and answer his witness in all people; then will you have the reward of life. For my part, I have walked in faithfulness with the Lord, and I have thus far finished my testimony, and have peace with the Lord, and his majesty is with me, and his crown of life is upon me: so mind my love to all friends.'

Then he spoke to Stephen Crisp, saying, 'Dear heart, keep low in the holy fear of God; that will be thy crown.' Afterwards he said, 'A minister of Christ must walk as I have walked.' Then he desired George Fox to pray, that he might have an easy passage: and friends seeing him begin to be heavy, desired him to go and lie down on the bed, which he did; and friends sat about him, and held him, and he was filled with the power of the Lord and seed of life, which was over all. So in that he departed away, in the arms of friends, as he sat on the side of his bed, and had a very easy passage into eternal life.

He died in London, aged thirty-five years and two months, in the year 1668.

He laboured in the ministry twelve years, and wrote many treatises, which are collected together in one volume.

FRANCIS HOWGILL, of Grayridge, in the county of Westmoreland, an early minister of the gospel of Jesus Christ, was convinced of the blessed truth by George Fox, at that notable meeting at Firbank Chapel, in Westmoreland, in the year 1652. He soon became a powerful minister, and preached Christ freely as he had received him. He came to London with Edward Burrough early, to visit that city; and travelled to Bristol and divers parts of the nation, and suffered imprisonment in Appleby jail, in the year 1652; and a nasty, stinking prison it was. He was set at liberty the latter end of the year, and grew valiant and bold for the name of the Lord, travelling up and down on foot, preaching the gospel. He went to the steeple-houses, and to many places, warning both priests and people of the day of the Lord that was coming upon them, directing them to Christ Jesus their teacher and Saviour.

He came also to London, on foot, with John Camm, to admonish Oliver Cromwell, soon after he was made protector; and he went with Edward Burrough to Ireland, and preached Christ under great sufferings there, until he and Edward Burrough aforesaid, were banished by Henry Cromwell out of Ireland. Afterwards he was imprisoned in London, in the year 1661, at the time when the Fifth Monarchy people rose up in arms, but was clear of that bloody act; and so was set at liberty, and continued labouring up and down the nation, in the work of the Lord, and turned many to God. In the latter end of the Fifth month, in 1663, he was sent for out of the market in Kendal, by the magistrates, who tendered him the oath of allegiance, and because for conscience-sake he could not take it, they sent him to Appleby jail; and at the assizes, for refusing to take the oath, sentence of premunire was given against him by the judge, in these words: 'You are put out of the king's protection, and the benefit of the law; your lands are confiscated to the king during your life, and your goods and chattles for ever; and you to be a prisoner during your life.'

F. Howgill replied, 'An hard sentence for my obedience to the commands of Christ; the Lord forgive you all.'

Judge. 'Well, if you will yet be subject to the laws of the king, the king will show you mercy.'

F. Howgill. 'The Lord hath showed mercy unto me, and I have done nothing against the king, or government, or any man, blessed be the Lord, and herein stands my peace; for it is for Christ's sake I suffer, and not for evil doing.' The court broke up, and many were sorry to see what was done against him; but he signified how contented and glad he was, that he had any thing to lose for the Lord's precious truth, of which he had publicly borne testimony, and that he was counted worthy to suffer for it. He was kept a prisoner in Appleby jail four years and a half; and his body being much spent in his public travels and labours in the gospel, was not able to endure such close confinement, though he bore his suffering in much patience and cheerfulness until the time of his decease.

He was taken ill the 11th of the Eleventh month, 1668, and though his departure drew nigh, yet was he kept in perfect understanding, being often very fervent in prayer, and uttered many comfortable expressions, to the refreshment of those about him. Two days before his death, his wife and friends being present, he said, 'Friends, as to matter of words you must not expect much from me, neither is there any great need of it, or to speak of matters of faith to you who are satisfied; only that you remember my dear love to all Friends who enquire of me, for I ever loved Friends well, and any other in whom truth

6*

appeared. Truly God will own his people, as he hath ever hitherto done, and as we have daily witnessed; for no sooner had they made that act against us for banishment, to the great suffering of many good Friends, but the Lord stirred up enemies against them, even three great nations, whereby the violence of their hands was taken off. I say again, God will own his people, even all those that are faithful; and as for me, I am well, and content to die; I am not afraid at all of death. Truly one thing was of late in my heart, and that I intended to have written to George Fox and others, even that which I have observed, which thing is, that this generation passeth away, when so many good and precious Friends, within these few years have been taken from us; and therefore Friends had need to watch and be very faithful, so that we may leave a good, and not a bad savour, to the next succeeding generation; for you see that it is but a little time that any of us have to stay here.'

Often he said in the time of his sickness, that he was content to die, and that he was ready; and praised God for the many sweet enjoyments and refreshments he had received on that his prison-house bed where he lay, freely forgiving all who had a hand in his restraint. And he said, 'This was the place of my first imprisonment for the truth at this town; and if it be the place of my laying down the body, I am content.'

Several persons of note, inhabitants of Appleby, as the mayor and others, went to visit him, some of whom praying God might speak peace to his soul, he sweetly replied, 'He hath done it;' and they all spoke well of him. A few hours before his death, some being come to visit him, he prayed fervently with many heavenly expressions, that the Lord by his mighty power would preserve them out of all such things as would spot and defile. A little after, recovering some strength, he further said, 'I have sought the way of the Lord from a child, and lived innocently, as among men; and if any enquire after my latter end, let them know, that I die in the faith that I lived in and suffered for.' These words he spoke, with some other words in prayer, and sweetly finished his course in much peace with the Lord, in the Eleventh month, 1668.

He laboured in the gospel sixteen years: there is a volume of his works printed in about 740 pages in folio.

THOMAS LOE, of Oxfordshire, was a faithful servant and minister of Christ Jesus, and converted many to truth, especially in Ireland, where he travelled through great hardships. His first going thither was about the year 1657; Francis Howgill, Edward Burrough, and others, having been there before him. He had an excellent gift, sound and clear in the ministry, powerful in speech, sharp and quick in his understanding; and many people flocked after him, and received truth by his ministry in that nation; and others he confirmed in the truth who were convinced before. He was often publicly engaged with priests and opposers, and the Lord made him a sharp instrument in his hand to confound the adversaries of truth, and the mouths of gainsayers were stopped. His company was very desirable, being pleasant and sweet in conversation, and sympathizing with his friends in affliction, so that he could speak a word in due season. He was several times a prisoner for the testimony of truth, and went out of England several times to visit the nation of Ireland, in which travels his natural strength was much impaired. He also laboured in the work of the ministry in London, being often there; and was taken sick in that city, expressing on his death-bed what exceeding encouragement and glory he saw and felt of the Lord, as followeth:

'Glory to thee, O God, for thy power is known. 'God is the Lord.' Then speaking to William Penn, whom the Lord had made him instrumental to convince, he said, 'Dear heart, bear thy cross. Stand faithful for God, and bear thy testimony in thy day and generation, and God will give thee an eternal crown of glory, that shall not be taken from thee. There is not another way that the holy men of old walked in, and it shall prosper. God has brought immortality to light, and immortal life is felt: glory, glory, for he is worthy. My heart is full, what shall I say? His love overcomes my heart; my cup runs over, my cup runs over. Glory, glory to his name for ever. He is come, he has appeared, and will appear. Friends, keep your testimony for God, live with him, and he will live with you.'

Another time he said to some friends, 'Be not troubled, the love of God overcomes my heart.' And again he spoke to George Whitehead, and other friends present, viz., 'George, the Lord is good to me; this day he has covered me with his glory. I am weak, but I am refreshed to see you: the Lord is good to me.' Another friend asked him, 'How art thou, Thomas?' He answered, 'I am near leaving you, I think; but as well in my spirit as I can desire, I bless the Lord; and I never saw more of the glory of God than I have done this day.' And then being expected to depart, the power of the Lord arose in him, and he sung to the Lord, 'Glory, glory to thee for ever.' And so continued praising God for some time, which much affected the standers by.

He departed in peace with God, on the 5th of the Eighth month, in the year 1668, at London.

ELIZABETH FURLY, daughter of John Furly of Colchester, in the county of Essex, was a child that loved the Lord, and also those who feared him. . Her delight was to hear truth preached, and to be with such who excelled in virtue; she feared and hated a lie, and lived and died in the faith which the people called Quakers profess. She was taken sick at her father's house in Colchester, the 11th of the Twelfth month, in the year 1669.

Two days before she died, being filled with the love of God, she uttered many precious sayings concerning the Lord, and his mercies towards her; praying to the Lord that she might be faithful to the end. In the presence of several persons she spoke as followeth: 'Whatever is not of thyself, O Lord, purge out of me; yea, purge me thoroughly, leave no wicked word in me, thrust away the power of darkness. O Lord, make me able to praise thee: let me not come into that way which is evil, for if I do, I shall dishonour thee and thy truth. I hope I shall never rebel against thee more, but have full satisfaction in thee, and in thy ways, and not in the evil one and his ways. Wash me, O Lord, thoroughly, let not an unadvised word come out of my mouth;' with more to the same purport. 'Show them, O Lord, the evil of their ways, that have done evilly, and lay a burden upon their spirits, that they may leave it. I feel no pain, the Lord is good to me; good is the will of the Lord. Let thy will be done in earth as it is done in heaven. Everlasting kindness hast thou shown me, and I hope I shall never forget it while I am in this world;' with more in admiration of the kindness and mercies of God, and her desire to serve him whilst she lived.

To one of her brothers she said, 'Improve thy time, for thou knowest not how soon thou mayest be taken away;' warning him of the danger of an evil life, and took him about the neck and kissed him, saying, 'Mind what I say, O dear brother;' and with many more words she exhorted him. She also admonished her other brothers with tender expressions, saying, 'Love the Lord, brothers, love good men: hate the devil; but oh, love the Lord, and then you will be a joy to your father and mother.' When she saw one of her sisters weep, she said, 'Weep not for me, I am very well. All serve the Lord, that he may be your portion. In my Father's house there is bread enough, there is fulness, want of nothing; yea, there is fulness of bread, durable riches and honour. I desire never to forget the Lord.'

As she walked in innocency, so she died in peace, and entered into glory, the 16th day of the Twelfth month, in the year 1669, aged thirteen years and five weeks.

MARGARET MOLLESON, wife of Gilbert Molleson of the city of Aberdeen in Scotland, was in her youth an enquirer after the best people, and joined herself in worship with the most strict and refined in profession then in that city. But it having pleased God, who beheld her hungering desires after himself and his righteousness, to send some of his faithful witnesses and servants called Quakers, from the nation of England into the north of Scotland, who preached the everlasting gospel; she was one of the first in those parts that received the same.

Coming to taste of the unspeakable love of God, she delighted often to retire therein, out of the cumbering cares of her family and business. And although her love to her husband, and cares of her many children, were great, yet her greatest delight and care was, to draw nearer and nearer to the true and living God, the chiefest beloved of her travailing soul. For that end she often resorted to the public meetings of the people called Quakers, as well as being frequently in private with the Lord in prayer; which gave her husband (who was not one called a Quaker) cause to say, that her knees were worn with kneeling at prayer.

For about four months before her departure hence, he usually found her, when he awaked in the night-time, in meditation; and after her departure, he also said before several people coming to visit him, that he had lost a true Mary and a Martha, none knowing how great his loss was, and he could not but much lament it.

On the 16th of the Tenth month, 1669, in the morning, she was taken suddenly sick, and the same day in the evening died, having been for some time before made sensible of her end; yet her physician, not supposing that she had been so dangerous, said to her, she needed not fear, his life for hers; to which she answered, 'Fear, I have no cause; but thou wilt see thou art mistaken.' Many relations and neighbours being in her chamber, were in great sorrow; among whom was a great professor, and an old acquaintance of hers, who desired those about her to pray for her; which she hearing, when others thought she had been dying, answered, 'My Advocate is with the Father, and my peace is made. I am feeding at a table none of you perceiveth.'

Some lamenting much her being like to be taken away from her nine children, who were all about her bed, she said, 'As many of them as shall truly fear the Lord, and follow him, shall be provided for:' which hath been since truly fulfilled. Fixing her eyes on her son Gilbert, who was then about ten years of age, she said in a heavenly frame of mind, 'Truth is precious, cleave to it.' She observing the people in her chamber much lamenting, said to them, 'Settle yourselves, and be staid in your minds, for ye are now to see the last.' Being to reap eternally the fruit of her great and spiritual labours, she had true cause given her then to declare before those present, viz. 'Now interruption is to cease, and my eternal joy is already begun;' the certain earnest of which she received, and [had] often preferred before all other enjoyments.

Her life and conversation, as well as her latter end, were such as gained her not only great love and esteem from friends of truth, but also from others of her acquaintance.

She departed hence on the 16th of the Tenth month, in the year 1669, about the forty-second year of her age, at Aberdeen, in the kingdom of Scotland.

JANE WHITEHEAD was the wife of Thomas Whitehead, of North Cadbury in Somersetshire. Her maiden name was Jane Vaugh, and she was born in Westmoreland, her relations living about Hutton in the same county; whom she left in obedience to the Lord, and travelled in his service, and bore witness against the false ways and worships of the world; and for the sake of her testimony endured much persecution.

In the year 1655, coming to Banbury in Oxfordshire, to visit her dear friend Anne Audland, then a prisoner for the truth, she, for bearing witness thereto, and against their cruelty and wickedness, was also taken and committed to prison, and lay there five weeks. Not long after, coming again to the said town, the magistrates tendered her the oath of abjuration; which she refusing for Christ's sake, who saith "Swear not at all," was imprisoned twelve months in a low, wet, nasty place, in the winter season, that sometimes she would be over shoes in water; which she endured with much patience.

In the Fourth month, 1662, she was again imprisoned at Banbury, for worshipping God at a meeting of the people called Quakers, where she lay in the same nasty prison three months. These things she suffered before she was married. Afterwards Thomas Whitehead, aforesaid, took her to be his wife, by whom she had five children that she left behind her.

At Ivelchester, she endured five months imprisonment, with a young child at her breast, in a cold winter, for speaking the words of truth and soberness to the priests of North Cadbury. But the Lord upheld her by the word of his power, in the manifold exercises and tribulations which she passed through, too tedious here to relate. Those abuses which she endured brought her tender body into weakness, which attended her several years before she died; and, under great exercises and weakness of body, she acknowledged that the Lord was wonderfully good to her. She often said that the Lord had broken in upon her, and with his heavenly presence did fill her, to the comfort of her soul: and said, 'O that the Lord may never take his presence from me.' To the last she was kept sensible, and declared that she had the testimony of God's love, and that it would be well with her, and that she had no desire to live any longer in this world. She charged her children to be obedient to their father, and that they should mind truth, and then the blessing of the Lord would be with them.

The morning before she died, being sensible her death was at hand, she told a Friend that she was going to her long home; and soon after departed this life, in the love and peace of God, on the 28th day of the Seventh month, in the year 1674.

WILLIAM BAYLEY, who was a Baptist teacher at Poole, was convinced of the blessed truth, as professed by the people called Quakers, in the year 1655, and travelled up and down in many places in the service of the Lord. His gift in the ministry, both as to matter and utterance, was plain and prevalent; he divided the word aright, for he fed the fat with judgment; and yet he had milk for babes, and stronger meat for those of riper age. He was mighty in the holy Scriptures, being well acquainted both with the history and mystery thereof, through the assistance of the Holy Spirit, which gave him a true understanding in both. It was given him, not only to believe and preach the word of faith, but also to suffer for the same, sometimes by cruel persecutions; being thrown down and dragged upon the ground by the hair of his head; and his mouth and jaws endeavoured to be rent and broken asunder, that the ground whereon he lay was smeared with blood. Yet as if this butchering of him had not been enough to make him a sacrifice, a heavy gross-bodied persecutor stamped upon his breast with his feet, endeavouring to beat the breath out of his body; and when this persecutor had done his pleasure, he commanded the jailor to take him away, and put him in some nasty hole for his entertainment and cure.

For the maintenance of his family, he several times adventured his life upon the mighty waters, being master of a ship; and many beyond the seas were partakers of his labours, and comforted by his ministry. In his return home from visiting friends in Barbadoes, he fell sick; and a little before his departure, desiring to be remembered to his dear wife and children, he said, 'Well, shall I lay down my head in peace upon the waters? God is the God of the whole universe, and though my body sink, I shall swim a-top of the waters. Remembering his love to Friends in general, and some by name, he immediately sung, being filled with the power of God, 'The creating word of the Lord endures for ever;' and spoke to them who sat by, and took several by the hand, exhorting them to fear God, and not to fear death. He said, 'Friends at London would have been glad to see my face. Tell them, I go to my Father and to their Father; to my God, and to their God. Remember my love to my wife; she will be a sorrowful widow; but let her not mourn in sorrow, for it is well with me.'

He then took is leave of the Friends on board, saying, 'I see not one of you, but wish you all well.' A Friend of New England asked him how it was with him : he said, 'I am perfectly well: and mind my love to Friends in Rhode Island, and New England, and to Friends in Barbadoes. I went freely in tender love to them.' He uttered more sensible words; and about half an hour past four in the morning, he departed this life, as if he had gone to sleep, being on 1st day of the Fourth month, in the year 1675, on board the Samuel of London, in the latitude of 46 degrees and 36 minutes

---

Concerning a Child about Thirteen years old.

JOSEPH BRIGGINS, son of William Briggins of Bartholomew Close, in London, having been a dutiful child to his parents, and ready to receive instruction, was taken sick the 20th of the Fourth month. Being, as it was thought, very near death; after he had lain silent for about an hour, he began to appear full of joy and pleasantness, saying, 'I shall praise the Lord, for he is only to be praised;' with many more words which they could not remember. He said, in admiration, 'Oh! I have never heard of any other God but thee, my holy One; I have heard of thee, but now I see thee in glory.' Calling for his father and mother, he said, 'Father, father, oh! father, oh! pure and glorious is my Saviour who hath appeared, and hath taken me into his kingdom. Oh! my eye hath seen his glory.' Then he prayed, 'Thou most glorious God, great and wonderful things are brought to pass by thy own pure holy power, by which thou hast revealed thy Son. Oh! my King, let all people fear and stand in awe of thy power, by which thou hast gathered many out of their sinful ways, into pure obedience to thee. Thou hast given us a living knowledge. Oh! pure, glorious, and holy God, let thy life reach unto all my dear friends, and keep them that know thee sure and stedfast upon thy holy foundation, Christ Jesus, my king, whose appearance is very glorious at this day, and of his government no end is to be, but thousands of thousands, millions of thousands, shall come to see, and be made partakers of his glorious, bright, shining day.'

Another time he said, 'There are many ways and baptisms in the world; but oh! thou pure, holy, holy One, we have known thy spiritual baptism into Christ Jesus my Lord, by whom the living water we have known and felt. Oh! it is indeed exceedingly pure, by which we have been washed from all our sins. Oh! my King, thou wast slain, and by the virtue of thy pure blood we have this given. Oh! that all may wait continually upon thee, that they may be kept from all the deceitful ways of the world.' To those standing by he said, 'Mind and serve the Lord in your day, for the holy truth received by you is the way in which you must wait and obey;' with much more. Then he lay silent a little while; but again said, 'The Lord hath taken me into his kingdom, he hath discovered the fresh springs of his love to my soul. All that know the Lord be obedient to his power, and he will discover himself more to you, and you shall know more. Thousands, thousands, millions, shall the Lord call.' With more words, after some time of silence.

Some who knew him very well, wondered to hear him speak as he did, and said they had never heard such words come from him before. He replied, 'The Lord hath fully made known that to my soul, which I had some feeling of before.' The next day he was very earnest in prayer softly to himself, but some words were heard, viz.: 'Oh! let all that know the pure truth, come and receive it, saith my soul.' He also sung of the olive tree, and of the fruit thereof, which he fed on, and of his refreshment thereby. He was asked what he meant by the olive tree. He said, 'The tree of life.' Many more sayings he uttered before he departed to his everlasting rest, which was on the 3d day of the Fifth month, in the year 1675, in the thirteenth day of his sickness.

ROBERT JECKEL, of Newcastle-upon-Tyne, in the county of Northumberland, having a desire to visit George Fox, who was then at Swarthmore, set out on his journey, in company with several friends, but began to be sick the same day that he went from home, and was ill at several places by the way; but still pressed forward, and would not be satisfied to stay short of Swarthmore, where he came the 2d of the Fifth month, 1676, and went to bed presently after he came in, and lay sick there nine days. During his illness, these following words, with many more, were spoken by him, viz.: 'No separation like unto this; soul separated from the body, the spirit returning to God that gave it, and the body to the earth, from whence it came. Great has the loving kindness of the Lord been to me, and not to me only, but to all my dear friends who are faithful unto death. I have always been faithful to the truth, as to what was manifested; for God hath loved me from a child.'

He added, spreading out his hands, 'O! the blessed precious truth is above all the world, and this is my living testimony I have to bear for the Lord, and his truth; for always I loved truth, and preferred it before all the world; for truth is precious; and to be valued before all things. Therefore, oh! my dear friends! prize this precious truth, for it abides for ever; let nothing divert your minds from that service of truth you have, for as that is kept to, truth answers truth in every heart. As to the principle of truth, it will reign over all. Though strange things may happen in this nation, yet the Lord will crown his blessed truth, and his glory is over all. Therefore, all my dear friends, be faithful to that manifestation in your own particulars, for a profession will stand none in stead, unless they live in the life and power of truth.' Another time he said, 'Though I was persuaded to stay by the way, being indisposed, before I came to this place, yet this was the place where I would have been, and the place where I should be, whether I live or die.'

George Fox visiting him, exhorted him to offer up his soul and spirit to the Lord who giveth breath and life to all, and he takes it again; and he lifted up his hands and said, 'The Lord is worthy of it, and I have done it.' George Fox then asked him if he could say, 'Thy will, O God, be done on earth, as it is done in heaven;' and he lifted up his hands and eyes, and cheerfully said, he did it. His mouth was often filled with praises to the Lord, exhorting those about him, saying, 'Dear friends, dwell in love and unity together, and keep out of jars, strife and contention, and be sure to continue faithful to the end, and be not weary in well-doing; for this is a good testimony, They that continue faithful to the end shall be saved.'

He said, 'If any bad spirits speak evil of me when I am gone, you are living witnesses' (speaking to two friends present, who were his neighbours) 'that I am an innocent man, and the Lord hath cleared me, and I lay down my head in peace. As to my wife, I give her freely up to the Lord; for she loveth the Lord, and he will love her. I have often told my dear wife, as to what we have in outward things, it was the Lord's first before it was ours, and in that I desire she may serve the truth to the end of her days. And now, my dear friends, I commit you all to the Lord, to be preserved and kept in his everlasting power, and bid you all everlastingly, yea, everlastingly, farewell. All is done, and to the Lord I leave you all; I commit you all, farewell.' Afterwards he said, 'Let us go hence in peace, for I shall go hence, and be no more seen in mutability.'

About two hours before he died, George Fox took him by the hand, and asked him if he was satisfied of his seeing him. He lifted up his hands, and with a gladness of heart, and smilingly, praised the Lord and said, that his comfort flowed in as a flood. George Fox asked him what he said; and he spoke those words over again. And in much patience the Lord did keep him; and he was in perfect sense and memory all the time of his weakness, often saying, 'Dear friends give me up, and weep not for me, but be willing to bear a part with me, for I am content with the Lord's doings.' He often said that he had no pain; but went away by little and little, lifting up his hands while he had strength, praising the Lord, and made a comfortable end, on the 11th of the Fifth month, in the year 1676.

WILLIAM SIXSMITH, of Warrington in the county of Lancaster, a young man about twenty-one years of age, was in time of health a pattern of piety and good example. When he was taken sick, he freely resigned up himself into the hand of the Lord, refusing a physician, saying, 'I am satisfied with the Lord's love;' and that he knew his Redeemer lived, who, if he pleased, was able to restore him to health, and if not, he was content. In the time of his sickness he was very patient and quiet, often praising God. A little before his death, calling his father, with an innocent look he gave him his right hand, saying, 'I desire thou wilt not be troubled.' And so laid down his life in peace, the 24th of the Seventh month, in the year 1677.

FRANCIS PATCHET, of Scotforth, in the county of Lancaster, was a prisoner for his testimony against tithes: the priest who prosecuted him removed him up to the Fleet prison in London, where he died a prisoner.

In the time of his sickness he prayed, 'O Lord God everlasting, glory and honour for ever be given to thy name. Thou hast made way for thy redeemed as in ancient days, when thou madest the sea dry land for thy people Israel to go through. O glory and honour for ever be unto thy name, who art unchangeable in all thy ways. Thou madest man in thy own image, but he lost it through disobedience. O Lord, in thy unspeakable love thou sent thy only Son Christ Jesus to redeem us again. Oh! everlasting praises to thy name for ever;' with many other words. Again he said, 'There is no God like our God; he has given his Son a light into the world, and his salvation to the ends of the earth. Oh! this blessed day wherein truth hath appeared: Oh! England's glory. Friends, obey the truth, love the truth, buy the truth, and sell it not: Oh! Christ Jesus, the way, the truth, and the life.'

Again he said, 'Glorious is the house of God, a house of holiness, a pure house, a house of love, and her gates praise. Our

God is a consuming fire; he consumes all that is bad, all impurity, all uncleanness, all that is unholy, all that is wrong.' Thus he went on praising God for sending his Son for the redemption of man, and spoke much of the Lord's making a way for his people in the nation of England. At another time he said, 'My strength fails me.' On which, one by him replied, 'I hope the Lord doth not fail thee:' he answered, 'Through mercy the Lord never failed me;' with more concerning the Lord's building of Zion, &c. Another time he said, speaking of the Lord, 'Oh! thy precious light, in which I see thy glory: what will become of them that despise thy light?' Again, 'The false prophet and the hireling the Lord will cut down, and all that resist his blessed work which he hath begun in this nation of England;' with more words of exhortation to friends, and praises to God; and so finished his testimony, a prisoner for truth, the 2d of the Tenth month, in the year 1677.

CHRISTOPHER BACON, of Polling-hill, in Somersetshire, was formerly a soldier in the king's army. About the year 1656, some of the Lord's servants, called Quakers, coming into that country to preach the gospel, he went to one of the meetings, not to receive good, but rather to scoff and deride. But, through the Lord's mercy, he was reached in his conscience, and received the blessed truth in the love of it; and afterwards received a dispensation of the gospel of Christ to preach, and was a diligent labourer in the work of the ministry. He travelled to London, and into Ireland and Wales, and many parts of the nation of England, and several were convinced of the truth by him.

In the year 1678, he came into the county of Cornwall, and there fell sick, being weak of body before, but had a good meeting of Friends in the town. Upon his sick bed he desired a Friend by him to write comfortably to his wife, if the Lord should take him away, and advise her, that she bring up her children in the fear and counsel of the Lord; and it was his fervent desire that his wife might be kept to truth; and [likewise] for all friends. And said, 'Since it is my lot, after many great labours and travels for the service of truth, to come here and lay down my body, I am well satisfied in God's will and pleasure, and am at this time free and clear in my mind, willing to be with God.' Then making some pause, he said, 'O! friends, keep in mind your latter end, and that will make you draw nigh to the Lord, and seek after him.'

He further said, 'Friends, take heed that you lose not an heavenly inheritance for an earthly.' The day before he died, being the First-day of the week, he spoke to friends as they were going to meeting, minding his dear love to friends, and said, 'The Lord's presence be amongst you, for his presence hath attended me in all my labours, travels, sufferings, and exercises, for his name's sake.' His end drawing near, and his body weak, he continued to the last moment in sweet harmony, lifting up his hands, and in much quietness and peace he gave up the ghost the 29th of the Tenth month, in the year 1678, aged about fifty-five years.

WILLIAM COALE, of Maryland, in America, was convinced of the blessed truth about the year 1657, and was a man of an innocent and tender spirit, of true judgment, and stood in the power and love of God against unrighteousness and false liberty; and for true liberty in Christ Jesus, and for holiness, peace, and unity in the church. He freely and tenderly preached the cross of Christ, and was living and weighty in his testimony. He suffered imprisonment in Jamestown prison, in Virginia, with George Wilson, a Friend of Old England, who travelled into America to preach the gospel, whom the magistrates of that town persecuted to death, after they had cruelly beaten and whipped him, and kept him long in iron chains; and the said William Coale was also much decayed in his body by that cruel imprisonment, and never recovered it.

His visit to friends in Virginia was very serviceable to many, some were turned to the Lord through his ministry, and many were established in the blessed truth. In the time of his sickness he was cheerful in spirit, freely given up to the will of God, as a living man prepared to die, saying, 'The living presence of the Lord is with me;' with many words more of the great satisfaction he had from the Lord concerning his peace, saying, 'I bless the Lord, I have finished my course, and I have nothing to do but to wait on the Lord to die.' So in a short time he departed very peaceably and quietly, about the year 1678.

SARAH BECK, wife of John Beck, of Dockra, in the county of Westmoreland, was an innocent woman, and one that feared the Lord. Even from a child, her heart was set to seek him and the prosperity of his truth, and the welfare of all people; and her chiefest care was to serve and obey the Lord. Being sick near unto death, it was thought she was dead, but recovering a little, she said, 'I was well, I was very well, if I had gone.' And after that, she praised and magnified the name of God, which much affected the hearts of many who were with her in her sickness. She said, 'O Lord, thou hast satisfied my soul. I desired that I might praise thee, and I am satisfied: honour, glory and hallelujahs be to thee, thou God of my life. I feel sweet peace and great joy: oh! the joy that is laid up for the righteous: oh! who would not fear the Lord! who would not be faithful!'

Taking her leave of her husband and her friends, one by one, she said, with a cheerful countenance, 'I am near going; this sweet end will come; it makes my heart glad when I remember my end; it will be the happiest hour that ever came to me.' Some observing her to be in great pain and very sick, said one to another, 'It is very hard;' she answered, 'Nay, it is very easy, for the Lord sweetens it. Oh! thou glorious God, thou hast satisfied my soul. I am filled with thy pure presence;' with these words, 'O that I may praise thee while I have breath and being!' as indeed she did, for even at the very hour of death she said, 'Call in the family;' and holding her husband by the hand, made sweet melody in her heart, saying, 'Dear God, what shall I render to thee for this evening sacrifice?' Thus she went on praising God till her natural strength failed, and then turned her face to the pillow and said no more; but died as if she had fallen asleep, being the thirteenth of the Sixth month, in the year 1679.

JOHN MATERN was a German, and educated in the learning of the schools, intending to be a priest. But it pleased God to visit him, even in his own country, in the year 1674, and his wife's father, Christopher Proham, who was a priest, was convinced also, and was a faithful friend, and died in peace with God in England, where they and their families came to live.

John Matern laboured about six years in great integrity, instructing youth in the knowledge of the tongues, and endeavoured to bring them to the fear of the Lord, and knowledge of his blessed truth. He lay sick about a week, and about four hours before he departed, at his desire, they called the youth of the school into his bed-chamber, where he had a meeting with the family, and he was filled with divine praises, magnifying the great power of God; and his prayer was fervent, that the Lord would carry on the good work begun among the children, and prosper his truth daily every where. He exhorted the children, as they sat around about him, to be faithful in their measures to a little, and more should be added. He gave thanks to God for many particular mercies, but more especially, that he had received the knowledge of the everlasting truth, and had walked uprightly therein; for which, he declared at that time, that he had the testimony of a good conscience, and was entering into eternal rest with the Lord.

He died in rest and peace on the 1st of the Seventh month, in the year 1680.

GILES BARNARDISTON, of Clare, in the county of Suffolk, came of a family of great account in the world, and had his education accordingly at the university, and his natural parts were answerable thereto; but when he received the truth, he saw not only the emptiness of those things, but of their way of worship also; and, like Moses, chose rather to join with the poor suffering people of God, called Quakers, than to enjoy the pleasures of sin for a season. After he was converted, it pleased God to commit a dispensation of the gospel unto him, and He laid a necessity upon him to preach the same; which he faithfully performed to the day of his death, not regarding the tenderness of his body so much, as to fulfil the will of God.

When he was about to enter upon an hard journey, or otherwise exercised, he would say, 'That is but for a short time, and we shall have done in this world; and I desire that I may be faithful to the end, that I may enjoy that of the hand of the Lord, that I received the truth for. If it had not been to obtain peace of conscience whilst I am in this world, and hopes of everlasting rest with God in the world to come, I would never have left the glory and pleasure of this world, which I had, and might have had, a share of, with them that are in it. Neither would I now leave my house and home, where I have a loving wife, with all that a man, fearing God, needs to desire, if it was not to obey the Lord, and to make known his truth unto others, that so they may come to be saved. For this cause do I forsake father and mother, wife and estate; and whosoever thinks otherwise of me, with the rest of my faithful brethren whom God hath called into his work, to declare his name and truth among the sons of men, they are all mistaken of us, and I would they knew us better.' He continued faithful in the Lord's work to the end; and he was blessed in his labour, for he turned many to righteousness.

It pleased the Lord to visit him with sickness, in his return from London to Chelmsford, and his sickness was short; in which time he gave testimony to the goodness of God, and said that the Lord was his portion, and that he was freely given up to die, which was gain to him. And on the 11th of the Eleventh month, in the year 1680, he departed in peace.

ALICE CURWEN, of Lancashire, with her husband Thomas Curwen, travelled in the work of the ministry in divers parts of America, as New England, New York, Long Island, Rhode Island, and Barbadoes; and after many long journeys, and much service, returned home about the Third month, 1677.

The said Alice, being upon her dying bed, was asked if she thought she should recover of her sickness; to which she answered, 'I do not know what the Lord has to do; but I am freely given up to his will, whether it be life or death; I am as clear as a child.' Another time, complaining of the unfaithfulness of some professing truth, she said, 'But those who are faithful, the Lord will preserve them, though they may meet with many trials and besetments, both inwardly and outwardly.' And again, 'All stand faithful for the Lord in their day, and none need be afraid of death, for it will be easy to them as it is to me.'

She often, in the time of her sickness, made melody to God in her heart, and said, 'Oh! my heavenly Father, how hast thou filled my cup, and made it to overflow; for I can do no less than bless and praise thy eternal name.' She often desired God's will might be done, whether it was life or death; 'For,' said she, 'to me to live is Christ, and to die is gain.' She exhorted friends to be diligent, and to know life and virtue in themselves; 'For,' said she, 'the time will come that words shall cease, and life shall more arise;' and said, if she lived she must declare it; and if she died, she must leave it as a testimony for the Lord. Toward the latter end of the last night she lived, her pain was great, and she spoke to friends about her, saying, 'Pray to the Lord for me, that he lay no more upon me than I am able to bear; that I may not offend this good God.' And immediately she prayed to the Lord, and had a little ease, and lay still as if she had been in a slumber, and so grew weaker, and was sweetly carried through to the end. She died in London in the year 1680.

MARY SAMM, daughter of John Samm, of Bedfordshire, and grand-daughter of William Dewsbury, of Warwick, aged about twelve years, being taken sick, and her aunt finding her under a concern of mind, asked her, why she walked so often alone in the garden, when she was well, for she would many times be weeping alone. She replied, 'Dear aunt, I am troubled for want of a full assurance of my eternal salvation. Not any knows my exercise but the Lord alone, what I have gone through since I came to Warwick. It was begun before I came, but it was but a little. This was my trouble, I thought I should not live long, and that if I did die, I did not know whither my soul should go; but I hope the Lord will give me satisfaction before I die. It is but hope, and though but hope, yet for this my soul shall praise his name for ever.'

The next day, having more assurance of her future happiness, and some friends coming into her chamber, she said, 'I have been twice in my days nigh to death, but the Lord in his tender mercy prolonged my days, that I might seek his face in the light of Christ, and come to be acquainted with him before I go hence.' Also she said, 'If this distemper do not abate, I must die; but my soul shall go to eternal joy; eternal and everlasting life and peace with my God for ever.' At another time, 'They that live longest, endure the greatest sorrow; therefore, O Lord, if it be thy will, take me to thyself, that my soul may rest in peace with thee.' With many more good words.

The day following she desired all to go forth of the room. After a considerable time, her mother and grandfather went in again, when she said, 'I have now received full satisfaction of my eternal salvation. It is now done, it is now done.' And after saying something to her mother, she said, 'I am very willing to die, that the Lord may glorify his name this day, in his will being done with me:' often praying to the Lord, to lay no more upon her than she was able to bear, saying, 'Help me, O my God, that I may praise thy holy name for ever.' Her grandfather advising her to stillness, she answered, 'Dear grandfather, I shall die, and I cannot but praise the name of the Lord whilst I have a being. I do not know how to do to praise him enough.' Her grandfather inquiring how she did, she replied, 'I have had no rest to-night, nor to-day. I did not know but I should have died this night, but very hardly I tugged through it; but I shall die to-day, and a grave shall be made, and my body put into a hole, and my soul shall go into heavenly joy, and into everlasting peace for evermore.' After more expressions, her aunt asked her if she thought she was upon her death-bed: she replied, 'Yea, yea, I am upon my death-bed. I shall die to-day, and I am very willing to die, because I know it is better for me to die than to live.'

After some time, and other expressions, she inquired the time of the day, which being told, she said, 'I thought it was more. I will see if I can have a little rest and sleep, before I die.' So she lay still, and had a sweet sleep, and awaked without complaint; and then in a quiet, peaceable frame of spirit laid down her head the same day in peace, being the 9th of the Second month, in the year 1680, in the twelfth year of her age.

MORDECAI HEARN was a young man whom the Lord in his mercy reached to in his tender years, and called by his holy Spirit in his heart, and he hearkened to the call of the Lord, so that he became a prepared vessel, by the Lord, for his use and service. God opened his heart, and mouth also, sometimes, to declare of his goodness and mercy, and speak to the praise of his grace in the congregations of his people, until the twenty-third year of his age, when it pleased the Lord to accept of his mite, offered in faithfulness and sincerity, and to cut his work short in this evil world, and give him his heavenly crown of reward.

He was visited with illness, which brought him into a consumption; and in his weakness and great affliction of body, he said to some friends who stood by him, as he lay in bed, as follows: 'Blessed be the Lord, that ever he made me to remember my Creator in the days of my youth, seeing old age is not likely to be my portion; but a portion hath the Lord provided for me among the faithful, in which my soul rejoices with you, dear friends; for this is our joy, and the crown of our rejoicing.' Another time he said, 'Friends, the Lord is wonderfully good to me in my sore affliction; he comforteth me with his sweet presence, which is more to me than all the fading things of this world. Oh! it is good to trust in the Lord, for he never faileth them that put their trust in him.' And so he lay in a sweet, quiet, and tender frame of spirit.

Many friends being about him, he exhorted them, with tears on his cheeks, to follow the Lord fully, and to go on in his work and service, and the Lord would be with them. This he spoke in so living a sense of the Lord's power, that those about him were much broken into tears, which, when he beheld, he, with a sweet heavenly countenance said, 'Friends, weep not for me; it is well with me. Death is no terror to me, for the sting thereof is taken away, so that I am not afraid to die. And although my body be laid in the dust, yet in this, dear friends, remember that I am now going but a little before, and you must follow me.' And soon after these words were spoken, he raised himself upon his knees, being in bed, and returned praises to the Lord for his goodness and loving kindness that was then shed abroad in their hearts. He besought the Lord that he would be with his servants and handmaids; and that he would prosper that work which he had begun.

At another time, a near relation came to visit him, whom he entirely respected and loved, who had much lost his former condition in the truth, to whom he spoke in much love and tenderness, saying, 'Oh! that our portion might be together. I fear thou despairest. Oh! do not distrust the Lord, for he is all sufficient; he is able to restore thee: but I fear thou dost distrust his mercy. The thought of it is more grievous to me than all my afflictions. Oh! that we should be separated; that grieves me.'

Being full of pain, and weak, he groaned, saying, 'Surely the Lord will release me in his time; surely the Lord will ease me of this pain, for I am pained. I do not desire to live here.' When he drew near to his departure, he awaked out of sleep or slumber; and soon after, his mother discerning him to breathe short, said to his sister, 'I think thy brother is now dying:' and he, hearing her voice, spoke these words: 'I am glad, I am glad; I go away with joy.' He called for his father, mother, and sister, to kiss them, and said, 'Weep not for me, for I have peace with the Lord.' He lived some hours after, and lay praising him, saying, 'The Lord is worthy to be waited upon; he will release me in his own time,' &c. Speaking to those about him, he said, 'To outward appearance my time is but short in this world; but this I have to say, the Lord hath been good to me in my pilgrimage, and therefore be you faithful to the Lord in his requirings, to the end of your days, and he will never leave you nor forsake you.'

He quietly departed this life, the ninth day of the Seventh month, in the year 1681, being twenty-three years and ten months old, at Sabridgworth in Hertfordshire.

SARAH CAMM, daughter of Thomas Camm, of Cam's-gill, in Westmoreland, and of Anne his wife, a child of nine years old, was visited with sickness the 13th of the Seventh month, 1682. She declared that she should be taken away by death, saying, 'I am neither afraid nor unwilling to die, but am freely given up thereto in the will of God.' When she saw her relations weep, she would say, 'Oh! do not so, do not so.' Being near death, her sickness increased; but she was very patient, only had deep sighs. Her father asked her if she could not pray to the Lord for help; her answer was, she could, and did pray. She further said, it was her belief, that the Lord, the great God of heaven and earth, would keep her, and preserve her soul, whatever might become of her body.

In the fifth day of her sickness, being under more than usual exercise of mind and spirit, after a little space she revived, and sat upright in her bed, and with a cheerful countenance said as followeth, 'My sins are forgiven me, and I shall have a resting place in heaven.' Then looking at her mother, she said, 'Oh! my mother, there is also a place prepared for thee in heaven, and thou shalt as certainly enjoy it as any here. I do not,' said she, 'desire my mother's death, or removal from you; yet we shall meet in heaven in God's time.' Seeing her friends weep, she said, 'Oh! you should not do so; I am well, I am well.' Her father desired the company to withdraw, lest they should trouble her but she soon called them in again, and said, 'Shall I go down to the horrible pit? Nay, the Lord hath redeemed my soul:' and called her brother, to whom she spoke very sensibly. To her sister she said, 'Be content, for it is, and will be well with me. I must go to a more fair place than ever my eyes beheld. It will be well with me, and all that fear the Lord, for we shall have everlasting joy in heaven, when the wicked shall be tormented in hell.'

Seeing her sister weep, she said, 'Do not cry, dear Mary, lest thou grieve the Lord: be subject to the Lord's will in all things, and love and be faithful to the truth, and do not forsake thy religion, whatever thou suffer for it.' And further said, 'I am satisfied with my religion. I will not forsake it, though I should be fed with the bread of adversity and water of affliction. Oh! praises, praises to my God, and my Father. Our Father, which art in heaven, hallowed be thy name;' and so said to the end of the Lord's prayer twice over; and the third time till she came to that petition, 'Thy will be done on earth, as it is done in heaven,' which she spoke deliberately, signifying to those about her, that they were all to mind that; 'For,' said she, 'I am freely given up to his blessed will in all things: praises to my God, bless his name, O my soul.'

Another time, her father having her in his arms, she said, 'Oh! my dear father, thou art tender and careful over me, and hast taken great pains with me in my sickness, but it availeth not, there is no help nor succour for me in the earth; it is the Lord that is my health and physician, and he will give me ease and rest everlasting.' Near her end she took leave of the family particularly, saying, with a pleasant voice, 'Farewell, farewell unto you all, only farewell; signifying, that now she had no more to say; and so went on praising the Lord, and continued in a sweet frame till she died, wanting eleven days of nine years old.

She died the 18th of the Seventh month, in the year 1682.

JOSEPH FEATHERSTONE, of Crowland, in Lincolnshire, was a man whom the Lord endued with much meekness, and he loved truth, and to do the will of God. In the time of his sickness he was freely resigned to the will of God, saying to his wife, 'My dear, give me up to the will of the Lord, for I can freely give up all.' When some of his friends came to visit him, he exhorted them to faithfulness, and said, 'The Lord will make a dying-bed comfortable to you;' that though he felt much sickness and pain upon his body, yet the refreshment he felt from the Lord made all his troubles easy.

He prayed that his wife and friends might be preserved in God's holy fear and undefiled way, to bear a testimony to the blessed truth to the end of their days. The day before he died, being somewhat restless, his wife said, 'Dear heart, thou art restless;' he answered, with a cheerful countenance, 'Dost thou not know where the weary go to rest?' and said, 'My rest and fellowship are with the Lord.' A little before his death, he rested a pretty while, and being asked how he did, he said, 'I am well, blessed be the Lord;' and desired his wife to be satisfied; and then lifting up his hands, he said, 'O Lord, thou art the eternal God.' And so fell asleep in the Lord the 26th of the Ninth month, in the year 1682.

JUDITH FELL, a young woman twenty-four years of age, daughter of Thomas and Anne Fell, near Ireby, in Cumberland, was never inclinable to vain company, nor to pride nor lightness of carriage, but always was very sober, and ready to be a good example to others, so that she abundantly enjoyed the love of the Lord; insomuch that on her sick-bed she was wonderfully filled, to the refreshment of others. Her sickness increasing, which was at times very severe upon her, some inquired of her how she did; she replied, 'I am well every way. If I should live ever so long, it can never be better; for my heart is fully satisfied, and my soul magnifies God, who is worthy for ever.' Another time she requested her father not to desire her health, for she said she felt that which was beyond all her weakness and sickness. Another time she said the sting of death was removed, and she felt victory over the grave; and so praised the Lord, saying, 'Surely it is thou, O God, that lives and reigns, and must reign for ever; and they are ever blessed who serve thee, and fear thy name. Thou, O God, reignest in the hearts of the sanctified, and thou hast sanctified my heart, so that I can truly praise thy name. Thou knowest, Lord, for what end thou hast cast me on this bed of sickness; surely it is for the glory of thy name; therefore, Father, glorify thyself in me.'

The day before she died, she said she saw that that day she was given to her friends; and so continued quiet and easy in her spirit, and several times slept very sweetly. At the end of that night her sickness increased, and she desired to see some friends, and spoke words to their great refreshment. The next day, after great fits of illness, she broke forth in praises, saying, 'He is come that brings joy: Oh! the streams of his love run over all, even to the skirts of the garment. Now is the fountain set open for Judah and Jerusalem to bathe in. Once more solace thyself, my soul, and delight thyself in thy Saviour; for I feel his love and life run afresh in my soul, so that now my spirit doth magnify him that lives for ever.' Her distemper prevailing upon her, they thought that she would not have spoken any more; but she lifted up her head and said, 'This is the way to rest; this is the way to rest for ever.' In a little time she drew her last breath, and ended her life comfortably, in the twenty-fourth year of her age, in the year 1682.

JONAH LAWSON, son of Thomas Lawson, of Westmoreland, aged about fourteen years, was a youth well inclined, of a peaceable spirit, and not known to tell a lie. He was taken sick of the small-pox; and in his sickness, his father putting him in mind of the difference betwixt this world and heaven, where is nothing but joy, the lad answered, 'Ay, father, I hope I have but little to answer for, and that I have a good conscience. I have abhorred lying and swearing, and what I saw to be evil; and am willing to die, if it be the Lord's pleasure, or to live to praise him.' His sister weeping, he said to her, 'Weep not, I hope we shall meet in a better place.' Soon after he uttered these words to the Lord: 'The time thou hast appointed for me on earth; give me grace to praise thy name.' Presently after, as if answered from heaven, he said, 'O, sweet God.' A little before his departure, his father and sister being present, he said, 'I am coming, I am coming. I must yield, I must yield.'

He died on the 23d of the Twelfth month, in the year 1683, aged fourteen years. After his death, his father found the following verses of Jonah's making, viz.:

Humility the spring of virtue is;
Humbling thyself, virtue thou canst not miss.
Delight in virtue; vice be sure to shun:
He 's happy that a virtuous course doth run.

ELIZABETH BRAITHWAIT, a young maid of seventeen years of age, died in prison for the testimony of a good conscience, at Kendal, in Westmoreland. From a child, God by his grace inclined her heart to love, fear, and serve him; and she was truly obedient to her parents, sober and chaste in her life and conversation, kind to all, and of a meek and quiet spirit. She was, with several others of the people called Quakers, taken up by a warrant, dated the 25th of the Fifth month, 1684, for not going to church (so called) and carried to Kendal jail. After some time, she had liberty for a few days to be at her brother's house; but complaint being made against the keeper, she was sent for, and she was not easy till she returned to prison, for she said, 'That is my place, and my present home; there I have most peace and content.'

About two months after her commitment, viz.: the 17th of Seventh month, she was taken sick in prison, and her mother coming to visit her, asked if she had a mind to go home; she replied, 'No, no; I am at home in my place, to my full content; and if my God so order it that I be dissolved, I had rather die here than in any other place. I am glad that I got to this place before I began to be sick: here I have peace and true content in the will of God, whether life or death. I am only grieved that there should be so little tenderness or pity in the hearts of my persecutors, to keep such a poor young one as I am in prison. The Lord forgive them, I can freely.' She further said, that 'her imprisonment was by the permission of the Almighty, who is greater, and above the greatest of my persecutors, who I believe will shortly set me free from these, and all other bonds, over all their heads; and in his peace, in true patience I possess my soul, and am contented, if it be his will, to be dissolved.' A friend asked her why she was so willing to die. 'Oh,' said she, 'I have seen glorious sights of good things.' The friend queried, 'What things;' she answered, 'They are so excellent and glorious that it is not utterable; and now I have nothing but love and good-will to all.' But more especially she was glad in the love and unity she felt with friends; 'with whom, said she, 'I have been often refreshed in our meetings together, with the refreshment that comes from the presence of the Lord. Oh! the good evening meetings we have had.' Another time she said to her mother, 'They say that we shall spend all our riches with lying here in prison; nay, our riches are durable, and our treasure hidden, laid up in heaven.'

Her mother seeing her lie under great weight of sickness, would sometimes weep; but she was always troubled at it, and said, 'Dear mother, do not weep, but resign me freely up into the hand of the Lord. Weep not for me, for I am well, Christ my Redeemer is with me.' And to her sister she said, 'Come sister, lie down by me, do not sorrow for me, I am well content to live or die; for my God hath blessed me, and will bless me, and his blessings rest upon me.' A little before she departed, her speech failed; after which she would sing in her heart; lifting up her hands with a cheerful countenance, and taking her friends by the hand with great affection, so fell asleep in the Lord on the 28th of the Seventh month, in the year 1684, in the seventeenth year of her age.

DAVID BARCLAY, of Urie, in the kingdom of Scotland, father of Robert Barclay, the great and eminent apologist for true Christianity, was convinced of truth in the Seventh month, in the year 1666, being then in the fifty-sixth year of his age; and abode in the truth, and in constant unity with the faithful friends thereof to the end; having suffered the spoiling of his goods, and many other indignities, besides several tedious imprisonments, after the sixty-sixth year of his age.

In the latter end of the Seventh month, 1686, being past the seventy-sixth year of his age, he was taken with a fever, which continued upon him for two weeks; during which time he signified that he had a quiet and contented mind, freely resigned up to the will of God. About two days before he died, being troubled with the gravel, and much pain, in an agony he said, 'I am going now;' but instantly checking himself, added, 'but I shall go to the Lord, and be gathered to many of my brethren, who are gone before me.' Upon the 11th day of the Eighth month, between two and three in the morning, he growing weaker, his eldest son drew nigh to him, and he said, 'Is this my son?' Robert answered, 'Yea;' signifying his travail, that he that loved him might be near him to the end. To which he answered, 'The Lord is nigh.' Repeating it once again, he said, 'You are my witnesses in the presence of God, that the Lord is nigh.' A little after he said,

'The perfect discovery of the day-spring from on high; how great a blessing it hath been to me and my family!'

Robert Barclay's wife desiring to know if he would have something to wet his mouth, he answered, 'It needs not.' She said it would refresh him; he then laid his hand upon his breast, saying he had that inwardly that refreshed him: and after a little while he added, 'The truth is over all.' He took his eldest son Robert to him, and blessed him, and prayed God he might never depart from the truth. When his son's eldest daughter came near, he said, 'Is this Patience? let patience have its perfect work in thee.' And after kissing his son's other four children, he laid his hands upon them, and blessed them. Perceiving one by, (who was not a friend in the truth,) weeping much, he wished she might come to the truth, bidding her not weep for him, but for herself.

A sober man, an apothecary that waited upon him in his sickness, coming near, he took him by the hand, saying, 'Thou wilt bear me witness, that in all this exercise I have not been curious to tamper, nor to pamper the flesh.' The man said, 'Sir, I can bear witness that you have always minded the better and more substantial part, and rejoice to see the blessed end the Lord is bringing you to.' He replied, 'Bear a faithful and true witness; yet it is the life of righteousness (repeating these words twice over) that we bear testimony to, and not empty profession.' He, supposing a man that was by him to be a carpenter, said to his son, 'See thou charge him to make no superfluity upon my coffin.'

About three in the afternoon there came several friends from Aberdeen to visit him, and he took them by the hand, and said they were come in a seasonable time. And after some words were spoken, and Patrick Livingston had prayed, which ended in praises, he held up his hands, and said, 'Amen, Amen, Amen, for ever.' After they stood up, looking at him, he said, 'How precious is the love of God among his children, and their love one to another. Hereby shall all men know that you are my disciples, if you love one another. How precious a thing it is to see brethren dwell together in love!

My love is with you; I leave it among you.' Perceiving some of his friends to weep, he said, 'Dear friends, all mind the inward man, heed not the outward; there is one that doth regard, the Lord of Hosts is his name.' After he had heard the clock strike three, in the afternoon, he said, 'Now the time comes.' And a little after he was heard to say, 'Praises, praises, praises to the Lord: let now thy servant depart in peace. Into thy hands, O Father, I commit my soul, spirit, and body. Thy will, O Lord, be done on earth as it is in heaven.' A little after five in the morning, on the 12th day of the Eighth month, in the year 1686, he fell asleep like a lamb, in remarkable quietness and calmness; there being standing about him, to behold his end, about twenty persons, who were witnesses to what is above said.

JOSEPH FULLER, a young man about twenty-five years of age, son of Abraham Fuller, of Queen's County, in Ireland, having been sick three days, his father desired some relations to sit down, and wait upon the Lord in Joseph's chamber. He being asked if it was not tiresome to sit so long, his answer was, 'I bless the Lord for this opportunity.' His brother's wife asking him how he did, he said, 'I have had a wearisome night; but I have had joy in the presence of the Lord.' Next night he sang praises to the Lord, and said to his sister, 'Never, since I was born, such words came from me; this is from the Lord.' More he said to the same purpose to his father, and further said to him, 'Tell all my brothers and sisters, that they take their minds from the things of this world, and have their minds fixed upon the Lord.' Taking his father by the hand, he said, 'Farewell, farewell.' Afterwards he said, 'Well, I thought to have gone when I bid you farewell, (his sister being also with his father,) but I shall not go yet.' A little while after he said to his sister, 'Jane, I am long a dying.'

About a quarter of an hour before he drew his last breath,

he said to his sister, 'See what hour it is.' She replied, 'It is seven.' Then he asked her, lies my head right for dying? If it doth not lie right, do thou lay it right.' She told him it did lie right. So he lay until he drew his last breath, which was a quarter past the seventh hour in the morning, on the 17th of the Seventh month, in the year 1686. Aged about twenty-five years.

ROBERT WIDDERS, born in Upper Kellet, in Lancashire, of honest parents, was a seeker after the Lord, and the knowledge of his way; and when George Fox visited those parts, he received the knowledge of the truth, which was in the year 1652. He was a faithful servant of Christ, and laboured for the good of souls; and to that end, in the year 1671, he travelled with George Fox in divers parts of America, as Barbadoes, Virginia, Maryland, Jamaica, Long Island, Rhode Island, &c., and great perils they went through both by sea and land, and in the wilderness, and lying in the woods, in danger of wild beasts, and through all the Lord supported him, and kept him faithful to the end.

He was many times concerned to go to the public places of worship to call the people to repentance, for which he endured hard sufferings, as at Coldbeck steeple-house, where the people threw him down among the seats, afterwards dragged him out into the yard, and threw him on the ground, punching and beating him so cruelly, that the blood gushed out at his mouth, and he lay for dead.

For speaking to the people at Acton steeple-house, he was sent to Carlisle jail, where he lay in a dungeon among thieves a long time, and was not suffered to come out day nor night, till he was released. At Lamplough steeple-house they tore the clothes upon his back, and the hair off his head; and in Bishop Aulkland, speaking to the people as he passed through the town, they stoned him with stones, which very sorely bruised his head.

He afterwards travelled into Scotland with George Fox, and there went to a steeple-house called New Munckland, besides many other places, where in the fear of God, and love to the people's souls, he was constrained to direct them to the word of God in their hearts. Through all which sufferings the Lord kept and preserved him by his power, blessed be his everlasting name for ever.

Also, for his faithfulness in his testimony against tithes, and for the true worship of God in spirit and truth, he had much spoil of his goods; but when his cattle, corn, and household goods were as it were by wholesale swept away, he was not in the least dejected nor concerned, knowing well for what he suffered: his loss on these accounts was of considerable value.

He was faithful, noble and valiant for God's truth, over all its gainsayers; though he was not large in declaration, yet he was large in integrity and zeal, and was endowed with a word of wisdom, and in discerning and sound judgment, and gave good advice and admonition to friends, for establishing them in the faith wherever he came; and the Lord prospered his work in his hand.

During the time of his sickness he was in a resigned frame of mind, given up to the will of God, and spoke of the mercies of God to his church, saying, 'God will comfort Zion, and repair her decayed places, and make her desert as a paradise, and her wilderness as a garden of the Lord: mirth and joy shall be found there, thanksgiving and the voice of praise.' At another time, speaking of his own experience, he said that the work of righteousness is peace, and the effect of righteousness is quietness and assurance for ever. He would often upon his death-bed say his heart was filled with the love of God; and that there was nothing betwixt him and the Lord. Saying to the Lord, 'Thou hast taught me the way of life, and makest me full of life, and makest me full of joy with thy countenance.'

His love to God, and good-will to his brethren, filled his heart with tender and heavenly comfort, so that within two hours before his death, he discoursed sensibly with friends about him, and passed quietly and patiently away, in the First month 1686, after he had been a believer in the truth thirty-four years, being then in the sixty-eighth year of his age.

ANN WHITEHEAD, wife of George Whitehead, of London, was an early believer in the blessed truth. In the year 1656 she travelled on foot about two hundred miles, into Cornwall, to visit George Fox and other Friends in Launceston prison, in that county; and in that journey convinced many people, some of whom were of account; and in her return confirmed and established several who were newly convinced. She continued a faithful woman to the end, and was very serviceable in the church of Christ, not only in respect to her ministry, but also to the poor widows and orphans, and to the sick, whom she did truly consider, and spared not herself to serve them who were in distress, so that nothing might be wanting.

In the year 1686, finding herself indisposed in health, she went a few miles out of London to a friend's house, where, continuing weak, about four days before her decease, she declared in the presence of several, saying, 'Friends, I would not have you too much concerned about me; as to my going hence. I am in the hand of the Lord. I desire the God of peace and love may be among all Friends, and that they may be kept in love, and peace, and concord, unto which we were gathered in the beginning; and that the same that gathered us in the beginning, may always preserve Friends in the spirit of love, and of the same mind: as the God of love and peace may please to dispose of me, I am content in his will.'

Her ancient friend, Mary Stout of Hartford, visiting her, and she being asked if she knew her, replied, 'Yes, very well; it is Mary Stout. I have my memory very well, and my understanding is clear, though I am very weak; but I am given up to the will of the Lord, whether to die or live; for I have been faithful to him in what I knew, both in life and death.' When she discovered any friends to be troubled, she would say, 'There is no cause for you to be troubled or concerned, for I am well, and in peace, and have nothing to do.'

Besides the many seasonable, tender and Christian exhortations and counsels, which on her dying-bed she gave, in the love of God, to particular friends, some friends from London coming to visit her, she said, 'What! do you come on purpose to see me! I take it as an effect of the love of God; and I pray God bless your children.' Another time to one of the same friends, she said, 'Remember me to all friends. I pray God bless your families, and if I never see thy face more, it is well with me. God doth know my integrity, and how I have been, and walked before him; and I am in charity with all Friends; and be not over careful, or troubled for me, but be retired and quiet.'

The evening before she died she said to her husband, George Whitehead, 'The Lord is with me; I bless his name; I am well. It may be you are afraid I shall be taken away; and if it be, the will of the Lord be done. Do not trouble yourselves, nor make any great ado about me; but, my dear, go to bed, go to rest; and if I should speak no more words to thee, thou knowest the everlasting love of God.' Another time, said she had done with all things in this life; that she had nothing troubled her, but was at true peace and ease every way. And but a few hours before she departed, said, 'Though I am in a dying condition, yet it is a living death; and though weakness doth seize on my body, yet my understanding and sense is as perfect and clear as when I was in perfect health.' And so, in true love and charity with all, she quietly departed this life on the 27th of the Fifth month, in the year 1686.

BARBARA SCAIF, daughter of William Scaif and Isabel his wife, of Blackside, near Appleby, in the county of Westmoreland, with her sister Mary, were both taken sick on the

30th day of the First month, 1686, within one and the same hour, of the small-pox; and were both of them dutiful children, fearing God, and making profession of the principle of light and life in Christ Jesus, to which the people called Quakers bear testimony.

At the beginning of their sickness, divers of the neighbours came to visit them; but Barbara said, 'Mother, suffer but a few to stay. When they have seen us, desire them to go into the house, for we have no need of such empty talk as is used amongst too many. We would be quiet, that we may pray to the Lord to forgive us the faults we have committed; and if he spare us our lives at this time, I hope and believe we shall amend, and have a care of displeasing the Lord while we live.' About the seventh day of her sickness she prayed to the Lord, saying, 'O, Almighty God! I cry to thee; blot out all my transgressions, O Lord, and all my sins; let them come no more into thy remembrance. I beg it of thee, in the name of Jesus Christ, with all my soul, and with all my strength; and let thy favourable countenance be upon me.'

She also prayed that the Lord would confirm and strengthen her weak sister, to give up herself freely, as she blessed the Lord she herself had done; and then prayed for her parents; and many supplications besides, for a considerable time, in the presence of several people that were not called Quakers, who said, 'How can any die better than she is like to do?' To her brother she said, 'Be faithful to the Lord, and to thy religion,' &c. Being asked if she could freely part with her dear relations, her answer was, 'I can freely part with, and leave them all, for the enjoyment of the comfort and happiness which my soul is made sensible of;' and praised the Lord for the riches of his grace and comfort that she had received from him to her immortal soul. Being pressed to receive some meat, she said, 'Do not trouble me with meat, for if thereby you think to keep me, it is all in vain, for I must die and leave you. Neither would I desire to live for all the world; for to be with the Lord is better than ten thousand worlds, with whom I shall rest for evermore, even with God and his saints, his faithful people and servants: glory to his name for evermore.'

In her sickness she manifested great love to her parents, and also to her sick sister Mary, saying, 'Go to her, do not stay with me, whatever may befal me; that too sharp sickness may not fall on her, until she know her peace with God.' To her brother she gave religious counsel, saying, 'Love the Lord with all thy heart, and with all thy soul, all thy life-time; love not the world, nor the pleasures thereof.' All the time of her sickness she was tender in her spirit, and circumspect, not an unbecoming word proceeded out of her mouth; kind and pitiful to those about her, not so much concerned at her own sickness, as for them who attended her, considering the trouble they had in helping her.

That day she had lain a month sick (being much like as she had been for three weeks before), she was very cheerful, and able to express herself, and said to her mother, 'What thinkest thou of this forenoon?' Her mother asked her what she meant: she replied, 'It will go far in my time in this world, for the Lord will ease me ere long, take away all my pain, and wipe away all tears from mine eye. Call in my father (said she) that he may see my departure.' Her father being come, he said, 'Barbara, how dost thou?' She replied, 'I am ready to leave this world; therefore, father and mother, be content, and bear me company a little while.' And about the first hour in the afternoon she departed this life, as if she had fallen asleep, on the 27th of Second month, in the year 1686.

MARY SCAIF was elder sister to the aforesaid Barbara, taken sick the same hour that she was, and for whom her sister Barbara had been often tenderly concerned in supplication to God, to give her the knowledge of his peace that hath no end. She lived about two weeks after her said sister, her sickness being also the small-pox; and in the Lord's time, who keepeth covenant, and shows mercy, and giveth the spirit of supplication and prayer to them that believe, he gave her a clear understanding, and she prayed unto God as followeth: 'O great God, Jehovah, of heaven and earth, whose splendour filleth heaven, and thy wonders fill the earth, have mercy upon me thy hand-maid, who am as a worm before thee, yet part of thy creation. Lord, help my weak soul, revive my drooping spirit: by thy consoling presence strengthen my faith, I beseech thee, and help me through this exercise. I beseech thee, Lord, that thy will may be done in earth, as it is done in heaven;' and continued in prayer a considerable time, supplicating for a willing mind, to resign herself up to God.

She was much inclined from a child to read the holy Scriptures; and she often spoke of Job, David, and others of God's servants in former ages. 'And now,' said she, 'I do know God's love to be the same to me as it was to them, so that I am neither afraid nor unwilling to die; for God blotteth out my transgressions, and lays nothing to my charge, and I do believe there is a place prepared for me in heaven. And, dear mother, do what thou canst not to sorrow. My love is great to thee, and my advice is, that you go and live near some good meeting, and bring up my brother amongst friends.' Her sister being dead, she spoke of her own death also, and was satisfied that her soul should ascend up to God in heaven, 'where,' said she, 'I believe my sister Barbara's soul is ascended, to rest with the Lord for ever.' Her sickness increasing, she grew weaker, and departed this life on the 13th of the Third month, in the year 1686.

AMARIAH DREWET, of Cirencester, in Gloucestershire, preached in his life and conversation; for he was faithful according to the measure the Lord had given him, and turned not his back in time of suffering, but rather blessed the Lord that he was found worthy to be one of that number to have his faith tried, often praying for his persecutors.

On the 11th of the Seventh month, 1686, he was visited with sickness, and the Lord so filled his soul with his love and presence, that three days before his death he signified, if it was the last testimony he had to bear, the love and presence and peace of God was with him; and that he could truly say, as good old Simeon did, that he had seen the salvation of God. The night before his departure he said to his wife, 'Go to bed, thou hast need of rest, and give me up to the Lord, whose presence I feel, and I resign thee up; may the Keeper of Israel, that good watchman, that neither slumbers nor sleeps, be with thee.'

At other times he prayed, 'O Lord, strengthen my poor body, that I may praise thy name; my rest is in thee. Oh! the largeness of thy love that I feel. O Lord, hear my cries, and bear up my head in all my exercises. Oh! thy sweet presence, and fresh springs that I feel! Glory and honour, and praises, be unto thy name for ever.' Again, 'Lord help me, and keep me close to thy power.' With divers other petitions that he put up to the Lord; admonishing people who came to visit him, and warning the young to fear God, and watch against those things that did corrupt youth; exhorting them to faithfulness, that it might be well with them upon their dying bed, as it was with him. He uttered many more heavenly expressions, which are omitted for brevity. He lay half an hour, as if he had been asleep, and went away quietly, without sigh or groan; and so departed this life, on the 25th of the Seventh month, in the year 1686.

BENJAMIN PADLEY, son of William and Elizabeth Padley, of North Cave, in the East Riding of Yorkshire, was a young man that walked in humility, zeal and love towards God, and to all who walked in his truth. The Lord was pleased to raise him to bear testimony to his everlasting truth, in the assemblies of his people; and his great delight was in the prosperity of the truth, for which he faithfully and zealously laboured to the end of his days, having regard to the motion of God's spirit in his ministry, and lived according to his testimony. He was sound, plain, and weighty in his declaration, and kept low and humble, in a deep sense of the need he had to wait upon God, for the renewing of his mercies, and fresh openings of the springs of life and love from God, to help him forward in his spiritual travail, that he might persevere to the end; and to which he did much exhort, and stir up Friends where he came.

He was taken sick the 17th of Sixth month, 1687; which sickness continued about eight days. In this time several Friends, and also neighbours and relations, came to see him; and in the sense of God's love he declared truth amongst them. There being some present who did not profess the same truth with us, he said, 'It is not for any outward thing we travel abroad; not any man's silver or gold that we seek or covet after; but it is for the gaining of souls. We have suffered the loss of our goods, scoffings, scornings, and imprisonments; so that it may appear that it hath not been the benefit of any man's goods or estate that hath been in our eye, but for performing the will of the Lord. Several of his neighbours being present, he said, 'It is well for them that can say, on their dying beds, that their sins and iniquities are blotted out.' He prayed to the Lord, that he would mix mercies with his afflictions; and exhorted friends to faithfulness and righteousness. Observing his wife to weep, he said, 'O, why dost thou so? thou must not do so; but keep to truth, and fear not but all will be well.' At night he said to her, 'Go to bed, and be not troubled about me.' Friends visiting him, he said, 'I am glad to see so many of your faces, which I thought I should not have done, being the Lord hath been pleased to visit me with sickness, so that I am not likely to continue many days here; but I feel nothing, but all is well.' When his friends would be careful about some physician to help him, he said, 'I have a physician the world knows not of.'

When he drew near his end he desired to be helped upon his knees, and was so powerful in prayer to the Lord, considering the weakness of his body, that it was an admiration to all present. After that, few words proceeded from him, but he weakened apace, and the next day departed this life, being the 25th of the Sixth month, in the year 1687.

SARAH FEATHERSTONE, daughter of Joseph Featherstone and Sarah his wife, aged about fifteen years, was inclined in her tender years to hear the voice of wisdom, and to remember her Creator in the days of her youth. From a child she was harmless, and obedient to her parents, and of a meek and quiet spirit. She was taken sick the 9th of the Seventh month, 1688.

Her mother coming to her, she told her that she thought she should be taken from her; and when her mother would send for a doctor, she said she was freely given up to the will of the Lord, whether to live or die. She farther said it was showed her that she was not of a long life; and, 'if this be the time of my change, I am content.' Her sickness increasing, her mother was much concerned; at which she was troubled, and said, 'Dear mother, thy dear and tender love to me hath been very great, and in that love I desire we may rest, freely given up to the will of God; for the Lord may not see meet to trust me in this wicked world any longer.' And farther she said, 'O! the abominable pride of this world! and there are some amongst us who can take liberty to fashion themselves in many things like unto the world, both in their habit and other needless things. Oh! but the Christian life is another thing; this is not the adorning that we are to put on; for if the righteous scarcely be saved, where shall the wicked and ungodly appear?'

Her distemper being violent, she then said, 'Never so sick in my life; O! sick at my heart! O Lord, in mercy remember me, and bear me up above all my afflictions, for my heart trusteth in thee.' Being asked by her mother whether she would be buried by her father, or at another burying-place, she answered, 'Dear mother, bury me where thou and my father

(her father-in-law) please, I leave it to you; it is no matter how many miles distant these bodies lie, our souls shall one day rejoice together;' with more words, bidding them about her not to trouble her, or give her any thing, without she desired it. She lay still in a good frame of mind, with a sweet countenance, bearing her sickness in much patience; often saying, 'O! my dear and heavenly Father! come away, come away, for my heart trusteth in thee.' And so fell asleep in the Lord, the 17th of the Seventh month, in the year 1688, aged fifteen years.

GEORGE GRAY, of Acquorthies, in Scotland, was a sufferer for the truth; a poor man in this world, yet rich in faith; of mean education, yet endowed with divine wisdom; and bore a sound and faithful testimony amongst the Lord's people.

A little before his departure, being filled with the power of the Lord, he gave weighty exhortations to all present, especially to his children. To some friends that came to see him, he said he had not kept back the word and counsel of the Lord from them; and now he could say, it was good doctrine, to leave nothing to do till a dying bed: so finished his testimony, and laid down his body the 8th day of the Twelfth month, in the year 1689.

GEORGE FOX was born in the Fifth month, 1624, at Drayton, in Leicestershire. At eleven years of age he knew purity and holiness. In the nineteenth year of his age, in the year 1643, he left all, and travelled up and down the nation, visiting many people who were seeking the Lord, until the year 1646, at which time he entered into his more public ministry; for he was sent of God, as the apostles were in the primitive times, to turn people from darkness to light, directing all to mind the light of Christ Jesus in their own hearts. In the year 1648, several meetings of Friends were gathered to God's teaching through his ministry; in which ministry he faithfully laboured forty-four years, through much suffering and many perils of various sorts, as by the journal of his life doth largely appear.

God gave him length of days, so that he saw his children in the faith, unto the third and fourth generation, to a great increase. Great was his care for the preservation of those who had received truth, that they might walk in the same; and to that end he gave forth many faithful epistles, and good exhortation and advice, for good order and discipline in the church of Christ, as appears in the collection of his epistles to friends.

He preached the gospel effectually but two days before he died, viz., on the 11th of the Eleventh month, 1690, at Gracechurch-street meeting-house in London. After meeting, he said, 'I am glad I was here; now I am clear, I am fully clear;' and then was the same day taken ill of some indisposition of body, and continued weak in body for two days, at the house of Henry Goldney, at White-hart-court, in Gracechurch-street, and lay in much contentedness and peace to the end, being very sensible. In this time he mentioned divers Friends, and sent for some in particular, to whom he expressed his mind for spreading truth and Friends' books in the world; signifying also to some Friends, saying, 'All is well, and the seed of God reigns over all, and over death itself; and though I am weak in body, yet the power of the Lord is over all, and over all disorderly spirits;' which were his wonted sensible expressions, being in the living faith and sense thereof, which he kept to the end.

On the 13th of the Eleventh month, in the year 1690, he quietly departed this life in peace, about the tenth hour in the night: so he ended his days in a faithful testimony, in perfect love and unity with his brethren, being about the sixty-sixth year of his age.

JOAN VOKINS, wife of Richard Vokins, of the county of Berks, was a faithful woman, and labourer in the gospel.

After she had received God's blessed truth, she was much concerned that her relations also might receive the same truth; and by her upright conversation and good example among them, with the blessing of God and assistance of his grace, her husband, father, and children received the truth; and her husband was a sufferer for the same, in his imprisonment in Reading jail, and her eldest son also. Having received a dispensation of the gospel of Jesus Christ to preach to others in this nation, she was also concerned in her spirit to visit divers provinces and islands beyond the seas; and in order thereunto took shipping from Gravesend in Kent, in the Twelfth month, 1679, and visited New York, East and West Jersey, and some parts of Pennsylvania, which at that time was not much inhabited, Long Island, Rhode Island, and New England, and several of the islands, as Antigua, Nevis, and Barbadoes.

In her journey to these places she endured many hardships and sufferings of several kinds; yet through all she was supported by the power of Christ, whose peace she felt in her soul. On the 3d day of the Fourth month, 1681, she returned from Barbadoes to England, and landed at Dover in Kent. At Sandwich she exhorted the priests and people of that town, in their public place of worship, to forsake their vanity, and to come to the spiritual worship of God; and laid before them the danger of the one, and the benefit of the other.

After her return home to England, she continued her diligence in the Lord's work, and care and service in his church, and among his people, to the end of her days. About the yearly meeting time, in 1690, she went up to London to visit Friends thereabout; and, but a few weeks before her death, by a letter, dated from London, in the Fourth month following, she signified to her dear friend Theophila Townsend, another faithful woman-labourer in the gospel, at Cirencester, that now her service was finished; and said, 'I could gladly have laid down my body here among the Lord's worthies; yet, seeing it is ordered otherwise, I submit to the will of my God, and do think to go homeward in a little time.'

Joan Vokins also said, not long before, to the said Theophila

Townsend, being then with her, that she had some papers, which she desired might be made public after her decease, expecting her time was not long to remain in the body, being well satisfied that she should lay down her head in peace with God, let death come when it would. And according to the sight she had, and what she said, the time of her decease was near at hand, for she did not live to get home, after she wrote the letter aforesaid in the Fourth month at London. Coming to Reading, she fell sick there, and upon her dying bed spoke to her son, Richard Vokins, as followeth: 'Son, my weakness is great, and my pains very strong; but the Lord is large in his love to me, and good to me; he gives me patience to bear my pains, which are strong. Ah, son, I have learned a good lesson; Paul's lesson; in all states to be content; and now I have nothing to do but to die.' Putting forth her hand to take her leave of him, she farther said, 'Son, remember the Lord, and he will remember thee: remember my love to thy wife, and to all my children.' And after a little stop, and her speech low, she spoke these words again, 'And he will remember you; and be you faithful to him, and he will bless you, and you shall be blessed.'

She departed this life the 22d of the Fifth month, in the year 1690, having finished her course, and kept the faith.

ROBERT LODGE, of the county of York, was convinced of truth in the year 1660, and was a faithful minister of Christ Jesus, and a valiant sufferer for the testimony of a good conscience. He travelled in the work of the gospel, both in England and in Ireland, and turned many to righteousness, and did build up many in the most holy faith: he was not only a planter but a waterer in the vineyard: a son of consolation indeed.

The time of his sickness was but short. A friend visiting him, he gave account of his infirmities, and questioned his recovery: but he said, 'The Lord knows my heart, that I have served him; and it hath been of more account to me, the gaining of one soul, than all my labours and travels.'

The friend going again the next day, and seeing him near his end, was sorrowful; to whom he said, 'What! we must meet again, we must meet again in eternity;' and put up many heavenly petitions to the Lord. Another friend taking leave of him, he called him by his name, and said, 'It is well with me, and I have no disturbance in my mind.' And again he said, 'The Lord knows I was never commissioned to go any way, or to do any thing, but I have willingly answered him; and the Lord, who hath been my rock and refuge, my shield and buckler, and a sanctuary to me, hath been with me all along to this very day.' He spoke much more in praises to the Lord for his many deliverances, praying for the continuance of God's life and love to his whole heritage. After which he spoke little, but that all was well with him; and said, 'Blessed be God, I have heavenly peace;' and so fell into a sweet sleep, and went away, being on the 15th of the Seventh month, in the year 1690.

STEPHEN CRISP, of Colchester in Essex, received the blessed truth about the year 1655, when he was about twenty-seven years of age, and was a preacher of the everlasting gospel of Christ Jesus about thirty-five years. In that service he travelled in many parts of England, Scotland, Holland, Germany, and the Low Countries, as by the printed journal of his life more largely appears, and endured many hardships for his faithful testimony to the blessed truth. He was greatly capable, through his long experience, to advise and give counsel to persons in all conditions.

In the latter part of his days, being unable to travel much, through an indisposition of body, yet he was diligent in preaching the gospel in Colchester and London. He lay some time under great exercise and weakness; and about four days before he died, being under much bodily weakness and pain, he said to George Whitehead, who came to visit him, 'I see an end of mortality, yet cannot come at it; I desire the Lord to deliver me out of this troublesome and painful body. If he will but say the word, it is done. Yet there is no cloud in my way. I have a full assurance of my peace with God in Christ Jesus; my integrity and uprightness of heart is known to the Lord, and I have peace and justification in Christ Jesus, who made me so; that is, upright to God;' and remembered his love to all the faithful in the church of God. To another friend he said, 'I have fought the good fight of faith, and have run my course, and am waiting for the crown of life that is laid up for me.'

To a friend who visited him, he said, 'Serve the truth for the simple truth's sake, and it will preserve thee to the end, as it hath done me.' In his great pain of body, feeling the word of patience to support him, he said to the friends watching with him, 'Grow in the word of patience, that it may keep you also in the time of need.' The day before he died, he said, 'I hope I am gathering,' (as his expression was understood,) 'I hope, I hope,' being then hardly able to speak out his words. George Whitehead, near parting from him, said, 'Dear Stephen, wouldst thou have any thing to friends?' After some pause, he gave this answer, 'Remember my dear love in Christ Jesus to all.' And on the 28th day of the Sixth month, in the year 1692, he died in the Lord, at Wandsworth, near London, about the sixty-fourth year of his age.

GULIELMA MARIA PENN was the wife of William Penn, of Pennsylvania, and daughter of Sir William Springet, of Durling. Her illness continued eight months upon her, in which time she uttered many living and weighty expressions upon divers occasions, both before and near her end. At one of the meetings held in her chamber, only her husband and children and one of the servants being present, in a living power she said, 'Let us all prepare, not knowing what hour, or watch, the Lord cometh. O! I am full of matter! Shall we receive good, and shall we not receive evil at the hand of the Lord? I have cast my care upon the Lord, he is the physician of value; my expectation is wholly from him; he can raise up, and he can cast down.' A while after she said, 'O! what shall be done to the unprofitable servant!'

At another meeting, before which much heaviness seemed to lie upon her natural spirits, she said, 'This has been a precious opportunity to me, I am finely relieved and comforted, blessed be the Lord.' At another time, her husband speaking to her of the peace of well-doing, she replied to him, 'I never did, to my knowledge, a wicked thing in all my life.' To a friend, aged seventy-five years, that came to see her, she said, 'Thou and I, to all appearance, are near our end.' And to another, about sixty-five years old, who came also to see her, she said, 'How much older has the Lord made me by this weakness than thou art! But I am content. I do not murmur. I submit to his holy will.' In the height of her sickness she said, 'It is the great goodness of the Lord that I should be able to lie thus still. He is the physician of value to me, can I say. Let my tongue set forth his praise, and my spirit magnify him whilst I have breath. O! I am ready to be transported beyond my strength. God was not in the thunder, nor in the lightning; but he was heard in the still small voice.' She called the children one day, when very weak, and said, 'Be not frightened, children; I do not call you to take my leave of you, but to see you; and would have you walk in the fear of the Lord, and with his people in his holy truth.' Speaking another time solemnly to her children, she said, 'I never desired any great things for you, but that you may fear the Lord, and walk in his truth among his people, to the end of your days.'

About three hours before her end, a relation taking leave of her, she said, 'I have cast my care upon the Lord; my dear love to all friends;' and lifting up her dying hands and eyes, prayed to the Lord to preserve them and bless them. About an hour after, causing all to withdraw, she took her leave of her husband, saying all that was fit upon that solemn occasion.

She continued sensible, and ate something about an hour before her departure; at which time her children, and most of the family being present, she quietly expired in her husband's arms, with a sensible and devout resignation of her soul to Almighty God, on the 23d of the Twelfth month, in the year 1693, in the fiftieth year of her age.

PATRICK LIVINGSTON was born in the year 1634, near Montrose, in the kingdom of Scotland. He received the blessed truth about the year 1659, and travelled much in the service thereof, bearing a faithful testimony to the same for above thirty years, in many parts of England and Ireland, and most places in Scotland, where he was made a good instrument in convincing and gathering many to the knowledge of the inward appearance of Christ Jesus, particularly that meeting settled at Kinermuck in Aberdeen county, the largest meeting in all the nation. In this county he valiantly and patiently endured several years' close imprisonment in Aberdeen, for his faithful testimony to the truth, viz., from the year 1676 to 1679; and he likewise bore a faithful testimony for truth, by imprisonment in Newgate, in London, for a considerable time, about the year 1684.

Valiant he was for the truth, especially in times of persecution. Like a good soldier, he never turned his back in the day of battle, but through the strength of the Lord was still amongst the first in suffering, being fervent and zealous for the cause of truth and honour of God. His persecutors were sensible that he was a strengthening to his brethren in prison; and therefore, that it might not be so, they would several times let him go, or miss some meeting he was known to be at. Faithful he was to his brethren in their afflictions, and would not leave them, till he saw an end to that persecution in Scotland in the year 1679; and from that time no Friend was imprisoned for several years in that city.

After this he returned into England to his dear wife, who at that time dwelt in Nottingham, but in his latter years, he with his family lived in London. He continued to the end a diligent labourer in the Lord's vineyard, several times visiting his native country of Scotland; and the year before he died, viz. 1693, he again visited his brethren there, and was attended with a plentiful measure of the Lord's power and presence, all the time he was among them, though at that time weak in body. After his return home he grew weaker, until he departed this life on the 15th of the Fourth month, 1694, at the house of John Kirton, in Kensington, near London, being removed thither for the benefit of the air, where several friends were present, witnesses of the following heavenly expressions, viz.

The day before his departure he said, 'I am in unity with all faithful Friends, and in love to all men.' About an hour before his departure, he said, 'O Father! O Father!' A little time after, mentioning his weakness of body, and as if he desired more strength to utter what was in his mind, which being then apparently given him, he said, 'Let life reach unto all here:' and pulling off his night-cap with his own hand about half an hour before he was removed hence, he said, 'Blessed, praised, magnified, and exalted be the mighty, powerful, great and everlasting name of the Lord God, for evermore. Oh! that thy life may arise in full dominion over all, and that Friends may feel it so in all their assemblies; that they may be kept in love, concord and unity together, and show it forth in word, work, testimony, life and conversation unto all;' adding, 'Life being over all; here we have all we need, and here there is a lying down in true submission to the will of the Lord, and laying down our heads in peace and rest with him for evermore.' Which last words he repeated twice, and said, 'Here is victory over death, hell, and the grave, and resting in peace with the Lord for evermore.'

He died on the 15th of the Fourth month, in the year 1694, about the sixtieth year of his age.

ANDREW SOWLE, of London, received the truth as professed by the people called Quakers, in his young years, and became obedient thereunto, and gave himself up to the living power thereof, which enabled him with much cheerfulness to undergo those manifold afflictions and persecutions with which he was exercised; for being a just and upright man, he was zealous for the propagation of the truth, to which, both by conversation and sufferings, he bore a faithful testimony.

He was a printer by trade, and engaged himself freely in the printing Friends' books, when he had large offers of advancing himself in the world, made to him by his other friends and relations, if he would have desisted therefrom. But his love to truth, and the desire he had to be instrumental in his calling for spreading it abroad, would not suffer him to hearken to any of those offers. He freely gave himself up to the service thereof, even in times of the hottest persecution, believing it his duty so to do, though therein he should hazard not only his life, but also that outward substance God had blessed him with. For several years together he was in continual danger upon that account, his house being often searched, and his printing materials, as presses, letter, &c., as often broken to pieces, and taken away, as any Friends' books were found printing by him; and this they did for many years together. During this time, though he met with great losses, and had, at one time, by his adversaries, about a thousand reams of printed books taken from him, yet he was never heard to complain, but he would say, he was glad to have any thing to lose for truth, and that the Lord had made him worthy to be a sufferer for it. This quiet resignation of himself to the will of God, caused one of those who came to seize upon his goods, to do what he could with his partners to put a stop to the seizure; and when he saw he could not prevail, he went out and wept. When at another time his adversaries came to take away his printing-press, he was so resigned and easy, in giving up all to his persecutors, that when they had done their work, and seized upon all, he, (as he often did in like cases,) set forth meat and drink before them, according to the command, Rom. xii., 19, 20, to feed even his very enemies; and his good so overcame their evil, that some of them departed under a concern; but one of the chief being filled with malice against the truth, survived not long after, but died in a miserable condition.

As this sincere man met with great sufferings, so had he also large experiences of the goodness of God towards him in many remarkable providences. At one time he was taken at a meeting of the people called Quakers, and carried to Newgate, and being examined by Sir Richard Brown, the persecuting mayor, who, understanding he was a printer, threatened to send him after his brother Twin, (as he called him, who some time before suffered in Smithfield for printing a treasonable book,) to whom this meek man replied, 'Thou wilt not live to see it:' and the event justified it, for Brown died soon after.

After many exercises and trials divers ways, which it would be too long to recite, he was visited with weakness of body the beginning of the Tenth month, 1695, and grew weaker and weaker till the 25th of the same month. His patience and resignation to the will of God, during the time of his weakness, were such, that he seldom was heard to complain, but would say, that he was given up to the will of God; saying often, that he had no dependence on any thing, save upon Christ Jesus, the good Samaritan, on whom was his whole dependence.

George Whitehead, with another friend, coming to visit him, he said he had served truth faithfully, according to what the Lord had been pleased to make manifest to him; and that in what he had done, he had not sought himself, but the honour of God. He would often exhort his family to faithfulness, and his young ones also to seek the Lord in the days of their youth. His reproofs to those who had done amiss, were so kind and so convincing, that a servant of his said he stood more in awe of a reproof from him, than the severest treatment of another. 'His end,' said he, 'being in love to convince me, that I have done that which is not right.'

William Penn, the night before he departed, came somewhat late to visit him, and finding him in a sweet composed frame of mind (for indeed he was to appearance as though he ailed nothing), asked him how he did; he answered with much cheerfulness, his satisfaction and peace of mind were great, and that he waited for his change. The said Friend, who had been many years acquainted with his industrious and innocent life, after some discourse with him, kneeled down and prayed that the Lord would give him the reward of his labour; for, through him, many blessed truths had been brought into the world, &c. After prayer was ended, he acknowledged William Penn's love, telling him he was well satisfied in his condition, and in the truth of God which he had professed; and that he had nothing to do but to wait in the will of God till his change came: and so in much love they parted, he signifying his love to, and unity with all Friends, in the truth.

After that, he lay sweetly retired, waiting for his change, and had his senses perfectly and clear to the last, which was about eight the next morning; at which time his wife came to his bedside, and asked him how he did; he answered, 'Oh Jane, never such a good night as this:' and the same minute shut his eyes, and with a hymn of praise to God, offered up his last breath, and fell asleep, not so much as fetching the least sigh, nor was any alteration seen in his countenance. So easily and so quietly did he leave this world, in which he had known much exercise, and is gone to his everlasting rest, with God's faithful servants.

He finished this life the 26th of the Tenth month, in the year 1695, about eight in the morning, at his house in Holywell-lane, London, in the sixty-seventh year of his age.

Rom. viii. 18. For I reckon, that the sufferings of this present time, are not worthy to be compared with the glory which shall be revealed in us.

SPRINGET PENN, eldest son of William Penn of Worminghurst, late of Pennsylvania, was a young man about twenty-one years of age. For more than half a year before it pleased the Lord to visit him with weakness, he grew more retired, and much disengaged from youthful delights, showing a remarkable tenderness in meetings, even when they were silent. But when he saw himself doubtful [as to health] he turned his mind and meditations more apparently towards the Lord, often praying with fervency to the Lord, and uttering many thankful expressions and praises to him, in a deep and sensible manner, saying one day, 'I am resigned: what God pleaseth: he knows what is best: I would live if it pleased him, that I might serve him: but, O Lord, not my will, but thy will be done.' One speaking to him of the things of this world, he answered, 'My eye looks another way, where the truest pleasure is.'

Another time, his father going to a meeting, at parting he said, 'Remember me, my dear father, before the Lord. Though I cannot go to meetings, yet have I many good meetings: the Lord comes in upon my spirit. I have heavenly meetings with him by myself.' With more to the same purpose, expressing his sentiments of the vanity of this world, and of his entering into secret covenant with the Lord, and his thankfulness for the Lord's preservation and goodness to him. Fixing his eyes upon his sister, he took her by the hand, saying, 'Poor Tishe, look to good things; poor child, there is no comfort without it. One drop of the love of God is worth more than all the world. I know it; I have tasted it. I have felt as much or more of the love of God in this weakness, than in all my life before;' with more that he said to his father.

Taking something one night in bed, just before going to rest, he sat up, and reverently prayed thus: 'O Lord God, thou whose Son said to his disciples, whatsoever ye ask in my name ye shall receive, I pray thee in his name, bless this to me this night, and give me rest, if it be thy blessed will, O Lord:' and accordingly he had a very comfortable night, of which he took thankful notice the next day. At another time he expressed his desire to serve the Lord if he lived. He one day saying thus, 'I am resolved I will have such a thing done;' immediately he catched himself, and fell into this reflection with much contrition, 'O Lord, forgive me that irreverent and hasty expression. I am a poor weak creature, and live by thee, and therefore I should have said, If it pleaseth thee that I live, I intend to do so or so. Lord forgive my rash expression.' He desired his mother-in-law not to trouble herself for such a poor creature as he; and to pray for him, that he might live and employ his time more in the Lord's service.

To his brother he said, looking awfully upon him, 'Be a good boy, and know there is a God, a great and mighty God, who is a rewarder of the righteous; and so he is of the wicked; but their rewards are not the same. Have a care of idle company, and love good company, and good Friends, and the Lord will bless thee. I have seen good things for thee since my sickness, if thou dost but fear the Lord; and if I should not live, remember what I say, when I am dead and gone;' with many more religious expressions. Taking his leave of his father, brother, and sister, he said, 'Come life, come death, I am resigned. Oh! the love of God overcomes my soul.' Feeling himself decline apace, and one seeing him not able to bring up the matter that was in his throat, went to fetch the doctor; but so soon as he came, he said, 'Let my father speak to the doctor, and I'll go to sleep;' which he did, and waked no more.

He died the 10th of the Second month, in the year 1696, in the twenty-first year of his age.

RICHARD BAKER, of Jordan's in Buckinghamshire, received the truth in the love of it, many years since, and he testified his love to it;

1st. In a circumspect walking, showing himself a pattern of good works.

2dly. By suffering cheerfully for it, and took joyfully the spoiling of his goods, and the imprisonment of his body; and would often say, 'If people knew the pleasure of godliness, they would not live in the earth as they did.'

3dly. By a hearty zeal for the prosperity and propagation of it. A vigilant watchman he was in his station, a sharp reprover of evil, and an encourager of the good, and a diligent labourer in the work of the ministry, earnestly endeavouring to bring those he ministered to into an inward exercise of spirit towards God, that therein they might be more acquainted with, and subject, to the divine power of God: concerning which he wrote a treatise, published since he deceased, although it was written about twenty-six years before; the reasons whereof he gave upon his dying bed, viz. That he had read of many in former days, and had observed some in his own time, who had made fair progress in the way of truth; and had said, done, and suffered much on behalf of it, who yet had not held out to the end; but through too great security, or self-confidence, and for want of a continual subjection to the power of God, in and by which alone strength and preservation are to be found, have by the violent assaults, the subtle insinuations, or mysterious workings of the enemy, been drawn back again under the power of Satan, to the invalidating (at least in the eye of the world) the testimonies such had before given to the sufficiency of the power of God. And he having by others' miscarriages learned to beware, had, from a godly jealousy over himself, suspended the publication of the said sheets, until he could with greater confidence, and more full assurance, say with the holy apostle, when the time of his departure was at hand, "I have fought a good fight, I have finished my course, I have kept the faith," * &c., which bespoke his great modesty. Upon his dying-bed, he had the witness in himself that God was pleased with him, and had a suitable word to every one's state that came to him; and would often clap his hand on his breast, and say, 'All is well here.'

The day before he departed, many Friends visiting him, he spoke to all in expressions of great love, and took his leave of them; and taking his leave of a child who wept, he said, 'Do not cry, I am well, my peace is made with the Lord. If thou cry, cry that iniquity may be brought down and righteousness brought up. The power of God and strength of God is with me. I am going the way of all flesh; I am going before, and others must follow after.' So he laid down his life, in the feeling of that power, about the year 1697.

---

* 2 Tim. iv. 6.

ROBERT BARROW, born in the county of Lancaster, but removed and brought up from a child in Westmoreland, was early convinced of God's blessed truth, and was a zealous labourer in the gospel for twenty-six years, and a faithful sufferer for the same in London, and other places; travelling much in this nation, and twice through Scotland, Ireland, and Wales, to preach Christ Jesus, the light of the world.

In the year 1694 he went forth in the love of God, in company with Robert Wardel, of Sunderland, both of them being ancient men, to preach the gospel in America. After they had visited Pennsylvania, and some other parts on the continent, they took shipping for Jamaica, where Robert Wardel died the 22d day of the Second month, in the year 1696. After Robert Barrow had finished his testimony there, he took shipping in order for Pennsylvania again, and on the 23d of the Sixth month, 1696, embarked with divers passengers and seamen on board the barque Reformation, Joseph Kirle, master. But on the 23d of the Seventh month, by a storm in the Gulf of Florida, the vessel ran aground, and to save their lives, they were forced among the savage cannibals of Florida, and underwent grievous sufferings of various kinds, being often in great danger of death; travelling naked in heat and cold, hunger and thirst, and having no proper food to eat from [the time of] their suffering shipwreck, viz., from the 23d of the Seventh month, to the 15th of the Ninth month following.

At last they arrived at a poor garrison town called St. Augustine, belonging to the Spaniards in America, maintained partly by the king of Spain, and partly by the Pope; but the governor, &c., were courteous and generous, according to their ability, who, after they had clothed and refreshed them, assisted them to Carolina, which province they reached on the 23d of the Tenth month, 1696; but several of their company died under the hardships they met with. Robert Barrow, by feeding upon such unwholesome food (that little which they did eat,) was taken with a flux, which continued upon him; and together with the great sufferings he underwent in his journeys, being ancient, he was thereby much decayed in his body; but his desire was to see his friends once more in Philadelphia, and he reached Philadelphia from Charleston, in Carolina, in fourteen days.

One remarkable passage I may not omit, viz., the company Robert Barrow was with, to save their lives, assumed the name of Spaniards, for the savage Indians stood in fear of them; and this true-hearted man being directly asked the question, 'Art thou a Nickaleer?' which is an Englishman; he answered, 'Yes.' For his plain dealing, he was stripped naked of his clothes, which till then he had saved. God suffered not these savages to touch his life, nor the lives of those with him; though at one time these bloody creatures placed themselves each behind one, having their arms extended, with their knives in their hands, ready to execute their bloody design, some taking hold of them by their heads, with their knees set against their shoulders, waiting for their chief to begin. They were very high in words, which the English understood not; but on a sudden it pleased God to work wonderfully for their preservation, and instantly all these savage men were struck dumb, and like men amazed, for the space of a quarter of an hour; in which time their countenances fell, and they looked like another people, and quitted the places they had taken behind them, and fell to plundering their chests and trunks.

But to return to our friend Robert Barrow, who behaved himself under all those calamities in great patience, and by faith overcame even the worst of men, looking to him who is invisible, who by his grace supported him under all. By prayer he wrestled with God, to be delivered from those unreasonable creatures, desiring to lay his bones among his faithful friends in Philadelphia. And God was so gracious that he sealed an assurance upon his spirit, even before he was yet off his knees, that his prayer was heard, and should be answered in due time. And great strength and comfort he was to his companions in affliction.

When he arrived at Philadelphia, divers friends went on board to help him on shore; but he was so weak that he could not be removed that night, being the 4th of the Second month,

1697, but he signified to Friends his great satisfaction that the Lord had granted his request that he might lay down his bones in that place; that his heart was strong, and he hoped he might see Friends again at the meeting. He made mention of the goodness of God to him, and that his presence had attended him in all his exercise. Next morning he was removed to the house of Samuel Carpenter, where he slept a considerable time: the same day friends coming to visit him, he rejoiced, putting forth his hand ready to embrace them, to whom he said, 'Although my body be weak, my mind is sound and memory good; and the Lord hath been very good to me all along to this very day, and this morning hath sweetly refreshed me.' And farther added, 'The Lord hath answered my desire, for I desired content, and that I might come to this place to lay my bones amongst you.' Afterwards he said, 'It is a good thing to have a conscience void of offence, both towards God and towards men.'

On the day that he died, he desired a friend to write to his friends in England, and to acquaint his relations that he had settled his affairs; and afterwards declared to divers friends that were by him, that the Lord was with him, and all things were well, and that he had nothing to do but to die. Accordingly, on the same day he departed this life in peace with God, being the 4th of the Second month, in the year 1697; and was buried the 6th of the same, in Friends' burying-ground in Philadelphia, in Pennsylvania.

TUDOR BRIAN, of London, a youth about seventeen years of age, was taken ill about the Tenth month, 1696, and from that time decayed daily, falling into a deep consumption, till the Tenth month following. Being in the country for his health, he was often observed to be in retirement in the fields, sometimes returning with wet eyes; and his friends apprehending it might proceed from his distemper, or else from fear of death, his frequent answers were, he was no ways afraid to die, but willingly resigned himself to the will of God, either for life or death. About a month before he died, he was taken so ill as not to be able to go out of his chamber; and so continued, being daily with a great sense of God upon his spirit; and would often repeat a full assurance of his future happiness, saying, 'Come, Lord Jesus, come quickly, and receive my soul.' A few days after, he called for a bible, desiring to read; his mother's answer was, 'Child, thou art weak;' he said he could read; and so read the 17th chapter of John, with trembling lips. When he came to the 20th verse, viz., "Neither pray I for these alone, but for them also which shall believe on me through their word," he took particular notice, and wept.

On the day before he departed, he fell so ill they thought he was smitten with death; and several friends, as well then as before, visiting him, he was much refreshed and comforted, and said, 'O mother, how merciful is the great God to me, that hath put into the hearts of good friends to visit me! There are healthier and younger lads than I, that are gone before me, a poor consumptive lad; he hath spared me; surely I shall never forget his mercies.' And to the Lord he said, 'Oh! glory, glory and praises, for they are thine for evermore.' Then sitting still, he said, 'Oh, thou merciful God, thou art merciful. I can say that I have found it so; that when I had no breath, I have sought thee, and it hath been given me.' His parents, hearing him, wept; but he answered, 'Wherefore are ye troubled, my dear parents? Be not troubled for me, for I am going to a better place. If it be the will of the Lord, he can raise me; but if not, his will be done: it may be he may spare me two or three days.' Turning his eyes on his parents, he said, 'You are the nearest in the world to me, but yet there is a nearer who is above.' After some silence he said, 'I can say that in my younger years I have gone by myself down into the meadows, and have cried to the Lord, but knew not where he was; and when I heard his voice I trembled; and as I gave up, the Lord Jesus made himself known to me. Then I knew what I sought for:' with more concerning a vision he had of his future happiness; and he testified against superfluity in the house.

About twelve hours before his death, a near relation desiring, on behalf of those present, that they might be fitted for their latter end, he said, 'You must pray, and hang and lean upon the Lord Jesus Christ: for it is of him, and through him, that we must expect salvation. Without him ye can do nothing. He died for sinners, and he is merciful to forgive, for he hath forgiven me, blessed be his holy name. Although some be hardened and stubborn, yet the Lord is merciful; he can and may forgive; but you that are in the truth, keep in the truth:' with more which he said, concerning remembering our Creator betimes, and concerning death.

About two hours before he died, he prayed thus: 'Lord God be merciful; thou art good, thou art bountiful. Lord have mercy on me! Come, Lord Jesus, have mercy: thou diedst for sinners; glory, glory to the God of heaven! oh! praises to thy name. Lord Jesus receive my soul:' with more that he said to his father and mother. Lying still a little, he said, 'O what a glorious kingdom I am going to! there are dainties enough. Lord Jesus thou hast pardoned me. O what a numerous army hath my God! He hath a great one.' And so lay praising God till he finished this life, about two in the morning, on the 3d of the Tenth month, in the year 1697.

THOMAS HAINS, son of Thomas Hains and Hannah, his wife, of Southwark, in the county of Surrey, was educated in the truth, as professed by the people called Quakers, by his father; and also for some time at the school of Richard Scoryer, of Wandsworth. He was a dutiful child, and had a sense of the fear of God upon his heart, so that during his sickness he behaved himself more like a man than an infant, (as he called himself) having a care, lest he should say any word amiss. If he refused to take any thing offered to him, and was again pressed to take it, he replied, 'Wouldst thou have me tell a lie?' Once having refused something, he was desired to promise to take it in such a time; his answer was 'Can I tell what is to come?' When he took that which he found refreshed him, he with much thankfulness acknowledged it; being also very sensible of the love and tender regard which his parents had towards him, and expressed it several times to them. He bore his sickness with much patience, and often expressed his willingness to die; saying, 'It is better for me to die; this is a troublesome world; and we should every day and every moment think upon the Lord.'

A few days before his decease, he uttered many expressions in prayer and praises to the Lord, saying, 'Thou art a God of love, thou art a God of mercy; thou knowest the hearts of them that love thee; thou knowest the hearts of them that seek thee. Lord remember thy people. Thou knowest the hearts of the ungodly; thou knowest the hearts of the wicked; thou hast nourished and brought up children, and they have rebelled against thee.' He also spoke of the care we ought to take of the never-dying soul, and that the Lord will send forth his messengers. Another time, expressing his inward satisfaction at a future state, he said, 'Glory, glory; joy, joy: come mother, come father, come all; it is a brave place, there are no tears nor sorrow:' and praised God, saying, 'Thou art worthy to have the honour and the glory for evermore; for to thee it doth belong. Thou art God of heaven, and of the whole earth;' and continued about a quarter of an hour in prayer, and said to the Lord, 'I am an infant, and cannot do anything without thee.'

One evening, several friends coming to visit him, he desired their prayers to the Lord for him: and the next day himself prayed again, saying, 'Our Father, which art in heaven,' &c. Afterwards he said, 'It is a brave thing to be at peace with the Lord.' His end drawing near, he said, 'Father, let me die.' And again called out 'Father, father.' His father being present, asked what he desired? He said, 'I do not speak to thee, but to my heavenly Father: have mercy on me;' and expressed much joy that he had with the Lord; and desired them about him that he might be still; and so lay secretly praising the Lord. A few hours before he died, he said, 'I come, Father, I come:' and being very weak, his voice was low, but he was heard to say, 'God is my father:' and so like a lamb he quietly finished his days the 12th of the Twelfth month, in the year 1700, aged nine years.

END OF THE FIRST PART.

PIETY PROMOTED,

IN A COLLECTION OF DYING SAYINGS

OF MANY OF THE PEOPLE CALLED

QUAKERS;

WITH A BRIEF ACCOUNT OF SOME OF THEIR LABORS IN THE GOSPEL, AND SUFFERINGS FOR THE SAME.

THE SECOND PART.

BY JOHN TOMKINS.

"Gather up the fragments that remain, that nothing be lost." — JOHN vi. 12.

PREFACE.

[BY ANOTHER HAND.]

WONDERFUL hath been the love of God to the children of men, and various have been the methods whereby he hath given demonstrations of it. All ages and generations abound with the testimonies of his bounty to them; for his goodness hath been always so plentifully extended, and also in such an indulgent manner; as if his happiness was not complete unless mankind partook of it. So that he had great reason indeed to ask, What could have been done more to his vineyard (the house of Israel), that he had not done in it? For he gave them his good Spirit to instruct them, he sent his servants, the prophets, to reprove them, and which was the most stupendous kindness of all, he also sent his only begotten Son to reclaim them, and to be a propitiation for them. Yet such was the obstinacy of that impenitent generation, that few would thereby see or do the things that belonged to their peace so that at last they were hid from their eyes; a doom dismal and just! May their calamities be our caution, that by their harms we may learn to beware.

We have also, in this our day, been honoured with a visitation from heaven, a high and holy calling indeed; a call to be holy in order to be happy. But few have obeyed, though Christ himself hath called by his Spirit and by his servants, by his judgments and by his mercies, that men might be reduced to the paths of the righteous, which are paths of pleasantness and ways of peace. But alas! instead of being melted to contrition by these endearing testimonies of his goodness, such hath been the ingratitude of many, they have done despite to the holy Spirit of Grace that was given for their eternal profit, and have also very evilly entreated his servants and messengers, whom he sent to proclaim that accepted time, the day of salvation. Yet these good men were not, by their hardships, weary of their well-doing, but persevered to the end in doing good to them, though they returned hatred for love, persecution for kindness, as thou wilt find by some instances in these collections, which the industrious author presents thee with; that the drowsy world might be awakened to holiness by the voice of the dead, since that of the living is so little regarded.

The matter thou wilt soon see is very excellent, since it shows thee that to live holily is the way to die happily. In short, it is a continued persuasion to virtue, and a compendious directory in the way to it, by the great means of example, which at once gives both light and strength in that indispensable duty of living well. It is free of what might excite thy displeasure, not intermeddling with the controversies of the times; so that charity persuades me that scarcely any can read it and not be bettered by it. This gives me the boldness to recommend these following sheets to the serious perusal of all; high and low, rich and poor, friends and enemies; that all may be humbled to the improvement of their time, that treasure of eternal consequence, and be wise, and consider their latter end; lest, when it is too late, they may desire to die the death of these righteous persons; and that their latter end may be like theirs, who breathed out their pious souls in faith, and full assurance of an immortal crown of glory.

For the voice was true, [which] the holy man declared he heard, and that bade him write, "Blessed are the dead which die in the Lord, that they may rest from their labours, and their works do follow them," to their comfort and everlasting consolation; and stay behind them too, for the example of the living, who desire to live to God, and follow them as they followed Christ, in humility, self-denial, brotherly-kindness; though thereby they are a proverb of reproach, and their life accounted madness, and their latter end without honour; yet they will be numbered among the children of God, and their lot will be among the saints.

I will detain thee no longer from what is better, only recommend thee to the holy Spirit of Truth, that is able and willing to guide thee into the same blessed Truth it led these happy souls into, and then thy latter end will be like to theirs, comfortable and glorious. This is earnestly desired for thee by the author of these treatises; for I know his sole design is thy profit and advantage. He desires none for himself, but the comfort of well-doing; being actuated by a better principle than to make gain of Godliness, too much the practice of men of great pretences.

PIETY PROMOTED.

THE SECOND PART.

WILLIAM DEWSBURY was one whom God raised up in the morning of his glorious day, broken forth in our age.

After that eminent servant of Christ, George Fox, was set at liberty, having been almost twelve months in Derby jail, whereof nearly six months he was in the dungeon, for his testimony to the truth, in the year 1651, he, passing from thence through several counties, came to Balby, in Yorkshire, where he was instrumental to convince several friends of note, who were afterwards serviceable in their days, viz., Richard Farnsworth, Thomas Aldam, Thomas Goodyear, Thomas and John Kilham, James Naylor, &c. George Fox having a meeting at lieutenant Roper's house, William Dewsbury and his wife came to it, and heard truth declared. The same evening, they having some conference with George Fox, confessed to the truth and received it; and after some time, William Dewsbury publicly preached the same truth.

In the year 1653 he went into Westmoreland, Cumberland and Lancashire, and declared truth both in steeple-houses and in meetings; and underwent great sufferings, beatings, &c., and was imprisoned at York, and also at Northampton in the year 1654. Indeed, God made him an eminent instrument in his hand, for the publication of his mighty day of power, preaching repentance in order to the remission of sins. He bore a faithful and universal testimony of the free grace of God to mankind: and the Lord was with him, and prospered him in his manifold sufferings, travels, labours, and exercises, in the gospel of Christ, and word of the ministry, as may be seen in his several books, testimonies and epistles, collected together in print. Many were made sensible of the benefit of his labours, counsel, admonition and encouragement, to the good and welfare of their immortal souls. For the Lord, in whose dread and zeal he laboured, endowed him with faith and courage, and great boldness for his name and truth; and he published the same in great plainness, and in the simplicity thereof. To the tender-hearted he was exceedingly mild, but to the stubborn and lofty he was sharp and plain; admonishing them, and declaring the righteous judgment of God against that state; watching with much patience and long-suffering the recovery of such, who through the subtility of the enemy, had fallen from the truth, and from unity with the people of God. But when any made it their work to cause division and discord, and to sow dissension among brethren, he would plainly testify against them, and reject them, as he did in his last visit to London.

A little time before his departure he had a concern upon him for the honour of God, and that those who had believed, and made profession of the truth, might answer it in an holy and blameless conversation; which he would often say, could not be done by largeness of knowledge, and strength of comprehension, but by a real dying to their wills and affections, by virtue of the daily cross.

The envy of wicked and unreasonable men was very great and fierce against him, especially in those early days of his travels and labours; and for the sake of his testimony he was often beaten, stoned, and imprisoned. He feared neither their malicious threats nor blows, but boldly went forth, publishing the truth, testifying to that of God in all consciences; and the hand of divine Providence often delivered him out of the hands of his enemies, for his name's sake.

A few weeks before his decease he came up to the city of London, and visited most of the public meetings there, and bore a faithful testimony to truth, and for love and unity; preaching up the cross of our Lord Jesus Christ, by whom the world "is crucified unto us, and we unto the world." Gal. vi. 14.

It being the Third month, 1688, when he was in London, and he intending to tarry there with friends till the Yearly meeting, which was approaching, was taken ill about the 29th of the same month, so that he could no longer be in the city. He then determined to return home; but before he went, he left a letter for the Yearly meeting, which is as followeth:

'Dear Friends and Brethren,

'I did not know till this last night but that I should have been with you at the Yearly meeting; but it pleased the Lord to visit me with my ancient distemper, which hath accompanied me in prison; and since I was released, the distemper was so sharp upon me, as to my sense, this last night I did not know whether I should have lived to see another day. But crying to the Lord, he ordered and cleared my way to go into the country, so that I cannot be with you at this Yearly meeting; but desire the Lord to assist you with his blessed power and heavenly life, to bring in the scattered ones to their everlasting comfort, and his glory for ever. Amen.

'And that it may be so with you, is the prayer of your loving brother,

'WILLIAM DEWSBURY.

'London, the 30th of the 3d Month, 1688.'

He lived but seventeen days after he left London; and making short journeys, got home to Warwick, and continued weak in body. A few days before his departure, some friends being together with him in his chamber, he, rising up in his bed, in great weakness of body, said to them as followeth:

'My God hath yet put in my heart to bear a testimony to his name and blessed truth, and I can never forget the day of his great power and blessed appearance, when he first sent me to preach his everlasting gospel, and proclaim the day of the

Lord to all people; also he confirmed the same by signs and wonders. Therefore, friends, be faithful, and trust in the Lord your God; for this I can say, I never played the coward, but as joyfully entered prisons as palaces, bidding my enemies to keep me there as long as they could; and in the prison-house I sung praises to my God, and esteemed the bolts and locks put upon me as jewels; and in the name of the eternal God I always got the victory: for they could not keep me any longer than the determined time of my God.

'And, friends, this I must once again testify to you in the name of the Lord God, that what I saw above thirty years ago, still rests as a testimony to leave behind me, that a dreadful, terrible day is at hand, and will certainly come to pass. But the time when, I cannot say; but all put on strength in the name of the Lord, and wait to feel his eternal power to preserve you through the tribulations of these days that approach very near. In the sense of which I have often been distressed and bowed in my spirit, with cries and tears to my God for the preservation of his heritage.

'And this I have further to signify, that my departure draws nigh. Blessed be my God, I am prepared. I have nothing to do but die, and put off this corruptible and mortal tabernacle, this flesh that hath so many infirmities; but the life that dwells in it, ascends out of the reach of death, hell and the grave; and immortality, eternal life, is my crown for ever and ever.

'Therefore, you that are left behind, fear not, nor be discouraged; but go on in the name and power of the Lord, and bear a faithful and living testimony for him in your day; and the Lord will prosper his work in your hand, and cause his truth to flourish and spread abroad; for it shall have the victory, and no weapon formed against it shall prosper. The Lord hath determined it shall possess the gates of his enemies, and the glory and the light thereof shall shine more and more unto the perfect day.'

He concluded in prayers to the Lord, with fervent breathings and supplications for all his people every where, but more especially for his dearly beloved friends assembled together at the

Yearly meeting at London, where he had intended to be, if the Lord had given him health: his dear love was to all Friends who inquired after him.

He departed this life at his house in Warwick, in a good old age, on the 17th of the Fourth month, in the year 1688.

ROBERT WARDEL, of Sunderland, in the county of Durham, received truth about the year 1661, and bore a public testimony to the same, not only in England, but also in Scotland, Ireland, Holland, and some parts of Germany. In the latter part of his days, viz., in the year 1694, he went with our dear friend Robert Barrow, to visit the churches of Christ in America. They travelled through nine provinces, or distinct governments, in those parts; among whom they had three hundred and twenty-eight meetings with the people, for the worship of Almighty God, to their comfort and mutual refreshment in the Lord. And God enabled them to perform their service to the desire of their hearts, in their old age; and by his power supported them under all exercises which they met withal.

They left the continent to visit the islands; and after they had been at Antigua and Bermudas, where they had considerable service among Friends and others in those islands, they arrived at Jamaica on the 10th of the Second month, 1696, intending, if the Lord permitted, to go to Pennsylvania, &c., again. After their arrival at Jamaica, they had several meetings; but, about the 18th of the said month, Robert Wardel was taken ill, for the climate was exceedingly hot, which made great alteration upon them both, especially on Robert Wardel, who was very much indisposed. A friend asking him how he found himself, he answered, 'I have been sick many times, but I never felt myself as I am now; therefore I know not how it may be with me: the will of the Lord be done: I am given up, and am content with God's will.' Another time he said to the woman Friend at whose house he was, 'The Lord reward thee for thy tender care; it makes me think of my dear wife. I know not whether I may ever see her more; but, however, the will of God be done. I am, and was willing to be, contented with the will of God, whether life or death, before I came hither; and I bless God I am not afraid to die.' He continued to the end in a resigned frame of mind, submitting to the will of God. On his dying bed he gave divers good exhortations to Friends who came to visit him, concerning the education of their children, their care in discipline in the church, and that things might be kept in good order, and that Friends might answer God's love to them. After a few days' sickness, he peaceably finished his course on the 22d of the Second month, in the year 1696, at the house of John Dobbin, in Elizabeth Parish, in Jamaica.

ELIZABETH HARMAN, wife of John Harman, haberdasher in London, and daughter of John Staploe, grocer of the same city, was visited with a lingering distemper, which continued upon her for about four months; in which time, God was graciously pleased to give her many opportunities of great comfort, inclining several friends to visit her, and to pray to the Lord on her behalf. She much desired retirement, to feel her mind stayed upon the Lord, that she might feel his living power to prepare her, that whether life or death, she might be freely resigned and given up to the will of God. But she said, 'Oh, how hard it is to come there! It is hard work to die without having a full assurance of the love of God.'

She had great travail and exercise of spirit, with strong cries to the Lord, and wrestlings against the enemy, who endeavoured to hurry her mind, and bring her into doubts and fears, so that she would often say, 'How busy is the enemy in a time of weakness, and how hard it is to have a mind stayed upon the Lord!'

After some time it was thought convenient, for the benefit of the air, to remove her into the country to Mill-hill, in the county of Middlesex; which being done, she was satisfied therewith, saying, she hoped she should have more opportunity of retirement to seek the Lord, and find him near her.

One day her father being near her, she said, 'Oh, it is a good condition truly to wait and feel the mind stayed upon the Lord.' Her father related something of his own experience, having been greatly distressed for want of the presence of the Lord, and help in the time of need. She acknowledged her father's experience, and spoke with great respect of him, and low thoughts of herself. At another time she said, 'Oh the enemy takes advantage of my outward weakness;' but faith arising, she said, 'I trust the Lord will drive him quite away.'

A few days before she died, her father and another friend coming late one night to visit her, found her under great inward travail for the enjoyment of the love of God to her soul, that being all she desired. The next day, waiting upon the Lord in her chamber, the friend signified the sense he had of the mercy and love of God towards her; desiring that she might wait to feel more of it, and trust therein, watching against the enemy; and he believed God would graciously answer her desire and breathing; and she acknowledged his regard to her. The friend added, 'I believe this day shall not pass over, before the Lord giveth thee thy longed-for desire;' (which was God's presence,) and she believing, answered, 'I believe the Lord will hear thy prayers for me.' About the third hour in the afternoon, whilst her husband and friend sat by her waiting upon the Lord, the same friend prayed, and God did in a large manner manifest his love amongst them, and by his living power drove away the clouds and darkness, to the refreshing of the mourner, and the comfort of her that could not be comforted without the feeling of his power and goodness. She said, 'Oh, now is the good time come! Now I feel the love of God towards me, in my soul! He hath opened my heart and brought me into liberty. How good a God have I! O the merciful God that I have to do with, that hath remembered me! He that said to the thief upon the cross, "To-day shalt thou be with me in paradise," hath looked upon me. Now I am satisfied. Now I am freely resigned, and given up to the will of God; for now hath the Lord given me the assurance of his love for ever' It was observable how careful she was all along of speaking anything beyond what she enjoyed.

All her near friends and relations sympathised with her in the deep exercise and travail of soul she underwent, before she received the full assurance of eternal happiness; which, when she had attained to, was occasion of comfort and gladness of heart to them.

Soon after, some came to visit her, to whom she signified something of the Lord's dealings with her, remembering them of their latter end, and the necessity of a preparation for that time; and, withal, how hard it was to die. One of them being under some convincement of truth, she declared the need there was to mind and have regard to the convictions of the spirit of truth, and discovery of light; certifying the principle of truth to be most excellent; and so many as are led by it, are fit to die; but if any professing the same did act contrary, the fault was their own. Desiring, that not anything of that kind might be a stumbling-block to them; with more that she said, speaking of the great assurance of the love of God which she enjoyed, and now was willing to die, having nothing else to do but to die. This so greatly affected the persons she spoke to, that they wept much, and said they never should forget what she had spoken. At night, her husband and father, and others, being present, she said, 'Come now, rejoice with me; the good time is now come, because the Lord is good. The Lord is good, and hath given me the assurance of eternal life! so that you may now rejoice with me, and I hope you will have a joyful parting. The Lord give you a good meeting, from whence I am to be buried, and bless the opportunity to them that may be there. O that all might be diligent who have been careless, and let their minds out after vain things;' desiring that all might love plainness.

The next day she signified to those about her the continuance of the favor and love of God, that she was engaged to speak of, and praise him for the same, who supported her under great weakness; and that she saw clearly through the secret and subtle workings of the enemy of her soul, who would have discouraged her; 'but,' said she, 'I know the power that hath driven him back, and he must enter no more. Now is my soul redeemed to God, and he that hath redeemed me is near me. The sufferings and death of Christ, and his agonies; the shedding of his blood, and what he hath done for me; I feel now that I have the benefit of [them] all: blessed be my Redeemer who is near me.'

On the sixth day of the week divers of her relations and friends came from London to see her, and were much comforted because of the good condition that they found her in; and the time was good, because the good God of life opened the living spring in their hearts; that which stopped the well being taken away, so that those who loved her most were reconciled to part with her. To one of those present, whom she loved much, she said, 'Oh, why hast thou stayed so long? If thou hadst been here before, I believe I had been gone. But oh, when I wrestled with the Lord for my own soul, thou wast still before me, and it was often in my mind to send for thee. Indeed, I may say, the Lord constrained me; and it was to tell thee this, that thy state is as mine was, not as mine is. No, no, thou hast hard work to do first. Oh the anxiety, the sorrow, the agony and perplexity of soul, the Lord hath been pleased to lay upon me; yet [I was] blameless as to my life and conversation. None can accuse me of any evil, neither do I believe they can thee; neither can I. Therefore take it not amiss, for in pure love to thy never-dying soul do I persuade thee and exhort thee; for I cannot but say, I have seen clearly into thy state. Because I love thee, I am concerned for thee. I know it is as I was: I have sometimes gone to a meeting, and not keeping on my watch, my mind was cumbered with many things, and I have gone away never the better. Answer me; hath it not been so with thee?' No reply being made, she spoke earnestly, and asked again, 'Prithee tell me, tell me.' Then an answer being given, she said, 'Watch and pray, dear friend, for thou wilt find it hard to die; live as well as thou canst: and thou knowest not but it may be thy turn next. Though thou art a flower, so was I; yet see how I am faded away. Forget not my dying words, forget them not; they are spoken to thee in pure love. Therefore, dear and tender friend, take them so.' Then she said, 'Farewell, farewell; I am going to eternal glory. But, oh! how hard was it to obtain an assurance thereof! But now, glory, glory to my God! I have obtained pardon, and am going to him. And one word more, dear friend; keep in all plainness both in house and apparel, for that becomes us best; that will last longest; that we shall have most peace in;' then bid her again, 'Farewell, farewell.'

That night another friend came to visit her, who, with her husband, father, and divers other friends, had a good meeting in her chamber. After which, she expressed her affection to her husband and tender children, desiring the blessing of God upon them, and that her children might be brought up in the fear of the Lord, and in that plainness which truth leads into; and said affectionately to her father, 'Thou hast been a tender father to me, be so to mine; a grandfather, double, double.' She further said, 'Though I have a dear, loving husband and two fine children, and plenty enough of the things of this world, so that there is nothing wanting; but oh, what is all that? It is as nothing in comparison of the overcoming love of God which I feel. Oh, how gracious a God have I. Now I want to go hence. I long to be dissolved. Come Lord, come Lord Jesus, receive my spirit.' And for the comfort of her friends, said, 'My gracious God hath given me the full assurance. Oh, the light that I see before me, and the glory of that kingdom I shall soon enter into!'

The night before her departure, it having been the monthly-meeting at Mill-hill, several of her friends came from London to visit her. After they were gone, her father took notice what a company of friends had been below. She replied, 'I pray God bless you, and grant to you all as happy an end as I am like to make;' with many more sensible expressions which she uttered. That night she received a letter from our friend William Penn, whom she much esteemed, and who had been to visit her in the beginning of her sickness; part of it is as follows:

'Dear Elizabeth,

'I am grieved that I am hindred from seeing thee, but the Lord I have sought for thee, and in spirit abundantly sympathized with thee. I beseech him, make all easy to thee in life or in death. The Lord God of thy life and the life of his dear people, be with thee, and do his blessed good pleasure: in the love of which endless life I bid thee farewell, farewell. Thy friend and brother in the Lord, where we shall meet again and live for ever.'

The which letter, a friend present, at her desire, answered, and she, at the conclusion, expressed these words, 'My love in the Lord Jesus, in whom I received his love, is dearly to him, and my dear love to his wife.'

The next day, being the second day of the week, she said in the morning to them about her, 'Dear friends, farewell; the Lord God of heaven and earth be with you, bless you and preserve you.' Having taken leave of her husband, and all in order, leaving directions not only about her children, as to the bringing them up, but also the family she left behind, and concerning several acts of charity, also her burial and the manner of it; about the third hour in the afternoon she said to a minister present, who often visited her in her sickness, 'A true friend, the Lord reward thee when I am gone.' And having an easy passage, she soon fell asleep, and is now at rest in the Lord. She remembered her love in the Lord Jesus Christ to friends. She died at Mill-hill on the 12th, and was buried in London the 15th of the Second month, in the year 1698, aged twenty-eight years.

ANNE MERCY STAPLOE, daughter of John Staploe of Aldersgate-street in London, a young maid between fourteen and fifteen years of age, was a dutiful child to her parents, a pattern of contentment in the family, and was seldom out of temper, whatever happened.

She had been at school the 18th of the First month, 1700, and was taken sick the same day of a violent fever, yet was preserved in her senses to the last. At the time of her first being ill, a neighbour being with her, she said she thought herself to be taken much after the manner that the servant-maid was, who died out of the family two or three months before. She was heard to say, as she lay in a quiet and still frame, 'Thy will, thy will be done.' Another time, her mother asking her how she did, she cheerfully answered, 'that she thought she should not recover; but desired to be contented with the will of the Lord.' When her friends came to see her, she affectionately acknowledged their visit, and said, 'A broken heart and contrite, was accepted of the Lord;' with many more words, but her voice being low, they could not well understand them. A friend taking leave of her, desired the Lord to comfort her, and she answered, 'He hath;' and said, 'I have been in the sweetest frame that ever I was in in my life. Praises, praises be to the Lord; for thou art worthy of it.'

She declared her willingness to die, and that she was happy in the Lord; and being asked to take something to moisten her mouth she said, 'None; for in a few minutes I shall be at ease:' and looking on her friends about her, she turned her face to the pillow, and said, 'Anne Mercy bids all farewell.' A neighbour asking her if she was willing to die, she said 'Yes, and go to God;' and departed in about two minutes after, having been sick four days.

She died on the 22d of the First month, in the year 1700, and was buried from the Bull and Mouth meeting-house the 25th of the same month, aged between fourteen and fifteen years.

MORGAN CADWALADER, son of Morgan Cadwalader, of Merion Township in Pennsylvania, being under weakness of body, said, when he was in health he was not so careful as he should have been; so that when he heard friends speak concerning the preciousness of the work of the Lord, and concerning being serious, and how needful it was to use but few words in our conversation; he was not careful enough concerning these things: and when it happened that he was among some who were light and vain, it was pleasing to him.

But when the Lord was pleased to visit him with sickness, and bring him in his apprehension very near death, then he began to consider his condition, and saw himself wanting. Then the fear of the Lord came upon him, and he took delight in his service; and the company of those who were most serious, and careful to keep close to the Lord, was most acceptable to him. He desired that they would pray for him; and the Lord put it into his heart to go alone to wait upon him, and pray unto him. It was his chief concern to be serious and grave, and to refrain from that company which he formerly delighted in. Such a fear was upon his heart, that he would desire his friends and relations, if they heard him at any time say amiss, to tell him of it. When he was in his last sickness, a friend visiting him, enquired how he did, he replied, 'I am not afraid of death, nor punishment after it; for I know and am satisfied that the Lord will have mercy on me: and yet I wait to come one step nearer to him.' To another friend he said, taking his leave of him, 'When thy heart is tendered, remember me; for it is good for one that is weak to have help.' He often said, 'The time of my going to my long home draws nigh;' 'How good is the Lord, and how great is his love!'

One time he asked his mother how much he wanted of twenty years, she replied, 'Three-quarters of a year.' 'Then,' said he, 'if I go to my grave in my youthful days, I shall escape a great deal of trouble that is in the world.' And farther said, 'I very often used to go alone into the woods, and fall on my knees to pray to the Lord, and make covenants with him, and that with many tears. Though I have sometimes been too short in performing my covenants which I made in my distress; yet the Lord has been merciful to me, and I am willing to die. This poor carcass, which is much decayed already, will go to the grave; but the purer part, or spirit that is in it, will go to the Lord that gave it.'

He said to his brother, 'I know thou art tender, and often broken into tears: if thou wilt be careful, the Lord will be good to thee. I desire thee, after meeting on First-days, and on other days, when thou hast time, to read the Scriptures, and Friends' books, and spend less time in reading history; though I do not say there is harm in so doing, if it do not too much employ thy mind, for these things will be of little worth at last. I hope thou wilt think on my words, when my body is in the dust.' He prayed on this wise, 'O! Lord, who doth hear and see in all places, let it be good in thy sight to look upon me a poor mortal. Comfort and strengthen thou me, against the time that thou mayest see it convenient to take me out of this world; and if there be any under great trouble, Lord, do thou help them.'

The morning before he departed, a friend asked him how he did; his answer was, 'I am very well. I can wait bravely to-day, better than at any time before;' and desired his father to wait with him that day; and also entreated both his father and mother to pray to the Lord for him. He gave good advice to his sisters, to shun vain company; adding, 'Through the goodness and mercy of the Lord I am going to a good place. Do not despise your father and mother.' Farther speaking to them all, he said, 'When I am departed, be you silent, and have a care you make no noise; but for weeping, you cannot help that.' Then he said, 'Turn me on my right side, and I will trust in the Lord.' These were his last words that he spoke, and so slept about half an hour, and departed this life without struggling, as if he had fallen into his natural sleep.

He died the 16th day of the Twelfth month, in the year 1698, aged nineteen years and three months

---

RICHARD SAMBLE was born at a place called Penn Hall, in the parish of Enoder, in the county of Cornwall, and baptized according to the manner of the church of England, the 24th of the Fifth month, 1644. His education was in that Society; and he continued in it until it pleased God to call him by his grace, and to reveal his Son in him, which was about the year 1666, at which time the Lord sent some of his messengers, called Quakers, into those parts, to make known the way of salvation, and to turn people from darkness to light. Their testimony he received and closed with, and, like Ephraim, lamented his mis-spent time, under a form without power; and then joined himself to the Lord and his people, as in a perpetual covenant that can never be broken. He was brought into deep humility, and sat down in silence in the assemblies of God's people for several years, in tenderness, fear, and trembling, waiting upon the Lord for that wisdom which is from above. Sometimes when his heart was filled with the power of the Lord, he would in much tenderness speak a sentence or two in a meeting of God's people, which was received and accepted. Though his presence was contemptible to the great men, rabbies, orators and disputers of this world, yet his testimony was made powerful to many.

He was improved in his gift for the work of the ministry, through great diligence; and in his last six years he travelled frequently from county to county, visiting the meetings of Friends in many parts of England and Wales. At his return from his journeys he fell diligently to his trade, which was a tailor, for the help of his family.

He gave up his weak body to spend and be spent in God's service, and was as careful of his time as if he had seen the shadows of the evening stretched out.

He adorned his testimony by a circumspect life, and was very temperate; and all things were so sanctified to him in the fear of the Lord, that he was a sweet savour in his day. His wife did not remember that ever she heard him speak one unsavoury word, during the twelve years she was his wife; and he was contented in every condition; exhorting her and his children to live in God's fear. In the church he was a nursing father; never sparing his labour, though many times through much difficulty, to visit the people of God, both in season and out of season; rebuking some, exhorting others, and comforting and confirming many, in that heavenly power that accompanied him; being willing to serve the Lord with all his heart, mind, understanding, and strength.

About the First month, 1680, being then on his travels, and having been weak some months before, he was taken sick at Poole, in Dorsetshire; from whence, expecting to see them no more, he wrote an epistle to Friends in Cornwall, the county where he was born, and where he received truth, and also where his family dwelt; which is as followeth:

'To Friends in Cornwall.

'Dear friends,

'I send this salutation, as though it were my last unto you, wherein I take my leave of you in the Lord Jesus Christ, desiring you all may obey the truth, and live and die in it. The many sweet and heavenly opportunities which my soul hath had with you, are fresh in my remembrance. And now, dear hearts, my body grows very weak, but my soul is strong in the Lord, who hath greatly renewed the lasting seal of his love unto my soul this morning. Oh! how could I sleep when my heart was so awakened unto the blessed sense of my acquaintance with the Lord, which sounded through my soul, that my name should not be blotted out of the book of life, and of the holy city, the heavenly Jerusalem, whose foundation is full of precious stones, and where the river of the water of life flows; where the gates are not shut all day, neither is any night there. Which, when my soul heard, my heart was dissolved and broken within me, and my head was as it were turned into water, and mine eyes gushed out with tears, in the consideration of the endless love of God to such a poor creature as I.

'Now, dear friends, who are truly near me in the Lord, you know the time of our first knowledge and acquaintance, which was a time of love; and to this day my heart is filled with the same towards you, though I am likely, as to the outward, to see your faces no more.

'O Friends! be not ensnared or entangled with things of this world, nor let your minds go out of truth, and so lose the everlasting stay and support of your souls in the last day; but rather let go all, and hold fast the truth, and keep your hearts from being overrun with the world's spirit; and so will the spirit of truth spring up in you as a well to refresh your souls.

'And all you, whose hearts are truly tendered to the Lord, whose trials and exercises are not a few, be not daunted nor discouraged, although the enemy may seek to frighten you with many temptations, and would seek to lead you out of the fellowship with your dying day; which exercise my soul has sometimes passed under. But blessed be the Lord for ever, the enemy is found a liar; for the Lord has been pleased to make this sick-bed to me better than a king's palace. I have great fellowship with my last day, and do rejoice in the Lord, who doth so sweetly visit me with the glorious light of his countenance. It is with me as it is with one who has travelled many weary journeys, and at last is come to the sight of his desired end, which, when he sees, he greatly rejoices in a sense of a further satisfaction which he shall after enjoy. Even so it is with me, who have passed no opportunity where I saw the way of life clear and open before me; but have been ready, night and day, to do the will, and answer the requirings of the Lord; and so running, as one in a race, knowing my time that it is but short. Blessed be the Lord, I have great peace and satisfaction in this my weak and low condition; and satisfied, seeing my lot was not at this time among you, that it is here in this place; and I hope it will be well, whether I live or die.

'My dear and well-beloved friends, dwell in love one with another, walking in the unspotted life, so shall you grow up as pleasant plants in the garden of the Lord, and the dew of life will more and more descend upon you, and this you will feel from day to day; and when you shall come to your latter end, your reward will be sure with the Lord.

'I have much in my heart towards you, but my strength fails me. Only this I desire of you, seeing I am likely to leave my wife and tender babes with you, whom I know not whether

I shall see more. Great is my love and tender respect to them, for we have lived from the beginning as two joined together by the Lord, who gives victory over the world; believing that, when I am gone, the care of my God will be over them. I have been a tender father to them, and they have been to me very tender children, and my wife hath been to me as bone of my bone, and flesh of my flesh, yet I must leave both her and them unto the Lord.

'And this would I leave with you, my dear brethren and sisters, who have known me from the beginning, that you esteem her, when I am gone, as one who was wife to him that was made willing in his day to spend and be spent for God's truth, and his church's sake. I desire you in the Lord Jesus Christ, that my dear wife may meet with no discouragements from you; she is a tender woman; and that you will be encouragers of her. I know when this comes to your hands, there will be no want of sorrow; but I trust in my God, that both my dear wife and you will be so endowed with the power and presence of the Lord, that if you should hear of my going hence, you will conclude, as becomes true Christians, that you must come to me, and that I cannot come to you.

'My dear friends, in the opening, free love of God, which this morning my soul is visited withal, I dearly salute you, desiring the Lord may be an husband to my dear wife, and a father to my children, and you friends to both.

'And whereas I have never been wanting in my labour and service for the glory of the Lord and your good, when with you; and if the Lord yet lengthen my days, I trust I shall be as ready and as willing as ever I have been; so I conclude in a sweet and living sense of that love which will never die, my wife's dear husband, my children's tender father, and your own dear friend and brother, in the immortal seed of life, where we are nearly and dearly related one to another.

'RICHARD SAMBLE.

'Poole, the 1st of the First month, 1680.'

Thus our dear friend had a true sense of his death; and this letter manifests that he was a true Christian, a good husband, a tender father, and a faithful friend and brother. They were his dying and last words to them, as he said, for he did not live to see his family and friends in that county, to whom he wrote, though he continued some weeks after this.

Recovering a little strength, he was desirous to be at home with his wife and small children, and relations in Cornwall; and in order to it, he travelled in much weakness to Topsham, and after a few days' rest he reached Champet, near Moreton, in Devonshire, and there he fell into a relapse, and his wife came to him. The day before his departure, taking leave of his wife, he said, 'Oh! my dear wife, come hither to me, and let me take thee in my arms once more. The Lord will be to thee an husband, and a father to our little children, as thou abidest faithful to the Lord.' Then, after a few words more to her, he prayed a considerable time; yea, as long as life lasted, he was praising and magnifying the Lord. To a friend who visited him a little before his death, as he lay weak on his bed, he declared how well it was with him; that he did give up to the Lord's requirings, to spend and be spent for the church's sake; and said he knew his time would be but short, and labours, travels, and exercises would have their end, and be no more; with many more heavenly expressions in much tenderness, with tears running down his cheeks; which was a great comfort to the Friends present.

So he finished his testimony, and slept with his fathers, the 15th of the Third month, in the year 1680, and is entered into rest from his labours, and his works follow him. Aged thirty-six years.

JAMES MARTYN, born at East Acton, in the county of Middlesex, in the year 1646, was convinced of truth in the year 1672. He was a man whose conversation adorned the doctrine of Christ Jesus, which he preached, and faithfully and zealously labored to spread the truth abroad; on which account he travelled in America as well as in England. The first time he went to America was in the year 1682, and he returned into England in the beginning of 1684; and went over into America a second time in 1685, and returned again in the latter part of 1687: after which he continued laboring in the ministry, according to the gift of Christ received.

He was a weakly man in body, and was taken sick when he was abroad on a journey in Essex; and being near his end, he said as followeth: 'Good is the Lord: great is his work which he hath wrought in the hearts of his people, to whom he hath given power to follow him faithfully in the regeneration, through great tribulations, and hath made their garments white in the blood of the Lamb, who hath cleansed and redeemed them from the vain conversation of the world; so that the image of the earthly is done away, and the image of the heavenly is borne. Their conversation and treasure is in heaven, and it is their hearts' delight to be there also.' In which blessed work, this dear servant of the Lord made a good progress, even to the finishing of his course with joy; and he received witness in himself that he pleased God, to his great consolation.

In the time of his sickness he had free access to the Lord, who was pleased to give him the returns of his divine love and life, to the overcoming of his heart and soul, and the comfort of them who were with him. O! the heart-breaking power that attended him night and day, which caused him to sing forth praises to the God of his life. He often said, 'Oh! precious it is to dwell low with the Lord! not to aspire too high, but to keep in the low valley, where the streams of life flow freely.' Again he said, 'O my dear God, how good art thou to me! thy goodness breaks my heart! My dear Father, I have loved thee ever since I knew thee! I have followed thee faithfully ever since I did know thy truth! Thou blessed God! let all that is within me praise thy name! thou hast given me a good reward! Death is swallowed up of life. Thou hast given me victory over the grave. My soul longs to be with thee, my sweet Father!' With much more, even continually praising the Lord, and rejoicing in his mercy. He admonished Friends who visited him to live in the life of their profession, saying, 'A profession without life will stand none in stead when they come to die. It is a dreadful condition to see death approaching, and the terrors of God lie upon the conscience for disobedience. O it is a blessed thing, when death approaches, to know peace and consolation with the Lord, and an answer of well done.'

He afterwards said, 'O what a blessed thing it is to feel life. Friends, life is that which will make your hearts glad.' When his speech was almost gone, those about him could many times hear him say, 'My soul praises the Lord. My soul is glad with thy joy.' He finished this life in great peace with the Lord, on the 30th day of the Eighth month, in the year 1691, at the house of John Salmon, of Bocking, near Braintree, in Essex, and was buried in Friends' burial-ground at Ratcliffe, near London, the 3d of the Ninth month following, aged forty-five years.

MARY MOLLINEUX, wife of Henry Mollineux, of Liverpool, in Lancashire, was one who in her childhood was much afflicted with weak eyes, which made her unfit for the usual employment of girls. Being of a large, natural capacity, quick and studiously inclined, her father brought her up to more learning than is commonly bestowed on her sex; in which she became so good a proficient, that she well understood the Latin tongue, and fluently discoursed in it, and made a considerable progress also in the Greek. She wrote several hands well, and was a good arithmetician; as also versed in the study of several useful arts. She had a good understanding in physic and surgery, delighting in the study of nature, and to admire the great God of nature in the various operations of his power and goodness.

She was one who loved the blessed truth, and those who walked according to it, from a child, being early convinced thereof, and was not satisfied with a profession of religion only, but earnest for the life of it, both in herself and others. Not proud or conceited of her parts and learning, but was adorned with humility; plain and decent in her clothes, which she valued for service more than sight. She loved to read the

Holy Scriptures, and delighted much in solitude, setting apart some time in the day for retirement.

She delighted in frequenting the religious meetings of the people called Quakers, and suffered imprisonment for the same in Lancaster castle, in the year 1684. Afterwards she was married to Henry Mollineux, to whom she was a loving wife, an affectionate mother to her children, and a kind, charitable neighbour, especially to such as were in distress, sick, or in affliction, though ever so poor, giving both advice and medicines to them that stood in need; whereby she was made an instrument of good to many. She was noble in enduring hardships upon the account of her husband's imprisonment, which was several times. For him and his fellow-sufferers she made application to Dr. Stratford, bishop of Chester, they being imprisoned upon the writ De Excommunicato Capiendo, for not appearing at the bishop's court, though they had no citation or lawful notice given them; and after her discourse with the bishop, he was so favourable, that they were set at liberty. But afterwards, the priest who prosecuted them before, threatened them again.

She wrote many poems upon religious subjects, which were printed for public service, having a gift that way.

Upon the 8th of the Tenth month, 1695, she was taken with sickness, under which she continued nearly a month. About nine days after she was taken ill, she said, 'I am well contented, if the Lord see meet, that he take me away; for my pain is great, and I know not what in this world I should stay to enjoy, except it be my husband, and my little lads;' her two sons; of whom she then said, 'I would rather have my children enriched with the fear of the Lord, than with all manner of worldly riches.' She grew daily weaker, inclining to sleepiness, yet would sit up five or six hours at a time towards evening, and discourse freely; and said to her husband, that she was well satisfied, if the Lord took her away by that distemper, she should be eternally happy; with more comfortable expressions that are not set down. One evening it was thought she would have died; but recovering somewhat, she spoke in

Latin of being clothed hereafter; whereby they understood that she was minding how the Lord would clothe her, when her mortal clothing was put off.

Her husband asking her if she had any thing on her mind concerning her children, or any other thing farther to communicate to him, she soon replied in Latin, 'Why speakest thou such things?' as if all temporal things were out of her thoughts; 'dost not thou understand me?' he replied, 'Yes, very well, she spoke of spiritual things;' she answered, 'Yes; but she had nothing concerning outward things farther to say.'

The next morning, her breath being short, and her husband expecting her departure, he expressed to friends present somewhat of his concern for her; to whom she said, 'Be not thou over-much careful or troubled.' When company was present she sometimes spoke in Latin, when she intended it only to her husband. Afterwards being asked how she did, her answer was, 'Drawing nearer and nearer;' with many other sweet and good sentences, and so departed without any noise, sigh or groan, on the 3d day of the Eleventh month, in the year 1695, aged forty-four years.

ANDREW TAYLOR received truth in the year 1672, when it pleased God to visit many about the borders of England, in Cumberland, by sending his servants to declare the word of life amongst them. Through his faithfulness and true zeal for the Lord, he came to be wonderfully changed, and suffered several imprisonments for meeting among the Lord's people. A man diligent in business, faithful and upright among men. His way was, to be better than he appeared, so that people loved and esteemed him. After several years, having approved himself just and honest towards men, God bestowed his heavenly riches upon him, and called him to the work of the ministry about the year 1679, fitting him for the same; so that by him many were convinced of the truth and right way of the Lord, not only in his own country, where he was best known, but in other parts; for he travelled diligently in many parts of England, and also in Scotland and Ireland.

He was zealous to reprove sin, and careful to preach the gospel freely, his own endeavours sufficiently supplying his necessities. At last his body being much spent through his many labours and travels, a universal weakness or consumption seized him. Having little pain or sickness, he grew weaker and weaker, and, being satisfied that his end drew nigh, there continued a travail upon his spirit, that the Lord God who had been with him, and borne him up in many deep trials and exercises, would receive him into his rest. The friends present were witnesses of the hope that he had in his latter end; and a little before he died, he prayed, saying, 'Come, Lord Jesus, come quickly; for now I am ready.'

Being filled with heavenly joy, he departed this life the 3d day of the Third month, in the year 1698, in the fifty-fifth year of his age, and about nineteen years a preacher of the gospel.

ELIZABETH COWPERTHWAITE, wife of Hugh Cowperthwaite, of Flushing, in Long Island in America, was convinced of truth about the year 1652, in the north part of Old England, and continued therein faithful to the end. She was a woman serviceable to the church of Christ in several respects, as well by a public testimony to the blessed truth, which she bore in much plainness and sincerity, delighting in the prosperity of truth, and of the people of God. She had true judgment when to speak, and when to be silent; and divided between the precious and the vile, being tender to the broken-hearted, but as a sword against that which was evil, and which tended to division in the church of Christ; very desirous that the young generation might grow up in the life of truth, as in the education thereof.

She was at times sick several months before she died, which she endured with great contentedness, often expressing the love of God to her, and said that she felt his heavenly presence.

In the time of her sickness she bore many faithful testimonies to the glory of the worthy name of God, strengthening and encouraging friends in his work and service, and against the spirit of separation; for the Lord had sealed it upon her heart, that that which leads out of the heavenly unity, and brotherly fellowship, was a false spirit, and not of the Father. She often said that such could not be heirs with the true seed, and exhorted those about her against the superfluity of the world; showing them the ill consequence thereof. Those friends who came to see her, she exhorted to faithfulness, saying there is nothing like it. She continued sensible to the last, and departed this life on the 15th of the Tenth month, in the year 1697.

WILLIAM WILSON, of Langdale-chapel, in the county of Westmoreland, was a man of an innocent life, and though he had little of outward learning, yet God was pleased to teach him himself, and called him to bear a testimony to his name; and he did it faithfully, not only in many parts of this nation, but in Germany, and was several times in Scotland.

He was a man of a lowly and meek spirit, upright and just among his neighbours, which caused them often to submit their matters in difference to his arbitration, in which he was careful to find out the truth and ground of things, and would never countenance deceit. In this service he had success, seldom missing his desired end, viz., to make peace. Faithful he was in his testimony for the truth, and a sufferer for the same in the prison of Kendal, in the year 1666, and several other times afterwards, as well as by distress on his goods. Besides that, he suffered cruel mockings, stockings, stoning, blows and wounds, by cruel usage, both from priests and people; particularly at Eshdale in Cumberland, where he exhorted the people to mind that of God in their consciences, and turn to that holy light and law which he had put into their inward parts, that by the same they might come to know the will of God, and do it.

Because of these and such like words, one Parker, a priest,

in cruel rage did beat and wound him, and with one of his crutches broke his head, and caused the blood to run down his shoulders. The priest being lame, and not able, as he would, to effect his cruel purpose, caused his horse to be brought, on which he mounted, and in the sight of the people broke his staff in three pieces upon William's bare head, which made the people cry out against such merciless work; but before the said Parker got home he was struck with sickness, that he never came more to the steeple-house; and during the time of his sickness he was very loathsome while above the ground, and so died.

A few weeks after, the said W. Wilson went to the same place at Eshdale; and for speaking a few words to the people, one Fogo, a priest, took him by the hair of his head, pulled him to the ground, and drew him out of the steeple-house; and also in rage and cruelty abused his brother, Michael Wilson. But a few months after, this same Fogo, riding over some sands, accompanied with several people, fell into a quick-sand, and was immediately smothered.

William Wilson left behind him a widow and two daughters, to whom he was a true husband and a tender father, instructing his children to keep in the fear of the Lord, and to walk in the way of truth, which he walked in himself, often saying to them, it would be the best portion that they could enjoy.

His sickness was short. Being lately come off a long journey, wherein his body was much spent and weak, he said, 'I have not served the Lord unfruitfully. I have no trouble upon me, and I am very sensible that all is well with me.' Again he said he was content whatsoever way the Lord pleased: he was as a dove, harmless; and as a lamb, innocent. A few hours before he died, he walked several times over the room, and said, as he had often before, 'My peace far exceeds my pain.' And standing upon his feet between two friends, he said, 'Oh that every one would mind the Lord, that they might keep life.' Then he sat down, and drew breath no more.

He deceased at his own house, at Langdale-chapelsteel, in Westmoreland, the 10th of the Fifth month, in the year 1682.

MARY WATSON, wife of Samuel Watson, of the county of York, was one who, for the sake of the blessed truth, denied herself, and was made willing to part with those things which she thought stood in her way, abhorring all manner of evil; and was a tender, nursing mother, nourishing, exhorting, and building up the young in the most holy faith. Though weak in body, she was much given to fasting on religious accounts, and giving of alms; spending much of her time in private retirement, frequent in prayer and praising the Lord, delighting in meditations; like Mary, of whom our Lord said, she had chosen that good part, which shall not be taken away from her. Luke x. 42. Whilst she had strength of body to go to public meetings, she had a word to speak in season, suitable to the states and conditions of many; and also was instrumental, in the Lord's hand, in keeping things in good order relating to church affairs.

In the time of her weakness of body, she was sometimes under fears of her great passage from mortality; but through travail of soul, in the living faith which she received of Christ the author of it, she was kept steadfast, and obtained victory, which God in his own time manifested to her soul. And afterwards she made acknowledgments of the same to the refreshment of others.

Several weeks before her decease, she gave an account, that the work of her redemption was wrought and completed, and all her doubts and fears were removed; and now she waited to be dissolved, and to be with Christ who redeemed and sanctified her; so that, as a wise virgin, she was prepared to enter into eternal joy. She was filled with praises while she had any strength remaining; and her eye was to that heavenly family, out of all the families of the earth, where she gladly desired to be rejoicing with her dear children and relations gone before, as often her expression was.

She had a tender regard to her offspring whom she left behind, that they might, through the grace of God, be gathered to Christ Jesus, the heavenly Shepherd; with many heavenly prayers for them. Her exhortation to them who were with her, and also for those absent, on her dying bed, was that they might walk humbly before the Lord their Creator, and watch against all the evil temptations of this world; the flesh, and the vanity and lusts thereof; that so they might not be captivated with pride, vain-glory, or intemperance; but, abiding in the holy fear of God, all evil would be suppressed and slain upon the cross; and humility, righteousness, meekness of spirit, and holiness, should grow up in them, and be not only to them as a comely garment, but as a never-failing portion.

At last, all visible helps and outward enjoyments failing, she had the Lord for her portion, and kept in possession of that heavenly treasure in her soul, and fed upon that living bread and wine of the kingdom, of which she is now in the more full enjoyment. She spoke often of her being surrounded with the glory of the Lamb, and was sensible in her expressions to the last few hours; and said to her husband, 'Love, pray for me.' So gave up the ghost, in a sweet, still manner, on the 2d day of the Ninth month, in the year 1694.

GRACE WATSON, daughter of Samuel Watson, of the county of York, was well inclined from her infancy, being subject to her parents, and hating a lie; and in the latter part of her time was much given to retiredness and reading.

In the time of her sickness she had more than ordinary concern in a travail of spirit and combating with the enemy of her soul; in which exercise she kept close to the power of an endless life inwardly; but made no great appearance until the Lord had given her victory over the enemy, and delivered her from his secret temptations. Having passed through the ministration of judgment, her enemy, the crooked serpent (as she expressed herself), was driven far from her dwelling, so that nothing hindered her refreshments; and the well springing up, her joy was great; and through her experience she sung the song of Moses, and the song of the Lamb, in a spiritual triumph, with humiliation and brokenness of spirit. She spoke seasonably and distinctly concerning the wiles of the devil, who, she said, had laid his snares in trades, dealings, and conversation in the world, and also in families. Though, according to common prudence, one would have advised her to silence (her weakness of body considered), yet she was so full, and had such constraint upon her, that words flowed from her a long time, in great sweetness and heavenly refreshment; insomuch that those with her were humbled before the Lord, in the sense of his presence, which caused many tears.

As any came into her chamber, whether her friends (called Quakers) or others, she had a suitable testimony, as if she had felt no weakness of body; so that much was spoken which was not taken down. Some of that which was taken, is as followeth:

'Oh, heavenly Father! what hast thou done for me this night? How hast thou removed the crooked serpent! and not only removed him, but taken him quite away; so that I can truly say, oh, heavenly Father! thy will be done! Thou hast shone in upon me with thy marvellous light; thou hast showed me the glory of thy house, the most glorious place that ever my eyes beheld: neither did I think thou hadst such a place for any, much less for me, a poor worm, a pelican, once ready to think myself destitute.'

Again she said, 'But now hath the Lord taken me up; he hath removed the crooked serpent; so that I can say, I defy him, I defy him.'

And further said to the Lord, 'If thou requirest my life this night of me, I freely give it unto thee. Oh, heavenly Father, thy will be done; and if thou hast farther work for me, keep me in that which I now enjoy, for there will my greatest care be;' meaning to be kept therein.

She said, 'Thou hast made my cup to run over, over, over. O heavenly Father, thou hast taken away all my pain. I am as if I ailed nothing, though of myself I could do nothing; scarcely move one of my fingers, my tongue being ready to cleave to the roof of my mouth; but thou hast been a light to my feet, and a lantern to my path. How can I cease praising thee, thou God of power! thou art more to me than corn, wine and oil. Thy love is sweeter to my taste than the honey, or the honey-comb. Oh! it is more to be valued than the costly pearls, and the rich rubies. The gold of Ophir is not to be compared unto it. O blessed, O praised, O magnified be thou for ever!'

When she was asked how she did, her reply was, 'I am but weak of body, but strong in the Lord, and in the power of his might.'

Once she was questioning something, but she checked herself. 'Why do I so? my case is no doubting one; the Lord hath created a clean heart and renewed a right spirit within me, so that all fears and doubts are taken away. For,' she added, 'the gates are open, and the angels are ready to receive me into the bosom of my heavenly Father, where I shall sing praises with his redeemed ones.'

It was not perceived, in all the time of her sickness, that she desired to live; but many times she said as above, 'If thou requirest my life this night, it is freely given to thee. Oh! Lord, do with me what thou pleasest. Oh! heavenly Father, thy will be done. What hast thou done for me, a poor stripling, in comparison of many? Thou hast made my bed, thou hast taken away my pain, and my sickness is gone.' And so lay all that day, with many other times, in this frame of spirit.

She said, 'The Lord has a people in this city, and other parts, that he will take to himself, and crown with glory and honor.' She exhorted those present to prize their time, and not to give themselves too much to the things of this world. 'How many,' said she, 'have laid up great riches, earthly treasure, and in one night have been deprived of all!'

Her sister weeping by her, she said, 'Weep not; remember David and be comforted. The tongues of men and angels cannot declare the wonderful greatness of God. O heavenly Father, how sensible of thee hast thou made me! Thou hast strengthened me, otherwise I should not have been able to speak so much of thee. With thee is fulness of joy, and at thy right hand are rivers of pleasure for evermore.'

She spoke of the parable of the ten virgins, 'Oh! therefore,' said she, 'keep upon your watch-tower, that whether he comes at midnight, or cock-crow, or dawning of the day, [you may] be ready; for that is the wedding-chamber indeed, and he is the heavenly bridegroom.'

Speaking of her parents and relations, she said they were as near to her as the flesh to the bone; and taking her sister by the hand, she said to her, 'Though we be separated outwardly, we shall meet in the kingdom of glory. O! what cause have I to bless the Lord on their behalf, whom I am sure never countenanced any evil in any of us, but reproved it. The words of my dear and tender mother I do remember, since I was but ten years of age, who said, she had fought the good fight of faith, and the crown of glory was laid up for her. These words having remained upon my mind, and taken deep impression upon me, I can now say, I finish my course with joy, and shall receive the crown of glory.'

She farther said, that the Lord was a God at hand in six troubles, and in seven; 'nay, if thou bringest me to the eighth, thou wilt never leave me:' such was her confidence in the Lord. She departed this life in London, the 20th of the Sixth month, in the year 1688, aged nineteen years and nine months.

GEORGE HARRISON, of the parish of Killington, in the county of Westmoreland, came of a family of note in the world, and underwent some hardships from his relations upon the account of truth, which he received in the year 1652, and soon after travelled in the service of the gospel in many counties of England, through great afflictions, sufferings, and persecution, from those who were high in profession of religion in that day.

He was an able minister of Jesus Christ, and valiant for the Lord. When he came into a meeting of professors, he would challenge of them the order of the true church, according to

1 Cor. xiv. 30, which is, "If any thing be revealed to another that sitteth by, let the first hold his peace."

In the latter part of his time he went southward, and came to Edmundsbury, in Suffolk, and declared truth through the streets of that town. Afterwards he went to an inn there, desiring some refreshment for his money, but they would not entertain him. So he went to Bradfield-manger, and put up his horse at an inn, and called for something to eat and drink; but they perceiving by his language that he was a Quaker, refused also to entertain him, and led his horse out of the stable; for which cruelty he meekly returned to them, in the words of Christ, Matt. xxv. 43, viz., "I was a stranger, and ye took me not in." This innocent young man was obliged to ride abroad all night; and it being a very wet season, and he having been tenderly brought up, took a great cold. He went to Haveril, a town between Suffolk and Essex, where the people grievously beat him for his testimony to the truth; which hardship, with the great cold that he had received by being forced abroad all night without food, greatly injured his health, and put him in a fever. After this, with difficulty, he got to Coggeshall, in Essex, and was kindly received by Robert Ludgater; and afterwards he removed to the house of Thomas Creek, of Little Coggeshall, a mile further.

During his sickness, he felt the love and peace of God to be with him, and said to the friends about him, 'Come, friends, rejoice with me:' and so lay praising God to the last hour.

He died at the house of Thomas Creek aforesaid, aged about twenty-six years, and was buried in the orchard of Thomas Sparrow, tanner, at Stansted, in Essex, the latter end of the Fifth month, in the year 1656.

ELIZABETH BARKER, wife of John Barker, merchant in Tower street, London, being sick, a Friend went to visit her; and when she understood that he was below, she caused those present to withdraw, and sent for him up. He asking her how she did, she wept, and said, 'I am a poor weak woman; and I have prayed to the Lord that if I am to die of this sickness, he would let me know it; and I do not see it yet, though I am weak enough to expect it.' She expressed much concern for her three children, if she should be taken away. The Friend answered, it was true that children are very near to tender parents, but we ought to be resigned, and commit them to God who gave them to us; and besides, if she should die, their grandfather and grandmother Barker were not only able, but willing to take care of them.

Upon which she seemed somewhat satisfied: after a space of silence she said, 'It is assurance of my peace with God that I do earnestly desire.' And further, 'For these two years past God has been at work in my heart, and I endeavoured to answer his will, and have denied myself of some things; but I have had a care not to do it in imitation of others, but from a conviction in my own conscience. I hope, if I live, I shall be faithful to God, and keep those covenants that I have made with God.' Afterwards she said, 'Oh the presence of God! it is that which my soul desires to enjoy. God has been good to me many times; for when I have been alone at home, as well as in meetings, the Lord has broken in upon my heart. When I have been troubled and exercised in my mind, I have gone in secret and prayed to the Lord, and I know he has heard me, and several times answered my prayer, not only for myself, but for my children also.' She particularly mentioned one time, when one of her children was in appearance near to death; 'I bowed my soul before the Lord, with earnest cries to him for my child; and the child fell into a sleep, and awakened much better, even before she took any medicines.'

After some pause, she asked the Friend who was with her, what his thoughts were concerning her recovery; to which he replied, he had little to say to that; and desired her to keep her mind stayed upon the Lord, whom she acknowledged had mercifully visited her, and she would find him still to extend his mercy and favour to her, with his good presence, which was the most comfortable support upon a sick-bed. She replied,

'God has been with me in this sickness, but I want more of his presence:' and added, 'In the first of my sickness, and before, at times, I used to be terrified with the thoughts of death; but now it is not so. I am not afraid of death; that fear is taken away. Yesterday they thought I was dying, and they were in a great hurry about me; but I was not so in myself, for I felt great sweetness and stillness upon my mind.' Afterwards she said, 'I do not find that the Lord doth lay any thing to my charge.'

Speaking concerning her child, she said, 'When I was last year in Yorkshire, God did many times visit my soul, and I had large enjoyments of him; and one time praying to him, I fervently asked the Lord to give me a son; and now God has answered me in this request; my desire is (which she spoke with much concern) that, when he is grown up, he may be a preacher of righteousness.' She spoke upon several things, which are omitted, for she had a clear understanding, and was in a right mind and frame of spirit.

Another time the same person visiting her, she desired all in the room might be still, and she waited in much retiredness of mind, secretly breathing to the Lord in her heart; and the Friend prayed by her, with whom she heartily joined. Upon his leaving her, she said, 'This has been a good time. I have many visitors, but too few of this kind. I have felt the Lord's presence, but he will be quickly gone again. I have not so much of these sweet enjoyments as I desire.' After some more that passed, he asked her if she desired to speak with any particular Friend in the city, and he would acquaint them with it; she answered, 'I have not; I am easy in my mind.'

About three days before her departure, when it was thought she was dying, the same Friend being sent for, she told him that she was willing to die, if it was the will of God; and gave him an account of the concern that she had upon her mind for a relation who came lately to visit her, whose sister had married one that was not called a Quaker. Said she, 'I entreated her not to do the like; also I prayed her mother, that she would not suffer it to be; and I desired her not to forsake the truth, and God would never forsake her; and they both wept; and when she comes again, I will endeavour to make her promise me not to marry one that is not a Friend.' The person replied, 'But then she must also keep her promise;' to which she earnestly answered, 'Ah! so she must.' The rest that she said at that time is omitted; only, that she had a great desire to speak to the other sister who is married; but she said she was in the country.

Her father and mother coming to visit her, found her in a heavenly frame of mind; and she said, 'O mother, thou knowest that I have been afraid of death, and how I have loved vain and foolish things; but I have prayed to the Lord to forgive me all my sins. And now, instead of that fear of death, there is much sweetness upon my soul; and all those vain things I once loved, I now loathe; and all the world is nothing to me:' with much more, expressing her satisfaction and peace of conscience. She spoke of the exceeding joy and comfort that she felt, and how sweet the presence of God was to her soul; and she made heavenly melody to God in her heart, which tenderly affected the minds of those present.

Her sickness increasing, she grew weaker; and though sometime before, she did not see that she should die, yet afterwards was satisfied concerning her departure; and, in order thereunto, bequeathed several things to her relations and children, and gave directions concerning the ordering of her children and family, and also where she would be buried. She received assurance of her future happiness; for, a few hours before her decease, the said Friend before mentioned, coming to visit her, found her very much spent, and her kindred and relations mourning about her; and he prayed, desiring that all might submit their wills to the will of God, who giveth and taketh away as he pleaseth. A considerable time after he was gone, lying very still, she said, 'The voice said, "Submit, submit;" and I say, I have submitted, I have submitted;' or to the same effect. When these words were spoken, a relation present said, 'Thou art going to leave us;' she replied, 'I shall be happy.' She also, in the time of her sickness, saw a vision of the difficulty of her passage out of this world, and of the felicity of the place she at last was to arrive at.

She peaceably ended her days the 6th of the Third month, in the year 1701, aged twenty-eight years.

JOHN CROOK was born in the year 1617, and received the blessed truth, as testified of by the people called Quakers, at its first being preached in Bedfordshire, which was about the year 1654. He was a man of note in that county, having been a justice of the peace; and the Lord by his spirit made him an able minister of the gospel of Jesus Christ. He had great discoveries in the mysteries of the gospel, was sound in doctrine, and a skilful archer, hitting the mark.

In former years, when he was out of prison, he labored much in publishing the gospel, and many were the seals of his ministry. As he had received a part of the ministry, so also he had a share of sufferings for his faithful testimony, being imprisoned in divers places, as at London, Huntingdon, Aylesbury, and Ipswich; and as he sealed to the truth by sufferings, so he was careful to adorn the same by conversation, and had regard to the power of godliness in life and doctrine, above dead forms, and to the spirit above the letter, yet highly esteemed the Holy Scriptures, with respect to the sacred doctrine thereof, being well read therein, and devoted for the faith and practice thereof, as the Lord gave him understanding.

He was eloquent, allegorical, and mysterious, many times in his ministry; but did not thereby deny or invalidate the history of Christ, &c., as recorded in the Holy Scriptures.

The mystery of Christ in spirit, and as revealed and formed in true believers, and their sincere conformity to him in spirit and conversation, he greatly esteemed; desiring the professors of Christianity might come into the true sense and experience thereof, by a true, living and feeling faith in Christ, and sincere obedience to him.

He spent his former years mostly in and about Bedfordshire

and the counties adjacent, and his latter years in Hertfordshire, being often disabled from travelling far by reason of several infirmities of body, so that he would say (with Israel), "I have been afflicted from my youth," Psalm cxxix. Under the sorrow and grief that he had with some of his children, he would sometimes, in a tender frame of spirit, comfort himself in the words of David, viz., "Although my house be not so with God, he hath made with me an everlasting covenant, ordered in all things, and sure," 2 Sam. xxiii. 5; and said, that the Lord did remember the kindness of his youth.

His patience under his bodily infirmities was very remarkable, and as a good Christian he made the best use of them, saying that the furnace of affliction was of good use to purge away the dross and earthy part in us; and that, did he not feel and witness an inward power from the Lord to support him, he could not subsist under his pains, they were so great, which continued with him to his end; yet he was not remembered to have uttered an unsavoury word, or impatiently to cry out; and when the extremity of his fits was over, he would express his inward joy and peace that he had with the Lord.

He would many times say, that many of our ancient friends were gone to their long home, and we are making haste after them; 'Thus,' said he, 'they step away before me, and leave me behind, and I that would go, cannot. Well, it will be my turn soon;' in which he seemed to rejoice.

He finished his course the 26th day of the Second month, in the year 1699, in the eighty-second year of his age, and was buried at Friends' burial-ground, at Sewel, in Bedfordshire.

SARAH BECKWITH, daughter of Marmaduke Beckwith, of Audborough, near Masham in Yorkshire, was from a child sober and grave in her deportment, not addicted to light and needless words, but behaved herself as one who was watchful lest she should offend the Lord, or be an evil example to others. She was obedient to her parents, and tenderly affectionate to others, one sincerely devoted to serve the Lord, and seek his kingdom and the righteousness thereof. She loved retirement, and when her business was over, would walk alone in the fields and other places, where she sought the Lord, and would sing praises to him, when she thought nobody saw or heard her.

In her sickness she was much troubled with shortness of breath, and often prayed to the Lord, to enable her to praise him whilst she lived.

About five days before her decease, having some ease, she desired to be raised up in her bed, and spoke largely of the tender dealings of God with her, desiring those who were young to prize their time, not knowing how few their days might be; 'For,' said she, 'many are the temptations of the enemy, especially to youth, presenting length of days, and persuading them that it is soon enough to trouble themselves with such a concern, for so he would have persuaded me; and many ways was I tempted, which caused such exercises that I was brought nigh to despair. I sought the Lord night and day. No ear heard me but the Lord alone, who heard my call, and afterwards gave me some comfortable assurance of my salvation: but the enemy hath been very busy, and has sorely hurried me, since I began with this illness.' Afterwards she prayed, 'O Lord, give me full assurance of my salvation before I depart hence! O Lord, let not my distemper overcome my senses, till I come to a full enjoyment! I pray thee, let not my desires cease, till thou answerest the desires of my heart; and let nothing quench thy love.' And the Lord answered her cries, and caused her cup to overflow, so that she sung heavenly praises to the God of her salvation.

She also gave tender advice to her sisters, and desired them to love and fear the Lord above all, and keep in the truth; saying, 'Oh! press after it, to feel the working of it in your own hearts; and when you are in it, keep in it, and under the government of it. Heed not to deck yourselves, but be meek and low. None ought to pride themselves in any endowment, either beauty, or any other thing; because it is not theirs, but the Lord's who gave it them, and can take it away when he pleaseth;' saying, 'What is all now to me?' She also spoke of the condition of some who were grown careless, and were got into liberty; 'Such,' said she, 'are ill examples to those that are coming up.' She said there were many who professed truth that knew little what truth is. 'It does not consist only in coming to meetings, and wearing plain apparel and the like, unless they come to feel the operation of truth in their own hearts; for all such outward appearances will stand in no stead, without the love of God be inwardly felt and enjoyed. It is an easy thing to come to meetings; and some are ready to think, that doing so, and behaving themselves soberly, is sufficient; but the Lord seeth at all times, and he will have no such mockery. I bless God, I have not been guilty of seeming what I was not.'

Her love was great to faithful friends, and she much desired their company, and wonderfully prized the love and mercies of God, saying, 'It is not for my deserts, for I had nothing to engage the Lord with, but it is his free love to me.' She said there was man's righteousness, and the righteousness of God; but man's righteousness must be rent off, and man covered with the righteousness of Christ Jesus, who said, "I lead in the way of righteousness, in the midst of the paths of judgment, that I may cause those that love me to inherit substance."' Speaking of the way of truth, she said, it was a strait and narrow way, and not to be kept in without a daily watch; and further said, 'But although a strait way, yet it is a pleasant path, and delightsome. Oh! here is peace in abundance. It is so sweet, I could delight always to enjoy it, and to live therein; gold is not worthy to be compared to it.' She thus continued, being taken up with heavenly thoughts, saying, 'Lord, give me fully to drink of the well of water that is within the gate, for thou hast raised my heart, and I am overcome with thy love. O! I long, I long! O! Lord, open thou the windows of heaven, and pour of thy blessings into my soul, until there be not room to receive, that I may bless and praise thy name.'

Her end drawing nearer, she prayed the Lord to give her

an easy passage; and taking her leave of her sister Hannah, she said if she was worse, some should call her. Taking her by the hand, she said, 'Dear sister, thou hast been near and dear to me, and careful of me: the Lord requite thee, and be near to thee when thou comest to lie on thy dying bed.' Near morning, her distemper growing upon her, she said, 'I am as sensible as any of you, and I am well content to die. I have no doubt of my salvation:' with many more good expressions, which could not be perfectly understood, her voice being low; but she was sensible to the last, saying within a very little time of drawing her last breath, 'Lord, take me away;' and presently after, she gently and comfortably passed out of this world, to live for ever in a world which hath no end.

She departed this life the 24th of the Ninth month, in the year 1691.

JOHN BURNYEAT was born in the parish of Lowes-water, in the county of Cumberland, about the year 1631; and when it pleased God to send his faithful servant George Fox, with other of the messengers of the gospel of peace and salvation, to proclaim the day of the Lord in the county of Cumberland, and north parts of England, this dear servant of Christ was one that received their testimony, which was in the year 1653, when he was about twenty-two years of age. Through his waiting in the light of Christ Jesus, unto which he was turned, he was brought into deep judgment, and great tribulation of soul, such as he had not known in all his profession of religion, and by this light of Christ were manifested all the reprovable things; and so he came to see the body of death, and power of sin which had reigned in him, and felt the guilt thereof upon his conscience, so that he did possess the sins of his youth. 'Then,' said he, 'I saw that I had need of a Saviour to save from sin, as well as the blood of a sacrificed Christ to blot out sin, and faith in his name for the remission of sins; and so being given up to bear the indignation of the Lord because of sin, to wait till the indignation should be over, and the Lord in mercy would blot out the guilt that remained, which was the cause of wrath, and sprinkle my heart from an evil conscience, and wash our bodies with pure water, that we might draw near to him with a true heart in the full assurance of faith, as the Christians of old did.' Heb. x. 22.

Thus did this servant of the Lord, with many more in the beginning, receive the truth (as more at large may be seen in the journal of his life,) in much fear and trembling, meeting often together, and seeking the Lord night and day, until the promises of the Lord came to be fulfilled, spoken of by the prophet Isaiah, chap. xlii. 7, xlix. 9, and lxi. 3. Some taste of the oil of joy came to be witnessed, and a heavenly gladness extended into the hearts of many, who in the joy of their souls broke forth in praises to the Lord, so that the tongue of the dumb, which Christ the healer of our infirmities unloosed, began to speak, and utter the wonderful things of God. Great were the dread and glory of that power, which in one meeting after another were graciously and richly manifested amongst them, to the breaking and melting many hearts before the Lord. Thus, being taught of the Lord, according to Isa. liv. 13, John vi. 45, they became able ministers of the gospel, and instructors of the ignorant in the way of truth.

After four years waiting, mostly in silence, he appeared in a public testimony, which was in the year 1657, being at first concerned to go to divers public places of worship, reproving both priests and people for their deadness and formality of worship, for which he endured sore beating with their staves and bibles, &c., and imprisonment also in Carlisle jail, where he suffered twenty-three weeks' imprisonment for speaking to one priest Denton at Brigham.

After he was at liberty he went into Scotland in the year 1658, where he spent three months, travelling both north and west. His work was to call people to repentance, from their lifeless hypocritical profession and dead formalities, and to turn to the true light of Christ Jesus in their hearts, that therein they might come to know the power of God, and the remission of sins.

In the year 1659 he went into Ireland, and preached the truth and true faith of Jesus in many parts of that nation. About the Seventh month following, meeting with Robert Lodge, a minister concerned in the same work, he joined with him, and they laboured together in that nation for about twelve months, in the work of the gospel, and returned to Cumberland in the Seventh month, 1660.

In the year 1662 he travelled to London, where he met with George Fox, Richard Hubberthorne, and Edward Burrough; and in his returning home through Yorkshire, at Rippon he was committed to prison, and kept fourteen weeks, for visiting the friends who were prisoners there.

After he was discharged of that imprisonment he returned home, where he abode, except at times visiting friends in adjacent counties, till the beginning of summer in 1664, when he took shipping again for Ireland, and visited most of the meetings in that nation. From thence he embarked for Barbadoes, in order to perform his journey into America, which had lain before him for four years; and from Galway he arrived at Barbadoes, after a passage of seven weeks, and stayed three or four months there, and had great service, and much exercise also, occasioned by the imaginations of John Perrot, and that fleshly liberty he had led many into, not only there, but in Virginia and other places. From Barbadoes he went to Maryland about the Second month, 1665, and afterwards to Virginia, labouring in the work of the gospel. In the Fourth month, 1666, he came to New York, so to Rhode Island, New England, and Long Island, till the Second month, 1667, at which time he went again to Barbadoes, and spent that summer there. In the Seventh month of the same year he sailed from thence, and arrived at Milford-Haven, in Wales, and laboured much in the gospel in this nation, from the time of his arrival from America, till the latter end of the year 1669, when he went over and spent that winter among friends in Ireland, and returned to London in the year 1670.

In the Fifth month, 1670, he embarked for Barbadoes again, in company with William Simpson, who died in peace with the Lord in that island. From thence he went to New York, Long Island, Rhode Island, and New England, and afterwards to Virginia and Maryland, where he met George Fox and several brethren, just come from Jamaica. Having spent much time and labour up and down in America, till the 25th of the Second month, 1673, they came from the Capes of Virginia, and arrived at Galway in Ireland, the 24th of the Third month, and from thence they came to the yearly meeting at London, in 1674.

From that time he continued in this nation, labouring among the churches, until the Eighth month, 1681, when he went to Ireland again, and tarried there till the Sixth month, 1684, and then he came into Cumberland, and so to Scotland, and into the north parts of England again, visiting the meetings of Friends, and so returned to Ireland the 25th of the First month, 1685, where he tarried till he departed this life.

In the latter part of his life he took a wife in Ireland, and had by her one son. After the death of his wife, he had some intentions to go for England, about the year 1688; but seeing the troubles and wars in Ireland coming on, and that many afflictions would attend Friends in that nation, and people being possessed with fears fled for England; our dear friend, though he had opportunity, had no freedom to go, but gave himself up to stay with Friends there, and bear a part of the sufferings that might attend them. In this time he was a precious instrument in the Lord's hand, able and skilful in the ministry, for the comforting of his people; for he was a cheerful encourager of them, a dear friend and true brother; a diligent overseer and tender father; a perfect and upright man in his day.

Having been at a province-meeting at Rosenallis, where he bore a living testimony to the comfort of friends, he went from thence to Mountrath and Ballinakill, and so to a monthly meeting at New Garden; after which he came home with John Watson, and feeling himself not well, took his bed, and was visited with a fever, and continued sick twelve days; in all which time he was preserved in his senses, and in a sweet frame of spirit. He often said he was finely at ease, and quiet in his spirit, and the Lord did attend him with his heavenly power and presence, to his comfort, and the satisfaction of those about him. He said that he ever loved the Lord, and the Lord loved him from his youth.

He peaceably departed this life on the 11th day of the Seventh month, in the year 1690, and was decently buried at New Garden, the 14th of the same.

Convinced at the age of twenty-two; a labourer in the gospel thirty-three; aged fifty-nine years.

HENRY HAYDOCK, of Warrington, in the county of Lancaster, was a faithful man in life and conversation, and walked as becometh the blessed truth, of which he made profession

When he was upon his dying-bed, and in outward appearance nigh gone, the Lord, who is the God of the living, raised him up by his divine power, to the admiration of those present, to bear a living testimony for him, which was in this wise, viz.

'Friends, I was never a public preacher in all my life; but now, by the power of God, I am one at my death. Glory be to God for evermore, who hath the life and breath of all men in his hand, and can lengthen at his pleasure; who knows how to dispose of us. Therefore, friends, be you all faithful to the Lord, for great things will the Lord bring to pass for his people, who are true in their hearts to him. Such as serve God faithfully, they shall have a living reward from him, and their rest shall be with the Lord Jesus Christ; which rest my soul is already entered into, and is set down with God in the Paradise of his pleasure, taking its repose with God the Father, and our Lord Jesus Christ, and all the holy men of God since the foundation of the world. And though my body go down to the earth, yet my soul and spirit shall have its residence with the living God in heaven, where they who are unfaithful to the Lord cannot come. 'I was well nigh my last breath, but the Lord loosed my tongue, that I might declare of his goodness.'

Again he said, 'The Lord in my healthful days did put his living word in my heart, and though I have been by some looked upon as a stripling, and as one that knew not much of the things of God, yet my soul hath had many sweet seasons and opportunities.'

Again he said, 'I have a very good wife, faithful and loving to me, and three sweet children; call them, that I may kiss them before I die, for my time here will not be long.' So they brought one of his daughters to him, and he said, 'Thou art Elizabeth, my youngest daughter,' and kissed her many times. He farther said, 'Silver and gold I have not much to leave thee; thou hast hitherto been a good child; the blessings of the living God rest upon thee, and the blessing of me, thy dying father, be with thee also.' So then he took his son, and said, 'Thou art Roger, my sweet son. In thee I have taken great delight; yet now thy father is about to take his last breath; and that which I desire of the Lord, is, that he will bless thee and thy two sisters, and bless you all, that you may keep up my name, and live as your father hath done. Though I have not filled up the number of many years, yet I, thy father, do witness peace with God.' Being pretty much spent, he said, 'The Lord bless thee, my son, and thy two sisters; the blessing of your father be with you all;' and so kissed him many times, and let him go.

Then he called for his daughter Alice, and said, 'Thou art Alice, my first born, and I love thee well. It hath been real and true; and though some men can show it more, yet I love you all well, and I hope the Lord's care will be over you when I am dead and gone; and I believe you will not want. Alice, (said he) kiss me, for thou must never kiss me more:' so clasping her in his arms, he kissed her, and bade her farewell. And then said, 'I have now made an end of what lay upon my mind; therefore, everlasting, living, pure, invisible God, into thy hand of power I recommend my soul.' He lay still and quiet till a little before his departure, when the very pangs of death seized on him; then were his sighings many, yet had the savour of life in them. Afterwards he lay still and very quiet, rejoicing in his spirit, and said, 'My soul doth magnify the Lord, and my spirit rejoiceth in God my Saviour, who hath saved me from sin; but what shall I say to the rebellious? If they will serve the devil, they will have a bad portion in the end.'

He said, 'Though there may some of all persuasions find salvation, yet that people, in scorn called Quakers, who are really faithful to God, are satisfied in God, and they know salvation to their immortal souls, having been redeemed by Jesus Christ, who is come to save many.' He prayed for his brother and sister, saying, 'O Lord, thou knowest I have one brother and sister, who are not in that faith in which I am about to lay down my head. Lord, bring them to it, if it be thy blessed will, and confirm them in the same, that they may receive that blessed reward thou hast made my soul a witness of.' And said, 'So my strength now failing, as to my outward man, I once more recommend my soul into thy hands, Lord Jesus Christ.'

He departed this life the 5th day of the Fourth month, in the year 1688, aged about thirty-three years.

THOMAS JANNEY was born in Cheshire, and received the blessed truth at the first preaching thereof in that county, which was about the year 1654, being then in the twenty-first year of his age. The next year he received a gift in the ministry, preaching the gospel of Christ freely; and travelled into many parts of England and also in Ireland, and had a fervent and sound testimony for truth; and his conversation and course of life accorded with his doctrine.

In the year 1683, he with his family went to Pennsylvania, and there settled, where he staid about twelve years; and in the year 1695, he came over again in company with his friend Griffith Owen, of Pennsylvania, to visit his brethren in England: and after he had staid some time in London, he went into Cheshire in the Sixth month of the same year, where he had many relations who were faithful friends; and though they were dear to him, and their houses might have been his home, yet he rested little, but visited the meetings of Friends in several neighbouring counties.

The next spring he travelled through several counties where he had been in former years; and as he had a desire to see the brethren at the yearly meeting in London, he was there at that time; soon after which he was taken so ill, having decayed in his natural strength before, that his recovery was much doubted; and some advised him to go out of the city for the recovery of his health. After some time he adventured by short journeys from London to Enfield, so to Hertford, and from thence to Hitchin, where his distemper increasing he could go no further, having a purpose to go for Cheshire. At Hitchin he lay a considerable time at the house of our friend William Turner; and friends there were careful and tender over him; and he having endured much hardship formerly in the service of truth, by travelling into several climates, and enduring heats and colds, his body was attended with much pain, so that few expected his recovery.

Two of his relations, who were friends, came from Cheshire to Hitchin to visit him, and one of them being with him in his chamber, he said to this effect: 'Cousin, I am glad that you are come. I hardly expect to recover so as to be able to get into Cheshire. It is some exercise to think of being taken away so far from my home and family, and also from my friends and relations in Cheshire. I would gladly have got down into Cheshire; but I must be content, however it pleases God to order it. Worse things have happened in this life to better men than I am. I shall be missed in America; friends there were troubled when I came away. I have laboured faithfully amongst them; they will be grieved at the tidings of my death. My family will want me. My care hath been for my sons, that they may be kept in the fear of God. I have been a good example to them. I have a care upon me, that they may be kept humble while they are young, that they may bend their necks under the yoke of Christ. If I am taken away, I am very clear in my spirit. I have answered the requirings of God; I have been faithful in my day, and I have nothing that troubles my spirit; my spirit is very clear.' He also expressed his concern for his brethren in the ministry, especially the young, that they might observe the leadings of God's spirit in their ministry, and not lean upon their own natural parts, which, he said, occasioned divers inconveniences; of which he spoke particularly in the time of his sickness.

After this, the Lord answered his desire, that he recovered, so as to be able to get down to Cheshire to his relations there; and he got abroad to some meetings that winter, but yet was weakly in body; and, towards the spring, he made preparation to get home to his family in Pennsylvania; but before the ship set sail, his distemper, which had not quite left him, returned sorely upon him. He went to his sister's, near where he was born, and she spoke something to him about his family; but he said little, only these words; 'If it be the will of God that I be taken away now, I am well content;' which was the most he said in his last illness, save to a Friend concerning his burial.

He departed in much quietness of mind, the 12th of the Twelfth month, in the year 1696, and was buried the 15th of the same, in Friends' burying-place, in Cheshire, aged sixty-three years: having been a public minister forty-two years.

HENRY STOUT, of Hertford, born at Ware, in the county of Hertford, in the year 1631, was convinced of the blessed truth by the ministry of a woman, in the year 1655, being then about the twenty-fourth year of his age. At which time some of the people called Quakers came into that part of the county, concerning whom he had heard evil reports, and that they denied the Scriptures; which had prejudiced his mind against them. But it so happened that there came a woman called a Quaker, and preached in Ware market; and afterwards a rude rabble followed her down the street, and he seeing them, followed her also, in pity towards her, and to rescue her from them. But she turned into a house where there was a meeting; and a Friend was speaking there, unto whom he listened, and heard him speak much Scripture, although he named neither chapter nor verse; at which he wondered, because he had heard that they denied the Scriptures.

After he thus lent an ear, the woman stood up and spoke; and such a power attended her ministry, that his spirit was much broken, and astonishment seized on him; and he saw others also with paleness of face, and they smote their hands. This brought great fear upon him, lest he should be deceived; yet was he afraid also that he should offend God, and resist the day of his visitation. This brought great sorrow upon him for a time, he not being able to distinguish; but afterwards going to another meeting, he heard another woman, by whose preaching his convincement was increased; and he was so confirmed, that he could set to his seal that it was the very truth which had long been veiled in him; but now, by the preaching of the gospel, was revealed. He could say, Christ was come, and he looked not for another; and it was confirmed by the work that was wrought both within and without. First, within, the eye which had been shut was now opened, and the ear that had been deaf, now heard, and the mouth of the dumb could speak, and the lame could walk, and the mysteries of the kingdom of God were known, which before were in parables.

He searched the Holy Scriptures, and found it was the good old way, though new to him and others; and the Scriptures were opened by the spirit that gave them forth, and a witness for God he had in himself, according to John i. 5, 10. "He that believes, hath the witness in himself." Then he took up the cross and denied himself, and so became a gazing stock to the world, as the Lord's people were in those days, as well as in former ages. Soon after he was moved of the Lord to go to the public places of worship, to declare against them, and to preach the truth. Persecution and sufferings soon followed;

for many and various were the trials and exercises which the Lord's people went through in their day.

He was the first called a Quaker who suffered imprisonment in Hertford jail, for the testimony to the truth; where his sufferings were great, the prison-windows being shut, that he might not have the benefit of the air, or the light of the day. After he was released of that imprisonment, he was a prisoner five times more in that town of Hertford; the last of which he was sentenced for banishment, and continued a prisoner nearly eight years, to the great detriment of his health, being often put into the common jail; which trials the Lord carried him through with much patience, contentedness and quietness of mind, he being given up to the will of God.

He was a serviceable man in many respects, and willing to do what offices of love he could for any. He travelled pretty much in the service of truth in his younger years, whilst he had strength of body, but some time before his death, distempers grew, and weakness increased upon him, which made him incapable of being much from home.

The last four months before his death, he went little abroad, but grew weaker and weaker; the which his wife perceiving, did much importune him to advise with some doctor; but he answered her thus, 'I would not have thee confide too much in doctors, for they will all prove physicians of no value to me. I thank God, I know that power which in former ages raised the dead, and healed all diseases; and if it is the will of God, he can restore and heal me; if not, I am satisfied; his will be done.'

His greatest infirmity was a stoppage at his stomach, and shortness of breath, which often brought faintings upon him; but he bore all with great patience. And when some friends came to visit him, he told them his weakness was such that he thought he should hardly recover it; but however it pleased God to order it, he was fully satisfied: for he had this testimony, that he had served the Lord with faithfulness, and with an upright heart, to the best of his knowledge: with more to that effect, which cannot be well remembered. At another time to a friend that came to see him, he said, 'None know the virtue and goodness of truth so well as when they draw near their latter end, when all outward comforts fail, and are leaving them, and sickness and weakness come upon them.'

He further said that he had travelled in the service of truth in former years, when he had strength of body, and the Lord had given him many living testimonies to bear for his name; in all which he was faithful, and the remembrance of it warmed his heart at that time; for he could say that his care was, not to speak more than what the Lord gave him to speak, that thereby his name might be honoured. Many times, and upon several occasions, he so expressed himself, as fully manifested the true satisfaction and peace he had with the Lord; often desiring to be dissolved, that he might go home to his rest.

The Lord's love and gentle dealing appeared very largely towards him, in giving him many times ease of body, and comfortable seasons of refreshment; and he generally rested well in the night, till about a week before his death. The sense of it would often make him break forth into praises and thanksgiving to the Lord, for his goodness and mercy to him in the night-season. When he awaked out of his sleep, and when his sleep was taken from him, he continued quiet, patient, and sensible to the last moment. And when his wife saw that he slept little, and took little, hardly enough to keep him alive, she was full of grief; which he perceiving, said to her, 'Thou must give me up, for I shall not long continue here: but it will not be long before thou and I shall meet again in that blessed state, where all tears shall be wiped from our eyes.'

He kept his bed but four days; and the day before his death, his children being by him, he said to them, 'You, who are likely to enjoy what I have, I would have you to remember the advice of your father when I am gone, and live in the fear of God, and as it becomes the truth; then you will be as monuments, when I am gone, and it will go well with you, and what I leave will be a blessing to you. Beware of earthly-mindedness, and pride, and prodigality, which is a dishonour to any family; and bring up your children in plainness, and not in the fashions and superfluities of the world, which passeth away. Remember my advice, who speak to you in love: for wo will be to the wicked. I would say more to you, but my strength faileth.'

The day he died he spoke little, but lay as if he slept; but sometimes fainting fits would come, that it was thought he would have gone away in one of them; but he did not, but fell into a slumbering; and when he awaked, he desired to be turned on the other-side, and then he stretched out his hands and feet, and said, 'Now I am going to the Lord;' which were the last words he spoke: and so departed in peace, without so much as a groan or sigh.

Thus he finished his course, and laid down his body, the 6th of the Tenth month, in the year 1695, in the sixty-fifth year of his age.

THOMAS ALDAM, of Warnsworth, in Yorkshire, received the glad tidings of the gospel of life and salvation very early, viz., in the year 1651, by the preaching of that eminent and faithful servant of Christ Jesus, George Fox, soon after he was delivered out of the dungeon in Derby prison. At this time, Thomas Aldam, John Kellam, Thomas Kellam, Richard Farnsworth, Thomas Goodyear, and several others of note, received the truth; and many sufferings, beatings, reproaches, spoiling of goods, and imprisonments he endured, for Christ's sake and the gospel's; being often concerned to go into market-places, and public places of worship, bearing testimony against the wickedness of the world, and against such teachers and leaders as caused them to err, through lightness, pride, and covetousness.

Before he was convinced, he was a great follower of the priests and teachers of those times, but his hungering and thirsty soul not being satisfied amongst them, he left them, and waited as alone, until it pleased the Lord to send his servant George Fox, as aforesaid, into those parts of the country. And he having received the truth, was valiant for the same upon earth, and gave up his strength and substance to serve the Lord. He was very zealous and fervent in spirit, severe against evil, but tender to the least appearance of that which was good, watching over his children in the fear of God; given to charity, and to do good to all.

He was one of the first called a Quaker, who was imprisoned in York Castle upon that account, in the year 1652. It was for going to Warnsworth steeple-house, and speaking to Thomas Rookbey, a priest of that place, who procured his imprisonment at York, where he was kept two years and six months so close, that he was not suffered once to come home, nor to see any of his children; and sometimes not permitted to see his wife and relations when they went to visit him. He was also fined during that imprisonment £40, at the assizes, for appearing before the judge with his hat on his head, and for speaking thee and thou to him.

During the aforesaid imprisonment, his adversary Rookbey, the priest, and one Vincent, an impropriator, sued him at the law for treble damages, and they made spoil of his goods to the value of £42; not leaving one cow to give milk for his young children and family. Thus he suffered for his faithful testimony to the coming of the Lord Jesus Christ in the flesh, and for his free ministry; at other times also he suffered the loss of goods for his testimony to the truth.

As he had been a sufferer himself, so he had a tender sympathy for the Lord's people, his brethren, who were sufferers for the truth, and would go oftentimes to Oliver Cromwell, and others, the rulers of those times, and lay the sufferings of Friends before them.

He also travelled into Scotland and Ireland, and went to the chief rulers there upon the same account.

He went to all, or most of the prisons in England, where there were any of the people called Quakers, to take a perfect account of their sufferings, that he might be the more capable to advocate their cases before the government, being ready at assizes, sessions, or elsewhere, to plead the cause of God's people.

He had a tender regard to love and unity among brethren, bearing good esteem in his mind for such as laboured in the gospel.

When he was about to undertake any journey upon truth's account, he would call his family together, and in much humility pour out his supplication to God to preserve them.

After thus having served his generation in faithfulness, he was visited with sickness, in which time he set his house in order; and in the time of his weakness, the Lord was good to him, and eminently appeared with him, so that he said to his sister, near his latter end, that he found his strength so renewed, that he believed he could get to London if the Lord required it: but he answered again, 'I am clear of the blood of all men. I find nothing to this man,' meaning king Charles the Second, then lately restored to his kingdom.

He was very sensible of his latter end; and the day he died he called for his children, and exhorted them to live in the fear of God, and to love and obey their mother: and so, being freely resigned into the hands of God his Creator, he departed this life in the Fourth month, in the year 1660.

His wife, Mary Aldam, survived him but three months. She was a woman fearing God, and served him in her generation. In all the exercises which her husband passed through in those early days, she never was heard to grudge or repine, but was given up in all things to God's disposing. Her remembrance is sweet, and her name to be recorded amongst the faithful of God's people. She received truth by the ministry of George Fox, at the same time her husband did, and bore testimony to the same truth, according to her measure.

He had also two sisters, faithful women.

MARGARET KELLAM, who was convinced about the year 1651, travelled much in truth's service in the breaking forth thereof, and many were convinced by her. She also suffered imprisonment for the same at Exeter, York, and Banbury in Oxfordshire; and great was the courage that attended her in preaching truth in the streets, markets, and public places of worship, and to the rulers of the people; and the Lord was with her.

She finished her course in faith, signifying before her departure the great peace she enjoyed with the Lord, and the clearness of conscience she had before him. And so departed this life in the year 1672.

JOAN KELLAM was also a woman that truly feared God, and a good example where she dwelt: she was of sound judgment, and well experienced in the work of the Lord; zealous for his honour, and faithful to the truth; an encourager of virtue, and watching over the young, and an instructor of them in the right way of the Lord. She could speak a word in due season to an afflicted soul, having passed through many states, and seen the wonders and goodness of the Lord therein; and was as a mother in Israel.

In the time of her sickness she was well disposed, and gave good advice to them she left behind her, that they might persevere in faithfulness, to the finishing of that work which the Lord had for them to do. So departed this life in the year 1681.

SARAH BROWN, wife of Capt. Brown, of Leicestershire, and mother to Samuel Brown, physician in the town of Leicester, was one who in her young years fervently and sincerely sought the Lord, and frequented the assemblies of the best sort of people in that day, called Puritans; afterwards she joined herself to the Baptists, among whom she walked inoffensively.

But when it pleased God to raise up his people called

Quakers, in the northern parts of this nation, and gave some of them commission to publish the way of life and salvation, she received their testimony with great joy and thankfulness to the Lord and was a nursing mother among that people. Her husband, at her request, gave up his house for Friends to keep meetings in, even at the breaking forth of truth in that day: and she counted nothing too dear to part with for truth's sake, and was a good example in conversation, in temperance, meekness and charity, towards those with whom she was concerned. She was a true wife and a tender mother, a loving relation, a good neighbour and firm friend. She had a word of comfort in due season to many when in afflictions; she loved to visit the widow and the fatherless, the prisoners, and the house of mourning; and to feed the hungry, and clothe the naked, and to wash the saints' feet. She suffered imprisonment, and spoiling of goods for the truth's sake, counting all as dross and dung, that she might win Christ.

When death came she received it with contentedness, being given up to God's good will and pleasure, and she lived to old age.

A friend visiting her in her last sickness, said to her, 'The Lord hath sent his messenger' (meaning, that her end was at hand); she made answer, 'He is come;' and desired the Lord to give her an easy passage. She was first taken ill in the night with a violent pain in her legs, and her son Samuel Brown being presently called, she prayed to the Lord to mitigate the violence of her pain, and to give her strength to bear his hand with patience. Her son was much grieved for her; which she perceiving, said, 'Child, do not do so; rejoice and be glad, for thou hast no other cause. Thou hast been a dutiful and loving son to me, even to the full.' The Lord answered her prayer; and in a short time took away the violence of her pain; and she praised the Lord, and blessed his name, for his mercies and goodness; speaking of his great mercy and favour to her all her life long, to the great comfort of her children about her; and blessed her son, saying, 'The Lord bless thee and thine, for thy love and duty to me; for I do rejoice that thou wast born unto me.' Also to her son's wife she said, 'Daughter, thou didst promise to take care of me, when weakness should approach; and now thou art as good as thy word: the Lord bless thee and thine, for all your love to me.' And in the sense of the love of the Lord to her she prayed, 'O Lord, guide thy poor hand-maid into thy everlasting kingdom, where I may sing hallelujahs to thee for ever.'

She gave order, two days before her departure, (being sick but six days) to be buried at Leicester, by her grandchildren; and so died in a good old age, at her son, Samuel Brown's, at Leicester, on the 30th of the Ninth month, in the year 1693, aged eighty-three years.

WILLIAM WALKER, an inhabitant of Pennsylvania, born in Yorkshire, but convinced in Pennsylvania, was one who bore a living testimony to the truth of God in the assemblies of his people. He came over to visit his friends and brethren in England, about the latter end of the year 1693, in company with other Friends from those parts, which was about the time George Keith came over from America. This our friend often expressed his great sorrow for George Keith, and the sore exercise and trouble he gave to friends in America, by his contention and jangling; and he had a testimony against that spirit but a few days before he died, that God would judge it.

After he had visited friends about London, he went into several counties, and also into Wales; and returned to London, in order to be at the yearly meeting in 1694; a little before which time he was taken sick there, and endeavours were used for his recovery, but they proved unsuccessful. In the time of his sickness he was often filled with the love and power of God in his soul, to the comfort of those present. Observing some to weep, he said, 'Weep not, dear hearts, lest you trouble me.' Afterwards he said, 'O the goodness of the Lord!' And lifting up his hands, he said, 'Lord, thou art altogether able to do wonderful things! Thou shalt be my physician. Oh the wonders of the Lord! What have I seen of the transcendant glory! Though I see but a little, yet it is admirable glory.' Again he said, 'The old enemy would have had me let go my hold; but I said, I have an interest in thee, and I will hold thee, Lord.'

Those about him being desirous that he might recover, he said, 'Nay, I have no promise of life.' Speaking of Christ, he said, 'I can see him; his arm is open to receive me.' After some time he said, 'The Lord is a physician indeed, a physician of value.' Another time he said, 'We must all double our diligence,' Another time, lying in a still frame of mind, he sang in sweet melody as followeth: 'His compassion fails not; he waits to be gracious: Oh the wonders of the Lord! The wonders of the Lord in the deep.' Another time he said, 'My faith is steadfast in the dear Son of God; that although I am under great weakness and afflictions, yet in the strength of my Father's love I shall be enabled to stand against the mists of darkness. The enemy would fain unpin my faith: God's people are always preserved while they wait still at home. Oh! Lord Jesus Christ! I will hold thee fast; thy compassion fails not. Oh! sweet Jesus Christ, I have great cause to hold thee fast. Oh! sweeten death unto me! Oh! thy sweet presence! In it there is life. Oh! Lord, give me strength; I will not let thee go: thou hast regard to them that fear thee, thy compassion fails not; thou art at my right hand to uphold me. Oh! my Saviour! thou art at my right hand to save me; thy compassion fails not, O Lord.' Afterwards he said, 'Oh! Lord Jesus! Come, sweet Jesus, I long for thee; now death is pleasant.'

His wife's sister being by him, he said, 'Fear the Lord God.' She said, 'Wouldst thou [say] any thing to thy wife.' He answered, 'My dear and tender love in the Lord Jesus unto her, and to all my dear friends every where; and that you may double your diligence, to your soul's comfort, the days you have here. My dear love to our dear friends in America, where I have been sweetly refreshed, and had many good meetings among them.' After a little repose, he said, 'Oh! Fountain of Life!' Then stopped, and thus spoke again, 'I cast the care of my dear wife and children, if living, upon the Lord; I trust in him.' After some rest, he said, 'Lord Jesus Christ, come, receive my poor soul: come, O my soul's beloved! Come, Lord, I long for thee. Lord Jesus Christ, if there be any iniquity in me, search it out.'

Afterwards he said, 'I feel the angel of thy presence to surround me: come, Lord Jesus Christ, come, come, receive my soul into thy bosom.' Again he said, 'Come, Lord Jesus Christ, let me entreat thee come away, and receive me out of all sorrow; come away, my Lord. After a little time he said, 'I feel the Fountain of Life; my soul's beloved, is come.' He died in peace with the Lord, as those then present can testify, that he was in a sweet, heavenly frame of spirit when he drew his last breath, which was on the 12th of the Fourth month, in the year 1694, at the house of John Padley, in Olave's Parish, Southwark.

RUTH MIDDLETON, daughter of Samuel Middleton and Rebecca his wife, was visited with a consumption in the Tenth month, 1700, and continued in much weakness of body till the 16th of the Fifth month, 1701. During her sickness, these expressions, among others, were observed.

One time, her mother being much concerned to part with her, the child lying still as if she was in a slumber, opened her eyes and said, 'What's the matter? what's the matter? My dear mother, do not be troubled for me; do not sorrow for me, I shall be happy. It is the Lord's will that I am thus afflicted, and we must be contented. Thou knowest that Abraham was willing to offer up his only son Isaac; and thou dost not know if thou couldst freely give me up, but that the Lord might spare me a little longer to thee; and if it be his good pleasure to take me to himself, his holy name be blessed for ever.' Another time her mother said, 'How art thou now?' She replied, 'But indifferent; but I am well satisfied, for it is the will of God that I am thus afflicted. Oh! my dear mother, I would be glad if thou couldst freely give me up.'

One time, going to slumber, she prayed thus: "Our Father which art in heaven, hallowed be thy name, thy kingdom come, thy will be done in me, as it is in heaven." 'Oh! sweet Lord Jesus, feed me daily with the bread that comes down from heaven. Lord, if it stand with thy will, grant that I may sleep to refresh this poor needy body: but thou, Lord, knowest what I stand in need of, better than I can ask. Lord, be with me, and my father, and mother, and brother.' Thereupon she went to sleep: and when she awoke, she said, 'Oh! blessed and praised be thy holy name, O Father of life! for thou hast heard my desires, and hast answered me; for I have slept sweetly.'

Another time she said, 'The Lord said to his followers, "Suffer little children to come unto me, and forbid them not, for of such is the kingdom of heaven." And if I be not happy, what will become of ungodly men and women? For truly I am afraid of offending any body, for fear I should offend the Lord.' One time she said, 'Pray, mother, have a strict eye over my brother, for he is very full of play.' A friend, after inquiring how she did, said, 'I hope thy eye is still to the Lord:' her reply was, 'Although I can hardly speak, I think upon the Lord, and he knows my thoughts, and answers them;' with more sensible words.

Another time she said, 'It will not be long before I shall be at rest and peace, where there is no more pain to the body nor to the mind; and where there is nothing but joy for evermore. Dear mother, be willing to part with me, for I am willing to part with you all. I am not at all concerned for myself, but for thee, poor mother, who doth and will make thy bed a bed of tears often for me.'

Hearing her mother question her recovery, she said, 'Oh! what the Lord pleases; for I am not afraid of death. I never wronged any body of a pin to my knowledge, nor loved to make excuses. I never told a lie but once; when I should have said yes, I said no: that has been a great trouble to me; but the

Lord, I hope, will forgive me, for I called the maid, and told her the truth.'

Near her end she desired to come out of the country to London, and said, 'The air does me no good, and the doctor does me no good: the Lord is the same at home as here.' And when she was removed home, she said, 'Now I am glad; if I die it is better to be here, and will save a great deal of trouble.'

A Friend asked her if she was willing to leave father and mother, and go to the Lord; after some pause she answered, 'If the Lord please, I am willing this very minute to leave all, for I shall be happy.'

The night before her departure, after a Friend had prayed by her, she said, 'I do understand well, and am inwardly refreshed. I am sorry that I cannot speak so that the Friend could hear, or else I would give an account of my inward peace with the Lord.'

A few hours before her death she thus prayed, but her voice was very low: 'Oh, Lord! withhold not thy tender mercies from me at the hour of death. Oh, Lord! let thy loving-kindness continually preserve me.' Afterwards she said, 'I desire to slumber; but if I die before I wake, I desire the Lord may receive my soul.'

She was thankful for the tender regard her mother had to her, and with a low voice said, 'Farewell, dear mother; in the love of the Lord, farewell.' And then desired to see her father and brother; and feeling for her brother's face, she stroked him and said, 'Farewell, be a good boy.'

Her father asking her how it was with her, she replied, 'I am just spent, but I am very easy, and shall be very happy My body is full of pain, but the angel of the Lord is with me, and his presence will for ever preserve me;' and so kissed her relations, and bade them all farewell.

Her last words were her desire to be remembered to the Friends who visited her in her sickness; and, in less than half a quarter of an hour, like a lamb she departed this life, on the 16th of the Fifth month, in the year 1701, being eleven years, two months, and four days old.

ALEXANDER JAFFRAY, of Kingswell, in the north of Scotland, born in the city of Aberdeen, was one who early remembered his Creator; and as he grew in years he increased in a religious concern towards God, and those who he thought feared him. He joined, when young, with the Presbyterians, though he was educated in another form of religion; but some time after, when those people got into rule and government, they forgot their former low and persecuted condition, and grew high, rigid, and fierce persecutors of others; therefore he soon disliked them, and signified the same to some of the chiefest among them, having been himself one of those commissioners who were deputed by the nation of Scotland to treat on articles with King Charles the Second, then in Holland, in the year 1650.

After he left the Presbyterian way, for some time he was among the Independents, and finding them also to be for setting up themselves, and persecuting others, he could no longer follow them. After this he remained in private for some years, a solitary mourner, not joining with any profession in religion; nor suffering several of his children to be sprinkled or baptized (as they called it), because he could not own their way of constituting national churches; and this was long before he was called a Quaker. In his solitary retirement he sought the Lord, waiting for a people who were spiritually touched with a divine coal from the altar, to kindle true and spiritual sacrifices to God.

When he first heard that God had raised up such a people in England, who directed all to God's pure light, spirit and grace in their own hearts, as the most sure teacher and leader into all truth, worship and religion, he said he felt his heart to leap within him for joy. After weighty examination concerning the people called Quakers, who preached the truth among them, he found his heart and soul united to them. This was in the year 1662, a time when it was as bitter a cross even as death to own them, especially to one of his repute; and shortly after, several more men of note, in that nation, were convinced of the same way of truth, as John Swinton in the southern parts, David Barclay, Alexander Skein, Thomas Mercer, and others.

This made the priests and others persecute them; but they stood their ground, through the grace of God, and boldly bore their testimony valiantly, particularly Alexander Jaffray, contending for the truth in solemn conferences with the bishop of Aberdeen, and the chief preachers of that city.

He was faithful in his testimony to the truth to the last; and in his sickly old age was imprisoned many miles from his own house, for non-payment of tithes. It is remarkable that, a little before this imprisonment, being near to death, as was judged by all who saw him, he signified under his hand, being altogether unable to speak, by a great swelling in his throat, that his God had yet a service for him to do, in suffering for his precious truth; and that he was not to die at that time.

He was taken sick the latter end of the Fourth month, 1673; and during the twelve days of his sickness, he uttered many living testimonies to the blessed truth, before many witnesses, both Friends and other people, who visited him; and a few of them are as follows;

He said that "it was his great joy and comfort in that hour, that ever he had been counted worthy to bear a testimony to, and suffer for, that precious testimony of Christ Jesus, his inward appearance in the hearts of the children of men, visiting all by his light, grace and spirit, that convinceth of sin; and that it was, and would be the great judgment and condemnation of many in this nation, particularly of the professors, that they have so slighted and despised, yea, hated the said light and witnesses thereunto."

Sometimes being overcome in spirit, he said, 'Now Lord, let thy servant depart in peace, for mine eyes spiritually have seen, my heart hath felt, and is feeling, and shall ever feel, thy salvation.'

He also prophesied of a great and near trial shortly to come, wherein some that were not what they seemed to be, should be discovered and fall; but the upright and lowly ones, the lowly shrubs should be preserved, when tall and sturdy oaks should be overthrown; which is since fulfilled upon some.

He farther said, that the Lord had given him the garments of praise, instead of the spirit of heaviness.

Sometimes, when very sick, he would bless the Lord, that now fighting with a natural death, he had not an angry God to deal with. 'Oh!' says he, 'the sting of death is fully gone, and death is mine; being reconciled to me as a sweet passage, through him that loved me.' Another time, seeing the candle almost out, he said, 'My natural life is near an end, like that candle, for want of nourishment or matter to entertain it; but in this we shall differ, that if it be let alone, that goes out with a stink, and I shall go out with a good savour, praises to my God for ever.'

A little before his breath ceased, he said he had been with his God, and had seen deep things; about which time he was filled with the power of God in a wonderful manner, which much affected those present, and in a little time after, he died like a lamb, being the 6th day of the Fifth month, in the year 1673, aged fifty-nine years; and was buried in a piece of ground set apart near his own house at Kingswell, the 8th of the same month.

MARY PADLEY, wife of John Padley, timber-merchant, of Olave's, Southwark, was a woman adorned with truth and innocency, chaste, upright, and sincere-hearted, industrious, yet void of covetousness, so that virtue shone forth in her conversation. She was also charitable to the poor, plain in apparel, adorning the truth in her conversation, punctual in performing her promise, and in the discharge of any trust reposed in her. She spent her days in the fear of God, so the Lord was gracious to her at her death.

She was taken with pains, the 6th of the Seventh month, 1695, at which time she said, in much tenderness and fervency of spirit, 'My God, and my father, deliver me.' And after she was delivered, she praised God for his mercies towards her: and afterwards being asked by her husband how she did, finding some unusual symptoms attend her, she answered, 'Weak, but well satisfied.' And as a confirmation thereof, she broke forth into sweet praises to the Lord; and died, leaving behind her four young children. Aged about twenty-eight years.

CHARLES MARSHALL, born at Bristol in the year 1637, was religiously educated by his parents in the Independent way. In his tender years he had inward desires after the knowledge of God.

After he had continued some years amongst the Independents, and also the Baptists, he grew more and more dissatisfied with the empty and lifeless profession of those amongst whom he walked. He spent much time in retirement alone in the fields, under a sense of his state and condition, crying unto the Lord, and seeking after his saving knowledge. In this state he continued, until it pleased God to send to that city his faithful servant John Audland, from out of the north of England, by whose powerful ministry he was turned to the light of Christ Jesus in his own heart, which had before discovered his state and condition to him. After he came to turn in his mind to the light of the Lord, and was thereby and therein resigned, he witnessed God's pure power, love and life to break in upon him; and after manifold exercises and troubles, was raised up a powerful minister of Christ Jesus, and an instrument in God's hand to turn many to righteousness.

He was moved in the year 1670 to go through the nation of England, and visit God's heritage, which he did within the compass of one year; and although it was then a time of great persecution, yet in all his passage through cities, towns, and all the counties of the land, no man was suffered to lay hands on him, or stop his way.

He continued a faithful minister, and laboured much in the gospel to the time of his sickness, which lasted several months; in all which time great patience and meekness appeared in him, although under weakness and affliction of body.

He had some sight and knowledge of his end; for a little

before he was taken ill he earnestly pressed a particular friend of his to ride out of town with him, having something of moment to impart to him. When they were a few miles from London, he said, amongst other things, that he was satisfied his departure drew near, and therefore had a desire to discourse with him about some particular things before he died. And when he was taken ill he sent for the same friend, and told him now he was satisfied he should go abroad no more; although in his first illness there was no such appearance to others, which the said friend told him; but whatsoever he said to take him off of such thoughts, it had no impression upon him; he continued fixed in his mind, that he should die of that illness.

Several of his friends pressed him to go into the country, but he desired only to go to John Padley's, a Friend that dwelt near the river side, which he much liked; and at his first going thither he was a little better, but soon altered again. He lay ill there about three months, under great weakness; and several Friends often came to see him, and he would be frequently giving them seasonable counsel and advice, in many heavenly expressions, and would often exhort them to keep in love and unity, and to the living divine power and life of truth, that thereby they might be kept a people fresh and green, and living to God, that so formality might not prevail over them. He pressed that a great regard might be had of the poor, and that some way might be found out for their employment; often saying to this effect, that in an inexpressible manner he felt their sufferings, by reason of their poverty. Indeed he was a man who greatly sympathized with those who were afflicted either in body or mind, being of a very tender spirit.

A little before his departure, he sending for John Padley and his wife into his chamber, said to him, 'Dear John, do what thou canst for the honour of truth, and the Lord bless thee and thine for generations to come.' To his wife he said that he desired the Lord might be with her when she came to such a time as that he was then in, i. e., a death-bed, and make her passage easy; and his desire was granted, for she died in less than a year after; and said, on her dying bed, that the

Lord had answered dear Charles Marshall's request, for she lay very easy, and freely given up. As he lay in this weak condition he was often opening his mind to divers of his friends; particularly when several ministering Friends came to see him, he spoke to this effect: 'I have loved the brotherhood; I have sought the unity and peace of the churches for these forty years, and to my great comfort I never did any thing tending to the breach thereof. I have two things that lie upon me to Friends, which I desire may be communicated to them.'

The first is, 'That they gather down into the immortal Seed and Word of life in themselves, and be exercised in it before the Lord, and duly prize and set a value upon the many outward and inward mercies, and blessings, and heavenly visitations, that the Lord has eminently bestowed upon them, since the morning of the day of his blessed visitation; then shall they grow and be preserved in a living freshness to him: and the Lord will continue his mercies to them, and they shall not want his divine refreshing presence in their meetings together before him.'

The second thing is, 'That those Friends to whom the Lord hath given great estates, ought to cast their bread upon the waters, and do good therewith in their lifetime; for those who are enjoyers of such things should see that they are good stewards thereof. Oh! the many poor families that such persons might be a help to! how easily might they, with a little, assist many a family to live in the world! and what a comfort would it be for such to see the fruits of their charity in their lifetime'

When our friend George Whitehead came to see him, with much tenderness of spirit, he signified his great peace and satisfaction, and that he always, from the first, had an honourable esteem of the unity of his brethren. A little before his departure, when our friend William Penn and divers others visited him, he lay as a man gathered up in his spirit unto God; and though he was almost spent, his voice being very low, hardly to be heard, yet by what was understood, it might be perceived that he had in possession the earnest of that blessed peace which he was going to receive the fulness of. The observation of his peace, and happy condition, much affected those present. He departed like a child, in a quiet frame of spirit, the 15th of the Ninth month, in the year 1698, aged sixty-one years, and was buried from Grace-church-street meeting-house, in Friends' burial ground, near Bunhill-fields, London.

SARAH PADLEY, second wife of John Padley, aforesaid, of Olave's, Southwark, was a woman of a meek and quiet spirit, and had great sympathy with those in affliction, and bore a public testimony for God in the assemblies of his people, and she had an honourable esteem of the faithful elders in the church.

She was taken ill the 26th day of the Fifth month, 1699, and was sensible her end was near, and on that account was concerned for her husband. The love of God, with which she was filled, caused her sweetly to praise his name, so that the sense of the pains and weakness of her body seemed to be taken away. One time, in the sense of the love of God to her soul, she cried out, "Oh! death, where is thy sting?" Often praying and praising God, and during the whole time of her sickness she was freely given up to die.

A few days before her departure she said to her husband, 'Thou art the dearest of any thing in the world to me; yet I can freely leave thee.' Another time she said to him, 'The Lord hath answered dear Charles Marshall's prayer for me;' remembering that C. M., who died at her house, had desired, upon his dying-bed, that she might have an easy passage when she came to such a time as he was in; 'for,' said she, 'I am very easy;' and often said that she was resigned to the will of God.

A little before her death, much through her husband's great affection to her and his earnest desire of her life, she seemed a little to desire life, but presently checked herself for it, and returned to her former resignation of spirit; and so lay supplicating and praising God, so that a neighbour present, not called a Quaker, said that she never saw any lie so sweetly in all her life. Seeing some about her weep, she said, 'Do not cry for me, for I am going to my rest.' A friend said, 'Art thou willing to leave thy husband?' She answered, 'I have often told him I am willing to go when the Lord pleaseth:' and in a little time after she said, 'In a few days, in a few days, they will say, Sarah Padley is dead.' It much affected those about her to see how reconciled she was to death, speaking very pleasantly concerning it, and of the felicity that would accrue to her thereby. She finished her course on the 8th day of the Sixth month, in the year 1699, aged about thirty-four years.

WILLIAM GARTON, of Ifield, in the county of Sussex, was an early fruit to God, a faithful believer in his blessed truth, and a servant in the church of Christ. He was zealous against all unrighteousness, and much for the unity of the spirit in the bond of peace among brethren; an elder indeed, watching for good over the flock, a sympathizer with the afflicted, and a mourner in the house of mourning, more in deed than in words. Though but a plain man, yet God endowed him with a large understanding and sound judgment, which has been approved in difficult cases. He was firm and constant in spirit in times of suffering and persecution, prefering the service of truth, and the testimony of it, before all worldly things.

He was an example of virtue in the church, also in his family; and his removal hence was a great loss to both; a true loving husband and tender father. He had a great care that his children might be trained up in the fear of God, and knowledge of his blessed truth; which labour God was pleased to answer to his satisfaction. He would often say, the greatest portion he desired of the Lord for his children was the blessed truth, and that they might love, fear, and serve the Lord, and then he did not doubt that they would want any good thing; and to that end he would often be giving them good counsel and admonition.

Two days before his decease, being visited by a friend, he said that he had always endeavoured [to promote] the prosperity of truth to the best of his understanding; and that he had nothing of trouble upon him; but did bless God that he had an opportunity to give this testimony to those present; exhorting an ancient friend to keep low in God's fear, and make straight steps, that he might lay down his grey hairs in peace.

Another time, several Friends coming from a meeting to visit him, he desired that his love might be remembered to all Friends.

Another time he said, 'I have always sought the peace of the church, according to my ability.'

Being asked by a young man that watched with him how he did, he replied, 'I am the better to see young men come up in the truth.'

A friendly person coming to see him on his sick-bed, he put out his hand to him, saying, 'Ah! thou lackest something: these be serious times.'

Two ministering Friends visiting him the day before he died, he seemed very much revived, and said, 'I never did any thing against the truth knowingly, since I was convinced.

One taking his leave of him, hoping for his recovery, he replied, 'If it be the Lord's will, let me go in peace:' he also said that he felt the Lord to come in upon his spirit. Near his end he prayed for his wife, and children, and grandchildren, that God would make up the loss of him to them. He further said, 'Oh Lord, I pray thee, remember the ancients, that they may still hold on their way; and, oh! my God, if it stand with thy will, visit more and more those who are not of thy fold, and bring them in by thine arm, that they may come to know rest for their souls, that at the last we may be bound up together in the bundle of life;' and so concluded with hymns and praises unto God.

Another time, after some friends had prayed by him, which

was to his great satisfaction, and the room being clear of company, he said to his daughter who was standing by, 'Oh dear child, I have known much of the goodness of the Lord, but not in such a large manner before as now: the very fountain is open, and the love of God is over all; praises, praises to the Lord.' He uttered many heavenly expressions, and gave good exhortation to those about him, which are not here inserted. A little time before he died, he called for his relations, embraced his wife in his arms, and took his last leave of her, and of his son and daughter; holding out his hand and taking leave of all Friends who came to see him, till his strength failed; and so sweetly died in the Lord, in an honourable good old age, the 8th day of the Seventh month, in the year 1701, being the sixty-sixth year of his age.

CHARLES ORMSTON, merchant at Kelso, in Scotland, was convinced of the blessed truth about the year 1665. He was a good example and pattern of godliness, which he showed forth in the upright life and conversation he had amongst men, and bore a faithful testimony among the Friends of that meeting to which he belonged, and at whose house the meeting was kept to his dying day.

He was in the year 1668 cast into Edinburgh prison, upon the account of his owning those people called, in scorn, Quakers. He remained prisoner about twenty-two months; and his wife, who was not at that time called a Quaker, having several times made application to the privy council for his release, did at length obtain an order for the same on the 20th of the Twelfth month, 1669. Afterwards, Friends settling their meeting at his house, the earl of Roxburgh, whose lodging was hard by, being angry that it should be so near by, caused the town-militia to be raised, and by force hauled Friends out of their meeting, and laid several of them up in prison, amongst whom C. Ormston was one. His adversary at length perceiving that neither keeping them out of their meeting-room, nor yet locking up his doors, would hinder them to meet under the pillars of the house, gave over his persecution.

This our friend fell sick about the latter end of the year 1684, and continued to grow weaker for about two months time.

Having before put his outward affairs in order, and feeling himself very weak and nigh his end, upon the 21st of the Twelfth month, 1684, in the evening, he called for his two sons, (his daughters not professing truth) the elder whereof came to him, whom he took by the hand, and exhorted him to a faithful walking in the truth, as he had formerly done, and instructed them in many things. About three quarters of an hour after, he fell asleep in the Lord, having left a good savour of his upright life and conversation behind him.

JOHN ORMSTON, eldest son to the aforesaid Charles Ormston, was an example of sobriety and godliness, having from a child shunned evil; and when he was mocked for refusing to bear company with others in their vain recreations, he bore it patiently, not reviling again. He was given to retirement, and a careful instructor of his younger brother. He was much troubled with bleeding, which brought him into a consumption, and he told those about him he did believe he should die. Being near his end, he desired his father to pray by him, which he did; and about three or four days before he died, he inquired of his sisters the day of the month, which being told him, he answered, 'The twenty-second shall be my day;' which proved true, for upon the 22d of the Tenth month, in the year 1682, he departed this life, and entered into that blessed rest prepared for the faithful. Aged twenty years and four months.

THOMAS ROBINSON, of Bridge-end, near Kelso, in Scotland, was convinced of the truth about the year 1669, in which he walked circumspectly, in a good conversation, to his latter end, being a good example in the place where he lived; and often exhorted his friends and brethren, in the meeting to which he belonged, to faithfulness.

He was several times imprisoned about the years 1672 and 1673 for meeting with the people called Quakers, to worship God. After having lived to a good old age, it pleased the Lord to visit him with sickness, which continued about twelve days, in which time he was kept in patience, and often signified that he felt the love of the Lord in his soul; and exhorted his neighbours and relations, who came to see him, to fear the Lord and to turn to him, while they had time. Many more seasonable expressions he spoke, even when he was in great pain, which much affected the standers by; to whom he said, 'Let patience have its perfect work:' he also signified that being walking one evening by himself, as his manner was, he prayed fervently to the Lord that he might have a seal of his assurance before his departure; and immediately he was filled with great joy, and the word of the Lord came to him, saying, 'Is not my grace sufficient for thee? That is done already: thy peace is made.'

A little before he departed some of his children, with others, being present, and he being about to take his last leave of them, said, 'Humble your hearts before the Lord, and make use of your time, and slip no opportunity of making your peace with God.' At last, recommending his spirit into the hands of the Lord Jesus Christ, he sweetly laid down his head in peace upon the 28th of the Ninth month, in the year 1698, being about the seventy-third year of his age.

THOMAS ROBINSON, son of the before mentioned Thomas Robinson, was convinced of the truth about three years before his parents, when he was about thirteen years of age, and but few Friends in those parts; and he was so effectually converted, that although many endeavours were used, both by promises and threatenings, they were not able to overturn his faith.

He was a youth of a sober and religious conversation, insomuch that he was a wonder to many; and by his faithfulness to the truth, though a child, he was very instrumental to the convincement of his parents, who afterwards lived and died in the same faith. Many disputes he had with priests and others, and was so furnished with arguments, that they were often astonished at him.

About the twentieth year of his age, God was pleased to call him to the work of the ministry; at which time he was concerned to go to public places of worship, and bear testimony to the people against their evil deeds. His ministry was living, and he had a clear discerning of the spirit of antichrist, that secretly worked for the hurt of God's heritage, which he advised friends to watch against.

He travelled through the northern counties of England, and also visited all the meetings of Friends in his own nation, and had several sights of things to come, some of which he saw come to pass; and also had a vision of his own death two years before he died. He was visited with sickness, which continued about seventeen weeks, and in all that time he was not heard to repine, or speak frowardly, though his sickness was attended with much exercise. Many times he sung praises to the Lord, to the affecting of others who heard him; and declared that he valued not the pains and trouble of his body if it was the Lord's will so to try him; but that the Lord's everlasting truth might be raised over all; and all lets and hindrances be taken out of the way, and he to feel preservation in the truth, to the end of his days. With many more good expressions.

The night before he died, he entreated his parents not to repine at the Lord's doing, saying it was his will to remove him from the evil to come. After a little silence his father asked him if he had any thing more upon his mind to say; he answered, 'Little more, but that all might be kept faithful who profess the truth, the precious truth.' And farther said, 'Let me rest, I have done, I have done;' and fell asleep, and slept till about break of day, and then departed this life on the 2d of the Eighth month, in the year 1678, about the twenty-third year of his age.

STEPHEN SMITH was born the 19th of the Seventh month, 1623. He received the truth in the love of it in the year 1665, and gave up to obey and walk therein. He truly loved God's faithful messengers and people, how despised and suffering soever they were; and he suffered with them, both in person and estate, by imprisonment and spoil of goods, for his tender conscience and testimony on behalf of Christ Jesus.

He was a man fearing God, and of good report in that county, being an exemplary preacher of righteousness in his conversation, and one truly kind and ready to do good in his day. God also endued him with a living ministry and experimental testimony to tell of his goodness, and speak of his praise to others, from an inward sense thereof in himself, and to the comfort and encouragement of many who heard. He travelled in divers parts of the nation, in the work and service of God, in the gospel of his Son.

In the time of his sickness, when he was in the greatest extremity of weakness, he often declared of the loving kindness of the Lord God, by which he was upheld above the fear of death.

To several who came to visit him on his sick-bed, he said, it was a blessed and heavenly thing to have the mind clear and holy, free from all troubles and cumbers of this world, as he said his mind was, having all given up to the will of the Lord, that it might be truly done on earth, as it is in heaven; adding, 'O what a blessed and heavenly habitation is this for the soul of man to rest in, which I have a full assurance of!' At another time, one who came to see him he exhorted to dread and fear the Lord God, and to repent of all, whatsoever that holy and pure witness in his conscience makes manifest to be evil, if happily he might find mercy with the Lord; which will be better to thee (said he), than all the world besides. A little after came into the chamber another person, and the power of the Lord being with him, he was refreshed in his spirit, and he desired the said person to fear the Lord, that thereby she might be preserved out of all evil; and added, 'Love the truth above all, for the truth is a very precious thing; and be sure keep low and humble to it, and be not high-minded nor exalted above the pure witness of God in thy conscience, for that would be hurtful.'

Another time, in remembrance of the tender dealings of the Lord to him, he said to his sons, who were present, 'My days are very near drawing to an end; and though my father and mother cast me off when I was a little lad, the Lord hath always preserved me, and his blessings did always attend me, having been often in many great dangers, both by sea and land. Having my mind sober and chaste to God, and having the fear of the Lord placed in my heart, by which I was preserved out of evil, I did the thing that was right in the sight of the Lord, so that I found favour of the Lord, and gained the love and favour of people, in dealing justly and truly with all people, not wronging any man.' This he gave in charge to his sons, that they might always be kept sober and chaste in their minds, having always regard to the fear of the Lord placed in their hearts, that thereby they might be preserved out of evil, doing always that which is just and right; and to be sure to be courteous and kind to all, loving the good in all, and bearing their testimony against the evil in all, wheresoever it did appear.

He farther said, 'And whensoever you go about that which is weighty, take counsel of good and sound Friends, so that all things may be done to the glory and honour of the Lord and his blessed truth, in which your blessings are all yea and amen.' He moreover advised his sons, saying, 'Do not run into the cumbers of the world, but wait upon the Lord, and he will find out a way for you in his time; for the Lord is calling, and taking me out and from all troubles and cumbers, and from the evil that is coming upon this wicked world, in a good time, wherein I am assured of that sound and perfect peace, wherein my soul will rest with the Lord for ever; so that I have no more to do now, but desire the Lord to make my passage easy to my heavenly rest.'

A little before his departure, being filled with the spirit, he praised and magnified God, and prayed, saying, 'Lord, and dearest God, oh! assist in this heavenly passage from death to life;' and soon after said, 'Now I am going into my sweet sleep;' and immediately and innocently laid down his head in perfect peace with the Lord, the 22d of the Seventh month, in the year 1678, at his house, near Guildford, in Surrey, aged fifty-five years and three days.

WILLIAM ALLEN, of Earls Colne, in the county of Essex, received the blessed truth in the year 1654, and the power of the Lord made a speedy change in him. Soon after, he had a dispensation of the gospel of Christ Jesus given to him from God, and he was stirred up with zeal in his soul against the false ways, worships, superstitions, and profaneness of those times; which zeal for God produced living testimonies from him, in divers towns and places where he travelled, against those things which were evil, which sometimes occasioned him to come under hard sufferings, bonds and imprisonments. In these he behaved himself as a faithful and courageous soldier of Christ Jesus, and a good example to his fellow-sufferers, preaching the gospel of peace, both in life and doctrine, and stopped the mouths of gainsayers. This had a sweet and comfortable effect upon many, who were reached in their consciences by his testimony and ministry, and by his innocent conversation; so that they embraced the truth he preached and suffered for, and became heirs of the salvation of God, to their everlasting comfort, and the furtherance of the gospel.

He was of severe carriage to such as made profession of truth, and walked not with a straight foot in the gospel; but he was very tender over all such as were young, and under exercise about their inward condition, and sometimes spoke effectually to their conditions, to the easing of their afflicted spirits.

He was an example in the county where he lived, encouraging Friends to observe the good order of the truth, and to keep the gospel void of offence; not exalting himself above his brethren, but carried a good respect to them, and to their counsel and judgment.

He served the Lord Jesus Christ, and his church and people, without weariness to the end of his days; and would lament those who sat themselves down at ease, and would often say that a terrible day would overtake them who were at ease in Zion. In the time of his health, when he was able to go abroad and visit Friends, he would say, 'God hath made me a huntsman, and I must visit many of them who are in their holes and caves; I must be clear of their blood:' and would relate the sore travails and pangs that he had for some, which often made his soul very sorrowful.

His labours in the gospel were chiefly in the counties of Norfolk, Suffolk, Cambridge, and Essex; and for his testimony to the truth he was imprisoned in Colchester castle, where he was instrumental to gain divers to the truth. He was also imprisoned at Cambridge, and at Ely, and Lynn in Norfolk, and many were turned to God by his ministry.

He was a diligent labourer in the Lord's vineyard for about twenty-four years, and the last year and a half of his time he was much afflicted with bodily weakness and sickness; but he would often say that he was content with the will of his Father. In the time of his sickness he showed the meekness and patience of Christ which dwelt in him; but the Lord, in due time, seeing his exercise to be enough, put a period to his days. He was filled with the peace of God to the last, so that he said he could shout for joy, but that he wanted strength of body; and which, he said, was but an earnest of what he should more fully enjoy when his earthly tabernacle was dissolved. He spoke largely of the enjoyment of the glory of God in his soul, and of the assurance he had of eternal life; some of his expressions in his sickness were as follows:

'The earth is filled with the glory of the Lord: praises, praises unto my God, who reigns over all, over all. He hath redeemed my soul from the grave, and my life from the horrible pit. He hath plucked my feet out of the mire and clay. Glory, glory be given unto thy great name, oh! my good God. As for my part I have fought the good fight, and have kept the faith; and a large share of the glory of my God is sealed in my soul. It is but an earnest that I have here of that crown of life and glory which my Father hath in store for me.'

Concerning his sickness, he said, 'It hath pleased the Lord to exercise me as he did Job, for the trial of my faith and patience. I have trodden his steps these twelve months. A full reward thou hast given me of life and glory. Oh! my good God, how good art thou to me! I have received abundance of good at thy hand, and shall not I receive a little evil? Blessed be thy name for thy goodness. My cup overflows, I cannot utter it;' and so continued, often speaking of the glory of the Lord, and the immortality that rested upon him. He charged friends to be faithful, that the dread of God might always rest upon their hearts, that they might answer his love, in yielding obedience to his requirings; and then, if they met with exercises for the trial of their faith, yet the Lord would be with them, if they abode faithful to the end; and the same crown of life they should enjoy, which he had assurance of.

'Therefore,' said he, 'watch, and keep your garments, and oil in your vessels, that you may be ready to enter with the bridegroom. But as for those that continue in hypocrisy and disobedience, and shun the cross of Christ, and neglect to work while it is day, the night will come upon such unawares, and the foolish virgins' state they will be found in; and though they may desire oil of the wise, the wise will have none to spare; but the door will be shut upon such, and misery will be their portion. He also gave good counsel to his two daughters, saying there was a blessing for them, for their father's sake, if they would bow to truth, and abide faithful therein.

He longed to haste away; but was also willing to wait God's pleasure. More was spoken by him as friends came to visit him, and as his strength would permit, which was not taken in writing.

After his speech grew low he could not well be heard, and seemed for some hours as if he was departing. At last he said to a friend, 'I was almost gone, but I cannot go yet; there is some secret counsel of God in it.' After some little time, more friends coming in, he was, beyond outward likelihood, enabled to declare much to them, exhorting them to faithfulness, and said, 'I am glad to see my friends about me. I go to my God and your God, my Father and your Father. My bosom is full of love to all my Father's children;' and then said, 'Now, Lord Jesus, how acceptable is it to leave all the world, and be gathered up to thee:' and so, committing his spirit to the Lord, soon fell asleep.

His end was honourable, and he is crowned with immortality and eternal life, and he left the world in a good age, having attained to about sixty-three years. He died the 21st of the Eleventh month, in the year 1679, at Earls Colne, in the county of Essex.

WILLIAM SIMPSON, born in Lancashire, where he also received the truth, was a faithful minister and prophet of the Lord, and was much concerned in going through markets and towns, and to great men and magistrates, and priests' houses, and public places of worship, declaring against their false worship, and evil ways and works; and was often imprisoned for the truth, and underwent cruel and hard sufferings by the jailors. He was moved of the Lord to go at several times, for the space of three years, barefoot through markets, courts, cities and towns, and to priests' houses, as a sign to the people; telling them so should they be stripped, as he was. Sometimes he was moved to put on hair sackcloth, and to besmear his face black, and to tell them so would the Lord besmear all their religion. Great sufferings did this poor man undergo; many sad blows, and sore whippings, with staves, and wands, and thorn-bushes, coach-whips, and horse-whips, on his bare body. This was before king Charles the Second came in; that that generation might have taken warning, and they would not, but rewarded his love with cruel usage: only the mayor of Cambridge did nobly to him, for he put his gown about him, and took him into his house.

In the year 1670 he went to Barbadoes, in company with that faithful servant of God, John Burnyeat, to preach the gospel of Christ Jesus in that island; and after they had some service for God there, he was taken sick of a fever, in which time he felt great peace and consolation of the spirit. After he had been sick several days, he signified to Friends about him that he should die. In the observation of his submission and innocent behaviour on his sick-bed, some shed tears; and he taking notice of it, tenderly desired that they should not be grieved. Growing weaker, and his voice low, he said to those about him, 'Friends, be noble, and do not hinder me in my passage, for I am an innocent man.' Being asked whither he would go, he said, 'I must pass away;' and by what more was said at that time, Friends were assured that his heart was wholly fixed upon the Lord.

A few hours before he died, a person came to visit him who had not been, though invited, at any meeting William had been at in the island, and taking him by the hand asked him how he did; he answered, 'I am a very sick man;' and looking towards the man, he was endowed with the power and spirit of the Lord, by which he marvellously preached the glorious gospel of our Lord Jesus Christ, for about a quarter of an hour, praising and magnifying the Lord; which was so contrary to the expectations of those about him, (considering the circumstances of his weak condition,) that it caused amazement, trembling, and tears.

He preached the doctrine of perfection, and freedom from sin on this side the grave, exhorting friends to be valiant for truth upon earth; and that they should not be again entangled with the yoke of bondage; but to stand fast in the liberty wherewith Christ hath made them free; that every bond and yoke might be broken, and that which is pure and holy, of the Lord God, might go free in all; that God might be glorified and honoured, and they preserved in the day of trial, which must come upon all flesh; and so to grow from grace to grace, and from strength to strength, and from one degree of holiness unto another, and that a daily growth might be witnessed in all. Farther saying, 'O friends! it is the life that the Lord looks at; for he that hath the Son hath life; and he that hath not the Son hath not life. Examine yourselves; no Son, no life; without the Son, without life:' and thus he declared wonderfully, often praising and glorifying God after this manner;---- 'Oh! all that is within me praise and magnify the Lord God, who is worthy for ever and ever of all glory. Everlasting praises to the God of my life, who is only worthy, and lives over all, and is above all, God blessed for ever. Amen.'

About three hours after he had given this testimony, he departed this life in much quietness, being the 8th day of the Twelfth month, in the year 1670, and was honourably buried in a garden belonging to Richard Forstal, at Bridge-town, in Barbadoes.

JOSEPH COALE, of Reading, in the county of Berks, a young man about nineteen years of age, was convinced of truth in the breaking forth of God's blessed day in our age. When the ministers of Christ Jesus our Lord came to Reading, he was one of the first that received their testimony, and was one of the first in the county of Berks that suffered imprisonment on the truth's account. In the year 1655 he was committed to the counter in Reading, by Henry Frewin, justice, and afterwards to the jail, for declaring, in the public place of worship, that Cain's sacrifice was not accepted, but was an abomination to the Lord.

He preached the everlasting gospel, and the day of God's visitation to the world; and his ministry was effectual, not only for the convincement but also for the establishment and confirmation of many, he being experienced in the work and dealings of the Lord God, and also of the wiles and baits of the enemy of the souls of mankind; a faithful witness-bearer to the truth, not in words only but in life and conversation also; walking in innocency and lowliness of mind, in which he was a good example and pattern, as became the gospel of Christ Jesus.

Being delivered out of prison, he was moved, in the year 1656, to travel abroad in the west of England, to visit his friends and brethren who were prisoners for the truth in Launceston jail in Cornwall, where, at that time, our dear Friend George Fox was also a prisoner, with other Friends. In compassion to their sufferings he was conscientiously concerned to lay before justice Anthony Nichols the cruelty of the jailor towards his friends, carrying also with him a letter from George Fox to the said justice; who, instead of relieving the oppressed, committed the said Joseph Coale to the rest of his friends at Launceston as a vagrant. He lay there many months, after he was fined at the assize, for the most part in a wretched place called Doomsdale, where they used to put murderers, after they were condemned to die. It was so noisome that it was observed few who went in ever came out in health; and the filth of the prisoners, that from time to time had been put there, had not been carried out, as the people said, for many years; so that it was like mire, and in some places to the top of the shoes in water, &c. The jailor would not let Friends clean it, neither would he let them have beds or straw to lie on. Being released, he went on farther westward to visit Friends, but was committed by justice Ceely again to Launceston jail as a wanderer, where he lay three months.

In the year 1657, he being with other Friends met to worship God, near Penryn, in Cornwall, captain Fox, governor of Pendennis-Castle, with a troop of horse, came and abused Friends in a wicked manner, and Joseph was much beaten, and some of his blood shed, to the hazard of his life.

He was also afterwards, for declaring truth in the public place of worship at Exeter, fallen upon by the rude people, and haled by the hair of the head, and had to the town-hall, and from thence to jail, a very filthy place; and they put a great pair of double irons upon one of his legs, and ordered the jailor not to let him have any bed nor straw to lie upon; but the next week he was set at liberty.

In the same year he was committed to Dorchester jail for exhorting people to repentance in the market-place at Lyme, and for declaring truth in the steeple-house at Bridport.

In 1661 he was again imprisoned at Exeter for not swearing; being taken from a peaceable meeting, and tendered the oath. Many other times he hazarded his life for the testimony of the blessed truth, in stocks, and stonings, and divers other hardships and difficulties.

He was once in Ireland with Edward Burrough, in the service of the gospel.

Last of all, he was committed to the jail of Reading, on the 13th of the Fifth month, 1664, by William Armourer, a justice of the peace, because, for conscience-sake towards the Lord, he could not break his command, who had said, "Swear not at all." After six years being shut up in prison, and much deprived of common air to breathe in, he was greatly impaired in his health. In the time of his sickness, he gave forth many heavenly exhortations to Friends who came to visit him; and this was his faith, which he declared on his dying bed, saying, that the light of that glorious everlasting day of the Lord, which is broken forth in this our day, shall never be extinguished, notwithstanding all that men can do: 'And though,' said he, 'it may be in the hearts of men to destroy and root out, if it were possible, the righteous from off the earth, yet the Lord doth not intend so, neither is it in his heart to suffer it so to be, but to exalt his own name and kingdom over all; and the wrath of man shall turn to the glory of God, and the rest he will restrain.'

Death was made easy to him; and near his departure he bid one of his fellow-prisoners farewell, and resigned up to him that office of love and care which he exercised amongst his brethren and sisters, in bonds for the truth's sake. Being filled with heavenly love and life, and fully satisfied, he laid down his head in peace, and full assurance of everlasting rest and joy in the Lord. Aged about thirty-four years.

WILLIAM SMITH, born at Besthorp, in Nottinghamshire, was formerly a pastor of an Independent congregation, and lived after the strictest manner of that people, and was convinced of God's everlasting truth about the year 1658. He was a faithful labourer in the gospel, and many were turned unto God by his ministry; for he approved himself a minister of Christ Jesus, in tumults, in labours, in travails, in watchings, in necessities and distresses, which came upon him through the often spoiling of his goods, and long and tedious imprisonments of his body. For refusing to pay tithes to an impropriator, he was kept close prisoner one time twenty-one weeks among felons, in a dungeon in Nottingham jail; and another time he had the value of forty-two pounds taken from him, at the same time he was in prison for seven pounds, demanded by Dove Williamson, priest of Elton.

Indeed, many were his sufferings for his testimony to the truth, which for brevity sake are omitted; all which he patiently endured, as seeing him who is invisible, that he might hold fast faith and a good conscience.

In the times of his imprisonment he wrote several useful books, which remain in the printed collection of his writings. When he was at liberty he travelled abroad, to the nourishing and strengthening of them who did believe. Though he was often visited by sickness, he was kept in much patience and contentment; and much of the power and presence of God appeared in him many times, when he was in great weakness of body, to the admiration of the beholders.

In his last sickness, he was a great comfort to them who visited him, being a living man in the life of truth. After he had been ill seven weeks, his pains began to cease, yet he continued in weakness; but other distempers came upon him, which he bore with great patience. Waiting quietly, and having his mind retired, he spoke little till one evening, when many Friends being in the room, sitting in silence, and he in his bed, he turned towards them, and plentifully declared of the great love of God: and Friends were much refreshed and tendered. He also testified of a large portion which he had in life eternal; and then he spoke to Friends to be mindful of truth, and of their service therein, more than of their daily food; and so committed them to the grace of God.

The day before he was taken away he called for all his children, who were six or seven, and tenderly exhorted them to keep in the fear of God, and to love the truth, and God would be a father and portion to them. The next day he departed this life, being the 9th of the Eleventh month, in the year 1672.

JOHN STEEL, of Cumberland, was brought to the knowledge of the truth in the year 1654, and was obedient thereunto; and the Lord gave him a public testimony to bear not long after he was convinced, which continued with him to the end of his days.

He was a man of an excellent spirit, and clear in discerning the states and conditions of many, to whom he was made very serviceable by good counsel, wholesome advice and instruction. His manner in public testimony was to deliver himself in few words, and not often, yet very weighty and profound. He was severe against deceit and wrong spirits, but very willing always to encourage the well-doers; a good example in conversation in his family, and abroad amongst men, as well as in the church.

When he was first taken sick he said to his wife, 'I must leave thee;' she replied, 'My dear, why art thou of that belief?' He answered, 'It is my belief, and that I shall be well, and get to the place of pleasantness that I have been travailing for above these twenty years;' exhorting her to take heed to the pure light wherewith she was enlightened, 'for,' said he, 'it is the way, and there is not another.' He bore a living testimony on his dying-bed, in the name and power of the Lord, to several who came to visit him, both Friends and other people, exhorting, warning, and reproving, as he was moved of the Lord.

The day before he died, several Friends being come to see him, he bade them sit down and mind well what he said; and he uttered many very weighty sayings, which were not written down; but this was remembered, that he said, 'None could die the death of the righteous but they that lived the life of the righteous. Though death may seem hard to some, it doth not seem hard to me; for I feel my passage sweetened this day.' He exhorted Friends to keep the unity, and beware of a wrong spirit, and then said, 'I have little more to Friends, but it may be I have something to say to others.'

After a little time he desired several of his neighbours, who were not called Quakers, to be sent for, and most of them being come, the power of the Lord came upon him, and he said, 'I am not ashamed this day to say the spirit of the Lord is upon me;' and so declared to them several weighty things, and said, 'Though some of you have been long in a profession of religion, if the question were put to you, What is the guide of your minds? I believe you will be put to a stand for an answer.' Some of their hearts were so reached that they wept. A few hours before he died, he uttered many heavenly expressions in prayer to the Lord, to the great refreshment of the standers-by. Thus the Lord, who alone is worthy of praise, accompanied him by his power to the last.

He was convinced of truth in the year 1654, and died in Cumberland, in 1680.

THOMAS LLOYD formerly dwelt at a place called Macemore, in Montgomeryshire, in Wales. In his young days he was brought up at the university of Cambridge, and afterwards removed with his family to Pennsylvania, where he was president and deputy-governor of that province several years; and in the last part of his time he had his share with other friends in the exercises occasioned through the contention of George Keith with Friends in that country.

Being taken sick, and near his end, he said to Friends about him, 'Friends, I love you all. I am going from you, and I die in unity and love with all faithful Friends. I have fought a good fight, I have kept the faith, which stands not in the wisdom of words, but in the power of God. I have fought, not for contention and strife, but for the grace of our Lord Jesus Christ, and the simplicity of the gospel. I lay down my head in peace, and desire you may all do so: friends, farewell all.'

He farther said to Griffith Owen, a Friend who was then intending for England, 'I desire thee to mind my love to Friends in Old England, if thou livest to go over to see them. I have lived in unity with them, and do end my days in unity with them, and desire the Lord to keep them faithful unto the end, in the simplicity of the gospel. After a few days' sickness, he departed this life on the 14th of the Seventh month, in the year 1694, aged about forty-five years, leaving six children behind him, and was buried in Friends' burial-ground in Philadelphia, in Pennsylvania.

ELIZABETH MOSS, daughter of Thomas Monk of South Liverton Hall in Nottinghamshire, whose mother afterwards married Samuel Watson of Knight Stainforth, in the county of York, and late wife of Thomas Moss, merchant in London, was educated under a tender, zealous, and religious mother, who brought her up in the nurture and admonition of the Lord; and she was a dutiful and obedient child. When she grew up, and came to receive the truth, she gave up to it, and continued faithful therein to the end. She was exemplary in her family, and took great pains to instruct her servants, that she might bring them to a sense of their dangerous condition without a Saviour.

She was a great lover of retirement, and much given to prayer, contemplation, reading of the Holy Scriptures, and spent much of her time alone in her chamber; so that frequently, when her husband returned home from his affairs abroad, he found her weeping; upon which he has sometimes said to her, 'If some persons saw thee at these times, they might think thou wast under discontent:' her answer was, 'No, my dear, there is nothing at all of that; but the Lord's power and presence hath broken my heart and tendered my spirit, in a living sense of his goodness and tender dealings towards me. I can say he is truly good to my soul, and I have tasted of the incomes of his heavenly love and life. I heartily wish that all who make profession of the blessed truth, were enjoyers with me, for my soul hath been overcome with his love; and although I have lost all my children, and many of my near relations, yet is the Lord pleased to sweeten all my afflictions, and make hard things easy to me.'

She was indisposed some time before she kept her chamber, and her sickness increasing upon her, she was advised to remove out of the city for the recovery of her health, which she did, and was some time at Shacklewell. But notwithstanding, she grew worse; and being sensible that her end drew near, she sent for Samuel Waldenfield, George Whitehead, and some other Friends, that she might see them before she died. The day before she died, Samuel Waldenfield and John Field coming to visit her, she was much revived, and spoke to this purpose, as followeth, directing her speech to Samuel Waldenfield.

'I had a desire to see thee, and to invite thee to my burial,' she having sent for him the day before; 'but I hope,' said she to John Field, 'thou wilt not take it amiss that I spoke first to Samuel, for I did not know of thy coming. Thy visit being altogether free, I kindly accept of it as freely, and desire thee also to be at my burial. Though I did not know that I should have seen the light of another day, yet the Lord having spared me, I am glad to see your faces, that I may tell you how good and gracious the Lord hath been to my soul; for I can truly say, I have sought him with many tears, in my secret chamber, and poured out my soul unto him; and said, O Lord, do thou come down and tabernacle in me, and take up thy abode with me. For I testify Jacob's seed hath wrestled with God for a blessing, and hath prevailed; and now he is become my portion, and the lot of my inheritance for ever. He hath poured of the oil of joy into my sorrowful soul, and hath fed me with the finest of the wheat, and with honey out of the rock hath he sustained me, and the sting of death is taken away. I say, my dear friends, I have not the work to do now, I bless my God for it, but am ready to be dissolved; and I do freely resign my life to my God. I remember my dear and tender mother, who was a woman that truly feared him, and her prayers and petitions were often put up to the Lord, on the behalf of her offspring; and we have reaped much benefit thereby. I have blessed the Lord many a time that ever I was born of her. I speak not these things boastingly; no, for what am I but a poor lump of clay? But only to extol the powerful name and goodness of my God, who hath been so bountiful and gracious to me, for there is forgiveness and mercy with him, that he may be feared. Therefore be encouraged to keep faithful to the Lord, all that are within the hearing of my voice, both husband, friends, and servants. I exhort you all, do justly, love mercy, and walk humbly with your God, that so it may be said unto us all, Come, ye blessed of my Father; which is what my soul hath desired, and that I might never hear that dreadful sound, Go, ye cursed. The Lord hath answered my desire this day, and hath loosed my tongue, that was ready to cleave to the roof of my mouth, and hath strengthened me to praise his great and honourable name. Oh! praise the Lord with me, my friends, and pray for me, as I shall do for you whilst I have breath, that I may be preserved and kept in patience to the end; for it is they that hold out to the end that shall be saved. And though I have a dear and tender husband, and want for nothing that is convenient for me, yet I can freely part with all. I hope the Lord will preserve him near to himself to the end of his days.'

Cornelius Mason coming in, she said, 'Remember my dear love to thy wife and dear children; she hath been kind in visiting me, and we have lived in much love and friendship together. I truly desire the Lord may keep you faithful to himself to the end of your days; and now I am comforted, and can say, Lord, here I am before thee, do with me as it seemeth good in thy sight.'

This is the substance of but part of what she said, for she continued a considerable time speaking of the mercies and dealings of God to her soul, and praising him for the same, to the comfort of those present. Samuel Waldenfield spoke a few words, and returned praise and thanksgiving to the Lord for his endless love and tender mercies to his servants and people; during which she was filled with heavenly joy, and spoke some words afterwards, desiring her dear love might be remembered to all faithful Friends, with whom, she said, she was in perfect unity; and so parted with them in much sweetness, love and satisfaction.

Soon after came our friend George Whitehead, whom she had desired to see, and she was refreshed and comforted to see him; and said, 'Dear George, I am glad to see thee, having always had much love and respect for thee, thou having been at my father's house, and known my mother well. Though I am weak of body, yet the Lord hath comforted me with his living presence, and death is no terror to me; but I am freely resigned and given up into the hand of my God;' with much more to the same effect. Being much spent with the other Friends, she could not raise her voice as she did before; but with love and sweetness, and a smiling countenance, spoke of the goodness of the Lord to her soul, and recommended her counsel to those that were present, that they might not leave that work to do, but labour to make their calling and election sure, before they were cast upon a bed of languishing, as she was upon; but through the love of her heavenly Father, she was waiting for her change, and desired that she might hold out to the end in true patience. She desired George Whitehead also to be at her burial, and after he had spoken a few words in prayer and supplication on her behalf, she parted with him in much love and unity. Afterwards she said, 'O that I had wings like a dove ! for then would I fly away, and be at rest :' with many other living and heavenly expressions.

These things are written, not only for the comfort but encouragement of those who are yet behind, to love the Lord above all, and follow him fully, that he may not forsake them in the day of distress. This Friend often said the eternal God was her refuge, and underneath was the everlasting arm of his power, to uphold and lift up her head above the floods of temptations and trials that she met withal; by which she was enabled to sound forth praises, and humble thanksgiving to his holy and blessed name.

She departed this life the next day, being the 3d day of the Second month, in the year 1702, aged about thirty-nine years, and was buried at Friends' burial ground in Bunhill-fields, London.

THE END OF THE SECOND PART.

PIETY PROMOTED,

IN A COLLECTION OF DYING SAYINGS

OF MANY OF THE PEOPLE CALLED

QUAKERS;

WITH A BRIEF ACCOUNT OF SOME OF THEIR LABORS IN THE GOSPEL, AND SUFFERINGS FOR THE SAME.

THE THIRD PART.

BY JOHN TOMKINS.

"For they that say such things, declare plainly, that they seek a country, that is an heavenly :—Wherefore God is not ashamed to be called their God, for he hath prepared for them a city." HEB. xi. 14, 16.

PREFACE.

Impartial Reader,

THE Author's design in continuing these collections, having already been discovered in his two former treatises upon this subject, to be no less than the promoting of piety, I hope I shall not need to recommend this third part of his so necessary, useful and commendable labours to thy serious perusal, especially in such an age as this, wherein impiety is so sensibly promoted, not only by the notoriously profane, but also by the presumptuously careless professors of Christianity.

How much conducing to obtain this excellent end, the dying words, even of the worst of men, and malefactors, have been esteemed, is evident by the practice of most governments in exposing them to public view, as a warning against vice, and incentive to virtue. How much more shall we count the dying words of the righteous, whose death is precious in the eyes of the Lord, likely to answer this end, and therefore worthy, with their lives and names, to be had in everlasting remembrance.

Although the short reflections given upon the birth, conversion, labours, travels, conversation, and sufferings of many of these precious servants and handmaids of the Lord, are very inviting, as well as instructive, in showing forth that free and universal grace of God, whereby they came to be what they were, and that arm of power whereby they were upheld in, and delivered out of many tribulations; yet the main intention of the Author is, to send us to the house of mourning, which, saith Solomon, is better to go to than the house of rejoicing; that we may learn so to live, as to be prepared to die, and enter upon an eternal state.

If death-beds were more frequented, and places of recreation less, we might hope the advantage would make amends for that part of self-denial. There we may often hear a more reaching sermon in a few broken words, than the most elegant in the pulpit; but especially from two sorts of experienced teachers, namely, sinners repenting, and saints triumphing: there we may hear all agreeing in one common prayer, viz. Oh! let me die the death of the righteous, and let my latter end be like his. There we may hear men discovering what they really believe, often very differently from what they formerly professed; and many with the repenting thief, come to have a better religion upon their death-bed, than all their life-long before. There we may hear those who have been eagerly pleading for sin, now crying out against it as the sting of death. Those who have exclaimed against good works, as dangerous to their faith, now wishing that all their time had been spent in going about doing good. Those who have charged God foolishly with an absolute reprobation, now trusting in, and begging his universal mercy. Those who have known Christ after the flesh only, now desiring to feel him within, as the hope of glory. Those who have grieved, resisted, and mocked at the holy spirit, now seeking for strength and comfort from it. Those who have opposed the light of Christ, now gladly embracing it in the dark valley of the shadow of death. Those who have lived upon outward observations, and been feeding upon husks with the prodigal, now looking towards their Father's house for the substance, the water of regeneration, the bread of life, and the new wine of the kingdom.

There we may hear teachers, tutors, confessors, and such like, who have had people's faith and conscience at their command, often exclaimed against, if not as bad examples, yet as miserable comforters, and physicians of no value. Now names, notions, creeds, traditions, controversies, honours, riches, compliments, pastimes, &c., are little regarded when death, the king of terrors, is in view, and the great Judge stands at the door, who, without respect of persons, judgeth and rewardeth according to every man's work. Now nothing will administer comfort but the inward absolution of our holy high priest, the

Lord Jesus Christ; nothing but the unction of the blessed spirit of intercession and adoption. Here those who have loved God above all, and their neighbours as themselves, are found to have the best religion, and to be the true believers in Christ, and witnesses of his redemption and salvation; and those to be the true and most honourable scholars, who have been taught by the grace of God, which brings salvation, and hath appeared unto all men, to deny ungodliness and the world's lusts, and to live soberly, righteously and godly in this present world.

There we may find the righteous, with Abraham, Isaac, Jacob and Joseph, advising, encouraging and blessing their posterity; with Moses going up to the top of the mount, to take a view of the good land, in retirement and solitariness with the Lord; with Joshua engaging others to fear and serve him alone, and to put away their strange gods; with Samuel, mourning and praying for those who have forsaken the Lord; with David, expressing their faith in his promises concerning their house, and their religious concern for their building of his; recommending truth, justice and mercy to succeeding generations; with Hezekiah appealing to God about their sincerity. In short, with Job, Simeon, Stephen, Paul, and others of the faithful servants and followers of Christ, embracing death, hastening to meet it, longing to be dissolved and to be with him, their captain, fore-runner and rewarder. Thus preaching and praying, and praising the Lord freely and fervently, boldly and experimentally, and all without book, as the holy spirit gives utterance, has upon a death-bed often proved an affecting, tendering and converting season to many hearers.

To such an house of mourning, or shall I say rejoicing, the Author of these collections kindly invites thee, Christian reader; where, by hearing the dying songs and sayings of the ransomed and redeemed, who knew in whom they had believed, thou mayest also come to know and believe in that great and true light, which enlightens every man coming into the world; for it was by the inshining thereof, that the feet of these blessed ones, now at rest with the Lord, as of all the righteous ages past, were guided into the way of truth and peace.

This opened their states, tried their reins, sifted their words, weighed their actions, stayed their minds, changed their hearts, condemned disobedience, justified faithfulness, counselled in difficulties, discovered the enemy, unveiled the painted harlot, the world, and the false church, and gave them the light of the knowledge of the glory of God, in the face of Jesus Christ, for whose sake they suffered the loss of all, and followed him in the regeneration and self-denial, and are now entered with him into that rest which remains for the people of God.

CHRISTOPHER MEIDEL.

PIETY PROMOTED.

THE THIRD PART.

JOHN BOWRON, was born at Cotherstone in Yorkshire, near Barnard-Castle, in the year 1627, which was the place of his outward habitation to his death. He received the truth by the ministry of George Fox and James Naylor, when they came into those parts; which was about the year 1653. Soon after he went to Stratford steeple-house, and preached to the priest and people, and from thence to the cross, and at Barnard-Castle, and at Rumbel steeple-house, and the people threw snow at him, as he stood upon a stone speaking to them. Then he went to Bowes, and stood up in the steeple-house yard, and spake to the people there; and one of the men cried out to the people, 'Hang him, hang him in the bell-house;' and some time after, that man hanged himself. After that he travelled into Allandale, and had a meeting there, and so to Scotland. At Edinburgh he preached to the people as he went through the streets of that city, and at the cross, and there were English soldiers who were kind to him; and he travelled through that nation. The soldiers were very kind to him, but the priests were in a rage against him, for he was a dread to them.

About the year 1656 he took another journey to Scotland, and at Birkwell he took shipping for Barbadoes, and was kindly received in that island, and had many good meetings there; and they would have had him tarry with them as long as he lived. When his service was over in that island, he took

20 *

shipping for Surinam, and travelled upon the coasts of Guiana, a country of South America, three or four hundred miles. He went to their sort of worship, which was performed by beating upon hollow trees, and making a great noise with skins, like a sort of drums; and he declared the word of the Lord among them by an interpreter. He travelled [among the Indian natives in several of their settlements], and spake to their kings, who were arrayed with fish-shells hung about their necks and arms; and they spake to him in their language, and confessed he was a good man, come from far to preach the white man's God.

After he had declared the name of the Lord in this barbarous country, he returned with his interpreter back to Barbadoes again, and staid a little time there, visiting Friends; and a ship presenting, he embarked for England, which proved a long perilous voyage of thirteen weeks. After they had been at sea about six weeks, they met with a violent storm, which took away their rigging, and their provisions grew scanty, so that for five weeks they were reduced to a pint of water, and a biscuit a day each man. There were about sixty persons on board, and some died; but at length they arrived at Dover, where he took passage by land for London, and met with George Fox, and Francis Howgill, to whom he gave an account of his voyage. This was about the time that Richard Cromwell was made protector of England, to whom he went with a message from the Lord, and warned him of the day of the Lord.

After John Bowron returned home into Yorkshire, and rested a little time, he took his journey into Scotland again, and so into Ireland, travelling through all that nation from sea to sea, and returned back again; and so continued visiting that nation of Ireland six times in six years. He was divers times in prison for the testimony of truth; as at Durham jail, and at Richmond house of correction twenty weeks in a sharp winter; and for being at a meeting at Croft-bridge, they took from him a horse and two steers, and imprisoned him again in Durham jail; afterwards he was released by the bishop of Durham.

He oftentimes travelled to London in company with John Langstaff, and to Bristol, and the west of England, till of latter years hindered by age and bodily infirmity. After many journeys, and sore travail and labour, the Lord gave him this blessing, that he lived to be full of days, and died in peace in the same house where he was born. About two weeks before his death he rode to the meeting as he used to do, and bore his testimony among Friends; and two or three days after, went to the burial of an ancient Friend; and his grandchild waited upon him, where he spoke at the grave-yard a pretty while.

The first-day after, finding his strength decay, he desired his son, Henry Bowron, to go to the meeting, and acquaint Friends that his days were almost spent, and he knew not that he should come any more amongst them; and his son answered his desire, and many Friends came to see him. Two days after, he arose without help, and came cheerfully forth of his chamber, desiring his son to trim him, which he did; after, he took his grandchildren by the hand, saying, 'Stay with me, go not away, for I am taking my journey to a city, New Jerusalem, that needs not the light of the sun, nor the light of the moon, for the Lord God and the Lamb is the light thereof.' He added, 'Zion is a precious habitation: he that dwelleth within the gates of Zion shall never want.' Again, 'What can be expected? I have seen many good days. I have seen the wonders of God both by sea and land. The sea saw the wonders of God, and fled, and Jordan was driven back.'

Sometimes he would pray to the Lord, saying, 'Lord bless this nation, and the city of London, which I dearly love.' The night before he died, Thomas Raylton came to visit him, and being told who it was, he said, 'Thomas, pray with me,' and he did so, and the presence of God was felt amongst them, and praises were given to the Lord. Though he was weak in body, yet strong in the inward man, and expressed his satisfaction with that opportunity. After, he said, 'Thomas, what meeting had ye yesterday?' meaning the quarterly-meeting; he answered they had a good meeting, of which he was glad; further he inquired, 'What way art thou going?' Thomas told him southward; he said, 'Tell friends of London how I am, and mind to give my love to them and to G. Whitehead;' and in great sweetness of spirit, and peace of soul, he continued till about midnight, sensible to the last.

He died the 5th day of the Eighth month, 1704, aged seventy-seven years; a minister fifty-one years.

HUGH ROBERTS, late of Pennsylvania, formerly of Wales, was a man fitted and qualified by God's power to be a serviceable minister of the gospel to the church of Christ in America, in which country he lived about eighteen years. His company was very desirable, being greatly edifying; he had passed through many trials and exercises, so could by experience speak a word in season to the travailing and weary soul. His doctrine in the meetings of God's people dropped as dew, and his speech as small rain upon the tender plants; for in the openings of life, things both new and old came forth of the treasury of wisdom. His testimony was comfortable to the hearts of the people, in the sense of God's love, who is the author of all good to his people; a man zealous for good order in the church, and skilful to accommodate differences when they happened. He travelled in the work of the gospel in Maryland, Long Island, Rhode Island, and New England, where his service was effectual to the people, and to himself a great satisfaction.

At his return homewards, being weakly of body, having been much spent, he lay sick at the house of John Rodman in Long Island, where his friend John Bevan visiting him, he said, 'Nothing lies in my way as an obstruction to hinder my peace with God.' After that he got home to Pennsylvania. A friend of his taking his farewell of him, said to him, 'I believe thy deep trials and exercises are nearly at an end, and that peace and joy everlasting will be thy portion from the Lord for thy faithfulness.' In much brokenness of heart, and sense of the presence of God upon his spirit, he answered the friend after this manner, 'I am satisfied thereof, and can bless my God for it.'

He departed this life the 18th of the Sixth month, 1702, and his body was buried at Merion the 20th of the same.

PRISCILLA COTTON, formerly wife of Arthur Cotton, who then dwelt at Plymouth in Devonshire, now of Colchester in Essex, was one of the first that received Friends in Plymouth; namely, John Audland and Thomas Arey, in 1654. She lived an honourable life, and was valiant for truth, and often bore public testimony to it in steeple-houses, and other places, against the priests and professors, who walked out of the truth; and for her testimony she suffered several imprisonments and cruel dealings from them, and other instruments employed by them. She travelled in several places, bearing testimony for truth in the living power of God. She also in her life-time gave forth several good papers, which are printed; and lastly, the day she died, she left a paper for Friends, as a testimony of her good will and love to them all; which is as followeth.

'The Testimony of Priscilia Cotton, to Friends, the day she died.

'All my dear friends, who have found your Redeemer, oh! wait upon him at all times, that you may stand continually in his presence where life is, that with the light you receive from him, you may see your thoughts, and deny them, that in stayedness you may be kept, when the hasty froward spirit would arise, and keep it down. With the measure of God's spirit all may be weighed, the words to what they tend, that no lightness may appear in your words, nor unsavouriness, that no offence come, but edification by all you speak. Let the elders watch, that at no time the younger may see lightness, laughter, or words of offence, but that you may always keep down the evil in yourselves, and may minister grace to all you have to do withal, that God's spirit be not grieved. So keep the field clean, that was once ploughed up and made green and beautiful, that no stones or hurtful weeds grow in it to oppress the Seed.

Friends, the cross is the power of God; when you flee the cross, you lose the power; that which pleaseth self, is above the cross, and that which pleaseth man, is above the cross; and that which shuns the cross, yields to the carnal part, and loses its dominion. Though the cross seems foolishness, stand in it; though it seems weak, stand in it; though it be a stumbling-block to the wise, stand in it; there the dominion, authority, and crown are received. This is not for you to be exercised in for a time only, as at your first convincement, but daily, even to the death, as long as a desire, will or thought remaineth in you, contrary to God's pure light, and judge it by it; and as you wait in the light, you will come to know a cross in the use of meat, drink, and apparel, and keep to the cross when alone, or in company; what the pure mind of God stands against in you, that the cross is against.

So friends, watch daily to keep Christ's command, 'Take up your daily cross;' be not at liberty one day, but deny thy own will, thy own thoughts, and thy own self. Taking up the cross, you feel the power, the strength of the Lord God, which breaks down all, keeps in order, in safety, and in peace. This preserves from stubbornness, wilfulness, and headiness, and brings all to be subject, as dear children, unto God, and subject one unto another as brethren. In the light and in the cross there are no evil thoughts, no hard speeches, no contention, no loving pre-eminence; but as brethren and sisters, pitiful, tender-hearted, courteous, forgiving, forbearing, long-suffering, and supporting one another. Here the power of the cross is known, which brings all to God's praise, and to his honour and glory, and to his children's prosperity and peace: so let it be. Amen.

PRISCILLA COTTON.'

After this, seeing her departure was nigh at hand, she desired several Friends to be called; being come, she desired to be lifted up in her bed; and in a sense of life she spake suitably to every one for some time, exhorting Friends to peace and unity, and to keep in the cross, which is the power of God, that all might witness a mortification to sin, and a renewedness to life, that the living God and his holy truth might be honoured by all; and that Friends might keep out of the fashions and customs of the world, both in words and apparel, every one answering the truth therein.

After this she called for her husband, who was at that time weak; embracing him, she said, 'My dear husband, the Lord hath largely manifested his love to us, and large has been our experience thereof, ever since he brought us together to this day. And now, my dear, the Lord will separate us, but grieve not; let thy eye and expectation be to him, and the Lord who hath hitherto helped us will be thy help and support; in whom let thy trust be for ever!'

In like manner she called for her daughter, and gave her charge to live in subjection to God's truth, and to forsake what she was convinced to be sin and evil, saying if she feared the Lord, and walked in his truth, it should be well with her; but if not, thou wilt be miserable. She also spake to other friends and relations, which for brevity is omitted. Afterwards she said, 'Let me lie down that I may die;' so in great stillness and quietness she departed this life, about four hours after she had spoken these words, the 4th day of the Sixth month, 1664.

ANDREW GRAHAM, of Cumberland, near the borders of Scotland, was a man of large understanding, a loving temper, and willing to do good unto all, which increased his esteem with all sorts of people. When the Lord was pleased to send his servants called Quakers to preach the gospel in the borders of England, in Cumberland, he with many hundreds came to hear their testimony, and did confess unto the truth. But he was before closely joined in fellowship with a people of good repute in the country, and it was hard for him to leave them, which occasioned his halting as between two, some considerable time, until the Lord was pleased to renew his visitation to him, and by his righteous judgments awakened him to a true sense of his state; so that he was deprived of peace, until he gave up to be faithful to what the Lord by his spirit discovered to him to be his duty.

He joined with the people called Quakers from that time, and was a good example in conversation among men, in humility, and in self-denial, and in suffering; and in about two years time the Lord committed to him a part of the ministry, and he faithfully laboured in the work of the gospel, in the churches of Christ, both in some parts of England, and in Scotland. His service was great in the meeting to which he more peculiarly belonged; and the more for his innocency, true zeal, and being devoted to the service of the truth, labouring to bring people to the life and power of godliness. He was as a nursing father, or cherisher of those in whose hearts he saw God had begun his work, as well as he was terrible against ungodliness.

He was suddenly seized with a great sickness, and lay sick but a short time; in which he said, 'I see they are happy who, when death comes, have nothing to do but to die; for the pains of the body at this time are enough to struggle with.' As he lived, so he died, ending his days in a travail of spirit, that Friends might be faithful; and Friends visiting him, the Lord's power and presence was plentifully enjoyed, to the tendering of the hearts of many. He finished his course in this life on the 15th of the Eleventh month, 1704. Aged sixty-two years.

THOMAS WRESLE, of Winteringham, in the county of Lincoln, was an early seeker of truth and righteousness; and for some time had his conversation among the Baptists. He received the truth in the year 1655, wherein he much improved, and approved himself a faithful man, loving truth, and the friends thereof, with all his heart, and serving it and them faithfully to the end of his days. He was exemplary in his conversation, and helpful to his neighbours; and having a good understanding, was able to give counsel and advice, which was esteemed amongst them. In his sickness he said, 'I have seen where the weary are at rest, and where the wicked cease from troubling; and I have received an earnest of that blessed inheritance, which is laid up in store for all the faithful.'

A day or two before he died, some of his friends visited him, which greatly comforted him, as he signified; to whom he said, 'I have loved truth with all my heart, and all the friends of it, and feel nothing, but that all is well with me.' In and with much fervency, he said, 'I desire that Friends would keep up their meetings in the name and power of the Lord Jesus Christ, and that the Lord may bless and prosper them.' He exhorted Friends to keep their ancient zeal, love, and integrity, which the Lord raised in them in the beginning, saying, 'That is my great comfort now upon my dying bed;' and taking his leave of Friends, said, 'It is life, it is life, Friends, that overcomes death. Give my dear love to all faithful Friends every where;' and life and truth was felt to flow among them at that time.

He died the 21st of the Twelfth month, 1704.

WILLIAM CAPTAIN came out of England with his parents into Ireland, after the civil wars; and was convinced at Mountmelick meeting. He was bred a scholar, and in his youth intended for a priest. He was a faithful, patient, and deep sufferer for the testimony of a good conscience, and often in prison for meeting to worship God, and for tithes; holding forth a good conversation, as became the gospel.

In the time of his sickness, some Friends being present, he said to them as followeth; 'The Lord hath appeared to me in a wonderful manner, when I was ready to sink under great affliction; then did he take me by the hand, as he did Israel of old, and raised me over mine afflictions. Whereas I had need of a physician, the Lord was unto me instead of a physician; and when I had need of patience, he gave me patience; and when I had need of sleep, he accompanied me with his living presence from time to time; whereby my soul was sweetly consoled, so that I can say with the Psalmist, "It is good for me that I was afflicted;" and with Simeon, that "Mine eyes have seen his salvation;" and with Job, that "My Redeemer liveth, and mine eyes have seen him." See how good the Lord is. Oh! my soul, praise thou the Lord, let all that is within me praise the Lord.' Another time he said, 'The truth which the Quakers profess is the way to salvation, and there is no other way.'

He died a prisoner for the testimony to truth, the 30th day of the Ninth month, 1672.

ROGER GILL, of London, shoe-maker, received the blessed truth, as professed by the people called Quakers, about the year 1683. He formerly went among those called Baptists, and I have heard him say that before he received truth he was guilty of many gross and enormous crimes. But by the power and virtue of the spirit of God, he came to know his heart changed, and being washed and sanctified, and the fear of God placed therein, which preserved him from those vices he had formerly been addicted to, for which he was very thankful to the Lord. Some years before he died, God gave him a dispensation of the gospel of our Lord Jesus Christ to preach, and he was faithful and diligent in that service, and was an able minister, having a word in season to speak to the weary soul; and very zealous he was for the prosperity of the truth.

In the year 1699 he had a concern upon his mind to visit the brethren in America, and to preach the gospel to the people on that continent. He went over the sea for that purpose, in company with his friend Thomas Story, concerned in the same work; where they had not travelled long, before they heard the people in Philadelphia, in Pennsylvania, were visited with a malignant distemper, which caused great mortality. At hearing thereof Roger Gill said he felt a great weight and exercise to come upon him, so that he had no ease in his spirit till he came amongst them at Philadelphia. The sickness increasing, he visited the sick, and preached in their public meetings, saying that when he was one hundred miles off them, his love in the Lord was such to them, that had he wings he would fly into Philadelphia.

It was the time of their yearly-meeting whilst he was there; where he, with others, was concerned in public, earnestly to supplicate the Lord for the people; and particularly Roger Gill fervently and devoutly interceded the Lord to stay his hand, and if he would please to accept of his life for a sacrifice, he did freely offer up his life to the Lord for the people. When meeting was over he often expressed the ease of his mind, and that it was with him that he had not much to do but visit Friends of Burlington, in West Jersey, about twenty miles off. He accomplished that journey; and at his return to Philadelphia was taken sick with the distemper, which filled him with great pain and affliction of body, and he remembered in his sickness the free-will-offering up of himself unto the Lord; saying to Friends about him, 'It is not in my heart to repent of the offer I have made.'

He was cheerful, notwithstanding his great affliction of body; and exhorted Friends to faithfulness, and said, 'The Lord hath sanctified my afflictions to me, and hath made my sickness as a bed of down:' and when some did speak of their hope of his recovery, he said in much love, 'Truly I have neither thoughts nor hopes about being raised in this life; but I know I shall rise sooner than many imagine, and receive a reward according to my works.' His sickness continued seven days upon him; and a few hours before his death he took his leave and said, 'Farewell, farewell, farewell for ever,' and sweetly passed away out of this life on the 2d day of the Eighth month, 1699. It was observed that the sickness stopped, and very few were buried of it after him.

He left a widow and two sons behind him in England. He was aged about thirty-four years.

WILLIAM SMITH, of Elsham, in the county of Lincoln, was an elder in the truth, having received it in the love of it, and walked faithfully therein to the end, and was a preacher of righteousness; in conversation a man of sincerity and godly simplicity, giving no occasion of offence to Jew or Gentile, neither to the church of Christ, and much beloved by friends and neighbours. When on his dying bed, several Friends visiting him, found him in a heavenly frame of mind. He being told Friends' love was to him, he answered, 'I have friends on earth, and friends in heaven, the Father, Son, and Holy Ghost, whom I have true fellowship withal, though yet in this earthly tabernacle; my treasure being in heaven, my heart is there also, where the Father, Son, and Holy Spirit dwelleth.' As he lived, so he died in the Lord, and is blessed, for so saith the spirit, and he is at rest from his labours.

He departed this life the 17th of the Twelfth month, 1701. Aged seventy-nine years.

MARGARET THOMPSON, wife of John Thompson, near Mountmelick, in Ireland, being upon her death-bed, and a few days before she died, calling her children to her, said unto them, 'Fear the Lord, and abide in the fear of the Lord. I do not allow you any thing further, than as you abide in the truth, and love one another.' After that she said, 'The Lord helps me, and I find all temptations taken away.' Another time she said, 'They that die in the Lord, have unity one with another;' and she confessed the love of God, and said, 'I will lean upon my beloved;' and further said to Friends present, 'Dear brethren and sisters, I exhort you in the Lord to love one another, and walk in God's truth for ever. Women Friends, I exhort you all in the love of God, govern well in your own houses, or else you cannot govern well in the church of Christ. Likewise, young women, be sober-minded, and fear the Lord, and be charitable, and walk in love to the end. Dear friends, I salute you all in the Lord; and I here give in my testimony against paying of tithes, for I never paid any tithes, nor ever condescended to the paying of any, this being my last testimony.' She also exhorted Friends to their first love, which they had received in the beginning, bearing her testimony against the vain fashions of the world. She died the 5th of the Third month, 1688.

WILLIAM GIBSON, born in Caton, near Lancaster, about the year 1629, being a soldier in the garrison in Carlisle, Cumberland, and he, with three others, understanding that a preacher called a Quaker, who was a stranger, had appointed a meeting in that city, agreed to go together to the meeting, with an intent to abuse the said Friend, whose name was Thomas Holmes. William coming first to the meeting, and hearing the Friend powerfully declaring the truth, was so affected and reached by his testimony, that he stepped up into the meeting, near the place where Thomas Holmes stood, and knowing the design of his fellows, waited to defend the Friend [against] any that durst offer to abuse him. From this time he became a constant frequenter of Friends' meetings, and quitted his place in the garrison, and employed himself in the trade of shoemaking, and waited upon God in silence, under the exercise of his power, for the space of three years. Afterwards he received a dispensation of the gospel to preach, and became very serviceable in divers places of the county of Lancaster.

On the 22d day of the Sixth month, 1662, he married Elizabeth Thompson, daughter of William Thompson, of Crossmore, in Lancashire, and settled in Sankey meeting, near Warrington, for some years; and some were convinced of truth by his ministry, who continue faithful to this day, and many others confirmed in the blessed truth; so that his memorial is of good savour in those parts. He afterwards travelled southwards in the work of the gospel, and was imprisoned at Maidstone, in Kent, for his testimony, which imprisonment was long; from whence being discharged, he went to London, and removed his wife and family thither, where his service was well known to Friends in that city, and many other parts of the nation, and many are the seals of his ministry. Though he was severe in reproof, and terrible in his ministry to the hypocrite and the workers of iniquity, yet he was as a tender father to the mourners in Zion, and divided the word aright, speaking a word in season to the tempted, afflicted, and travailing soul; a cherisher of such as loved and feared the Lord; and oftentimes his ministry was to the refreshment of the weary, and the overflowings of his cup administered true comfort and consolation to the thirsty, panting souls.

He was a lover of unity amongst brethren, but as a sword against that spirit, which, under pretence of love to the light of Christ Jesus in their consciences, would plead for a liberty that was out of the truth, and sought to draw others from the footsteps of the flock of Christ: to which purpose he wrote a book, entitled, 'An Epistle of Love.' He was a man devoted to the service of God, and was an example to believers, even in word, in conversation, in charity, in spirit, in faith, and in purity, and gave attendance to reading, and to exhortation, and to doctrine, given to hospitality, and apt to teach, and was approved as a minister of God. He had suffered hard imprisonments, and the spoiling of his goods, for his testimony's sake against hireling priests, who feed themselves and not the flock, and against their maintenance by tithes.

In the Third month, 1684, he travelled into his native country, Lancashire, though he had been out of health; and in his return home was taken sick of an ague and fever at Coventry, yet got to London, and continued ill for three months. On his sick-bed he exhorted Friends who came to visit him, to faithfulness, and trust and confidence in the Lord, and to the love of the brethren; and testified against that spirit which leads out of unity into a self-separation.

He left two sons and one daughter, to whom he gave good advice in the time of his sickness, directing them to that blessed and divine light of Christ, which he had preached, and by which he had received the knowledge of God, and by walking in it, salvation to his soul; desiring that they might know the same, and walk in it. 'It will show you,' said he, 'what is good, and what is evil: refrain from evil, and do the good; take heed to God's word in your hearts, so you will know your ways cleansed by it.' He charged them to avoid all vain and idle company, and to be diligent in frequenting assemblies of the Lord's people, and to have an ear open to receive the good counsel and advice of them who fear the Lord, and are faithful to him, and to keep society with such, and to flee youthful lusts, which war against the soul. Moreover he said, 'Love the righteous judgments of the Lord, and have regard to the fear of God, and love humility; so shall you receive wisdom and understanding. Be obedient to your mother, and be tender over her; and be not conceited, nor high-minded.' He also charged them to read the Scripture, and other good books.

Thus did this good man, like Abraham, charge his children to walk before the Lord. He was very resigned, and given up to die, and expressed his love to the brethren, saying, 'My love in the Lord Jesus is to all the faithful. Remember my dear love to them, and to all the faithful labourers.' Not long before he died, John Field visiting him, he looked earnestly on him; his wife asking if he knew him, he answered 'No;' she told him; he replied, 'He is the first man I did not know.' At this time he seemed very retired in his mind unto the Lord, his rock, and his refuge; several times lifting up his hands, and showed a willingness to be turned, and then said, 'I have spoken my mind while I could speak, and now I cannot.'

He died the 20th of the Ninth month, 1684, about five in the afternoon, and was honourably buried at Friends' burying-ground, in Bunhill-fields, many hundreds of friends and brethren accompanying his corpse to the grave. Aged fifty-five years, a minister twenty-six years.

ELEANOR BARCROFT, daughter of William Barcroft, near Edenderry, in King's County, Ireland, was a young woman of a clean and innocent conversation, obedient to her parents and loving to all, but especially to the godly, whose company was her delight; and as her life was good, so was her death. In the time of her sickness, she desired to have the tenth chapter of Luke read, wherein two passages were remarkable to her; the one of the man inquiring who was his neighbour, the other of Martha and Mary; at the reading of which she was much refreshed.

The morning before she died, it was observed she prayed with a low voice, and did wrestle in spirit with the Lord; and in the afternoon the Lord did so appear, that the pangs of death were as it were taken away, so that she sung hymns and spiritual songs of praise to Christ her Redeemer; and afterwards said, 'Oh! that I might live with thee for ever, and for evermore.' Then she took leave of her parents and relations. Being asked how she did, she answered, 'I feel neither pain nor trouble;' and hearing her mother weep, said, 'Why doth my mother weep, for I am well.' With these and some other words which cannot be well remembered, because of the sorrow of those about her, she departed this life with the seal of assurance in the true faith, and is gone to her rest, and hath left a good memorial behind her.

She died the 27th of the Eighth month, 1678, in the nineteenth year of her age.

THE words and testimony of THOMAS GETTOS, of Bandon, in Ireland, about eight hours before his departure out of this life. He was weak in body, but fervent in mind, and perfect in memory; taken from his mouth the 22d of the Third month, 1682.

'I have known the terrors of the Lord for sin, and for transgression committed against him in the time of my youth. But he that is an everlasting fountain of life and mercy, did not leave me in the greatness of my wickedness, but in the abundance of his pity and compassion visited me, and found me out, and laid hold on me by his judgments, and did awaken me, even in that dead state and condition he found me in. He made manifest his living truth, viz. Christ Jesus, the light of the world, which enlightens every one that cometh into the world, of the whole stock of mankind. So the light and life being made manifest to me, it became the joy of my heart, and the life of my soul. I was brought to see that I must come to deny the world, and the glory and riches thereof, and the honour thereof, and all things that are beneath. It became a very great cross to the fleshly part, which I saw I must daily keep to; for when I went from that which crucified me to the world, and the world to me, my enemy prevailed over me; so that I saw the words of Christ fulfilled in me, in that respect, according to his testimony, who declared on this wise; 'Whosoever doth not bear his cross, and come after me, cannot be made my disciple.' When I came to see that heavenly treasure, made manifest, and revealed in my soul, and kept my affections thereunto, the yoke of Christ which seemed to be so heavy became light; even so it is unto all them that keep in faithful obedience unto him, and take up his daily cross. I have known a travel towards that spiritual kingdom of our Lord and Saviour Jesus Christ; for I saw a race set before me, and I saw, if I did run with all my might, it was possible for me to obtain the prize. Therein I have had an exercise of my faith; for had I not believed in the object of my faith, Christ Jesus, it had been impossible for me to run that blessed race. As I was faithful and obedient to the manifestation of Christ, who is God's righteousness, which is manifest and received in the internal parts, I received daily supplies of strength in my greatest exercises. Unto whom then shall I return the glory and the praise of this wonderful work of my salvation, and eternal happiness, but unto Christ Jesus, the great fountain of life, mercy, and truth, and righteousness! which I do desire to return at this time, and at all other times, unto him who lives and reigns for ever, God over all, blessed for evermore.

'And now, my friends, as the Lord brought these things unto my remembrance, I could do no less than declare unto you the wonderful dealings of the Lord to my soul, that all thereby might receive the instructions of the Lord, who is forewarning the sons and daughters of men, according to the greatness of his wisdom. Certainly, although the Lord never created man to destroy him, yet his determination shall stand for ever; that is, they that take warning in the day of their visitation, and return with all their hearts, and with all their souls, shall find the way of life made manifest, and revealed in them, which leads unto the Father, who is an eternal fountain of life. But they that neglect the day of their visitation, must be shut up under darkness, until the great day of the Lord. And then they shall come to know they have rebelled against him, and must know his righteous judgments, although it be to their everlasting destruction. Here they shall see and know that their destruction was and is of themselves; and God will be glorified, even in the destruction of his enemies.

'And now it is the desire of my heart and soul, even before the Lord God Almighty, that all may be warned and awakened out of that state of deadness and security which the god of this world hath brought them into, so that the righteous judgments of the Lord might be made manifest unto them; that so they may lay hold of his mercy in the day of their visitation. And as for my dear friends, who have known the gathering arm of his power into the holy habitation of our God, which is Jerusalem, which is from above, the mother of us all, I warn you all in the fear of the Lord to be careful to keep your habitation, for in that consists your safety.

'While Israel kept the place wherein God ordained them to be outwardly, Balaam could not curse them, nor could any enchantment be found to prevail against them; but when the wiles of their adversaries enticed them out of their habitations, how many thousands were destroyed thereby! The enemy stands without this holy habitation of the people of the Lord, to entice his people to mix with a wrong seed, and then we give our strength to our enemies, and so befool away that heavenly treasure which God hath committed to our charge. Notwithstanding the enemy hath prevailed over many upon this account, yet

I have taken notice of the goodness of this heavenly shepherd, and great bishop of our souls, who hath sought after them also, that have been scattered out of the fold by that means. Many he hath laid hold on by the crook of his judgments, and brought them back to the fold again. And behold how many have perished, to the grief of the shepherd, and of the flock also. But oh! for ever blessed and praised be the Lord, that hath kept and preserved a remnant that have faithfully followed him, who are built upon the rock Christ Jesus, where they stand steadfastly, showing forth the greatness of his love. They are as a city on a hill, that are seen far and near, and are become the light of the dark world, by the shining of their holy conversation; and so shining by reflection, receiving their light continually from Christ Jesus, the true light of the world. Blessed are all they who know the gathering into this blessed city, and abide steadfast unto the end; for the Lord hath chosen Mount Sion unto himself, that from thence his glory might be proclaimed throughout all generations.

'And now, my dearly beloved friends, whom I dearly salute, even in the bowels of our Lord and Saviour Jesus Christ; oh! my love unto you all is beyond expression, who have kept in faithful obedience to the truth. Oh! the blessed satisfaction that we have found in him, when we have been gathered into his name, and there drank together in one spirit, so that our souls have been exceedingly refreshed, and we have been made partakers of the heavenly bread, which hath been broken plentifully unto us, even at the table of the Lord. Oh! never forget those blessed opportunities; but as you are kept in spiritual health, you will feel a hungering after the bread of life, day after day, and a thirsting after the water of life also. So being kept here, you are capable of the blessing of the Lord, and will see the Scripture fulfilled in yourselves, which saith, "Blessed are they that hunger and thirst after righteousness, for they shall be satisfied."' About eight hours after he had delivered this to Friends present, he died in peace the 22d of the Third month, 1682.

JAMES BLACKHOUSE, of Yelland Conyers, in the county of Lancaster, was born of believing parents, called Quakers, in the year 1668, and when he grew up he received the same faith, and for several years professed truth in much sincerity and plainness. He was a man of a blameless conversation, and a good example, and of great service in divers affairs of truth, until, in the year 1697, he was, at the suit of the dean and chapter of Worcester, apprehended and committed to Lancaster castle for his Christian testimony against tithes. Here he continued for some time a faithful sufferer, until he fell sick of body, which increased upon him to the finishing of his life in this world.

When he was, as to outward appearance, nigh unto death, the Lord revived his spirit, and he sang, and made pleasant melody unto God in his heart; and said, 'The Lord hath appeared in a wonderful manner unto my soul, and hath removed and taken away the pains of this my outward body, and hath received me into his bosom, and hath set me upon his holy mountain, which is as sure as Mount Sion, that cannot be moved, and it is better for me to die than to live.'

He died, a faithful sufferer for the testimony of Jesus Christ, in Lancaster castle, the 13th day of the Fourth month, 1697. Aged twenty-nine years.

MERCY JOHNSON, wife of Elihu Johnson, of Manchester, and daughter of Samuel Watson, of Stanforth, in the county of York, was born the 7th day of the Fifth month, 1670. She received a gift of the ministry while unmarried; and in the year 1697 travelled with Jennet Stow in the work of the gospel into the western and southern parts of England, and in some part of Wales. In the year 1699 she went, with her father, Samuel Watson, into Scotland, to visit the meetings of Friends in that nation. She was a tender woman, of a weakly constitution of body, though many times, when in the Lord's service, she seemed very strong, and was concerned in her spirit for the good of all, and for the prosperity of truth, and desired no long life in this world.

In the beginning of her illness she often desired of the Lord to give her patience to undergo what might be suffered to come upon her. Her illness abated, but in some time came again violently upon her; also she was sensible her end drew near, and often desired it in the time of her sickness. The Lord favoured her with his presence, and made her sick bed pleasant to her, insomuch that she sang praises to the Lord, the giver of all good things. Many Friends visited her in her sickness, and it was a comfort to them and her relations to feel the Lord's presence with her; and she declared of the goodness of God, and how well content she was to be taken off the stage of this world, saying, 'I am not in love with it.'

Many were her excellent sayings, which are not remembered. Near her latter end she was more filled with God's salvation, and some of her words were as follow; some Friends being present, 'Happy are you whose kingdom is not of this world, but of the Father's; the Father's kingdom, your kingdom! Friends, love God better than all. Be faithful to the Lord every one, although you are but few. I could have been glad that the whole meeting had been here; surely they will remember what I said the last meeting I opened my mouth among them; that was, to prize their precious time, not knowing how long they might have time, neither what exercises they have yet to meet withal. Now the time draws near that I shall go to an everlasting kingdom, where all sorrow, tears and sighing shall be done away. Glory, glory in the highest, to the Lord my God, who hath been with me, and borne up my head in time of great exercises. I have nothing to do but to die. Keep you near to the Lord, that so when you come to lay down your heads you may have nothing to do but die.'

Speaking to her husband, she said, 'Oh! my dear, I have in the time of my health desired to live with the Lord, and to be faithful to him, and now I see I have nothing to spare; what will become of those who live a careless life, and do not make a right use of their precious time?' She was, in the time of her speaking these words, filled with the love of God, and the sweet spirit of life did attend her, to the comfort of those present; and she said, 'This outward body grows weaker and weaker, yet blessed and praised be the Lord, my inward man grows stronger and stronger.' In time of silence she made songs of melody to God in her heart; and after a Friend prayed by her, she said, 'I am so filled with God's love, I shall never be emptied again.' She much longed to go out of this world, waiting for the coming of the Lord to remove her, and said, 'My dear children, I have prayed for them who are near and dear to me; but now I can leave them freely, and commit them into the hand of my God.'

Speaking to her husband and them, she said, 'I must part with all, and I will bid you all farewell; the Lord bless you all, and keep you all, in all your exercises that will come upon you. I believe the Lord will be with you, as you have an eye to him.' Another time she said, 'Have nothing to do with them of ill spirits, but keep to God, and he will give you power over them.' She was much grieved to see any professing truth to be light and airy, out of the savour of it, and said, 'A day of trial will come upon them. Another time, being in a quiet frame of mind, she said, 'The sooner a period is put to this life, the sooner I shall go to my everlasting comfort.' One wishing her a good night, she said, 'I shall have a good night, let it be how it will; blessed and praised be the name of the Lord, I am full of his goodness. What a great difference betwixt being thus, and in some of my sick fits! There is a great comfort in one, but not in the other; only that I think that it is doing the work, and hastening me to my everlasting joy.'

A little before she was taken away, having got some rest in sleep, when she was awakened, said, 'Now I am very sensible I must go soon to my joy, that will last for ever;' and speaking to her husband, said, 'Fare thee well, my dear, now I shall be well in a little time.' She lay still a little while again, then said to those present, 'Oh! the Lord is the best master you can serve while you live, for he will reward you in your afflictions as he rewards me. Oh! he is a fountain set open for me in a full manner in my affliction. Glory, glory, praises, praises to his eternal name. I will praise him whilst I have breath in my nostrils; he has been a merciful God to me, and has helped me over many things, and has blotted out my sins, and will remember them no more. Oh! praise, honour, and glory to him for evermore. Now into thy hand I commit my dear husband and children, whom thou hast bestowed upon me, and will take me from them; bless and preserve them to the end.'

Thus she was drawn forth to supplicate the Lord for all, saying, 'I love all, and God above all, for what he hath done for me.' After this, she asked what hour it was; they told her four in the morning; she said, 'I shall surely be gone in a few hours to my everlasting rest;' desiring her dear love might be remembered to all Friends in general. Then she lay down quietly, waiting for her change, and desired all might be still, and none come to disturb her in her passing away; after she awaked, she said, 'Let us praise the Lord once more; we will love him above all. All glory, praise, and eternal renown to his most worthy name; he hath filled my heart, and is near to crown my soul. I would not live if I might choose to have the whole world. Oh! thou, the Lord, art better than all; my soul magnifies thee; honour, glory, and eternal praises be given to thee for ever, and for evermore; I will praise thee to the end. Lord be with my dear husband and children to the end.' She said, 'I hope you will remember me when I am gone, to the comfort of your souls.' She said to her husband, 'The Lord united us in his own love together, and in his love he will part us. I was always satisfied before and since, that the Lord's hand brought us together.'

The First-day of the week several friends came to visit her, whom she exhorted to be faithful to what God had made known to them; and her words had power with them, to the tendering the hearts of them she spoke to. A little before her departure, she had a mind to send for her father to her burial, who was an ancient man, about eighty years of age, and dwelt forty miles off. He coming, she was glad, and told him how good God had been unto her in the time of her sickness, and said, 'If it was not for the hope of glory which is to come, I had fainted.' After this, she said, 'Now, Lord, when thou pleasest, remove me; I am content with thy will, when thou seest meet.'

She continued in a heavenly frame of mind; and a young woman who used to go to meeting coming to see her, she gave her good advice; and afterwards fell asleep. When she awoke, her husband asked her if she would drink any thing; she said, 'I have had a full draught of the goodness of my God; I did not so much as think of cordials;' and so continued praising the Lord for his goodness, and the enjoyment of his presence. She said, 'My troubles in a little time will be over, and I shall be at rest and peace with my God, where I shall praise him for ever;' and she said, 'Methinks in a vision I have seen my dear mother and sisters, in shining garments, where I shall be soon. He is a great and mighty king that I am going to. Oh! love so, that you that stay a little behind may come after.' A little before she died her husband asked her how she did, and she said, 'Come near,' and she kissed him, and bade him farewell; and presently again she said, 'Let us bid farewell again;' and so died, as if she had fallen asleep, about the tenth hour at night, the 14th of the Twelfth month, 1704, in the thirty-fourth year of her age.

A few words of tender counsel and advice to Friends, given forth by Mercy Johnson upon her dying bed, two days before she died; which she desired might be communicated to Friends.

'Dear friends, both old and young, wherever these may come, my love salutes you dearly, desiring the welfare of your bodies and souls. I have in my measure laboured amongst Friends in many places whilst with them, for the prosperity of truth and good of souls, and now shall be taken away. I find great concern upon me to leave as advice and tender caution to all, that you may keep near to truth, and love it, seeking the honour of it above all things. Dear Friends, love one another, and as you have an eye to truth, and seek the honour of it before your own, then will your love flow one unto another; and whispering, with backbiting, and tale-bearing, will be removed from you, for I have seen the ill effects of such things many times. And, dear Friends, in your meetings for business upon truth's account, have your eye to the Lord, and wait to have your minds stayed upon him, respecting one another above yourselves for truth's sake, and you waiting upon the Lord to work in you, and for you, and to open your mouths to speak a word in season.

'Reason not, but give up freely to act and speak for truth, whether you be young or old; not in high-mindedness, but in true fear before the Lord. For I must tell you, the humble, and those that abase themselves, the Lord will exalt; but the high-minded, and those of an exalted spirit, the Lord will abase and humble, and make them know he is God, and will be bowed to by every high spirit.

'Therefore, dear friends, let the truth have the reign in you, to govern your words, though never so few, that they may be rightly seasoned with grace, that so you may edify one another. Suffer no unruly spirit to appear in your meetings, neither in old nor young; but stand in the counsel of God, and he will give you a word in due season, to stop the mouths of all gainsayers of the blessed truth, and of the work you are called to do in your days. Thus the Lord will bless, and more and more prosper his work in you, to your comfort, and his eternal praise, to whom all is due. I can tell you, it will be well with you to be faithful to the Lord, when you come to a dying-bed, as I now am. I feel peace and true consolation with the Lord, and my love herein dearly salutes you, and bids you all farewell, who am your dear and tender sister

'MERCY JOHNSON.'

TACY DAVIS, wife of Richard Davis, of Welsh Pool, in Montgomeryshire, formerly dwelt in London, but after her marriage, removed with her husband to Pool aforesaid, where were few or no Friends at that time, which was about the year 1659. She had a public testimony in meetings, and was instrumental to bring many to the truth, and was an entertainer, with her husband, of strangers, and a nursing mother to those in prison for the testimony of a good conscience. They lived together to old age, and she cheerfully went through the various exercises and hard sufferings which attended, in those days, those that professed the blessed truth.

She was taken sick the 29th of the Second month, 1705, and had been at a meeting the same day, which was kept at their house about forty years. After the extremity of her pain was somewhat abated, she said, 'People do not think it so hard to die, as I find it;' and prayed thus; 'O Lord, accept of me in thy well-beloved Son, Christ Jesus. I have loved thee with all my soul and spirit. I have kept thy commandments. Oh! Lord, bless my family with all heavenly blessings; grant to them that they may live in thy fear.' She said to the servant-maid, who was not a Friend, 'Remember thy Creator in the days of thy youth; leave off thy vanity before such a day as this overtake thee. I have nothing to do but to strive with this natural distemper. I loved the Lord in my young days, and he kept me from many evils; and when he was pleased to make known his blessed truth to me, he helped me to work out my salvation with fear and trembling. That work I have not to do now; the Lord Jesus Christ did it in me, and for me;' upon which the maid wept much.

At another time, pain coming on her, she said, 'I feel I am of a strong constitution, and that nature would not yield to my distemper;' and prayed fervently, saying, 'Come, Lord Jesus Christ, come quickly and put an end to my pain. Lord, I long to be with thee for ever.' Another time she prayed, 'O Lord, I am the workmanship of thy hands; thou hast often helped me in the time of need, for thy name's sake help me now in the time of my distress; thou art my God, my hope, and my help, I will trust in thee, oh my God! Oh God! hasten thy coming for thy son Christ Jesus's sake.' Another time she said to her husband, 'I have done too little for the Lord.' Her husband put her in mind of her many former services, and particularly visiting his servants when in prison for Christ's sake, feeding them when hungry, entertaining strangers, and when sick, very tender in helping them, &c., she replied, 'All this is too little to do for the Lord Jesus's sake, who hath loved us. We must not depend upon these things, but we must depend and trust in our Lord and Saviour Jesus Christ; and when we have done all, let us account ourselves unprofitable servants, for we have done but that which was our duty.' A little before she died, she desired her husband to praise the Lord with her for all his mercies, and said, 'At this time I feel his living presence to my great comfort.' She prayed herself, saying, 'O Lord, thou hast been a father to me, thou hast kept me from evil, and now I trust in thy great name, that thou wilt not forsake me; for thy Son Christ Jesus's sake, take me to thyself.'

And she was heard: about the sixth hour in the afternoon, on the First-day of the Third month, in the year 1705, the Lord in his love and mercy took her to himself, in great quietness and peace of spirit, in about the ninetieth year of her age.

MERCY EMES, was the wife of Charles Emes, of Warwick, and daughter of John Garner, of Kinningsworth, of the same county, yeoman. Her first husband's name was Charles Devale, a Frenchman, who was formerly a priest of the church of England, and chaplain to the Earl of Essex, but for conscience-sake he left that church, and joined with the Baptists in London; amongst which people he continued until his death. The said Mercy, before she was his wife, attended upon the countess of Ranclagh, from which family Charles Devale married her. She did from a child seek after the kingdom of heaven, and when she was among the Baptists, was dissatisfied with the doctrine which she often heard preached of God's absolute reprobation of men; and upon that account sought for a people who had better tidings to preach. In her inquiry she came to a meeting of the people called Quakers, where she heard preached the "free grace of God, which bringeth salvation, that it appeared to all men, teaching them to deny ungodliness and worldly lusts; that we should live soberly, and righteously, and godly, in this present world, &c."

From that time she, with two other of her acquaintance who were with her, left the Baptists and embraced the truth, and joined in fellowship with the people called Quakers; among which people she married Charles Emes. She often praised the Lord for the knowledge of his truth, which she loved and valued above all outward enjoyments, and ordered her conversation according thereto, unto the end of her days.

Her sickness held her about five weeks, in which time she said it was a good thing to be ready to die, and not to have that work to do when we are to leave the world. The Lord was large in his love to her; for which she blessed his name in the sense of his mercy; and as her friends and neighbours came to visit her, she exhorted them in great love and tenderness, which caused much brokenness of heart amongst them. One visiting her, she said, 'I have a love to thee; thou art convinced, but not converted; hold on thy way, the Lord will do thee good.' Another time, two friends visiting her, one inquired how she did, she answered, 'I am a dying woman; I am going to my God and thy God;' she said, 'Why so long coming to see me?' he told her the reason: she replied, 'Thy heart is towards Zion, and so is the other friend's; keep your shoulder to the work which God hath put upon you; hold him forth to the nations; be not ashamed of Christ, he is a glorious Saviour; if I should live I must declare it; if I live I cannot hold my peace.'

She testified to the service of women's meetings, saying, 'Women have a service for God as well as men, and women's meetings are of service, and this is my testimony before I die.' To a friend who was under some doubtful thoughts, she spoke by way of encouragement, saying, 'Thou wilt meet with many troubles, but it will be well with thee in the end;' with more words to that purpose. She spent much of the time of her sickness in praising God. The day before she died, she spoke to several friends concerning their states and conditions in the truth. She was freely resigned to die, and nothing seemed hard to her to part with, except her two little children, of whom she often said, 'My little babes;' but she declared her satisfaction that the Lord would provide for them, which is in part fulfilled already. A few hours before she died, her husband coming to her bedside about midnight, found her pouring out her soul to the Lord, and she said to him, 'The sting of death is taken away; I am not afraid to die. I have the evidence of God's love sealed to me: my bed is a bed of roses;' which expression she used several times in her sickness; so resigning her soul unto the Lord.

She finished this life the 31st of the Eighth month, 1697, and was buried among friends at Warwick.

SARAH KIRKBRIDE, wife of Joseph Kirkbride, of Pennsylvania, and daughter of Mahlon Stacy, of West Jersey, in America, was virtuous from her childhood, and very dutiful to her parents, and an example of piety to her latter end. She was taken sick the 24th day of the Ninth month, 1703. In the time of her sickness she uttered many living and weighty expressions, desiring to be dissolved, saying, 'I have not been afraid of death these many years; death is no terror unto me; my God hath taken away its sting.' She being under great weight of bodily affliction, and seeing her husband under trouble for her, said, 'My dear, if it please the Lord to strip thee of thy meet-help again, my God will be thy rock, he hath been thy stay hitherto, and he will never leave thee. The Lord will bring me to his holy hill, and I shall praise him upon Mount Zion, with the saints and holy angels.'

She again said, 'I shall praise thee, O my God, and my Christ, world without end.' Soon after, her husband was moved to pray by her, that the Lord would be pleased to support and strengthen her in her distress and great affliction, and to bear up her exercised soul, and to make them truly willing to submit to his holy will, whether in life or death; at which words she said, 'Amen, Amen.' A little after, her husband asked her how she did, she said, 'I am sweetly comforted in my affliction; the Lord is exceeding good to my soul.' Many more good expressions she uttered upon several occasions, that cannot be remembered. The evening before she departed this life, some friends being come to see her, she said, 'I am weak of body, but the Lord is very good to my soul, and hath filled me with his love; but my bodily weakness is such, that it renders me incapable of praising him as I ought to do.' To her husband she said, 'The Lord hath heard thy prayers for me this morning, and hath satisfied my soul to the full;' more she said to the same purpose, taking her husband's children by the hand, embracing them, and exhorting them to fear the Lord, and to love and obey their father; and said, 'He hath been a good father to you.' A little before she died, she said, 'My God, I come, I come;' and soon after she departed this life, and is entered into that rest that will never have an end.

She died the 28th of the Ninth month, 1705, aged twenty-nine years.

SARAH THOMPSON, daughter of George Thompson, of Crook, in Westmoreland, was a maid who, in her life-time, did truly fear the Lord, and remembered her Creator in the days of her youth. She sought the honour and promotion of truth, according to the measure of grace which she had received; and according to the understanding God had given her, she was faithful, and her understanding was good, and capacity large in things natural, as well as religious. She took great delight in reading the Holy Scriptures, and other religious books, and was careful to put in practice what she did read, and would often be speaking of heavenly things in the family, and exhorting to virtue and patience; for it was a great trouble to her when she saw any impatience or indifference in the family. She was obedient to her parents, and very tender over them; kind and compassionate to all, and was beloved of them that knew her. Her temper was sweet, and of a cheerful spirit and good courage, but not rash, and of few words, and very careful not to give offence to those she was at any time in company with, who were not of our profession in religion, and very sorrowful when she saw any professing the truth, who did not walk answerably to the same.

She was much afflicted with shortness of breath, which she patiently bore, and would say she durst not murmur at it, lest she should offend the Lord. She often retired alone into solitary places, and said that when she had been alone, and meditating upon the things of God, that the Lord did wonderfully break in upon her soul, by his glorious light and good spirit, and let her see over the world, time, and mortality, into eternity, which appearance of his presence did very much affect her. She also said that the Lord had showed her that the time would not be long until he would ease her of all her pain and sorrow, and take her to himself. Another time she said the Lord was present with her, and comforted her in the midst of all her afflictions, and spoke peace to her soul in the midst of her troubles, which she said made hard things easy to her.

She sickened the 1st of the Twelfth month, 1702. In the time of her illness the Lord's power and presence attended her, and she uttered many weighty expressions, with wholesome counsel and advice, to the comfort of those about her. Observing her friends sorrowful, she said, 'You trouble me to see you so; why are you so unwise? It would be more satisfaction to me, if you did not one of you shed a tear for me; must we not all part? What! is death a terror to you? It is no terror to me. I am not at all daunted at it, for I am content whether I live or die; for if I am spared at this time, you must not keep me long, having been sensible some time, that I have not long to live. Cannot you freely give me up, and part with me? I am but a poor infirm creature, and it will be well with me. I shall be freed from many troubles, and from many dangers, which you will be exposed to that stay behind; for I see as long as we are here, we are liable to many temptations. I know they will be exercises to you, but keep to that which is good, and God will keep you, for he hath kept me many a time, as I have kept my mind to him.' This she spoke on the Sixth day of the week, in the afternoon.

At another time, her father and mother, and two sisters, standing at her bed-side, she said to them, 'I must die; and I have a word of counsel to you all; be faithful to your gifts that God hath given you; I beg it of you; and overcharge not your minds with any thing of this world, for you see how frail flesh is, and how soon we are gone;' with many more weighty expressions which were not remembered. After this she said, 'I desire you to remember my words when I am gone, that it may be well with you at your latter end, that you and I may meet in the mansions of glory, where we may never part. And be all of you content, for it is well with me. I have made my peace with God, and I feel nothing to rise up in judgment against me, for the Lord hath forgiven me my sins and mine iniquities, and I feel my mind is very quiet and still, and hath been ever since I begun with this illness. There is nothing cumbereth my mind, not so much as a temptation is presented, and I have been borne over my exercises far beyond my expectation.'

Her brother Isaac being from home, in the service of truth, she said, 'Remember my dear love to my dear brother. If I die, tell him from me, that my soul is gone into everlasting rest, where I hope we shall meet again in the heavenly joy, where we shall never part. I think I have done, and I will take my leave of you;' then taking them one by one by the hand, she kissed them, and bade them all farewell; and said, 'I do not know when my life will go; I would gladly die.' She prayed to the Lord, and continued in prayer a considerable time; in which she was very powerful, and was filled with divine praises, and the power of God was felt by them that were present with her, and their hearts were abundantly comforted, and were made to bless the name of the Lord on her behalf. She prayed fervently for the preservation of those who should be left behind when she was gone; he had kept and preserved her from the many hurtful things that are in this world, and that he would help them through their exercises, as he had helped her many a time, for which she blessed his name, and so concluded her prayer with returning living praises and thanksgivings unto God. Then she signified to them how she had felt the Lord's power to support her in her life-time; 'for,' said she, 'I have often cried to the Lord to help me through my exercises, and he hath answered my prayer many a time, to my great admiration.'

She lay still a while, and afterwards began to pray again to the Lord, with a heavenly sweet melody, which did attend her; but she spoke so low, few of her words could be distinctly understood by them that were present. Then she asked for her grandmother, who was above eighty years of age, who coming to her, she took her by the hand, and said to her, 'Thou art now very ancient: the Lord hath been very merciful to thee, and hath given thee many years, far above what many attain to; and if thou comest short of making thy peace with God, thou canst not say it was for want of days. But see to the improvement of thy gift, I beg of thee before thy days be over, that it may be well with thee at thy latter end, that thy soul and mine may meet again in heavenly joy.' Her cousin, Robert Thompson, a young man, coming in, asked her how she did; she answered, 'I am passing away in peace, and so may all do that keep faithful to their God.'. Then lying quiet, and slumbering a little, afterwards said, 'I have had a sweet dream;' her mother asked what: she answered, 'I thought there were four angels that were conducting me to the land of rest. I have had this dream,' said she, 'twice over, but I am here yet. I am long a going, you have waited long:' her mother said, 'Thy death is hard to win;' she said, 'It will come by and by, I have prayed to the Lord to make my way easy through death.'

Her sickness increasing upon her, she grew very weak, so that it was thought she would not have spoken any more, it being about two hours before her departure, yet the Lord was pleased to give her strength again, so that many weighty words proceeded from her, to the tendering of the hearts of them that were about her, both friends and others. Speaking to her father and mother, desiring them not to mind the things of this world, but to serve the Lord in their day, who is worthy to be served, who is the Lord of lords, and the King of kings; desiring them to remember the words of their dying daughter; exhorting to love and charity, and to be prepared for their latter end, where they might meet in everlasting joy, never to part. Then asking for her cousin above-named, he came to her, and she said, 'Dear cousin, whom I love as my own soul, thou art young, and in the prime of thy time, see thou serve God in the flower of thy age. The Lord hath created thee that thou mightest serve him; see thou answer the end for which thou wast created. And dear cousin, I believe the Lord hath a service for thee if thou be faithful to him, and I wish well for thy soul, as for my own, desiring thou mayest be faithful to God in thy day, that thou mayest have thy account ready, against the day of dissolution, that thou and I may meet again, where we shall live to sing Hosannah to the Lord for evermore.'

Asking for one who was related to her, she said, 'I have something to say to him;' he coming to her, she said to him, 'I remember there was a time when thou thoughtest thou shouldst have died, and thou wast under great exercise, for I believe thou hadst lived a very loose life, and the Lord smote thee with his judgments, and I remember thou madest a vow, that if the Lord would spare thee at that time, thou wouldst amend and do so no more; and it pleased the Lord to spare thee; but oh!' said she, 'hast thou fulfilled thy vow?' She exhorted him to more faithfulness, that he might obtain peace to his soul, before the day of his visitation went over his head. She said to her sisters, 'Be sure you be good to my mother when I am gone, and mind not the fading things of this world;' after which she spoke not many words; but if she was asked how she did, she would reply, 'I am very well, and in a sweet frame; I am going to a sweet place!'

She departed the 6th day of the Twelfth month, being the Seventh day of the week, about the first hour in the afternoon, 1702. Aged nineteen years.

JAMES BAINES, son of William and Sarah Baines, of Strangerthwait in the county of Westmoreland, was one who began to seek the Lord in his young years. As he grew in sincerity and zeal for the blessed truth, and increased in his concern for the promotion thereof, some time before he died, God opened his mouth in a public testimony for the Lord Jesus Christ and his pure religion; in which he was very fervent, having a sight how eminently God would appear for those who were faithful. He had a word of encouragement to them, but was sharp in judgment to the backsliders and unfaithful: and although he was under much affliction, by reason of bodily infirmities and distempers which grew upon him, yet he was more and more devoted to truth's service, as if he had known that his time was not to be long in this world, even to within some hours that his last sickness seized upon him. Notwithstanding he was under great pain and exercise of body, yet the power and presence of the Lord were with him, which was his great support and strength. He often spoke of the goodness of God to his soul, and of that inward sweetness, peace and comfort, that the Lord was pleased to afford to him in his afflictions, to the great satisfaction of those who were present.

He gave much wholesome advice in the time of his sickness to Friends and others, and spoke of the prosperity of truth, and said in particular to his relations as followeth: 'As we are children of believing parents, and have had our education amongst Friends, so I would not have you to rest contented there, but be solid, and weighty, and humble yourselves under the mighty hand of God; and as you abide here you will feel the goodness of the Lord to spring in your souls, to your great comfort and inward peace and satisfaction. I know our natural tempers are inclinable to be light and airy, like other people, therefore we have more occasion to be bowed and weighty in our minds.' Speaking concerning tithes, he desired Friends would keep up their testimony against them; 'For,' said he, 'I could have slipped sufferings if I would have given way to it, but it was a thing I durst not do; but I accounted it a great mercy that the Lord had blessed me with something to part with for his name and truth's sake.' Although he suffered pretty much at times, upon the account of tithes, yet the Lord's goodness to him did overbalance all, so that he had a word of encouragement to others on that account.

Upon occasion, speaking of the uncertainty of riches, he said, 'At some time I pursued them, and they fled from me;' but this use he said he made of it; 'to conclude it was not a city here I was to look after, but one in the heavens, whose maker and builder is God.' This he spoke as caution to others. At several times he expressed his great peace with God here, and full assurance of eternal blessedness in the world to come, through the atonement made by the Lord Jesus Christ, and the work of sanctification of his Spirit. The day before he died, hearing that that ancient Friend, Anne Camm, was deceased, he said, 'Ah! that honest, honourable woman, is she gone to her eternal rest before me? I shall follow her very shortly, where we shall meet never to part again.' Many were the comfortable expressions and seasonable advices which he gave forth in his sickness, that cannot be remembered; and as, in his lifetime, he honoured the truth, so was his latter end comfortable and full of peace; in which he departed this life, the 1st of the Tenth month, 1705, aged fifty-one years; and was buried at Friends' burying-ground, at Sedbergh meeting-house.

Postscript.—The Testimony of Isaac Alexander concerning James Baines, in a letter dated the 8th of the Tenth month, 1705, who also died the 11th of the Twelfth month, after him.

'Our truly beloved and esteemed friend, James Baines, departed this life the 1st of this instant; and though he was afflicted with great pain, yet he bore it with admirable patience. Though I live remote from him, and notwithstanding my unfitness, I went often to visit him; and I do not remember that since I came amongst Friends, any Friend was so universally visited by all sorts of people as he was, especially by faithful Friends. Neither did I ever visit a Friend in such a case, who had that reach upon all sorts of people, both in the expressions he declared in the time of his sickness, and also the frame of his spirit. It was admirably reaching and melting, beyond what I can express, and so continued to the end, as sweet and sensible as ever. He died with the greatest esteem and love to Friends and truth, and in great esteem and interest in the hearts of Friends; he died in a most happy and blessed condition.

'ISAAC ALEXANDER.'

JOHN BLAIKLING, of Draw-well, in the parish of Sedbergh, in Yorkshire, bordering on Westmoreland, was born in the Ninth month, 1625, and he and his wife, and his father and mother, were people of good repute and esteem amongst all that knew them, being all very religiously inclined from their youth. They were all convinced of the truth in the Third month, 1652, by the ministry of that truly honourable servant of Christ, George Fox, whom they received into their house with joy, because of the glad tidings of salvation that he brought to them; soon after which John Blaikling accompanied George Fox to Firbank chapel, where many were also convinced of truth. About the latter end of the year 1654, or beginning of 1655, John Blaikling received a dispensation of the gospel to publish to the world, and was very serviceable therein to many, and soon after, he was called by the Lord into the county of Durham, Northumberland, and the east of Yorkshire, where he had then, and many times since in his frequent visits of those places, good service, and was with great respect received and loved whilst he lived. A few years after, he travelled into Scotland, visiting a great part of that nation, and in his return, as well as going out, visited the northern counties of England. After it pleased God to raise up others to bear testimony of his truth in the meeting John Blaikling belonged to, and the adjacent meetings, to answer the service in part, which before lay much upon John, he was not only glad thereof, but a great encourager of them, and all others at all times that came up in a public testimony for the Lord Jesus Christ, who is the true light.

He also travelled into many other cities and counties; as at London, Bristol, Lincolnshire, Norfolk, Suffolk, and Essex, and most counties of England, and many times to London; in which service he faithfully continued till weakness of body and old age prevented. The last time he visited London, was when he came up to the yearly meeting in 1698; that service being over, he visited the most of Friends' meetings in the county of Kent, and his service was very acceptable amongst them.

He was endued with a great gift of discerning, of solid judgment, and deep understanding in heavenly things, as well as in the things relating to this life; his ministry was attended with power, and though his utterance was not eloquent, yet full of profound and weighty matter, suitable to the several states in the auditory where he did minister. He was an example in a tender, humble life and conversation, and zealous for good order in the Church of Christ, as well as steadfast in opposing and bearing testimony against such as would endeavour to break unity, and so lead into a loose liberty, disorder, and confusion, as well as other evil works. It was at J. Blaikling's house, which is called Draw-well, that the memorable meeting was held for the endeavouring the recovery of John Story, and John Wilkinson, and others, who opposed the good order and discipline now established in the churches of Christ. The said meeting began upon the 3d day of the Second month, 1676, and continued four days: but notwithstanding the labours of many brethren met at that time from divers parts of the nation, and particularly four Friends from the city of London, the said John Story and John Wilkinson continued in their contention and opposition to Friends; and not long after William Rogers published a book against Friends, which J. Blaikling, &c., answered, entitled 'Antichristian treachery discovered, and its way blocked up;' a volume in folio, of about 50 sheets.

He was a great supporter of such as were in low circumstances in the world, often assisted them in difficult cases, to the exposing himself to great hazard of loss; and many times he was blessed with good success therein. He obtained the blessing of a peace-maker, being of a good understanding, was qualified with judgment and patience to reconcile differences about temporal affairs, which was a means to bring him into many concerns of trust for orphans, &c., which is always attended with great care and trouble, and which often fell to his lot. The loss of him in the church, as well as among the neighbourhood, is great. He was not only called to believe in, and preach Christ Jesus, the truth, the way, and the life, but also to suffer for his name's sake, not only by loss of goods to a great value, but also by imprisonments several times at York, about sixty miles from his family, both on account of meetings for the worship of God, and in a firm testimony against tithes. Whilst he had strength, he was diligent in attending meetings; but old age and bodily infirmities growing upon him latterly, sometimes prevented him. Several times he expressed to friends in private the comfort that he had in the Lord's peace and presence with him to his satisfaction in his old age, and that his day's work was nigh done, and his reward and rest with God sure. This testimony agrees with the last letter I received from him, save one part, as followeth:

'Dear John,

'I love thee in the truest love that springs from Jesus Christ the fountain thereof, by and in which my life standeth; though as to bodily health and strength I grow weak and feeble, but my life in God standeth, whose I am, and I am comfortably content. I am scarcely able to walk to the door, nor have I been at a meeting these several weeks, but the Lord's will be done. I am comforted in the remembrance of my former services for the Lord, his truth, and people, for which I want not my reward in this my old age. I take time to read. I am almost blind, yet well content.

'J. Blaikling.'

He often signified his preparedness to leave this world, with fervent desires for truth's prosperity, and the preservation of unity and concord amongst brethren, in a faithful and steady testimony for the same in every part thereof, as led into by God's power in the beginning. Not long before his death, his ancient and intimate friend and acquaintance Thomas Camm being with him, he said to him, 'Thou and I have not sought our own interest, but have devoted ourselves to serve the Lord, his truth and people; he is, and will be our great reward in the end of all our troubles. I am greatly satisfied that I have faithfully served the Lord, and done my day's work, and enjoy the earnest of that peace and rest God hath laid up for his people; and if thou and I shall never have opportunity to meet again in the outward, yet in eternity our spirits, with the spirits of just men made perfect, shall meet never to part again. I pray God with all my soul, if it be his will for his truth and people's sake, to lengthen thy days, and grant thee that strength of body and health, that at least thou mayest be able once more to visit London, Bristol, and the southern parts of this nation, which will be of great service, and acceptable unto many.' This he spoke with great tenderness of spirit; to which Thomas Camm replied, 'The will of the Lord be done, I am in his hand:' so in much brokenness embracing and kissing each other, they parted; this was four or five days before his death. He had a short sickness, and an easy death, falling into a fainting fit, as sometimes before.

He passed quietly away out of this world, without sigh or groan, wanting about four months of eighty years, and was honourably buried at Friends' burial-place, at Sedbergh meeting-house, the 4th day of the Fifth month, 1705.

THOMAS GILPIN was born in the year 1622, son of Thomas Gilpin, of Mill-hill, in the parish of Caton, near Lancaster. His parents had five sons, and five daughters, whereof Thomas was youngest son; they were people of good repute in the country, and were religious, being called Puritans, who educated their children very strictly. After his father's decease, his mother removed with her children to Kendal, in Westmoreland, five of her children being dead; and she was so zealous as to force them into acts of religion before they knew what they did, as to pray without a form, &c. Thomas being but about ten years of age, considered it was not right, for he said he knew not who to pray to. After he grew up in more years, and his mother deceased, he ran into foolish and wanton delights, as sports and pastime, music and dancing. He went to London as apprentice to a tallow-chandler, and after went into the wars, (being the time of the civil wars in England,) where he was tempted into more evils. Yet in all this time the Lord followed him by his good spirit, reproving him in his own conscience for his sins, which brought great fear and trouble upon him; but by one means or other he endeavoured to get over these convictions, and so continued a considerable time striving against the good spirit of God. But oftentimes the Lord again did awaken him, and brought the consideration of death upon him, even in the time of sickness, and of battle, which he was often in. Then he would cry to the Lord for mercy, and that he would deliver him from death at such times, making promises of reformation for the future. And God was merciful and spared him, yet he forgot his promises and covenants, and fell into the same evils again; after which the Lord brought double fear and torment upon him.

At last he received the blessed truth, as preached by the people called Quakers; and in believing in and obeying the light and spirit of Christ manifested in his own heart, he came to receive power over those sins which had prevailed in times past over him, and so came truly to know repentance, and remission of sins, in the name of Jesus Christ, the true light of the world. And afterwards, in the remembrance of the unspeakable long-suffering and mercy of God unto him, he said in his life-time, 'Shall it not be recorded to posterity for the benefit of my children, and my children's children, that it may be a warning to the obstinate and rebellious, to turn from the evil of their ways, whilst the spirit of the Lord striveth with them, lest the day of their visitation go over their heads.'

In 1653 Ambrose Rigg, Thomas Robinson, and Jane Waugh, came into the county of Oxford, to preach the free gospel of the grace of God; at which time Thomas Gilpin received their testimony. After eight or nine years waiting upon God in silence, God gave him a dispensation of the same gospel to preach to others, and he became an able minister, showing himself approved unto God, a workman that need not be ashamed, rightly dividing the word of truth. In this service he laboured much, travelling through many parts of England, but chiefly in the counties of Oxford, Berks, and Bucks; he was a prisoner for his testimony to the truth twice at Oxford, and once in Newgate in London. His settlement was in the parish of Warborough, in the county of Oxford, where he married Joan, the daughter of Thomas Bartholomew, of the same parish, husbandman; in which place he was instrumental to settle a church or meeting of the people called Quakers, which remaineth to this day, as well as in many other parts where he travelled. He was successful by his ministry to turn many to righteousness, and for building them up, and establishing them in the most holy faith.

In the year 1702, and the eightieth of his age, he was weak in body for the most part of the winter, but complained little of either sickness or pain, his body gradually decaying. In the time of his sickness he desired one of his sons to remember his dear love to friends, and give them account of his sickness and departure. As he was zealous for God and his truth in the time of his health, so he was to his end, for he went to Friends' meetings for the worship of God as long as he was able, saying, 'I am willing to be a good example so long as I have strength to go.' When he was so weak that he could hardly go out of his chamber, he desired friends to meet in his room, which was not long before he died; at which time he signified to friends that he was satisfied, that as to words he must cease, but this was his comfort, that he enjoyed the power of the Word of life, which is beyond all words. He exhorted friends to faithfulness, and to keep their meetings, and not to look out at his being removed from them; putting them in mind of the goodness and love of God, which had been largely manifested both to him and them, in carrying them through many trials and exercises, and in preserving them in love and unity one with another, which he desired they would be careful to continue in. When he had done speaking, a friend prayed, and Thomas Gilpin's heart was much comforted in feeling the presence of the Lord, as well as those present, who were much tendered and broken into tears, and at the conclusion he again recommended love and unity one with another; and also declared that he was given up in the will of the Lord, and took his leave of them all.

This was the last meeting he had with friends; but he was much visited by friends, and it was a comfort and delight to him to see them, and sometimes it was hard for him to part with them, saying, 'This is such a parting as we never had before.' The Lord was very good to him all the time of his sickness, and did often cause his heart in the feeling of life to sound forth praises to the name of God; and he said he believed he as much desired to die, as ever any one did desire to live, although he wanted for nothing in this world; but said, 'I long to be dissolved, and be with the Lord, yet am willing to wait God's good pleasure.' The day before he died, viz. the 2d of the 12th month, some friends visiting him, he desired one of them to supplicate the Lord on his behalf, to put an end to his days, and make his passage easy. After some time the friend prayed to that purpose; when he had done, Thomas Gilpin lifting up his hands, said, 'The Lord grant thy request which thou hast made to him this day.' Though at that time to outward appearance he seemed likely to have lived some days, yet he quickly altered, and the morrow, about the fifth hour in the afternoon, he departed this life, being the 3d day of the Twelfth month, 1702. He left behind him three sons and two daughters, and all of them had children.

He was buried honourably the 8th of the Twelfth month, 1702, after he had professed truth forty-nine years, and had been a minister of the gospel forty years.

RICHARD ANDREWS, son of Richard Andrews, late of London, silk-man, and his mother, one of the daughters of our ancient friend, Thomas Gilpin aforesaid, was educated by his father-in-law, Moses West, of Hempsted, in Hertfordshire, and his own mother, not only in useful learning, in order to his accomplishment for trade and good settlement in the world, but also it was their great care to have him brought up in the way of truth. He was put apprentice in London to the silk trade; but after some years, what by the examples of others, and temptations of the enemy, he declined from his former simplicity and sobriety, and good inclination to truth, into more liberty and vain company and fashions of the world, which was a grief to his father and mother.

He was taken ill about eight or nine months before he died, of a decay of nature, which terminated in a consumption; and such was the goodness of God to him, that he was awakened in himself to a consideration of his inward condition, the visitation of God by his spirit being upon him, and he had frequent visions in the night of the near approach of his latter end. Being at Hempsted with his father and mother, he had opportunity to retire alone into private places, where he poured out his soul to the Lord in supplication, and great travail of soul came upon him, especially towards his latter end, for he was bowed in deep humility, praying for the light of God's countenance, in whose presence is life, peace and comfort. But the Lord was pleased to chastise him, by hiding his face from him for a time, yet he kept his hold, trusting in the Lord; though in this state he met with many assaults from the devil, and temptations to despond of God's mercy. Now he knew what it was to read in the book of conscience, and for his works to go beforehand to judgment. Now he disliked the company of those young men, his former companions, with whom he used to walk abroad in the fields, sometimes on First-day afternoon, and neglecting going to meeting for the public worship of God, which now became a very great trouble to him, and that he should spend his precious time so vainly. His powdering and apparelling, and such like follies, he particularly expressed a great sorrow for, promising that if the Lord should prolong his days, he would endeavour to follow the best examples and strictest way of living amongst faithful Friends; calling to mind, and praising the good life of his grandfather Gilpin.

A friend visiting him, together with the good advice of his father concerning the Lord's hand that was upon him, it being not in anger but in mercy, that he might turn unto him, with fervent desire after him, and enjoyment of him, and when he should obtain that, his wants should be supplied; so after some time the Lord did appear in him, and did lift up his spirit as a standard against the enemy of his soul, who came in like a flood, and tempted him to doubt of his mercy, so that he was comforted like a man reprieved from judgment, though not as yet having a full assurance of his pardon; but a living hope sprang up more and more, which became as an anchor to his mind. His company became delightful, because of those serious reflections he made on things, and religious discourses which he had with those about him. One time he said to his father and mother, 'I will appeal to you, if you ever heard me repine at the exercise and pain I have gone through since I have been at home, all this time of my great weakness? No,' said he, 'I have desired the Lord to let me have all my punishment in this life.' Indeed, he was sweet and cheerful under all his pain, which was very great; and he grew very bright and living when he had got dominion over his doubts and fears.

Near his latter end, through the prevalency of his distemper, he was somewhat broken in understanding, and wandered in his discourse, though his talk was inoffensive; yet, as if he had foreseen this, a little before, a kinsman of his, not one called a Quaker, offered to tarry with him; to which he showed himself unwilling, giving this reason to his father and mother, saying, 'May be I shall be light-headed, and ramble in my words, and he or others may inconsiderately reflect upon my profession.' Though his sickness was long, his death was pretty sudden, having kept his bed but four days, in which time, whilst sensible, he was kept in a most sweet, resigned frame of soul; being by his bed-side was like being in a well-replenished meeting.

Near his end, he said to his father and mother, 'Do not grieve, the Lord is with me,' with much more to the same purpose; so lying still and quiet, he went away with a smile, and is at peace with the Lord.

He died about the twenty-first year of his age.

PRISCILLA RICHARDS, daughter of John Richards, of Howsey, near Liskeard, in the county of Cornwall, and of Priscilla his wife, was born at Liskeard the 18th of the Sixth month, 1680; and though educated in her father's family, who were mostly strangers to the living way of truth, now in this our age revealed, only her mother frequented the meetings of the people called Quakers; yet did this young maiden begin according to the advice of the wise man, to remember her Creator in the days of her youth. She not only came to the meetings of the said people, but turned with her heart to the Lord; and as she came towards seventeen years of age, she grew in the fear of God, and in plainness and solidity, not regarding the gaiety of this perishing world so as to set her heart thereon, but became very modest in her habit, speech, gesture, and in all her deportment, and was greatly in love with the company of the best Friends, to whom she also became very acceptable. Though the family in which she lived might minister occasion to her, to look out at the ways and glory of this world, yet she was as one weaned therefrom, and delighted in retirement of spirit, and in that society which might be helpful to her in her way to that heavenly habitation to which she was travelling, and whereunto the Lord brought her in the very prime of her blooming years.

She was scarcely twenty years of age when she was visited with some infirmities of body, which still drove her nearer the Lord; and although she met with some exercises grievous to her tender spirit, yet she was resigned to the will of God. About the beginning of the year 1704, it was perceived by some symptoms, that her distemper tended to a dropsy, in which abundanee of care, both of parents and able physicians was used, yet her disease increased, so that it was apparent some months before she died, that there was little or no hopes of her recovery, which she foresaw, yet was very well satisfied and resigned to the will of God, in which she had peace and great quietness of mind, and would often testify as much to her mother and those about her, as well as friends who frequently visited her; for she having her affections drawn out of the world, it became easier to her to leave it.

In a letter to a particular friend, who married her near relation, written about fourteen days before she died, she says thus:

'Dear Cousin,

'I should have given an account of my sickness, but exceeding illness hindered me, and my mother, what with sorrow for me, and want of time, occasioned the same neglect. I am now very ill, being swollen all over my body, except my hands and arms, and am scarcely able to walk the chamber without help; but I am freely given up to the will of my heavenly Father, whether for life or death. I should be glad to see any of you here, for my time in this world is not likely to be long. I have been a little better at my heart this four or five days, but how it will please the Lord to deal with me, I know not. My dear love is to thee, thy wife and children, wishing you health and peace in this life, and happiness in the life to come; being, dear cousin, thy affectionate, &c.,

'P. Richards.'

This was written in a time of great weakness of body, but her spirit was strong in the Lord, having kept the faith, and by it was made a conqueror. About this time, her mother sitting by her, she said, 'It is well for me that I feared the Lord in my youth, seeing old age is not likely to be my lot.'

Those friends who visited her in the time of her weakness, were greatly comforted in the testimony she gave, and sense they had of her living condition of soul, in a dying state of body. To a friend who said to her, 'I hope, if thou dost recover, thou wilt live to praise the Lord;' she replied, I do not desire life upon any other terms.' Her expressions were many and frequent as to her peace and acquiescence of mind, but, her friends not supposing her end to be so near, they were not duly written down. Her mother at a certain time, hearing her speaking of her willingness to be with the Lord, said, 'What! hast thou no sympathy with my sorrow and grief, at the parting from thee,' &c., she replied, 'Mother, thou beginnest to grow old, and it will not be long ere we meet again in a better place, if we are found doing the will of God.'

In this sweetness of temper she abode without reluctancy or impatience at her state of body, which decayed daily. On the twelfth of the Seventh month, 1704, she was taken with some fainting fits, which made her attendants stir more than usual, at which she reviving said, 'Why did you not let me alone, I was very easy, and in much quiet;' and then turning to her mother, she said, 'Time will come; do not grieve, nor make the Lord angry.' To some about her, 'Do not leave repentance until a dying hour, for the body hath enough to do to bear its pains.' At night, her father going to bed, took leave of her. She said, 'If she never saw or spoke to him more, she was well.' But then her pains returned on her, yet she got up the next day, but had again some such dying fits, however continued till the next day after, always being very sensible, under no manner of disturbance in mind. On the 14th of the Seventh month, being sensibly weakened, and feeling the approaches of death, she said, 'Come, come, come, why so long;' and in a very little time after called out, 'Lord Jesus, receive my spirit,' and presently breathed forth her last, according to her prayer to the Lord, that she might not go stupified out of the world, for she died in full understanding, and soundness of mind, and is gone to rest in the Lord, blessed be his name for ever.

On the 18th of the Seventh month, 1704, her body was decently buried, from her father's house, in Friends' burial ground, in the parish of Liskeard.

Thus we have here an example of what one of old said of youth that is soon perfected, which shall condemn the many years and old age of the ungodly.

WILLIAM TURNER, of Hitchin, in Hertfordshire, was one who sought after truth and righteousness from his childhood, and when but a youth complained to a professor that he much desired an inward acquaintance with the Lord, and to be acquainted with the spirit of God, was what his soul longed for. The professor advised him to be acquainted with the Scriptures, which he had done before, and could not be satisfied with the reading of what God did for his people in former ages, without feeling after God and knowing him for himself. And it pleased the Lord in the riches of his love to answer the desires of his soul, and to open the way of life, and to manifest the truth, as believed by the people called Quakers. He was convinced thereof, when he was about twenty years of age, by the ministry of Thomas Green, and having attained to that which his soul longed for, viz. the true knowledge of God, he presently became obedient to the good spirit of God, and suffered both spoiling of his goods and imprisonment for the truth's sake; his love to which he manifested by bearing a faithful testimony to the same. He was a man of a blameless life and godly conversation, having regard to the honour of truth in all things, seeking the advancement thereof over and above his own temporal interest. He was a hearty lover of the friends of truth, and especially of the faithful publishers of the gospel, whom his heart and house were always open to receive. He was a lover of peace and unity in the church, and steady in his testimony against looseness and undue liberty, and those who opposed gospel order. He was indeed a pillar in the church, and a careful overseer in the flock, whom sometimes he was concerned to exhort in a brief testimony; which being delivered in much tenderness and brokenness of spirit, was of service and comfort to the faithful people of God.

He was much afflicted with pain and weakness of body a considerable time before he died, but bore it with much patience. His wife cannot remember that she ever heard one unadvised word proceed out of his mouth all the time of his illness; and he would say, that his affliction was not laid upon him in anger, but whom the Lord loved, he chastiseth. When his wife bewailed the loss she should have of him, he said, 'It will be better for me to go hence, for I shall be at rest and peace, where there shall be no more trouble.' About three days before his death, he called for his children and said, 'What I have to say, I shall speak in a few words, but remember them when I am gone. Mind truth above all, and then God will bless you! and be kind to your mother, and do nothing without her advice; and do not marry to any but them that love truth well.' He charged his children to be none of them that strive to stay at home, but strive who shall go to meeting. A little before he died, he said, 'I find nothing but that it will be well with me to all eternity.' To his eldest daughter Elizabeth, wife of John Pryor, he said, 'Be an upright-hearted woman, and walk uprightly before the Lord.'

He departed this life the 6th of the First month, 1704, in the sixty-first year of his age, after he had believed in truth forty-one years. His body was decently buried in Friends' burying-ground at Hitchin.

FRANCIS BLAIKLING, of Winder, near Sedberg, in Yorkshire, was a harmless man from his youth, born of good sober parentage. He was convinced of the blessed truth about the the time of George Fox's first coming to publish truth, which was in the year 1652. He gladly received the truth in the love of it, and faithfully walked in it, and cheerfully suffered for it, not only extreme spoiling his goods, but by a pretty long imprisonment in York castle. The Lord not only gave him to believe and to suffer, but also gave him a part of the ministry, to testify unto the blessed truth, which he had believed in, and to that word of reconciliation, nigh in the heart. In work, according to his measure, he was a faithful labourer, though he did not travel far abroad; neither was his testimony long, but it was very easy and comfortable to the faithful; and he, in a plain testimony, hit the mark, both in reproof to the wicked and the comfort of true mourners in Sion. He was a man well beloved, and esteemed both by Friends and others; wherefore, in the time of his sickness, many came to visit him, who found him in a comfortable frame of spirit; he patiently enduring those bodily infirmities which he was under, and much resigned in his mind to God's will, whether for life or death, often saying, the Lord was, and always had been, very good and favourable to him, and he found nothing but peace to his soul from the Lord, and he was ready to leave this world whenever the Lord pleased to call him out of it.

Thus in much patience and cheerfulness his spirit was borne up in his sickness, increasing in sweetness of spirit, and in expressions which are not written down, being not perfectly remembered. As he lived in love and unity with his brethren, so he died, saying to many friends who came to visit him, 'Dear friend, my love and life is with thee.'

He departed this life the 20th of the First month, 1704, aged seventy-three years, a believer in truth fifty-two years.

An Account of some remarkable words spoken by HAYES HAMILTON, son of Hugh Hamilton, of Ireland, a little before his death. Aged twelve years.

HE said he had been several times in a place by himself, where he wished he had been for ever, he enjoyed so much of the comfortable presence of the Lord in silent waiting upon him, and meditating in his law, which drew his soul in a rapture. He also told his schoolmaster, about twelve days before he died, the day he left the school (as the said schoolmaster did testify), that his said master should see him go no more that way, until he saw him carried to his burial. His master asked the reason for his saying so. He said he knew that he had taken the small-pox, and that he should die of that disease, which accordingly came to pass about twelve days following.

He hearing his mother reading the first of Cor. xv. 50, where the apostle Paul says, "Flesh and blood cannot inherit the kingdom of God," he asked his father what he thought of that saying; the father turned that question to his son, and asked his opinion of it; he replied, as God was a spirit, that which was for his use, he would make it spiritual, and therefore no longer flesh and blood.

When troubled with several questions about baptism, he said he could prove from Ephes. iv. 5, that there was one Lord, one faith, and one baptism; and he said, 'them that will be satisfied with that of water, let them hold it; for my part, I depend nothing upon it. I depend only upon the baptism of the spirit, and I doubt there are many that talk most about baptism, know very little what it is.'

He was taken sick, and about a quarter of an hour before he died he sat up in his bed, his mother and sisters by him, and he asked what day of the week it was. She told him, and he asked the hour of the day, the which she told; then he said, 'Heaven is not far from me;' his aunt asked him if he was willing to leave his father and mother, and all the world, to go to heaven; he said, 'Yes, I am;' and further said, 'It is a sweet change.' She desired the Lord to prepare him, and clear the way for him; he looking in her face, said, 'I know the way, and who hath cleared it.' And so died in peace, the 7th of the Third month, 1697, in the twelfth year and seventh month of his age.

THE dying words of THOMAS VOKINS, son of Richard and Joan Vokins, of West Charlow, in the county of Berks. The day before his departure he prayed thus: 'Oh! blessed God, if it be thy will to take me this night, make my passage easy; not my will be done; thy will be done. Oh, Lord! thou deliveredst Jacob out of all his troubles.'

Another time he said, 'There is a good spirit as well as a bad spirit; and if the good spirit be taken heed unto, it will be felt as strong to lead into good, as the bad spirit is to lead into wickedness.' Not one hour before he died, his mother and others being present, he said, 'Mother, the Lord is exceedingly good to me, and hath been all along the eight or nine weeks of my exercises, and when I could hardly speak, his sweet presence hath been with me, and his life hath sweetly refreshed me.'

As his mother sat by him, she felt the power of the Lord, and spoke to Friends in the chamber to be still, and this innocent young man died like a lamb, without sigh or groan, and those present felt the power of the Lord with him at his departure, and were greatly refreshed; much was spoken by him of the goodness of the Lord, but his voice being low, it could not well be heard.

He died the 23d of the Second month, 1683.

RICHARD VOKINS, brother to the aforesaid Thomas Vokins, in the time of his sickness, kept feeding in retirement within, and when he first took his bed he examined himself before the Lord thus; saying, 'Lord, have I done any thing to offend thee, have I wronged any man?' and desiring the Lord would take off all reproach from his people. During his sickness he was preserved in a quiet frame of mind, no impatient words coming from him; expressing how the Lord had preserved him in true simplicity, which was his great comfort, and gave good advice to several who came to see him; saying to them; 'It is well with me, you cannot think what I enjoy.' In the time of his health, he was an humble, tender-hearted man, considerate of his servants and poor people that worked for him; often saying that he would not enrich himself out of their labours; and was glad when he could do good to any. One time he called for his two children, and prayed the Lord to bless them; his wife asked him, if it did not seem hard to part with them; to which he replied, 'No, all is well, there is nothing troubles me, all is well;' desiring his dear children might take him for an example, and live no worse a life than he had done.

After this, his wife said, 'The Lord is able to raise thee again if it be his will;' he replied, 'I know he is able, but he doth not intend to restore me again;' and he told his doctor he could do him no good. In the time of his sickness, the impropriator and servants cleared his orchard of apples to the value of £4, for tithes. His wife asked if those people plundering them did not trouble him, he replied, 'No, not at all, the Lord forgive them, they know not what they do.' When his wife perceived his speech to alter, she again asked him if he was willing to leave the world; he replied, 'Yes, very willing;' soon after, his speech went quite away, and next day he died in peace, being the 12th of the Eighth month, 1696.

ELIZABETH WILLS, daughter of Daniel and Mary Wills, of Northampton River, in West Jersey, in America, was on the 2d of Eighth month, 1687, visited with an ague and fever, which continuing some days hard upon her, she often called upon the Lord, saying, 'The Lord help me, the Lord ease me;' patiently begging of God for help in her great exercise, and her cries were felt to proceed from the stirrings of life. About the tenth hour of the sixth day of her sickness, her extremity being great, she desired to be remembered to her mother, who at that time was very ill in another chamber, and her mother understanding it, she came to her, which much satisfied the child. Turning to her mother, she embraced her, and said, 'O mother, I will lie with thee;' and when she had manifested her kindness and tender love to her mother, for a little time lay still; there being her father and sister in the room, she raised herself upright without help, and said, 'Now I am well;' giving living praises and thanksgiving to God, saying, 'Lord God of power and glory; all power, glory and honour be given to thee for ever, Amen; for thou hast helped me, thou glorious God of life. Thou hast eased my heart, O thou powerful God of glory; praises, and glory, and honour, be given to thee for ever, Amen. O thou God of eternal glory! what shall I say unto thee? all praises be given unto thy name, thou glorious God of life, thou hast helped my soul; praises for ever be given unto thee, for ever, and for ever. Amen.' Often saying in this wise, 'What I speak, God gives me to speak;' and then speaking much more to the same effect, all tending to the praise and glory of God, and to the extolling of his great and wonderful name; often saying, 'God is good, God hath touched my heart.'

Thus she remained praising and giving thanks to God for the space of an hour, and it grew towards midnight. Then she desired her two brothers, and her younger sister should be called, who were in their beds, and when they came, she looked upon them, but still remained praising and glorifying God, often saying, 'Now I am well, I feel no pain. I am willing to live; I am willing to die. I am willing to leave the world, or I am willing to stay in the world;' often saying, 'I am content to live or to die;' which expressions greatly tendered the hearts of all present. She again spoke much, praising and magnifying the great name of God, to the same effect as before; several times saying, 'What I speak, God gives me to speak;' also saying, 'I did not know God would have given me so much to speak, for I was never sensible of these things before.' Then she took her father by the hand, and kissed him, saying, 'Farewell, my dear father;' and then took her mother by the hand, and kissed her, saying, 'Farewell, my dear mother;' and then her brothers, taking each of them by the hand, and kissing them, saying, 'Farewell, my dear brothers;' and lastly, took her sisters by the hand, and kissed them, saying, 'Farewell, my dear sisters.' Her father hearing her use that expression to every one of them, he called her by her name, saying, 'Where is that farewell thou speakest of?' she looked upon her father, and readily answered, saying, 'It is in my heart.'

Her speech was so affecting, that it exceedingly tendered the hearts, and caused tears to run much from the eyes, of all present; which she beholding, as one without all sense of sorrow, looked upon her father, saying, 'Father, thou art troubled;' he answered, no, he was not troubled, but glad; saying it was more to him to behold her in that condition, than life, or length of days. Then she said, 'I am well pleased.' She beholding her mother weeping, said, 'My mother is troubled;' her mother answered, saying, she was not troubled, but desired her to be content in the will of God. Then she said, 'I am content.' She caused her brothers and sisters to speak their minds one by one, of their satisfaction concerning her condition, which was done by them. She hearing their sayings, was well satisfied; she often said, as she was parting with them, 'God has eased me of my pain.' And after a little time she talked familiarly with them, as one that ailed nothing; and in her discourse, spoke in this manner, saying, 'James Martin (who was a minister of the gospel) is a good man; I would I could see him, but he is gone to England; I shall see him no more; and John is a good man;' her father, standing by, asked her what John; and she said, 'that John who had a meeting in the barn,' (which was John Hayton); likewise she said, 'I shall see him no more.' She also said, 'Thomas Olive is a good man, and I shall see him to-morrow,' which accordingly she did. When James Martin went away, she said, 'I am sure I cried;' and said again, 'Would I could see him.' Her father desired her to be satisfied, saying, 'God has given thee a share of that same life which James hath;' so she mentioned him no more, but something further of the goodness of God to her, and spoke of one Sarah Kem, saying she was a good child, she died well.

She lay still, and after a little time her sense of pain came again, and then she called upon the Lord, saying, 'The Lord help me, the Lord ease me;' and as it increased, the more earnestly she called upon the Lord, saying, 'O Lord, how shall I ascend to thee, that thou mayest hear me?' And in time the

Lord gave her some ease, and she took some rest; and the ninth day, being the first day of the week, Friends coming to the meeting, several came to see her before the meeting, unto whom she put forth her hand, and tenderly asked several of them how they did; but after meeting she seemed to be somewhat more weakened, and not so quick of memory, but took her leave of several friends, as they came to her.

That day she several times inquired for a servant boy, who she knew to be negligent, and often would lie out all night, and at the same time was gone, and that night late he came again. She desired to speak with him, so soon as she heard he was come. When he came to her, she turned herself, and steadfastly looked upon him, as one renewed with sense and strength, saying, 'God gave me much to speak last night, and thou wast not here. It is better for thee that thou shouldest walk with God. Thou must die as well as I; thou must go to the grave as well as I; and if thou dost not do better thou shalt have torment, and I shall have peace. It would be better for thee that thou wouldest walk with God, but time is past and gone, and cannot be recalled.' Saying to him, 'Is it not better for thee to do well than ill?' Her father standing by, asked her what she would have him to do then, if time were past. She answered, she would have him do well, but she believed he would not; she then said he might go away; and some time after called to him again, saying, she would not have him forget what she had said to him.

On the 11th of the Eighth month, 1687, she departed this life, having laid down her head in peace and rest with the Lord.

RICHARD PIKE, late of Cork, in Ireland, was born at Newbury, in England, in or about the year 1627, and came from Ireland, belonging to the horse in the army, which were sent from England, for the reduction of that nation, upon the rebellion of the natives. While he was in the army he had the character of a very sober, conscientious man, but of great courage, for which he was much esteemed by his superior officers. In those days he was accounted religiously inclined, and one who sought the Lord, and the Lord was pleased to be found of him, and revealed his truth to him. In or about the year 1655, the Lord sent some of his faithful ministers, called Quakers, to that nation to preach the everlasting gospel, by whom he was convinced of the way of life and salvation, to which he became truly obedient, and soon denied the use of carnal weapons for the destruction of mankind; and in other things taking up the cross of Christ, despising the shame, and for truth's sake became a great sufferer, by patiently enduring reproaches, abuses and imprisonments, as well as loss of outward substance. As he was a faithful follower of the Lord Jesus, so he was greatly beloved by all faithful friends who knew him; and his deportment, conversation and commerce among the world, were such as adorned the blessed truth, being a very upright and just, as well as a very inoffensive man; insomuch that his greatest persecutors have been heard to say, if there were any good or honest men among the Quakers, he was one.

In the year 1668 he was, with several friends more, cast into prison by one Rye, then mayor of Cork, for meeting together to worship God; in which place he got a violent cold, which ended in a flux, that brought him very low, the prison being thronged, and without convenience at that time for the sick. The jailor indulged him for a little time to be a prisoner in his own house. After his coming home, the distemper increasing upon him, brought him exceedingly weak and low; though in much pain, yet very patient under it, and much retired to the Lord, and in a sweet frame of spirit. The Fifth-day before he died came that worthy mother in Israel, Susannah Mitchel, to visit him; who, sitting in silent waiting upon the Lord by his bedside, was moved to pray, which she did with great fervency of spirit. At which time also the power of the Lord fell upon him in a wonderful manner, greatly melting and tendering his spirit, causing him to give forth several sweet and heavenly expressions; and though he was exceedingly weak in body, and neither able nor fit to rise out of bed before, yet the presence and power of the Lord so strengthened him, that he immediately rose out of his bed, as one that ailed little, and put on his clothes, in order to go to the prison, to see and meet his dear companions and fellow-sufferers. His wife and friends present, seeing this great and sudden alteration, were in great hopes the Lord would restore him to his health again.

He went abroad to prison, as one that was not sick, and had a good meeting with Friends there; the jailor gave him leave in the evening to return home again, which he did, with little appearance of illness; but soon after his return, as one that was only raised from his death-bed to give his last visit to his beloved friends, his distemper returned again, and he grew exceedingly ill that night, and so continued growing worse till about the Third-day, in the evening, at which time he was so bad that it was concluded he was dying. In his weak condition the power of the Lord came upon him again in an extraordinary manner, so that he was revived, and as one that had new life and strength given him, and he spoke of the wonderful love of God to his soul, and the preciousness of truth, with seasonable exhortation to all that were about him. Thus he continued with the Lord's power upon him until the Fifth-day, whereon he died; having a spirit of discerning given him from the Lord, by which he saw and spoke directly to the inward states and conditions of most or all that came to visit him, giving counsel and advice accordingly, and in particular to some who had been unfaithful. He spoke so home to their states, that they were almost amazed, warning them to prize their time, and be more faithful for the time to come.

He also called those of his children who were come to some years of understanding, in particular Joseph, Elizabeth, and Ebenezer Pike, and gave them heavenly advice and counsel; and among the rest, he spoke to them to this purpose: 'Fear the Lord, and be faithful to him, and be obedient to your mother, and then the Lord will be a father to you, and provide for and bless you, and the rest of you every day, and let the blessing of your dying father rest upon you;' with more that cannot now be remembered. It would require a volume to contain the many blessed and heavenly sayings and exhortations, if they could be remembered, which came from him in the time of his sickness, especially the last two days of his life, some of which were taken from his mouth, and committed to writing by a friend present, and read at his burial; which paper is through some neglect mislaid or lost.

He quietly departed this life, and died in the Lord, the Fourth month, 1668, being about forty-one years of age.

THOMAS THOMPSON, of Skipsea, was convinced of the truth of God by that ancient and faithful minister of the gospel of Christ, William Dewsbury, in the Eighth month of the year 1652, and shortly after had his mouth opened to declare the name of the Lord, and preach repentance to the people. He was preserved in faithfulness to the truth to the end of his days, not turning his back from sufferings, but patiently endured reproach for Christ's sake, and spoiling of goods, with many years' imprisonment. When it pleased the Lord to visit him with the illness whereof he died, which began on the 26th day of the Sixth month, 1704, his heart was filled with the love of God, and he was enabled through the goodness of God, though very weak in body, to go to several meetings, in which the Lord's heavenly power did livingly attend him. On the sixth day of the Seventh month, he was at the monthly meeting held at Harpham, being the last public meeting he was at, where he bore a plain and powerful testimony to the ancient truth, labouring to encourage all Friends to be faithful to God, and to be diligent in the service of truth, according to their several abilities, gifts, and endowments, that so an increase of the peaceable government of Christ might be witnessed, both in the particular and also in the general.

He was indeed a laborious man in the work of the gospel, having travelled in truth's service several times through Scotland, and in many places in this nation; and, as he said when upon a dying-bed, for many years had not omitted any opportunity of being serviceable. His testimony was plain, but powerful; sound and convincing, and severe against wickedness; but to the young and tender-hearted he was very loving and affectionate, even as a nurse that cherisheth her children. On the tenth day of the month, in the year aforesaid, being the First-day of the week, several Friends visited him in his chamber, he being then very weak, to whom he declared the loving-kindness of God, and of his tender dealings with his soul, from his youth to that day; and that he felt the Lord, who had been the guide of his youth, to be the staff of his old age; and exhorted Friends to faithfulness and confidence in God, that they should depend upon the arm of his power and providence for ever.

On the 13th day of the month, several Friends being with him, he said that he was content to live or die, as the Lord pleased, in whom he had peace; and that he was in no doubt concerning his salvation, but was satisfied for ever, and could say with Job, the Lord had granted him life and favour, and his visitations still preserved his spirit. The next day, being the 14th, and the day of his departure out of this world, he spoke little in the forenoon, being under much bodily weakness and pain at times; but about the second or third hour in the afternoon, in a heavenly, melting manner, he said, 'The Lord is my portion, and the lot of mine inheritance for ever. I am not dismayed;' and after a little time, 'I have peace with God;' and after a considerable pause, 'Since the day that the word of the Lord came unto me, saying, As thou art converted, strengthen thy brethren; and if thou lovest me, feed my lambs; I have spared no pains, either in body or spirit, neither am I conscious to myself of slipping any opportunity of being serviceable to truth and Friends; but have gone through what was before me with all willingness possible. And now I feel the love of God, and the returns of peace in my bosom;' which words were spoken in so living a sense of God's heavenly power, that it wonderfully broke and tendered Friends present.

Another time he said, 'The Lord Jesus Christ has shed his precious blood for us, and laid down his life, and became sin for us, that we might be made the righteous of God in him. O, this is love indeed.' Again he said, 'My heart is filled with the love of God. Oh the excellency! oh the glory! oh how glorious and excellent is the appearance of God! the rays of his glory fill his tabernacle:' and so he sung melodiously, saying, 'O praises, praises, high praises, and hallelujah to the King of Sion, who reigns gloriously this day.' All which being spoken in a heavenly sense of the aboundings of the sweet life of the divine and living Word, which was with the Father in the beginning, mightily overcame and melted the spirits of Friends. To a neighbour who came in to see him, he said, 'We must put off these mortal bodies; but for them that fear the Lord there is an immortal one prepared.' He continued very cheerful and sensible to the last, and spoke very cheerfully to several neighbours who came to see him. About three quarters of an hour before his death, he spoke to one that had been under convincement several years, but had not been faithful, exhorting him to repent and be faithful to what God had manifested to him, that so he might find mercy; with many more words not remembered, telling him that he would find it a terrible thing to appear before an angry God. He said that he spoke to him in love, and would have him take it so; and bade him remember the words of a dying man, and so bade him farewell.

Another time he said to friends, 'Ye are my witnesses, that I have not withheld from you the counsel and mind of God, and have laboured to provoke you to faithfulness and diligence in his service, that so ye might receive a crown of glory at the hand of the Lord, which is laid up in store for all the righteous, and my conscience is clear in God's sight.' Being filled with the living power and love of God, he often praised his holy and glorious name; and about the seventh hour he passed away like a lamb, into his Father's bosom, without so much as either sigh or groan, and is at rest in the Lord for evermore.

He departed this life in the seventy-third year of his age, the 14th of the Seventh month, 1704. A labourer in the gospel about fifty years.

The testimony of Hugh Stamper, of Lurgan, in Ireland, near his departure out of this life.

About twenty friends being present, he said, 'I die in the same faith that I have made profession of, and lived in, and suffered for these twenty-three years, and I am as willing to die as to live. All the desire I have to live, is to see truth prosper, and if sufferings come, I am willing to suffer for it. There is no weight or burden lies at my door. I have wronged no man, neither have I been burthensome to any, but always if there was any difference, I suffered wrong for peace-sake. I have not oppressed any man. So, my dear friends, beware of oppression, walk in love one to another, passing by infirmities, forgiving one another, for even as Christ said, if ye forgive not one another, how shall your heavenly Father forgive you? even as he who would not forgive his brother, missed of pardon. Keep your hearts clean, and let no rottenness remain therein. Keep the heart void of offence towards God and man, and when any evil doth appear, judge it down with the light, and be not peevish, nor fretting; it hindereth the springs of life. Walk humbly before your God, and be of a pure mind to him, Walk in true love one towards another, and stand not at a distance one from another, for envy and strife lead from God, and eat as a canker, so miss of the blessing which is poured down upon the righteous, as showers of latter rain. Blessed be the Lord God for ever. Bear up your heads, and give not away your crowns for any visible thing here below, for they are but trifles, and things of no value. Dear friends, keep your crowns sure, and then you need not care what scoffers, mockers, liars, backbiters, and drunkards say, for their way leads to hell, and they cannot inherit the kingdom of heaven.

'Dear friends, in the suffering of all things, you shall come to wear the crown. No cross, no crown; take notice of that. Friends, keep your crown, that your bow may abide in full strength in the needful time, when the pains of death come upon you, which will come upon all in due time. Death troubles me not, for blessed be the Lord for ever, the enemy durst never so much as once set up his head, either to twist or twine;

since I lay on this my bed of sickness, there is nothing but peace on every side.'

'My dear friends, I desire you in the bowels of tender love to love one another, and you will be a comely people, and an honour to God and one to another. Bear the daily cross, that you may be crowned when time shall be no more, and come to partake of the mercies of David, viz. an everlasting covenant which hath no end. If the righteous scarcely be saved, where shall the wicked and ungodly appear? Oh! the joy and endless felicity that shall be upon the righteous, and what horror and misery shall be upon the wicked!'

'And, dear friends, let not a bare profession serve your turn, for it will not stand you in any stead in such a needful time as this, but walk answerably to what you profess, that your bow may stand in full strength, as mine doth at this time. Blessed be the name of the Lord for ever, I have no more lying upon me that I know of, to hinder my journey, than a child. So, my dear friends, do not will and run in your own wills, but wait daily upon the Lord, and let your whole dependence be upon him, that you may come in at the right door, for whosoever climbeth up another way is a thief and a robber. Cast your care upon the Lord, and he will in no wise cast you off, but he will work in you, and for you, and you will become the children of the day, and of the light. I do not speak these things to exalt myself, for there is no exalting in the grave, but I must bear my testimony for God, and for his truth. Friends, you know these things before; this is to stir up your minds to stand steadfast in the truth, and let not your crown be taken from you. Be faithful in the day of small things, and despise them not, and the Lord will make you rulers over much, so shall you be honourable men and women, and he will shower down multitudes of blessings upon your heads.'

'O friends, I desire you again not to slight this glorious day, which is now dawned, for it can be called no less than salvation upon earth, but walk faithfully to the receiving of your crown, and you will return with sheaves in your bosoms.'

Thus often exhorting Friends to faithfulness, and to be of

an honest heart, and to keep nothing there but that which is of a right nature, saying, 'Take notice of my words, for they are the words of a dying man, and they are very weighty; and if you will not hear, you shall be made to remember hereafter when I am gone.'

When the time of his departure came near, he said, 'Come Lord Jesus, come when it is thy blessed will, for I am ready for thee.'

Just before he died he sat up in his bed and spoke these words, 'Now, Lord Jesus, receive my soul into thy everlasting kingdom of glory, for thy kingdom is from everlasting to everlasting;' and so departed this life about the ninth of the Seventh month, 1676. Aged about sixty-five years.

REUBEN SATTERTHWAITE, born at Skinerhow, in the parish of Hawkshead, in the county of Lancaster, came of believing parents, who used a godly care in educating him in the way of truth as professed by the people called Quakers. This young man had a care over his own words and actions, that they might become truth, and he received a gift of the ministry about the twenty-third year of his age, wherein he did much improve himself until the twenty-sixth year of his age, wherein he died; in which time he faithfully laboured in the gospel. He travelled into Scotland in company with his friend George Knipe, who was a nursing father to him, and they visited every meeting of Friends in that nation. Being clear of that nation, he came back through Northumberland bishoprick, and the east parts of Yorkshire, and so home: and in the Second month of the year 1694, he with his said friend set forward for London, and was at the yearly meeting there, and afterwards visited Friends in the west of England, even to the Land's-end in Cornwall, and so back by Bristol. In this journey he had very good success, and was much enlarged in his gift of the ministry; and from Bristol travelled through Wales to Lancashire home again. He travelled into Derbyshire, Nottingham and Lincolnshire;

and in the Third month, 1696, again into Scotland with his former friend, George Knipe, and returned thence through Cumberland, which was the last journey he had, for he was removed out of this troublesome world the same year.

He was a good example and pattern in righteousness and holiness, and was valiant for the truth upon earth, and was of a sound mind, and preached sound doctrine, and often opened the Holy Scriptures, to the edification of the hearers. When he was visited with sickness, he bore it patiently, and in the first part, he got up and walked about the house, but feeling himself weak in body, he said, 'I am a poor mortal, a worm, and dust and ashes.' Though his body was weakened and decayed, yet he was strengthened inwardly, and often spoke of the kind dealings of the Lord with him, and how mercifully he had helped him in his travels. His sickness increasing he kept his bed, and many came to visit him; to whose conditions he spoke, to the admiration of those about him. Not long before he died, his sister-in-law being present, he said, 'Oh! Lord, thou knowest I have passed through many exercises for thy name's sake, and thou hast rewarded me well for the same, for which I praise thy holy name. The Lord God is my staff, as he was to David, who said his staff did comfort him.'

Some young friends visiting him, he said, 'I desire you to wait upon the Lord all your days, for the promise of the Lord is to you, if you will wait upon him, and love him to the end;' with more expressions that could not be remembered. He passed that night in a very good frame of spirit, breathing to the Lord. On the morrow, being the First-day of the week, several young people came in, to whose conditions he spoke distinctly, exhorting them to remember their Creator in the days of their youth. He was very weak in body, but his words did so affect them, that they were tendered and broken into tears, and divers Friends present were much comforted thereby. That night, Margaret his sister, and another Friend sitting up with him, he taking his sister by the hand, said, 'Dear sister, tell my father and mother that I must go, I must go home.' After some sight which he had, which brought some exercise upon him, he broke forth into an inward rejoicing of spirit; and after that he expressed the travail that was upon his mind for some Friends and meetings in parts which he had visited, and prayed to the Lord to be gracious and merciful to them, and spoke many more seasonable words that are not here mentioned. That same night he departed this life, being the 12th of the Eleventh month, 1696.

JOSHUA BUNION, who lived near Ipswich in Suffolk in England, went over to preach the gospel in Ireland in the year 1696. He was remarkable for his extraordinary innocency in his conversation, chiefly minding the discharge of his duty, with respect to his ministry, which was edifying. He was taken sick going from Dublin to the north of Ireland, and coming to Ballyhagan in the county of Armagh, was so weak that he could scarcely alight off his horse without help, yet his zeal was such that he bore a faithful testimony for truth in the public meeting the same day. Afterwards he went to bed, continuing very ill about two weeks. In the time of his sickness he was very fervent in prayer, and the day before he died, sitting in a chair, desired another to be set before him, on which he leaned, and prayed fervently and powerfully to the Lord. The next day he departed this life, the 23d of the Fourth month, 1696. Aged about forty years. He was buried in Friends' burying-place, near Ballyhagan aforesaid.

PETER FLETCHER was born near Pardsay, in Cumberland, in England, and educated in the profession of truth. He came over to be an apprentice in Dublin; and after he had served his apprenticeship he settled in the said city; he was of a good conversation, both in respect to his Christian duty towards God, in duly attending meetings for the worship of God, and other religious performances, and ready and cheerful in doing those offices of love which we owe one unto another. About three years before his death the Lord was pleased to call him into the ministry; in which he was sound and deliberate in his delivery, being careful to minister from that ability which God had given him. He was under weakness of body some months before his death, in which time he spoke of the Lord's dealings with him, and how he inclined his heart to seek him when he was young, and had kept him all along to that day, in a sense of his goodness and power which had preserved him. He was freely given up to the Lord's disposing, and rather willing to leave the world than stay any longer therein, if it were the Lord's will; and further said he found nothing but sweet peace to abound in his heart from the Lord; and so being prepared for his latter end, he departed this life in Dublin, the 29th of the Fourth month, 1698. Aged about thirty years.

ABRAHAM FULLER was convinced of the truth in or about the year 1660, being about the forty-first year of his age. He lived most of his time after his convincement at Lyhensa in King's county; he feared the Lord, and was a serviceable man on several accounts in the church of Christ, and bore a testimony for the truth, and was a free and open-hearted man to his friends, distributing of his substance unto those that were in necessity. He was taken sick about the beginning of the Eighth month, 1694, of an ague and cholic.

In the time of his sickness he expressed his concern for the prosperity of truth, and sent to speak with some that made profession of it, and did not walk answerably thereto, and did admonish them to repent, and amend their lives. He was often in his illnesss in supplication to the Lord, and in returning praises to him for his mercies which he had received from him. About the 4th day of the Ninth month, most of his children being about him, and sitting awhile in silence, he then prayed the Lord that he would bless his children, and preserve them from the evils that were in the world.

One day having a pretty sharp fit of the ague upon him, his daughter-in-law who attended him said, 'Father, the fit thou hadst yesterday went away easily;' he replied, 'Yes, the Lord's power took the pain away.' He gave his children good counsel and admonition, according as he had a sense of their states. He often in the time of his illness expressed how good the Lord was to him. Six days before his death, being gone to his bed at night, he desired to speak with his children that were in the house, there being two of his sons and his son's wife. After they had sat a little time silent by his bedside, he said he had a desire to let them know, that if the Lord had no further service for him to do, he was willing to die; and then spoke to one of his sons, giving him good advice; and then called to his other son by name, and said, 'The Lord make thee a sanctified vessel fit for his use.'

His eldest son, living nearly a mile off, being newly recovered from a fit of sickness, came to see his father, and when he was about to take leave of him, which was but about two hours before his death, he spoke to him, admonishing him to take care of his soul, for it was of great value. He desired several times in his sickness, if it were the Lord's will that he might be sensible at his departure, and have an easy passage. His desire was answered, for in less than a quarter of an hour before his death, he laid his hand on the bedside, and turned himself, and desired to be a little raised in his bed; and so departed quietly, and finished his course about the twelfth hour at night, on the 4th of the Tenth month, at his son Isaac's house at Lismina, and was buried at Friends' burial-place, at the Moat a Green.

ROBERT BARCLAY, of Urie, in Scotland. This worthy man of God, whose character is written, as well for their example and encouragement who have or hereafter may receive the eternal truth, in which he lived and died, and lives for ever, as for a testimony to the power and goodness of God, in raising him up to his church, and to his lasting memorial in the churches of Christ, which is blessed for ever. The said Robert Barclay was the son of Colonel David Barclay, descended of the Barclays of Mathers, in the kingdom of Scotland, an ancient and honourable family among men, and Katherine Gordon, from the Gordons of the house of the duke of Gordon. He was born at Edinburgh, in 1648, educated in France, and had the advantage of that tongue as well as the Latin.

He returned to Scotland about 1664, being sixteen years of age, where, by the example and instruction of his honest and worthy father, who in his absence had received the everlasting truth, and his conversation was with other servants of God, he came to see and taste an excellency in it, and was convinced thereof about the year 1667. He publicly owned the testimony of the true light, enlightening every man, and came early forth a zealous and fervent witness for it, enduring the cross, and despising the shame that attended his discipleship, and received the gift of the ministry as his greatest honour, in which he laboured to bring others to God, and his labour was not in vain in the Lord. He was much exercised in controversy, from the many contradictions that fell upon truth, and upon him for its sake, in his own country chiefly, in which he ever acquitted himself with honour to the truth, particularly by his Apology for the Christian divinity professed by the people called Quakers, which contains a collection of our principles, our enemies' objections, and our answers augmented and illustrated closely and amply, with many authorities for confirmation. He wrote divers other books which are printed, and make a volume of nigh two hundred and thirty sheets, which contain many standing books of sound judgment, and good service to the truth and church of God.

He travelled often in Scotland and England, and also in Holland and Germany, to spread the gospel of our Lord Jesus Christ. He loved the truth, and the way of God, as revealed among the people called Quakers, above the world, and was not ashamed of it before men, but bold and able in maintaining it, sound in judgment, strong in argument, cheerful in travails and sufferings, of a pleasant disposition, yet solid and plain, and exemplary in his conversation. He was a learned man, a good Christian, an able minister, a dutiful son, a loving husband, a tender and careful father, an easy master, and a good and kind neighbour and friend. These eminent qualities in one who had employed them so serviceably, and who had not lived much above half the life of a man, having outlived his father but four years, and died at least thirty years short of his age, aggravate the loss of him.

His sickness was short: our friend James Dickinson, of Cumberland, in his travel into that nation, visiting him when on his death-bed, as he sat by him, the Lord's power and presence bowing their hearts together, Robert Barclay was sweetly melted in the sense of God's love, and with tears expressed his love to all faithful brethren in England, who keep their integrity to the truth. He added, 'Remember my love to Friends in Cumberland, and at Swarthmore, and to dear George,' meaning George Fox, 'and to all the faithful everywhere;' and said, 'God is good still, and though I am under great weight of sickness and weakness as to my body, yet my peace flows; and this I know, whatever exercises may be permitted to come upon me, it shall tend to God's glory, and my salvation, and in that I rest.'

He died at his own house in Urie, in Scotland, the third day of the Eighth month, 1690, leaving behind him seven children, four sons and three daughters.

He was born 1648; convinced of truth 1667; wrote his first book for truth 1670; and his notable Apology in and about the 27th year of his age, 1675. He died in the forty-second year of his age.

HANNAH TURNER, daughter of Thomas Turner, of Coggeshall, in the county of Essex, in visiting her acquaintance, was taken sick at Goussingbeckingham-hall, in the said county, and quickly after being taken sick was sensible she should die. Her mother being with her, she desired her to bear it with patience, and remember how it was with Abraham, and with many in our day, in parting with their only child. 'Dear mother, consider, it may be this great trial may prove to our sanctification; bear it with patience.' For several days she lay in a composed state, praying to the Lord to forgive her offences. She was troubled that she was so far from her friends and neighbours, and would have been glad to see them. She expressed her concern for an acquaintance of hers, entreating her mother to say to her as followeth: 'Consider my death as a precedent, and remember she must come before the bar of the great God, as well as I, and can no way shun it; and how doth she think to stand there without great repentance.'

Another time she desired to have her love remembered to Friends at London, and ordered the manner of her burial. Her father coming off a journey to see her, she said, 'Dear father, how often have I been comforted to consider how the Lord hath preserved thee through many jeopardies of thy life, both by sea and land.' She also admonished her nurse not to go into jollity and pastime, nor be ashamed of the cross of Christ. 'What if people mock thee, be not ashamed; remember Solomon's words, that "know thou for all these things God will bring thee into judgment."' Many other exhortations she gave to this lass, saying, 'Take notice of what I say;' to which she answered, breaking forth into weeping, 'I hope I shall.' At other times she spoke several weighty and seasonable exhortations, which are not taken down, and so passed away, inwardly breathing to the Lord, which was a great comfort to those with her; and died on the 8th day of the Twelfth month, 1705, in the nineteenth year of her age.

THOMAS UPSHER was born in the parish of Lexden, in the borough of Colchester, in the county of Essex, and was sprinkled or baptized, as they call it, a few days after, according to the manner of the church of England, the 11th of the Sixth month, 1672, but was educated in the Presbyterian way, and was religiously inclined from his youth, often seeking the Lord for the good of his soul, and delighted in reading the Holy Scriptures. About the fourteenth year of his age he left the Presbyterians, and joined himself with the people called the General Baptists, and was zealous in that way, and became a preacher among them when young, and was well esteemed by them, until it pleased the Lord more effectually to visit him by the light of Jesus Christ, unto which he turned his heart, and came to see the emptiness of his former professions and talk of religion, without the knowledge of God and Christ by the revelation of the Spirit.

A few days after he was convinced of truth, he wrote a letter, which was sent to the Baptist meeting, to be read on the First-day of the week, showing the cause why he left them. This letter was dated the 13th of the Ninth month, 1692, so that he was twenty years of age when he came among the people called Quakers, and was a diligent attender of the meetings of that people for the worship of God, waiting upon him in silence and retirement of mind, for his teaching and counsel, until he was pleased to give him a gift in the ministry, which he received in great humility, and entered upon his ministry, in speaking a few words amongst Friends, in much fear and tenderness, to the comfort and refreshment of many. God in tender mercy did increase his gift, so that he became an able minister of the gospel, to the turning of many from darkness to the light of Christ Jesus; and in that service he travelled in most parts of England, and also in Ireland.

As he often in the time of his health remembered and spoke of his death, so he did in his sickness, saying, 'I do not expect to live long in this world. I have been preparing for a better. I do not desire to live here on my own account. I long more and more to be at home with my God, yet I would not be of that sort to desire my reward before my work is done. There is nothing here can invite my stay, but if God hath further service for me in this world, I am resigned and given up to his will.'

In a letter to a particular friend, written in the time of his sickness, he expressed himself in these words:

'When I consider those many unaccountable changes which we, and ours, and all we have in this world are subject to, it seems a sufficient antidote against the inordinate love of it, and it appears to me, that it is the want of due thoughtfulness which makes many so much engaged in it, as almost wholly to sequester all those religious endeavours which are really necessary to make sure of an eternal interest.'

'It is now a long time since I have enjoyed one day of perfect health as heretofore. I consider it as a preparatory summons from this frail state of life; and to conclude, I thank God I am not altogether unmindful of my duty, in setting my house in order against the time shall come that I must die, and not live. I hope to live in a far better state, and there to enjoy all the generations of the just that are gone before, and shall hereafter follow.'

About the same time, several Friends being with him, he, speaking of his death, desired they might bear him witness, saying, 'My dependence, hope, and trust, is only and alone in the Lord Jesus Christ, and that I do not value myself upon any qualification or endowment, but lay all down at the feet of Jesus, and am as nothing before him.' About two days after, though weak in body, he was carried in a coach to Ipswich, to the burial of a Friend. When he came there, he seemed very unfit for the service of the day, there being much people at the burial; but the Lord strengthened him to declare, as at other times, the truth and word of life for about an hour and a half, which much affected the people in general; and Friends, who knew his weakness of body, admired the love and goodness of God to him. He prayed also, and spoke at the grave some time, and appeared stronger after the meeting than before, and continued better a few days after. But his sickness returned again, and he was very patient under the extreme pains, which he said no tongue could express, desiring to be resigned; and the Lord blessed him with resignation, faith, and patience, under all.

To a Friend that came to visit him, who made some observation of the prevalency of his distemper, he said, 'Now, in all likelihood, I am about to take my last leave of you all, and I pray God from my heart to bless you.' Many sound expressions were spoken to those who visited him in his sickness; to some, counsel and advice; to others, his own experience of the mercy and goodness of God. Being desired to send for another physician, he answered, 'No, I am satisfied: if God had been pleased to have said amen to means, there has been sufficient means used for my recovery, and therefore I shall have my eye only to the Lord for help.' At another time he said, 'My tongue is not able to express what I feel of the love and goodness of God now when I have most need of it; that saying used by that plain, despised people is very true, that life is better than words. There is one thing I cannot find out, why the Lord should so abound in his love and mercy to me, who am unworthy of the least of his mercies.'

There was a great refreshment felt many times in being with him in silence, in time of his sickness. On a First day, in the morning, several Friends being in his chamber, he desired that they might wait upon the Lord together; and the Lord was pleased to open his mouth to praise his holy name. Although very weak in bed, some Friends desiring him to say little to those who came to visit him, his answer was, 'I know not whether I may have another opportunity to do it.' He remembered the faithful, and spoke of their blessed estate; at the sight of which, he was even as it were in a rapture of joy, praising the Lord to the comfort of those present, saying, 'Oh! that I might declare of the wonders of the Lord that I have seen in the deeps, but I am resigned to the will of the Lord.' His pains and exercises were very great, and, as he often said, unknown; yet he also said, 'The Lord is very good to me, and bears up my spirit in the midst of them all.' Taking leave of several friends who visited him, he said, 'Oh! that you may so live, that we may meet again in the mansions of eternal rest.' He remembered his dear love to friends every where, saying, 'They are near my life, I have true unity with them in spirit.' At another meeting in his chamber, about fourteen days before he died, the state of the church, and many precious truths were opened to him, and in a heavenly frame of spirit he spoke of the wonderful wisdom, love, and goodness of God, exhorting Friends to be more faithful and diligent in the service of the Lord.

About ten days before his death, finding himself, as he thought, somewhat better, he went to the meeting, being the First-day of the week, and prayed fervently in the forenoon meeting, praising the name of the Lord, in a true sense of his mercy and goodness. But in a day or two he altered much, his distemper prevailing upon him. He desired to be carried decently to his grave, saying, 'I love decency, and desire to die in great humiliation, and commit my spirit into the hands of the Lord Jesus Christ.' About the time of his death, he was in a heavenly frame of spirit, and spoke of a glorious meeting, and said, 'The Lord in the riches of his mercy will keep all them that trust in him, under all their trials to the end.' And so departed this life, the 10th of the Eighth month, 1704. Aged thirty-two years two months. He left behind him three children; and his wife, in the time of his sickness, was much indisposed, which was an addition to his exercise.

PRISCILLA CUTHBERT, born at Brentford, in Middlesex, in 1697, was the daughter of Thomas and Isabella Cuthbert, of the same place. Some months before her sickness, she was observed to have a religious concern upon her mind, and retired from the rest of the children, and denied herself diversions among them, and got into solitary places, and read in good books, and sometimes weeping by herself, and other times praising the Lord. She had a sight of her death before she sickened, and spoke of it to several. When her sickness came, which continued three weeks, she bore it with much patience, praying to the Lord to be her comfort, and said, 'I hope the Lord will comfort my dear father and mother;' acknowledging the labour and tender care and cost which her parents had been at for her bringing up, and the education of herself and sisters and brothers. When her father came to her, upon her inquiry after him, she laid her arms about his face to wipe off the tears, and said, 'Lord, comfort my father and mother, and bless my poor sisters, and my brothers;' and gave good advice to her brother to obey his parents, and fear the Lord, saying he will bless thee. She said to her father, 'I am willing to live to praise the Lord, and I am willing to die, if it were at this moment of time.' She desired that when she was buried, none that laughed or were vain should be there, but such as feared the Lord; and in a sweet frame of mind praised the Lord.

Another time she said, 'I have, in the time of my health, been afraid when I have seen any dead nailed up in their coffins; but now the Lord hath taken away that fear, blessed be his name. Therefore take you notice, who stand by me, that I am neither afraid of death nor the grave, but I am willing to die when it pleaseth the Lord;' and soon after fell asleep. She often prayed for her parents, to whom she expressed more than ordinary affection and regard for their love and tenderness to her, expressing her willingness to die, and her comfort in the Lord. Her school-mistress visiting her, she said, 'I am going where I trust in the Lord I shall have rest, for the Lord is my rest.' Near her end, her father speaking of his purpose to stay with her that night, she replied, 'No, no, for I shall not die this night, though it will not be long before I do.' He went to bed: and the next day her father coming to her, she having had some rest in the night, she praised the Lord; a neighbour present supposed she might, by her praising God, disturb her father, to which she made no answer, till after some time, she said, 'Is my father disturbed at my praising the Lord? no, no, I know he is not. Indeed if I was dying, as some have done of late, rending and tearing with bad words, my father and mother too would have great reason to be troubled, but to have a child die in the Lord, I hope great is their comfort. I know their trouble is mixed with joy, blessed be the Lord for it;' upon these words several young women present broke forth into tears.

About two hours before she died, her father asked her if he and her mother should turn her to see if she could have a little rest, she answered, 'Do what you please.' A friend present advised all to be quiet and still, and in a little time hearing one weep, she said, 'Who is that, my sister Elizabeth?' reply was made, no; she replied, 'For the Lord's sake do not cry for me, do not cry for me.' These were the last words she was heard to speak: and so departed this life without sigh or groan, about the ninth hour of the sixth day of the Sixth month, 1701, in the fourteenth year of her age.

ELIZABETH WHIDDON, wife of Henry Whiddon, of Cork, in Ireland; was from her childhood given to sobriety, beyond what was common in one of her years, when she was about fourteen years of age, and was a woman of an exemplary life and conversation. She was called of the Lord to give testimony to his name and truth, though she was backward and unwilling to be concerned in so weighty a work, yet afterwards grew more strong, and declared of the wonderful things of God.

In the time of her sickness she enjoyed a great refreshment from the presence of the Lord, which tendered the hearts of friends present, and caused her to praise and magnify the God of her salvation, some days before her death.

Her brother, Joseph Pike, visiting her one morning, and inquiring how she did, she said, 'Oh! dear brother, though I have not slept all this night, yet I am as one that wants it not. Though my body is extraordinarily weak, yet I am strong, the power of the Lord carrying me over all weakness; but above all, the Lord said this night to me, in the powerful and fresh openings of life, "Thou shalt praise me in the heavens;" which hath so overcome my soul, and raised my spirits, that I am as one that wants no sleep, nor is sensible of pain or weakness;' and so went on in praising and magnifying the Lord, with many good expressions that cannot well be remembered. About a day before she died, observing her sister Elizabeth Allen to weep, looking upon her with a composed countenance, she said, 'Sister, why dost thou weep?' She answered, because unwilling to part with her. She replied, 'Oh! I shall go to everlasting joy and felicity, where I shall be at rest.'

She departed this life the 23d day of the Fifth month, 1693, to receive the recompense of reward, even a crown eternal, of which she had received before-hand a full assurance.

ROBERT SANDHAM, born near Petworth, in Sussex, in England, was convinced very early of truth at Youghall, in Ireland, where he then dwelt, and he soon became a faithful follower of it, and sufferer for it, bearing a steadfast testimony to it against its opposers; and was a preacher of it in his life and conversation amongst the inhabitants of that town until the end of his days. He lay sick two weeks, in which time he often exhorted Friends that came to visit him to be faithful to the truth; and to some, negligent therein, he said much in warning them to be no longer so, but to hasten out of a lukewarm state, lest the portion thereof should be theirs. Some relations and neighbours visiting him, he exhorted them to receive the truth; 'For,' said he, 'I bear my testimony now on my dying-bed, that it is the truth which the Quakers profess; therefore be faithful to the Lord and his truth, whilst you have health and strength, and delay not till you come to a dying-bed, as too many are apt to do, for then oftentimes men and women find it enough to bear their sickness and pains;' which affected most present.

To his wife, with whom he had lived about twenty-four years in much love, he said, 'I am freely given up to the Lord's will. I therefore desire thee also to give up, and bear my death with patience, and the Lord will make up thy loss of me in being near unto thee.' He often exhorted his children to love the Lord and his truth, and be obedient to their mother, and love one another, and all honest Friends, and delight to go to meetings. One of his children being of age to remember what he said, he said to her, 'Tell thy two young sisters when they are grown up, that it is my charge to them so to do, for they may not remember what I say to them now, and the Lord will be a father to you and a husband to your mother.' Seeing one of them crying, he said, 'Be good children, love the Lord, and obey your mother, and though I am taken away, you will have your mother left with you, and she will take care of you.'

Soon after he drew nigh his end, being in a sweet frame of mind, resigned up to the Lord's will, often speaking of his mercies to him. He said, 'The Lord hath fully satisfied my desires;' and took a solemn farewell of his wife and children. A friend being present, prayed to the Lord to be near him in that present exercise, and make his passage easy; after which he took the said friend by the hand, and expressed his great peace and satisfaction, and passed away, being sensible to the last. He died the 28th of the Eighth month, 1675.

DEBORAH SANDHAM, wife of Robert Sandham aforesaid, was born near Youghall, in Ireland; she received truth soon after her husband, and was a faithful, serviceable woman to her end, bearing a true and sound testimony for God and his truth, and was very exemplary in conversation. She survived her husband about twenty years, taking due care of her children, which fulfilled their father's dying words to them. When it pleased the Lord to visit her with the sickness whereof she died, she perceiving one of the family to be much concerned at it, said, 'Be not concerned, I am freely given up to the will of the Lord, either to live or to die. If the Lord have any further service for me, he can lengthen my days, if not, I am freely resigned to his will.' She was often in her sickness inward with the Lord, being kept in great patience and quietness, exhorting Friends, and inviting some of her relations and neighbours who came to visit her, to receive the truth; also warning some unfaithful ones, not to let slip the day of their visitation. She also exhorted her children to mind her frequent advice and counsel to them, and to fear the Lord, and to keep out of all that which grieves his righteous spirit; as (said she) your dear and tender father on his death-bed exhorted you, even so do. Love the truth, and love one another, and then the Lord will be a father to you, as truly he hath been a husband to me. My desires have been, and are still, that you may fear and love the Lord, and reverence him, for your mother doth not die without a hope, that the Lord who hath begun his good work in you, will carry it on, and that the blessing of the Lord will rest upon you, which is more than all visible things; as my soul hath been a witness of, as my mind hath been kept from coveting after them, having seen, that godliness is great gain, and in the gain of it is great peace.

One of her daughters not being with her in the time of her sickness, she desired to be helped up, that she might write a few lines with her own hand, as her last words to her, which were as follow: 'I not knowing as yet, whether it be the will of my heavenly Father to finish my days, I am, through the great mercy of God, freely given up. Oh! this I have in my heart to say to thee, be faithful, be faithful, and dwell in holy patience; and the same is to thy husband. Oh! that you may come to holy silence with fear and dread, then will the work of the Lord prosper, which is more than all works. Thou hast many of my exhortations, which get together, and keep and mind, and the God of peace support thee; thou not being in a condition to come to me, so farewell in the Lord.'

The day before her departure, she was fervent in prayer to the Lord, that he would bless his people, and enable them to walk faithfully before him, and that his truth might prosper, and that he would please to raise more faithful labourers for the gathering many more unto righteousness; also that he would be pleased to bless her children, and their offspring, and make them his; with much more which cannot be remembered. The day she died, she said to one of her daughters, 'Thou art my first-born, and always very dear to me. I cannot now say much more to thee, but mind my former exhortations, and remember that truth was more than all, and truth was over all with me, and truth was thy mother's chiefest treasure;' often saying, 'My dear child give me up, give me up; entreat the Lord to enable thee to give me up, for I am freely given up to the Lord's will. Taking her last farewell of her children and grandchildren, with friends and the family, she desired to have her dear love remembered to Friends at Cork, and elsewhere; my love also (said she) extends farther, to all Friends in England. Some time after, turning herself about in her bed, she said, 'I am now a going to leave you.' And so she quietly, and in great peace, departed this life the 15th day of the Fifth month, 1695, in Youghall, where she dwelt.

EDWARD PARKER, of Thornbury, in Gloucestershire, was convinced of the blessed truth by John Audland and John Camm, at their first coming into those parts, which was about the year 1654. He bore a public testimony for truth, and continued faithful to his death; and on his dying bed gave very living testimonies to the truth, to many Friends and others about him. His last words were, 'Lord, come, thy servant is ready:' and then departed this life in the year 1667, in the fiftieth year of his age.

ELEANOR CANNINGS, wife of Joseph Cannings, of Thornbury, in Gloucestershire, was convinced by John Audland and John Camm, about the year 1654, when they came into that county. She was a zealous woman, and often exercised in bearing a faithful testimony for the truth against the priests, for which she suffered many and great abuses from the rude people. She continued a sincere-hearted Friend to the end of her days, and on her dying bed gave many good exhortations to friends about her, saying, a little before her death, 'I am well satisfied, and am going to a better habitation.'

She was buried at Hasel, the 19th of the First month, about the seventy-third year of her age.

HENRY PONTYN, of French-Hay meeting, was a faithful labourer in the ministry of our Lord Jesus Christ, as well beyond sea, as in this nation of England, and endured many sufferings and hardships, and several years' imprisonment at Gloucester for his faithful testimony for God, and continued faithful to his death. On his dying bed he said that the Lord had done well for him, and the chastisements of the Lord are good; exhorting his children and friends about him to live in the fear of the Lord, that they might die in his favour, saying, 'The end will crown all.'

He died in the sixty-seventh year of his age.

ISAAC ALEXANDER, son of Thomas and Alice Alexander, of Bendrig, in Killington, in the county of Westmoreland, was born in the year 1680, and convinced of the blessed truth in the year 1694, in the fourteenth year of his age. In his seventeenth year he received a gift of the ministry, and became an able minister of the gospel of our Lord Jesus Christ.

In 1698 he travelled abroad in the work of the gospel, and went into Yorkshire, and through the east parts of England, till he came to London; and after his return home he travelled in the same service into Scotland, and visited all the meetings of Friends in that nation. After his return thence, he went into the southern and western parts of England; and three years after, he visited all the meetings of Friends in Ireland, and most of the meetings in England and Wales.

In the Eighth month, 1705, he began to be much out of health, and yet attended Friends' meetings till the middle of the Tenth month following. On the 21st of the same, several friends sitting by him, he, being sensible of God's salvation, said in admiration thereof to the Lord, 'To thee, to thee, be salvation and praise! This is a day of great salvation.' He signified what great mercy it was that the Lord should visit us in our young years, and reveal his blessed truth to us, and how unworthy many were before the Lord did make bare the arm of his salvation; further saying, 'How near has the Lord been to me in the time of my sickness! Although I have formerly felt much of his power and presence, yet never enjoyed such plenty thereof, as since I have been visited with this sickness;' instancing one night, wherein he could not sleep, he enjoyed more abundantly of the love of God than at any other time before. He said, 'Oh! what an excellent thing it is to keep in the truth, and visit one another in the life of it.' He made a great difference between those who visit the sick in the sense of the divine life, and other visitors, who no sooner meet but they begin to talk of their worldly affairs. He said, 'Friends, get into an inward acquaintance with the Lord in spirit, for it is a good thing to retire to the rock; there is safety, there is good standing, an excellent bottom, and room enough.' He further said, 'If any go out of the bounds of truth, thinking thereby to bring others in, they will find themselves to be in slippery places;' and 'Beware of joining with false, unsettled spirits.' Another time, two friends sitting by him, he felt the power and presence of the Lord, and sang praises to him after an heavenly manner, saying, 'My heart is full, though I can truly say, I have no desire to speak, but as I feel it spring from the life.'

On the 28th of the Tenth month he said, 'As I lay on my bed very weak of body, I thought I could never die better, for I felt my salvation sealed unto me. Oh! love God, love God, for he is worthy. You may love any thing else too much, but you can never love God too much. Oh! what hath he done for my soul; he hath given me everlasting comfort; it is enough; it is enough, indeed.' He said, moreover, 'There are two things which are to my great satisfaction:

'1st. That ever since the Lord manifested himself to me, I

have freely given up myself to his requirings, and delivered his word faithfully, and have not sought to please men, neither did I look for great things. What I desired was, that I might have a place amongst the sanctified.

'2dly. I have always been against libertine spirits, and have had no familiarity with them; these things are now my comfort.'

He also said, 'Oh! I have seen glorious things, yea, such things as I never saw before. I beheld a friend lately deceased in a glorious place, and that I was to be with him; and I said it is enough to be there. Oh! such salvation!' Again, 'I am glad I can say, O death, where is thy sting; and grave, where is thy victory?' Another time, some friends visiting him, he related to them how the Lord had raised him from nothing to bear a testimony for him, and wheresoever the Lord drew me I have followed him, both in this nation and other nations, and sought not favour and interest among men. He warned and cautioned the negligent to be diligent and faithful, and come up in the service of truth; and said, 'The Lord will cause a dreadful day to overtake the disobedient and the negligent;' saying, 'It is sealed to my soul, that it hastens on apace.'

He often said at times, in great weakness of body, 'I desire to be dissolved and to be with Christ, but the Lord's will be done;' adding, 'The Lord's presence is here;' giving thanks for his divine help, saying, 'I never wanted comfort from him in this time of sickness. Friends, it is an excellent thing to have a conscience void of offence towards God. Keep your hearts clean. I have discharged my duty to all people, so that I find nothing but that I am fully clear; I am fully clear.' After a little time he broke forth in a sweet harmony, and lifted up his voice in prayer to the Lord, which had been very low several weeks, saying, 'O Lord God! though my exercises and pain of body abound, thy power and life do much more abound, and carry me over all;' fervently begging of the Lord to be with all his faithful labourers all the world over, rendering thanks for his glorious appearance, saying, 'Worthy, worthy, art thou, O Lord, of all honour, thanksgiving and praise.' He prayed for an easy passage out of this world, which the Lord granted him; for about the second hour the same day, in the afternoon, he fell asleep, and twelve hours after, he said to a friend present, 'Lay my head better;' which done, he said, 'Now I will fall upon my sleep,' and immediately went away as if he had fallen into a natural sleep.

He died the 12th of the Twelfth month, 1705, at the house of James Wilson, at Aba, near Kendal; and the 15th of the same month was buried at Brigflats, near Sedberg

---

ANNE CAMM, late wife of Thomas Camm, of Camm's-Gill, was daughter of Richard Newby, in the parish of Kendal, in Westmoreland, a family of good repute, being always religiously inclined. Her father was convinced of the blessed truth in 1652, and died therein a faithful man. Anne Camm was born in the Eighth month, 1627; and was well educated in learning proper for her sex. About the thirteenth year of her age, she was sent up by her parents to an aunt at London, where she became acquainted with a religious people called Puritans. Her stay in London was about seven years, from whence she returned to Kendal. After some time there, she removed to the city of York, and dwelt in a family of great account in the world, her mistress being a pious woman, after whose decease she returned again to Kendal, her society still being with the most religious where she came.

At Kendal there was a seeking people, who met often together, sometimes sitting in silence, other times in religious conferences, and often in fervent prayer. John Audland living remote, yet sometimes fell in amongst them; and about the year 1650, John Audland and she married, and they were both convinced of truth in the beginning of 1652, by the ministry of that honourable servant of Christ, George Fox. So powerfully did God, by his sanctifying word and spirit, work upon them, that they were thereby made effectual instruments in his hand, to preach the gospel unto others in the next year, 1653, and so forward, until the Lord put a period to their days.

The first place the said Anne Audland was called of the Lord to visit, except about home, was the county of Durham, about the beginning of the year 1654, and she preached truth to the people in the town of Aukland, in the said county, on a market-day, for which she was imprisoned in the town jail, where she spoke to the people through the window, and several were affected with her testimony; and towards evening she was discharged. John Langstaff, who was of great repute among his neighbours, owned her testimony, and went with her into prison, and when released brought her to his house; but John's wife being no Friend, chid with her husband, which made Anne very uneasy to stay there. So she walked out in the fields to seek some covert place to take up her lodging in; but Anthony Pearson, of Rampshaw, a late justice of the peace, who lived some miles distant, having knowledge by George Fox, who was at his house, of Anne's coming to that town, came with a horse and pillion, and took her home to his house that night.

After her service in those parts was over, she returned home; and in the winter following, she, with Mabel Camm, wife of John Camm, travelled through Yorkshire, Derbyshire, Leicestershire, into Oxfordshire, to the town of Banbury, where Mabel Camm had a concern to go to the steeple-house; and spoke to the priest and people, and Anne accompanied her. Whereupon the people rudely hurried them out of the house, and abused them in the yard. The priest passing by, Anne Audland said, 'Man, behold the fruits of thy ministry.' Next day they were sent for before the mayor, who had got two witnesses to swear Anne had spoken blasphemy, for which they committed her to prison. Mabel Camm was dismissed, and travelled to Bristol, where she met with her husband, John Camm. After some days, two men in Banbury gave bond for her appearance at the next assize, by which she was a kind of prisoner at large, which gave opportunity for her to have several meetings with the people in the town. Her two bonds-men, and several hundreds more, came to be convinced of truth, and turned to the Lord Jesus Christ, being the fruits of that effectual powerful ministry God had called her to bear, so that many were added to the church, and a large meeting of Friends there was in that town, and several other meetings in the country adjacent were settled. For this cause their adversaries were angry, and they threatened that she should be burned when the assize came.

When the assize came, John Audland, John Camm, and Thomas Camm were there, and some Friends from London and Bristol; and the substance of the charge or indictment drawn up against her was, that she had said God did not live, because she had said concerning the priest at Banbury, that 'True words may be a lie in the mouth of some that speak them;' alleging, Jer. v. 2, "And though they say the Lord liveth, (which nothing can be more true,) surely they swear falsely." The judge of the court was moderate, observing her sober and wise answers to his questions, and her innocent boldness, and comely personage, and seeing the uncertainty of the evidence against her, and that the matter of fact charged, did not amount to what was designed, gave the matter to the jury thus, viz., 'That she acknowledged the Lord her God and Redeemer to live, and that there were gods of the heathen and of the Philistines that were dead gods.' Some upon the bench perceiving their end would not be answered, went off to influence the jury to bring in something against the prisoner, lest they should come off with discredit. One of the bench observing the injustice in that matter, stepped off also, telling them, he would sit no longer with them, till more justice was amongst them, and was convinced of truth. Other officers in the court threw away their staves, and bore testimony against their arbitrary proceedings.

The jury returning into court, and being asked if they were agreed, they answered they were; and being asked what they found, they made answer, 'Only misdemeanour.' A friend present told them it was illegal to indict her for one fact and bring her in guilty of another; for they ought to have found her either guilty or not guilty, upon the matter of fact charged in the indictment. The judge told Anne, if she would give bond for her good behaviour, she might have her liberty. She refusing, they sent her to prison again: but the judge was heard to say, that the prisoner should have been discharged, but the judge had a mind somewhat to please the angry justices. Her adversaries were confounded, and slipped off the bench one after another, in disorder, without dismissing the court, so that truth was that day exalted, and the Lord's power magnified in frustrating the designs of wicked men. The prison where Anne was sent to, was a close nasty place, several steps below ground, on the side whereof was a sort of common-sewer, that received much of the mud in the town, that at times did stink sorely; besides frogs and toads did crawl into the room, and no place for fire, yet she was in great content because it was God's cause. Her fellow-prisoner was Jane Waugh, a labourer in the gospel, who came some months before to visit her, and was committed to prison with her; but God's presence and peace being with them, made their nasty stinking jail a palace, where she remained seven or eight months, and from her first commitment, about a year and a half, and was at last discharged by the mayor and aldermen. The same day Richard Farnsworth was set at liberty, who, with other men Friends were prisoners in another room; but Jane Waugh still continued a prisoner.

Anne had frequent meetings in Banbury before she left it; and also went to the mayor to demand the liberty of her friend Jane Waugh, who was imprisoned for no other fact, than for coming many miles in love to visit her in prison, and she was soon after set at liberty. Being clear of those parts, she travelled through the counties to Bristol, where she met with her husband John Audland. John and Anne Audland continued in their service and labour in the ministry in several parts of this nation, south, west, and northward, until John Audland fell sick, and died in the latter end of the year 1663, having been married to his wife Anne about thirteen years, and left behind one daughter, since dead, and one son named John, born a few days after his father's death.

The 30th of the Third month, 1666, Thomas Camm married the said Anne Audland, and they lived together in true love, serving the Lord forty years wanting six months. She was one with her husband in all his services and sufferings, as at one imprisonment three years at Kendal, he not being permitted so much as to see his family; another time at Appleby, near six years, during the first part of which he was straitly confined, the latter, through favor of the sheriff and jailor, he had much liberty. They travelled together in the work of the ministry into the southern parts of the nation, as London and Bristol, &c., especially at London. About twenty-six years ago, she had like to have died in that city, as also of later years at Bristol. The last time she was there, she was brought nigh the grave; at which time she expressed many heavenly sayings, that will not be easily forgotten by some, warning all to prize their time, and prepare for their latter end, as God had inclined her to do, so that she enjoyed unspeakable peace here, with full assurance of eternal rest and felicity in the world to come, which, said she, I have desired to enter into as gain, rather than to live, if God so please.

It was her manner often to retire alone in her closet, or some private place, exercising herself in fervent prayer, and to set apart some time almost daily for reading the holy Scriptures, and other good books, and she was very diligent in frequenting meetings for the worship of God, &c. She was not forward to appear in preaching or prayer in public meetings, but when she did, it was fervent, weighty, and with the demonstration of the spirit, and with power, to the refreshment of the church, her doctrine dropping as dew, but with zeal to lay waste the mountain of Esau. She had wisdom to know the time and season of her service, in which she was a good example to her sex, for without extraordinary impulse and concern, it was rare for her to preach in large meetings, where she knew there were brethren qualified for the service of such meetings. She was grieved when any, especially of her sex, were too hasty, forward, or unseasonable in their appearing in such meetings; and would give advice to such, not without good effect. She behaved herself as an humble servant of her Lord and Master, Christ Jesus, washing his disciples' feet, and helping and serving, as a nursing-mother, the weakest and tenderest of the flock of Christ, and was an encourager of those who came forth in a testimony for God, though but of a stammering tongue.

The last opportunity she had amongst friends was the 2d of the Ninth month, 1705, at a monthly-meeting at Kendal; and notwithstanding her great age and weakness of body, with the coldness of the season, she would not excuse herself from that day's service; and the Lord was with her in good counsel and advice to friends, pressing all to faithfulness and diligence in their service for God, that they might receive their reward with those who had nearly served out their day. The next day her illness began. About the 16th of the said month, finding her husband under concern, because of her sickness, she said as followeth:

'My dear, if it be the Lord's good pleasure, who joined us together, and has blessed us hitherto, to separate us outwardly, I entreat thee be content therewith, and give me freely up to the Lord, for thou knowest we must part, and if I go first it is but what I have desired of the Lord many a time. I believe the consideration of the desolate condition I should be in, if left behind thee, will have that place with thee, that thou wilt the more freely commit me to the Lord, whose I am, and whom I loved, feared and served with an upright heart all my days. His unspeakable peace I enjoy, and his saving health is my portion for ever. I pray thee be content with what the Lord pleaseth to do with me; whether life or death, his holy will be done. Let us, my dear, leave all to the Lord. However it be, it will be well. I have loved thee with my soul, and God has blessed us, and will bless thee, and be with thee, and make up all thy losses. Death is gain to me, though it be thy loss, and for my gain's sake, I hope thou wilt bear with patience thy loss. I bless the Lord I am prepared for my change. I am full of assurance of eternal salvation, and a crown of glory, through my dear Lord and Saviour Jesus Christ, whom God the Father has sent to bless me, with many more, by turning us from the evil of our ways into the just man's path, which shines more and more to the perfect day. If God now please to finish my course, and take me out of this earthly tabernacle, I am well content. I am clear, and have discharged myself in the sight of God to all Friends, except something of late has been upon my mind, to send Friends in the south a farewell epistle, especially to Friends about Bristol and Banbury. She said the substance thereof was the remembrance of her dear love to them all in the truth, with tender advice to the professors of truth, to walk in, and keep to, the simplicity thereof, out of heights and exaltedness, under the power of the cross of Christ, by which they will be more and more crucified to the world, and baptized into Christ, and put him on, the new and heavenly man, in whom they will become new creatures, and enabled to serve God in spirit, and keep to the unity thereof in the bond of peace and love, which the god of the world is still labouring to break and dissolve. I have seen him at work to make a breach and separation amongst Friends, and if he prevail, it will be under specious pretences of a more angelical appearance than at any time before, and will be a bait taking to all that live above the cross and true self-denial. I would all were warned to stand their ground in the power of God, which only can bruise Satan, and preserve out of his subtle baits and snares.'

Next day several Friends came to see her, to whom she gave good advice and counsel, 'To prize their time: and oh! I bless my God,' said she, 'that I lie now in great peace, and content of mind and soul, though my body be held with pain. Oh! that it may be so with you all, my dear friends.'

When she was very weak, some Friends would ask her if she knew them; 'Yes,' said she, 'I know you every one. I have my understanding as clear as ever, for how should it be otherwise, since my peace is made with God through the Lord Jesus Christ. I have no disturbance in mind, therefore is my understanding and judgment so good and clear, for it were sad to lie under affliction of body and mind, to feel pinching pangs of body, even to death, and to want peace with God. Oh!

that would be intolerable to bear. Oh! let my soul praise the Lord for his peace and plenteous redemption.'

Her son-in-law, John Moore, having skill in physic, administered somewhat to her, after which they thought she was better, and he was gone towards Swarthmore. She soon grew worse again; upon which her husband would have sent for him back, and also for her daughter, but she was unwilling, saying, 'Be not careful in the matter; the Lord my God is near me, and I have thy company, and it is enough, and all will be well. If this lump of clay, in which I dwell, be dissolved, I have full assurance of an house and dwelling, God is the maker of, that will never wax old, nor be dissolved. Oh! my soul, bless thou the Lord, and be glad in his salvation for evermore.'

Her illness increased upon her, and many friends came to visit her, to whom she said, 'Oh! the cross is the only way to the crown immortal. Shun it not, therefore, lest you fall short of the crown; and stand up nobly for your testimony to the truth in all things, and particularly against the popish antichristian yoke of tithes, for which many have not only suffered great spoil of goods, but imprisonment till death, and have received a crown of life. Oh! if all that have been called to this testimony, had stood firm and true therein, God would have wrought wonders more abundantly, but unbelief makes a long wilderness; it is well if some die not in it, and never see the promised land.'

About two days before she died, she gave good advice to her grandchildren and servants, and said to her husband, 'My dear, thou hast spent much time and strength in serving truth and Friends; thy reward with God is sure. I never grudged thy absence in that good service; and if it be the time of our parting, as I think now it will, I pray thee quit thyself of the things of this world, as much as may be, that thou mayest with the more freedom pursue that honourable service for truth to the end of thy days. I hope the Lord will give thee strength to travel into the southern parts again, and remember my love to all friends, and warn all, but especially the rich, to keep low, and not be high-minded, for humility and holiness are the badge of our profession. God Almighty keep us all low and humble; it is a safe and blessed state. And, my dear, one thing I beg of thee; give me up freely to the Lord. The Lord joined us, and gave us to each other; let us bless his name, if he now take us from each other in the outward, that is all; for our joining in spirit stands and remains for ever. Oh! therefore let me go easy out of this world, where I have had a great share of trouble many ways thou knowest, and get to that haven of rest, that I have the full assurance of sealed upon my spirit.'

A little before she died, some fainting fits taking her, she revived again, and said, 'I was glad, thinking I was going to my eternal rest without disturbance.' Again she said, 'I have both a sight and sense of eternal rest with God in the world to come; and therefore I labour hard to be swallowed up in immortal life, and to be made possessor of that rest that cannot be disturbed, where sorrow will cease, and be no more for ever. Oh! my soul, this is thy glorious portion; therefore bless thou the Lord, and wait patiently his good and appointed season.' Then she desired to be helped up in her bed; but her pains increased: she grew very weak and faint, and said, 'Methinks I grow weak and cold. My hands and feet are grown very cold, yet my heart is very strong before it yields. I must meet with sharper pangs than I have yet felt. My God has hitherto laid a gentle hand upon me.' She desired to lie down again, but could not stay, but being set up in bed again, she said, 'This pain is hard to flesh and blood, but must be endured a little time; ease and eternal rest is at hand. I am glad I see death so near me. Oh! remember me to all my dear babes and grandchildren. I shall with these eyes behold them no more. God Almighty bless them all, and make them all his children, that I may enjoy them for ever in the heavens above. Neither shall I see my sons and daughter. Ah! my prodigal son, what shall I do for him? I have prayed and longed for his return. The time may come, God grant it may, but I shall not see it in my time. He is my son, the son of a godly father, and therefore I cannot but love him. Tell him it is his immortal soul's well-being that I am concerned for; not so much his outward state here, for that, though never so miserable, will quickly end, but the misery of the soul separated from God will never end. And, my dear, though our counsel has not had the desired end, yet I do entreat thee, remain a father to him in repeated counsel. Leave him not to run on in the way of misery, but labour and pray for his return. Oh! thou hast been true to me in bearing with me many a heavy burthen, and hast done abundance for him every way, for my sake;' with more to that purpose. 'My love to his wife; I desire she may mind heavenly things, and pray God bless their offspring, that they may walk in the steps of their grandfather, who is gone to his eternal rest;' with well-wishes for her son and daughter Moore, and blessings upon their children.

The day she died, many friends came to see her, being their monthly meeting-day, to whom she gave good advice, and expressed her joy and comfort in the salvation of God, peace and perfect redemption. Seeing friends weep, she said, 'Be not concerned, for all is well; I have only death to encounter, and the sting of it is wholly taken away; the grave has no victory, and my soul is ascending above all sorrow and pain. So let me go freely to my heavenly mansion, disturb me not in my passage. My friends, go to the meeting, let me not hinder the Lord's business, but let it be chief, and by you all done faithfully, that at the end you may receive your reward, for mine is sure. I have not been negligent, my day's work is done.'

Friends went to the meeting, and in a little time her pains increased, which she bore with patience, but sighed deeply, praying the Lord to help her through her agony of death. After some words, she said, 'Oh! my God, oh! my God, thou hast not forsaken me, blessed be thy name for ever. Oh! my blessed Lord and Saviour who suffered, for me and all mankind, great pains in thy holy body upon the cross, remember me, thy poor hand-maid, in this my great bodily affliction. My trust is in thee, my hope is only in thee, my dear Lord. Oh! come, come, dear Lord Jesus, come quickly, receive my soul. To thee I yield it up; help me now in my bitter pangs.' These indeed were very great, and her husband prayed by her, that the Lord would make her passage easy; and she had no more such pangs, but drew her breath shorter by degrees, and said very little more, but that it was good to leave all to the Lord; saying, 'Oh! pray, pray, pray,' and so fell asleep in the Lord, in a good old age, being in her seventy-ninth year, as a shock of corn in season. She died the 30th of the Ninth month, 1705, and was honourably buried: many ancient Friends of about thirteen adjacent meetings accompanied her to the grave, the 3d of the Tenth month, 1705.

END OF THE THIRD PART.

PIETY PROMOTED,

IN A COLLECTION OF DYING SAYINGS

OF MANY OF THE PEOPLE CALLED

QUAKERS;

WITH A BRIEF ACCOUNT OF SOME OF THEIR LABORS IN THE GOSPEL, AND SUFFERINGS FOR THE SAME.

THE FOURTH PART.

BY JOHN FIELD.

"Let the saints be joyful in glory: let them sing aloud upon their beds." PSALMS cxlix. 5.

"Blessed are the dead which die in the Lord, from henceforth: yea, saith the Spirit, that they may rest from their labours, and their works do follow them." REV. xiv. 13.

28*

PREFACE.

[BY ANOTHER HAND.]

Friendly Reader:

Give ear to that advice which was given by the lawgiver in Deut. xxxii. 29, in the words of that song wherein he broke out, saying, "Oh! that they were wise, that they understood this, that they would consider their latter end." Herein is expressed his care for the good of that people; but how little many regarded it is apparent by their forgetfulness of the Lord, who had done marvellously for them. For how did they provoke the Lord to anger, after divers manners, as is recorded of them, some by a vicious course of life, thereby neglecting both their present good and future happiness; which might well occasion the prophet Amos to say, chap. iv. 12, "Prepare to meet thy God, O Israel!" Here is an agreement, and holy harmony of these good men, in a matter of so great moment. A cloud of the like-minded might be produced on this occasion, which for brevity sake are here omitted, to show the care of the religious on this account, and also the negligence of the irreligious. They wanted not a profession, but for want of fearing the Lord, and serving him, although they had the law dispensed to them by the disposition of angels; nevertheless they were disobedient, and rebelled against the Lord, and cast his law behind their backs, and resisted the Holy Ghost, as said the blessed martyr Stephen, whom they stoned to death, though they were not able to resist the wisdom and spirit by which he spoke. Let none professing Christianity follow their example, but by these foregoing instances beware, and learn to mind the grace of our Lord Jesus Christ, that so they may choose the things that belong to their peace, before they are hid from their eyes.

The promotion of piety was intended by the compiler of the three former volumes of dying sayings, which met with such general acceptance, that many have desired the continuation of so good a work, which doth in a measure conduce, through the good Spirit of God, to awaken people to a preparation for death; a work, indeed, so very necessary for the children of men to observe, and be concerned about, that none ought to neglect it; for death most certainly will overtake all flesh; but when, where, or how, is generally hid from men; it is a secret that the Almighty has kept from them.

How doth it therefore behove all to be in readiness against the coming of the Lord. There are few but will readily confess such a preparation ought to be, though by too many it is neglected; in order to which, I entreat that it may be thy chiefest care to fear God, and keep his commandments, for that is the conclusion of the whole matter; without which, profession, worship, and confession to the very truth, profit little. Wherefore let godliness be thy chiefest concern, that thou thereby mayest have the profit of this life, and of that which is to come, life everlasting.

Oh! prize the season of the love of God unto thee, in affording thee heavenly light, by which thou mayest see his way, and how to walk therein in well-pleasing to him, who calls to thee by a word behind thee, saying, "This is the way, walk in it."

Reader, take heed to this teacher, which is come near to thy soul, that thou mayest be guided into all truth, by the Lord Jesus Christ manifested in spirit. Let him be thy counsellor; and if sinners entice thee, consent thou not; for blessed is the man who walketh not in the counsel of the ungodly.

Awake, oh! daughter of Zion, and wait for the coming of the bridegroom. Thou hast a lamp: take oil in thy vessel, that thou mayest enter in with him. Be wise betimes, for wisdom saith, "I love them that love me, and they that seek me early shall find me." And again, it is advised to get wisdom, and with all thy getting, get understanding; the first is got by fearing the Lord, the second by departing from evil.

The exhortation of old was, "Remember thy Creator in the days of thy youth, while the evil days come not, when thou shalt say, I have no pleasure in them; in the day when the keepers of the house shall tremble, and the strong men shall bow themselves."

Prepare for such a day, for what knowest thou but it may be near to thy door? Wherefore spend not thy time in vanity, or excessive care, saying, "What shall I eat, or what shall I drink, or wherewithal shall I be clothed? But first seek the kingdom of God, and his righteousness, and all these things shall be added; for your heavenly Father, (said our blessed Lord,) knoweth that you have need of these things." The Psalmist said, "I have been young, and now I am old; yet have I not seen the righteous forsaken, nor his seed begging bread." By all which it doth appear, that the Almighty, who feedeth the ravens, provideth a necessary supply for his children, and a little with the blessing of the Lord is sufficient, although with some a great deal hath not served. For want of a moderate care, some, like the prodigal, have spent their portion; others through sloth, which comes to what the wise man said, "He that is slothful in business, is brother to him that is a great waster." Wherefore let thy moderation appear in all things; neither be over thoughtful to get, nor careless in spending.

Live not unto thyself, but unto him who died for thee, and rose again, who was our great pattern of self-denial; and taught, that if any man would come after him, he must deny himself, and take up his daily cross. This, alas! proves hard to some, as it did to the young man, Mat. xix. 22, who went away sorrowful, and would no more sell all that he had, though for the gaining eternal life, than many will now forsake evil, and do good, that they may do well for evermore.

What argument shall be used, to persuade men to seek after peace with God, and acceptance with him? to choose with Mary, the good part; which may be attained to by true humility and the fear of the Lord, as was evidenced by her patience and true contrition, which is but little regarded by some, especially of the youth; who rather are pleasing themselves with the gaiety and other vanities of this world, spending much of their precious time in adorning themselves after the foolish modes and vain fashions thereof, which pass away.

How many spend their days thus, and in a moment go down to the grave, and their candle is put out. So little is eternity thought on, that when death comes, it is the greater surprise to such, who are ready to say, "Woe unto us, for the day goeth away, and the shadows of the evening are stretched out," Then a little more time to recover strength, or make their peace with God, would be greatly acceptable to such whose glass is nearly run, who are travelling through the valley of the shadow of death; and the glory of this world is stained, and the beauty of it is fled away. What would a soul in such distress give, if it were to be purchased, for an inheritance in the kingdom of heaven.

Much might be said on this subject, of reminding the living to prepare to die, that a volume might be written on purpose, without meddling with the sayings of the deceased; but the words of the dying may make a deeper impression than what is here written.

I therefore recommend thee, serious reader, to the perusal of what follows; and to the grace of God, by which it may be made advantageous to thy everlasting well-being, when time here shall be no more.

THE INTRODUCTION.

Pursuant to the title is the following collection made, viz. to promote piety, and excite all to live the life of the righteous, that they may be blessed in their death, and welcomed after, with the loving invitation of the Lord Jesus Christ, viz. "Come, ye blessed of my Father, enter into the kingdom prepared for you from the foundation of the world." Also to show that they are those that truly believe in God, and the Lord Jesus Christ, his dear Son, who came from him, who receive that power through which they are enabled to do righteousness, and by him only are made righteous; it is such that promote piety.

The knowledge only of what is right and good, the profession thereof, or being educated in the doctrines of the Christian religion, will not entitle any to eternal happiness, if the doing part be wanting. For piety is not promoted by a bare notion and profession, or saying prayers, hearing sermons or declarations, but by a holy life, and a rightly ordered conversation. Nor is salvation known to any of the professors of Christianity, from sin whilst here, or from eternal wrath hereafter, by any other way than by faith and obedience unto Christ. For they that fear God, and work righteousness whilst here, will find acceptance with God, and enjoy his favour. As they continue faithful therein unto death, they shall have the crown of life, whether young or old. As they fear the Lord, he teaches them, and they learning of him, come to be established in righteousness, and know their peace to be great whilst here, and inherit glory in God's kingdom hereafter. But if any pretend to love Christ, and continue doing evil, such keep not his commands, abide not in his doctrine, nor love him; for by their evil doing they declare they hate the light, and by living in iniquity are found in that which is hateful in God's sight; from all which he in great love sent his Son to redeem mankind.

It is therefore by me tenderly desired, for the promotion of piety, that all may think of God, and seriously consider their latter end; love, receive, and learn of the light, grace, and spirit of God, which is in them, and shows what is evil, and reproves them, when they think, speak, or do amiss. This spirit will give unto all who join with it, a good understanding, teach them to prize and improve their present time, and strengthen unto every good word and work, and preserve them, whether young or old, in that fear towards God, which Abraham had, who was God's friend, of whom, when God had tried him, he said, "Now I know thou fearest me."

Oh! how excellent is the fear of God! so generally and worthily commended; though by many too little minded, and lived in; which is the cause piety is no more promoted. But that it may be by all that profess and desire to be God's people and children, let them learn and live in that holy fear, which Moses wrote of, Deut. iv. 10. saying, that the people should learn to fear God all the days that they should live upon the earth; for all those that do not fear God, but love and live in sin, the Lord of hosts, said he, will be a swift witness against them. But if mankind fear him as they ought, and think upon his name, the Lord of Hosts hath said, they shall be his.

Let not, therefore, the love of the world, or the things of it, or the fading vanities, sinful pleasures, or evil lusts that are therein, either of the eye, the flesh, or pride of life, be followed by any that would promote piety, and die happily, and live eternally.

Note 1. I esteem myself obliged in the following account to give hints of some of the labours, services, and sufferings of the deceased, the better to lead to the meaning of some of their expressions, and to show forth the virtue and excellency of that faith they had in Christ, who suffered and died for them, and that it was not only given to them to believe, but also to suffer for his name's sake.

2. To excite all that have not received Christ, the true light, to receive, believe in, love and obey him faithfully unto death.

3. As a memorial of the deceased, and for the sake of the living, that they, by the dying sayings of the deceased may be stirred up, as aforesaid, to remember and prepare for their latter end, and to make a blessed conclusion here, and then to be favoured with the like assurance in their last moments, as the deceased mentioned in the following accounts had, to the comfort of their souls, and satisfaction of their near and dear relations and friends, who were the more confirmed in the belief of what they said, being then about to launch into eternity, at which time the awakened conscience dares not dissemble, that desires to be happy hereafter.

If reading the following treatise, written for these ends, be in any wise instrumental to the good of the living, to excite them to prepare for their latter end, as I pray God it may, my design will be answered, and the Great God, through Jesus Christ, shall have the praise, for he is worthy for ever, saith my soul.

J. Field.

PIETY PROMOTED.

THE FOURTH PART.

JOHN WHITING was of Naylsey, in the county of Somerset, yeoman. In the year 1654, when John Audland and John Camm, two eminent ministers among the people called Quakers, were first sent from the north of England to Bristol, and the adjacent counties, freely to preach the gospel of the grace of God, and to turn people from darkness to light, and from the power of Satan unto God; the said John Whiting was convinced of the blessed truth, and received it in the love thereof, as it was professed by those called Quakers. He also received the ministers of it into his house, as he had the truth they declared into his heart; and had meetings held at his house, to wait upon God, and worship him in the spirit of his dear Son; and for his ministers freely to preach the gospel of peace and salvation, as they were sent and required by him.

Although the truth, and those that received it, were greatly despised in those early days, yet this disciple of Christ, being made partaker of the like precious faith that was once delivered to the saints, was zealous for the truth, it being given to him not only to believe, but also to suffer for the sake of Christ, amongst the first of those people to whom he was joined, in that county, and remained faithful unto death.

In the time of his sickness, and near his end, in a sense of the love of God, and in love to his wife, with desires for her, who was then young in the truth which he had received, professed, and had suffered for, and found peace and comfort in; he exhorted her, saying, 'As thou hast believed in the light, so walk in it;' which showed, as he loved Christ the true light, he desired she might walk therein. Truly there are none but those that do evil, who hate the light; neither can such be saved, until they come to believe and walk in the light, as all the nations of them that are saved do, and it is not doubted but this our friend did, and died in the faith of Christ, and in peace with God through him.

He died the 9th of the Fourth month, 1658; aged about twenty-seven years, having been convinced four years.

ANNE DEWSBURY, wife of William Dewsbury, then of Wakefield, in Yorkshire, an hand-maid of the Lord, in the beginning of the Seventh month, 1659, had a revelation or dream from the Lord, that her life was nearly finished, and though she might be exercised with much weakness, yet in the midst thereof the Lord would strengthen her with his presence, and in him she should overcome the last enemy, which is death. Having assurance of what was revealed, though at that time she was in good health, she made ready what might be serviceable when her change came. About the 29th of the said Seventh month, some weakness came upon her, which increased so much, that she was many times, to outward appearance, near laying down the body; yet the Lord preserved her in much patience, and fresh in his love.

Her husband, being gone to the farthest part of Scotland in the service of truth, and to publish the day of the Lord, and preach the gospel of Christ, was moved of the Lord, the 9th of the Eighth month, to return to her, and on the 28th of the Eighth month, 1659, he was brought to her with joy in the Lord. After this she was weaker in her body; but the Lord gave her strength by his living presence to wait till her change came, which drew near, and being exercised in her affliction, which lay heavy upon her, she called to her husband, with certain friends, saying, 'Pray to the Lord that he may ease his afflicted hand-maid.' And the Lord moved them to call upon him, and immediately he took away the heavy affliction. Then she magnified the Lord, saying, 'Blessed be his name, he hath heard our prayers, and caused his hand-maid to rejoice.' Then she embraced her husband in her arms, saying, 'Thou art my dear husband; thou art my dear husband; thou art clear before the Lord, and hast discharged thy duty, and answered thy place, like an honest man to thy wife. Thou art blessed of the Lord; large is thy reward.' Then she expressed these words, saying, 'Dear husband, I am clear before the Lord thy God. I have no guilt upon my spirit in the covenant of light and life, sealed with the blood of Jesus. I am at eternal peace with him.'

She exhorted the friends present, saying, 'Oh! friends, get into the covenant of light and life, get into the covenant, be faithful to the voice that cries, "This is the way, walk in it."' Her strength was much gone, yet prayed to God a season longer, and breathing to the Lord till much spent, some that stood by her, seeing her lips and mouth move, but did not understand what her words were, asked her if she spoke to them, and what she wanted. She answered, 'I spoke not to you, neither do I want any thing of you.' Some time after she called for her husband, who was near, and presently spoke to her, saying, 'Dear wife, what wouldest thou with me,' she answered, 'I would have thee be with me and see me die.' He sat down by her; then embracing her husband in her arms, and with breathings to the Lord, she laid down her body with joy in peace with him.

ANTHONY PATRICKSON, formerly of Stockhow, in the parish of Lamplugh, in Cumberland, received truth in those parts of the country with the first, and was made by the Lord a minister of the everlasting gospel, and travelled in several places of the nation of England, and through Scotland, Ireland, and the Isle of Man, and was diligent in attending meetings, and admonishing and instructing the weak, and remained steadfast to the end. He was of a lamb-like spirit, meek, gentle, not easily provoked, ready to do good, and walked honestly; was of godly conversation, and preached therein to those that were enemies to the gospel; so that they would confess, if all the Quakers were like him, surely they were a good people. When taken sick, he saw he must depart this life, and immediately the incomes of the love of God did break in upon his spirit, with sweet comfort and consolation, and he said, 'The Lord hath given me an assurance of that blessed inheritance that never will have end.'

Thus did this faithful witness finish his testimony, and end his race of this mortal life, the latter end of the Sixth month, 1660.

MARY PAGE, wife to William Page, of Wellingborough, in the county of Northampton, a true and faithful hand-maid of the Lord, was taken sick at Warwick prison, where she had been a prisoner during the space of eleven months and upwards, for the testimony of the name of the Lord, which faithful testimony she sealed with her blood, to the joy of all that beheld her innocent passage, in the power of the eternal God. This hand-maid of the Lord was enlarged through the pourings forth of the spirit of the Lord, and upon her death-bed, in great power, exhorted all to be faithful and abide in the covenant of light, and be truly obedient in the meek, lowly, humble, and self-denying spirit of our Lord Jesus, that, in the pure love and righteousness of God, all the dear babes and children of our Father might live in pure union with the Lord, and one with another, to bear a bold and faithful testimony for the Lord. Whatever became of the body, it would, she told them, be well every way, both to the inward and outward man, and to the praise and glory of the Lord for ever.

Many times, when she ended her exhortation, she poured forth her spirit in supplication to the Lord with great fervency, and what follows is noted. 'Oh! thou powerful God, who art the searcher of all hearts, behold thy hand-maid; and if there be any thing that is not upright before thee in the heart of thy hand-maid, make it known to me, thou searcher of hearts. Thou knowest I delight to stand approved in thy sight in all thy ways; for thou art my dear Father, and hast not failed thy hand-maid in whatever thou hast called me to unto this day; but thy presence hath attended me, and comforted me through every trial and besetment, that the enemy of my soul hath compassed me about withal. Oh, blessed God! how hast thou kept and preserved me to thyself, and through the power of the Lord Jesus Christ made me to trample upon the enemy of my soul's peace. Therefore in the name and power of the Lord Jesus Christ, doth my soul praise thee, O my God, for my preservation in the power and authority of thy spirit, to bear my faithful testimony for thee my God, all my days until I have finished my course in thy will, oh Lord! my strength and life for ever and ever.

'And, dear Father, look upon thy poor oppressed ones, that have no life but in thee. Oh! how do they cry in a sense of their misery, Lord help, or we die. Oh Lord! thou knowest their necessities, and their wants are not hid from thee, whose righteousness without thee is as filthy rags. Therefore do they cry unto thee. Nothing will satisfy them but thy presence. Oh, powerful Father! raise up thy own begotten in the power and authority of the Lord Jesus Christ, to reign over all its besetments, that the mourner may rejoice, and the bowed-down head may be lifted up, and every hungry and thirsty soul satisfied with the bread and water of life, which thou freely handest forth by the hand of our Mediator, Christ Jesus our Lord, not for any thing that we have done, or do, but for thy own name's sake, that all flesh and boasting may be laid in the dust, and all crowns cast down before thee, that thou alone may have all the glory, whose right is over all, saith my soul, for ever and ever.

'And yet notwithstanding that all we have or receive, is in thy free mercy in Christ Jesus, yet this giveth not any liberty to sin, oh! Lord, thou knowest, but rather engages us that are born again to abhor ourselves, and to stand upon our watch diligently, that the enemy may not enter with any of his wiles, to cause us to abuse thy grace and free mercies, which thou hast so freely manifested to us, in the name of the Lord Jesus, when we had not any power to help ourselves. Therefore doth my soul, with the souls of thy dear and faithful children, cry unto thee to keep us pure in thy holy power, that in meekness and true sincerity of heart, we may wait upon thee, and be obedient in whatever thou callest us unto, even to the loss of husband, or wife, or children, or whatever else thou requirest. If it be to the laying down of the outward man, for thy glorious truth, it will be well every way with all that have not any comfort or help but in thee, thou ever-living God, to whom be all glory and honour for ever.

'And holy glorious Father of life, bless and preserve all the people that make mention of thy holy and eternal truth, here, and here-away, and all my fellow-prisoners, with all thy suffering members every where, and my dear husband and children. God bless and preserve them, and take care of them. Oh! my God, do well for them every way, in keeping them faithful, with my own soul, unto the end of our days; whether they be few or many, thy will be done. Oh! thou holy eternal God, keep thy dear children from whence I came. Oh Lord! thou knowest how dear they are to me; but I commit them wholly to thy care, oh! my God; whom I know certainly will never fail them that are of an upright heart, and cannot be satisfied but with thy living eternal presence in the Lord Jesus, to whom I commit them all, if I never see their faces in the outward any more. I know it will be well both with me and them, as we give up unto thee, to be ordered according to thy will, our little time we have here to be upon the earth; to the glory and honour of thy great name, thou everlasting glorious Father of life, to whom alone it doth belong, saith my soul, with the souls of all thy beloved and faithful children and servants, that thou hast chosen to glorify thee, who alone art God over all, blessed for ever, and evermore.'

When she had done, a friend asked her how she did, she said, 'I am weak, but I would go home.' 'What,' said the friend, 'to thy eternal home?' she smiled and said, 'Yea, when it pleaseth my heavenly Father.' Her tender and loving husband being there with her, drew near unto her, and she in much love stroked him on the face with her hand, when tears trickled down his cheeks, and friends weeping by her, after a little time she put her husband from her, and said, 'Give me up freely into the arms of my heavenly Father.' She spoke no more, but within a little time finished her course with joy, and laid down her body in peace, near the fourth hour in the morning, the 17th of the Tenth month, 1665.

ROBERT HATTON, of Hatton, in Cheshire, was an eminent minister of the gospel, and faithful in his labours and travels to preach the same for many years, of a good example, and adorned the doctrine of Christ, and in his innocent life preached righteousness at home and abroad. He was a man of substance, solid and grave, and had a good sense of God upon his spirit, and a divine understanding of things that tended to the honour of God and the church's peace. He dearly loved unity, and laboured earnestly to promote it. Every appearance of that which obstructed it was grief to him, but the increasing fellowship of the church his soul rejoiced in. He was zealous for the holy truth, and concerned for the glory of God; his soul hated the very appearance of evil, and [he was] a sharp reprover of the loose, profane, heady and high-minded, and such as were lovers of pleasures more than lovers of God. Being a possessor of the wisdom that is from above, he was mild in exhortation, and loved tenderness in whomsoever it appeared, and was ready to help the weak. In suffering, of a noble spirit, bold for the truth, wholly resigned in the will of God, come what would come, being a man of courage, and gave great encouragement to suffering friends. He was a faithful follower of the Lamb, whatever tribulations or imprisonments he met with, or fines that were imposed upon him, for the testimony that the Lord had given him to bear. When spoken to not to preach, he mildly answered, 'If the Lord kindle a sacrifice, who can forbear to offer;' and wherever he travelled, he left a good savour behind him.

The day before he departed this life, some of his friends were with him, to whom he spoke of things relating to the inner man, and said cheerfully, 'My spirit is very easy, and there is no guilt or burthen upon me;' and at their parting, he said, 'The Lord knows whether we may see the faces one of another again.' The day following, he laid down his head, no doubt in peace with God, and is at rest.

ELIZABETH HUNTINGTON, daughter of Robert Huntington, of Bowsted-hill, in Cumberland, was of an innocent life and blameless conversation, and a good example, of a meek and gentle spirit, careful and tender over all in whom the least appearance of truth manifested itself. When it pleased the Lord God, by his mighty power, to raise her up as an instrument in his hand, to declare his wonders and show forth his praise, her travels and labours were great for the truth's sake, to turn people unto the Lord; being not satisfied to eat her morsel of bread alone: and her faithfulness to truth, was as her crown to her latter end.

About the Seventh month, 1678, her mouth was opened by the power of the Lord, in which she grew exceedingly in the truth, and the Lord gave her wisdom abundantly, and she became valiant for the Lord, and bore an honourable testimony for his name and truth, and was a good example. By her faithfulness many were turned to the Lord, for she laboured earnestly for the good of all people; and in the year 1679 she travelled with William Johnson, and Jane Seally, into Northumberland, Bishoprick, and Yorkshire.

In 1680 she visited Friends in Scotland, with her companions Frances Liddle and Richard Perkin, and returned to her father's house after about three months' travel. Soon after, she went again into Northumberland, Bishoprick, and Yorkshire, and returned to her father's in the Sixth month. Upon the 3d of the Seventh month she was taken sick, and after some time said to her sister, 'I must leave this troublesome world, and go into immortality.' The Lord kept her near to himself; and as though she had fallen asleep, she laid down her head in peace on the 9th of the Seventh month, and was buried the 10th, in the twenty-third year of her age. In the ministry two years.

EDWARD JEFFERYS, of Charlecot in Wiltshire, was concerned, after he had spoken several precious words to those that were with him upon his death-bed, to give forth the following paper, which was taken from him by Andrew Shepperd, and being remarkable and prophetical, it is here inserted, viz.:

A word of exhortation and warning from the servant of the Lord, Edward Jefferys, written on the 4th of the Eleventh month, 1685. The power of the Lord was in him, and it constrained him powerfully to exhort all to faithfulness, saying,

'Dear hearts! a trying day is yet coming on this nation; for the Lord will yet farther visit it, and he will sweep away thousands to the grave. I prophesy of it in the pure fear of Almighty God, who speaks through me his instrument, who have followed him faithfully, and now heaven's joys are prepared for me, and for all those that faithfully follow him, as I have done. I have walked in the narrow way of life and peace; but how many are running in the broad way that leads to destruction? All my time, from my youth upward, I was inclinable to that which was good. And who would spend away his day in vanity and folly? seeing the shortness of time that we have here, to that we shall have hereafter. Dear hearts, be not concerned for me, although the Lord is pleased to remove me, he will raise up many Friends when I am gone, for I must certainly go the way of all flesh, and it will be but a little time, until you will come after me. Therefore I desire you may so walk, as becomes the blessed truth of our God; for because of pride, the Lord is offended with many that are under the profession of the blessed truth, which I have sought to promote in my day, and that the Lord would carry it on to his own praise. Often hath my heart been bowed down in the night season, intreating the Lord in behalf of all; often crying to the Lord for the restoration of poor fallen man, universally for all. Often hath my spirit been poured out to the Lord for this king, James the Second, that now is, that he might be a promoter of the blessed truth and righteousness in his day. But I fear whether this will be the man; yet, I say, the Lord will raise up one in his stead, that shall be as a nursing father, and as a nursing mother in Israel. God's truth shall prosper in this land.

'Fourth of the Eleventh month, 1685.'

The deceased was an honest, faithful man in his day, and a minister of the gospel of peace, and laboured therein freely for the good of souls, and died in peace with God, and is at rest.

MARGARET BERRY, wife of William Berry, of Choptank, in Maryland, was a mother in Israel, a teacher of good things, desired the good of all, and the Lord was with her. She was of a meek spirit, diligent in meeting, and stirred up Friends thereunto, faithful to the Lord in all her trials and exercises she met with in this world, not willing to gratify the world's spirit; but ready to testify against all superfluity in what kind soever, as in apparel, or other ways. She went plain and decent, in modest apparel, with sobriety, and was exemplary therein to young women, preferring a meek and quiet spirit as the best ornament, willing to do good to all, especially to the household of faith, careful to see all things in order in her family, discreet, chaste, obedient in her place, ready to give up her husband freely to the Lord's service even to the last, and loved unity amongst Friends.

And as she lay upon her death-bed, her husband being from home in the service of truth, with Daniel Gould, of Rhode Island, in and about Accomack, before several Friends, she said, 'I am freely given up to the will of the Lord, and if it be his will to remove me hence, I am well satisfied with what his will and pleasure is, and am satisfied that I shall lay down my head in peace with him, blessed be his name for ever. And though my pain be great upon my outward man, I am kept and borne above my pain, through the goodness of the Lord, in that I have nothing laid to my charge; but that I have discharged my conscience in his sight by his assisting power.' Finding herself very weak in body, not knowing how short her time might be, she desired her brother Pitt to write what she had on her mind by way of a will; and said, at that time, 'I would have all left to my dear husband, if living; and if any part of what I have done, or the whole, be not agreeable to his mind, he may make it void at his pleasure; for I would not do any thing that should grieve him, for he never deserved it at my hands.'

Then she also desired him to write a letter for her to her husband, as followeth:

'Dear and loving husband, William Berry. After my endeared love to thee and dear Daniel Gould, I thought meet to let thee know that I, being very weak in body, and not knowing what the will of the Lord is touching my outward man; yet in this am I comforted and refreshed, that the Lord is not wanting to refresh me with the smiles of his countenance, and am satisfied it shall be well with my inward man, and that, when I shall lay down my head, it will be in peace with the Lord, into whose hands I commit myself, being freely given up, whether life or death, which is more satisfaction than my tongue can express.

'So, dear heart, having something in my mind, to have a few lines written as a will, and I could not see thy face, which thing I more desired than any outward enjoyment, so could not confer with thee; yet what I have done in that kind, if I should not see thy face in mutability, it is not my mind to do any thing to grieve thee, or against thy mind. But when thou perusest what I have written, thou mayest, if it please thee, perform or make it void at thy pleasure, which I leave to thy consideration, not desiring to grieve thee, nor that thou shouldst be straitened in thy mind or otherwise upon this account, or bring thyself under upon any account, but as I have said, it may be with great clearness. So committing thee, with myself, to the Lord, I take leave, and remain thy true and loving wife,

'MARGARET BERRY.

'The 12th of the Second month, 1688.'

The day she departed, several friends being there, she desired them to be called together, and said, 'I have something to say, if the Lord enable me. As touching my burial, my dear husband being from home, it must be left to you; and I desire there may be nothing of great preparation for the same; though some may say it is covetousness, it matters not. We have enough, but I am against gratifying the world's spirit; for since I professed the truth, I never had unity with superfluity at burials or marriages, especially at burials, and have borne my testimony often against such things, as some of you are my witnesses; and my dear husband is one with me, and I know if such a thing should be at my burial it would grieve him, who is gone upon truth's account, and I have freely given him up. So if any Friend have anything to object, they may freely speak.'

All Friends were one with her in that concern, and she further said, 'I desire you may all keep in unity, and be of one mind.' She desired James Berry to make her coffin, being cheerful in her spirit; and desired friends to remember her dear love to her dear husband, and dear Daniel Gould and friends. At another time she said to friends that were with her, 'Have your eyes to God, whom I desire may support the little remnant that is left behind. There are but a few, but the Lord is all-sufficient; and as you are faithful, you will be preserved; for indeed there are a few that have the weight of truth upon their spirits. The Lord, if it be his will, raise up standard-bearers, and carry on his own work.'

At another time she said, 'Surely people had need have nothing to do at this time but to wait upon God, when it shall please him to remove them; and if it be so with me, O how will many do when their dying hour approaches!' Then said, 'Lord, hasten thy work, for there is no ease upon this feather bed for my body, but I shall be at ease when my body is laid in its cold bed of clay.' Some hours before she departed, she desired all friends to go to bed, and took her leave of them, as if she was going to her long home, as indeed she was. A little before she departed, the Lord gave her ease, which she said she never expected in her body, for which she praised the name of the Lord; so lay still afterwards, and all was well with her, being freed from the pangs of death, as appeared by her patient waiting the appointed time of the Lord, as if she was slumbering. In that quiet stillness she continued till she gave up the ghost, and no doubt but she is blessed: as she lived in the Lord, she died in him, and rests from her labours, and her good works follow her.

She had given many other heavenly exhortations, not noted, to several friends, and to her youngest son, and others of her family, and several relations, exhorting all to faithfulness, diligence, and true humility before the Lord.

Her age, the day of her death, and place of burial, I have no exact account of.

THOMAS FELL, late of Chapel-house, in the parish of Ireby, and county of Cumberland, was convinced in the year 1653, it being soon after the Lord had revealed his truth in the North; and he was also the first married amongst Friends, at least in those parts. Although he owned marriage as an ordinance of God, yet he could not find in all the Holy Scriptures that God ever appointed any of his priests or ministers to marry any, or appointed they should have money for so doing; yet he was cast into prison at Carlisle for not being married by a priest, and giving him money. There the said Thomas Fell remained prisoner one year, and before he had his liberty his wife died.

Afterwards he was a prisoner nearly ten years at the suit of one Edward Relf and Hugh Simpson, impropriators, for not paying tenpence per year for tithes, which they called prescription-money; for which he suffered cheerfully and with patience, and never murmured. After it pleased the Lord that he got his liberty clearly, he travelled in the public service of truth, bearing testimony thereto, freely preaching the gospel of Christ in England and Scotland, and divine openings of heavenly things he had. He was of a blameless life and conversation, and serviceable where he lived; and as he grew in years, he grew in gravity and zeal for the Lord, and for the promotion and prosperity of the great work the Lord hath begun in the earth, even to the day of his departure.

A friend visiting him near the hour of his departure, his memory was perfect, and he said, 'Truth is as precious as ever, for which I have been freely given up to suffer, labour, and travel, both in our own country and in Scotland. Indeed, he became as a pillar in the Lord's house, and when, by reason of bodily weakness, he could not travel, he was concerned that Friends might be kept in unity, and walk in the fellowship of the gospel. A little before his departure, he inquired whether they were in love one with another, and if there were no rent or division; and when it was reported to him that Friends were mostly well, and truth prospered, he was comforted, and in great peace he departed this life in 1697, in unity with the brethren, aged seventy-three years.

WILLIAM TOVEY, late of Henley-upon-Thames, Oxfordshire, malster, was convinced of the blessed truth in his young days, and lived to a good old age, and had many children, whom he had a care to train up in the way they should walk, and therein he, through faithfulness, hath found peace. He was a just and religious man, careful to discharge his duty to Almighty God, and to preserve his peace with him, through Jesus Christ his dear Son, whom God hath sent a light into the world, that all men through him might believe. By that power, which through faith he received, he was enabled to show a godly and exemplary conversation, and therefore did adorn the doctrine of Christ our Saviour, and in the time of his bodily weakness was kept in a sweet and tender frame of spirit.

A few days before he departed out of this mortal life, his children being by him, he, in sweetness and tenderness of spirit, said to them, 'Be faithful to the Lord, and serve him in your generation.' And in particular, calling his son Caleb unto him, and taking him by the hand, said, 'Dear Caleb, the Lord hath a blessing in store for thee, be thou faithful;' and repeating it, said, 'Be thou faithful, and the Lord hath a blessing in store for thee;' with more weighty expressions not noted; and he added, 'I desire thou mayest succeed in my place; but some may say, thou being but a young man, art too forward; mind it not, but be thou faithful, and keep thine eye to the Lord, and he will be thy reward.' Then he said, 'Oh! that a young generation may be raised up in this place, (Henley) if it be the will of the Lord, that may bear a faithful testimony to his truth, his living truth. I am not without hopes, though at present not very likely, for there is a great deal of rubbish to be removed out of the way.' Adding, 'It is not high notions or a bare profession that will do, it is heart work.' Being asked to drink some cordial, he said, 'It is my cordial to do the will of my God;' adding, 'I did not know I should have any thing to say; but it is the Lord's doings.' Then said to them present, 'Be not backward in going to meeting, and say, we are hindered; no, no, that is the devil's work; but be valiant, miss no opportunity; for as you are diligent in waiting upon the Lord, that may be revealed to you at one time, that may not at another, or afterwards.'

Speaking of the goodness of the Lord to the humble, and

how he guided those whose hearts are upright towards him, he said in much tenderness, 'Seek the Lord whilst he may be found, call upon him whilst he is near: let the wicked forsake his ways, and the unrighteous man his thoughts, and let him return unto the Lord, and he will have mercy upon him, and to our God, for he will abundantly pardon.' He then prayed tenderly and fervently to the Lord for the prosperity of his truth in that place; and expressed the satisfaction he had in discharging his duty in the sight of the Lord, saying, 'The quarterly-meeting was pleased to confer the care of the church in this place upon me,' (i. e. he being desired to take care of the poor, and to have an eye over the professors of truth there, that they might walk as became their holy profession.) 'I never did any thing in an overly way. No, no, but in humility and tenderness. I watched over them for good, though I have been spurned at by some for it, but the Lord forgive them.'

He was preserved very sensible, and in great patience all the time of his illness, several times saying he had no clog upon him, but was freely given up, saying, 'I am ready, come my Lord when thou pleasest, I am ready.' Another time he said, 'The Lord doth not withhold his living presence from me;' so lifting up his hand again, said, 'All is well, all is well, I am ready.' Near his departure, several of his children being by him, he looking upon them, said, 'The Lord bless you all, the Lord bless you altogether, and preserve you in his blessed truth until your last breath.' Giving order who should be invited to his funeral, he said his end in desiring many should be there was for the salvation of their souls; and if but one should be reached and come to the knowledge of the truth and be saved, it would be well, and that which he desired. Then said, 'I am wholly given up to the will of the Lord, and I hope he will make my passage easy;' and indeed the Lord was pleased to answer his desire, for he went away without sigh or groan, the year 1700, being seventy-seven years old. He is entered into the joy of his Lord, and by faith, he being dead, yet speaketh, or is yet spoken of, as it is said of righteous Abel. The weighty sayings following, being found of his own hand-writing, some years after his decease, by his son Caleb, are here printed, being worthy of observation.

'Stand in awe of the living God, that created thee to glorify his name.

'Refrain from all evil, and love righteousness.

'Do nothing that may bring dishonour to truth, if the whole world might be gained thereby.

'According to the ability or talents the Lord doth give thee inwardly or outwardly, do thou serve the Lord, his truth, and people. Those that profess and possess the truth, that love it above all things, that can venture all for truth's sake; such do thou have true unity with, but not with backbiters, or careless professors of truth.

'If any difference doth arise betwixt Friends or others, do thou endeavour to put an end to it, in the spirit of meekness. The rough nature is Esau, but the meek and lowly is the true seed.

'Do justly, love to be merciful, that thou mayest walk humbly with thy God; that when thou hast ended the days of thy natural life, thou mayest lay down thy head in peace with the living God; which far exceeds all the world, or the world's enjoyments. And in so doing, thou wilt not only answer the requirings of the Lord, but of thy dear and tender father also.

WILLIAM BEVAN, of Swansea, in the county of Glamorgan, aged seventy-four years, being sick and weak in body, and judging the time of his dissolution to be nigh, said unto his son Silvanus Bevan, his daughter Hester being present, 'I desire that you may live in love together when I am gone, and keep to meetings, and let your houses be open to those that bring glad tidings of the kingdom of peace, for they are faithful labourers, and if you have but little, God will add a blessing.' Being asked if he would take any thing to support his spirits, he refused, and said, 'All is well, and that he saw no cloud of darkness before him, but blessed God, that he had brought him into the inner court, and if he had strength he could sing for joy;' with many other comfortable expressions. At another time when weak in bed, his son Michael, James Picton, and kinsman William Bevan, and his son Silvanus Bevan, being present, he said to this effect, 'Grandson William, be obedient to those thou art under; fear God always, and run not into the fashions of the world; but behave thyself humbly and lowly, and God will add a blessing to thy endeavours. And son Michael, thou knowest much, and God hath given thee much understanding. Thou hast a large memory of the Holy Scriptures; mind the gift of God's Holy Spirit, and then thou wilt be a good man, and a serviceable man, and a preacher of righteousness in thy life and conversation.'

He also exhorted his sons to be kind to their sister, and to honour and assist her in the choice of a husband, that he might be one that fears God, and lives uprightly, and on all occasions; 'For,' said he, 'she hath been careful and tender of me since your mother died, and a support to my old age: so live in love together, that others may behold you as a family of love, and then the Lord will bless you.' At another time, his son Silvanus, and many of his grand-children being by his bed-side, he said, 'Fashion not yourselves after this world, but transform yourselves to the image of the dear Son of God. Be not puffed up in pride and gaudy apparel, but in the fear of God: adorn yourselves modestly, as becomes Christians to do, and keep to the small grain of the kingdom, and then you will grow and flourish in holiness to the praise of God, and lie down in peace, as you see me now.' And renewing his advice, of being a family of love when he was gone, said, 'Strive not who shall be greatest, but who shall be the humblest and most serviceable amongst you, for that will be joy and peace in the Holy Ghost. But an exalted mind brings pain and trouble; I know it. If you will be careful and obedient to that small grain which God hath sown in your hearts, he will fulfil his promise; I am sure he will fulfil his promise, and you will lie down in peace. I have left something to every one of you. If you do well, it will be a blessing, if not, a curse; as the children of Israel desiring flesh, not obeying the Lord, not content with their condition, God gave them flesh in his wrath, and they died whilst it was between their teeth. So to the Lord I leave you, desiring him to bless you, which is the best portion I can give you.' His children all kissing him, concluded at this time in much tenderness and tears.

Many other comfortable expressions dropped from him, which were not taken in writing, nor can it be justly remembered, importing tender advice and exhortation to his children, showing forth greatly the joys of a peaceable conscience in our Lord Jesus Christ. At another time, though very sick, and in much pain, about midnight, on a sudden he was still and quiet, and in a little while said, 'The Lord hath removed the pains of death, his glory shines in his weak servant. Hallelujah, hallelujah, praises, praises be to him for ever;' with other good expressions, and so continued singing a minute or two, as one whom the Lord had assured of his salvation, and exalted above the fears of death, or the terrors of the world to come, being supported by the spirit and power of religion, which the agonies of death are not able to shake. So having seen twenty of his children's children, and growing weaker and weaker in body, he resigned up this life in that quietness and innocency in which infants go to sleep, the 5th of the Twelfth month, 1701, and was buried by his wife in Friends' burying-place in Swansea. This good old man, through faith and obedience in and to the Lord Jesus Christ, and by a patient continuing in well-doing to the end, hath no doubt the reward of immortality, eternal life, and inherits glory, honour, and peace with God in his holy kingdom, and will do for ever and ever.

NICHOLAS BEARD, of Rottingdean, in the county of Sussex, was in his youth a tender, seeking young man after the knowledge of the Lord, and for nearly twenty or thirty years would often ride many miles to hear the best reputed teachers the times afforded.

In the year 1655 he was convinced of the blessed truth of God, by the ministry of that eminent servant of Christ, George Fox, and received it in the love thereof, and was faithful thereto. It pleased the Lord to call him into the ministry, and he laboured in the work thereof in the county wherein he lived, and the neighbouring counties. He was a constant attender of quarterly, monthly, and weekly meetings, as long as strength of body would admit; and after that failed, that he could not go far, continued visiting the nearest meetings, constant, sound in doctrine, fervent in prayer; and to his children would often say, 'That which is right do, and the Lord be with you.' And in the sense of the Lord's goodness, would often say, 'Be thou bowed before the Lord, oh! my soul.' Growing weak in body, being in his chamber, and some of his children with him, with lifted up hands and eyes, he said, 'I must leave you to the teachings of the Lord, and the Lord in mercy be with you.' Being weak in his bed, in melody of spirit, he was heard to say, 'Oh! Lord, my soul blesseth thee, and all that is within me magnifieth thy holy name.' He often desired to depart, and be with Christ in peace, which he also signified would be his portion in the world to come. So departed this life, in peace with the Lord and unity with the brethren, the 2d of the Fifth month, 1702, having ordained in his will that his executor should entertain his friends, the people called Quakers, in his house, as he in his lifetime did: aged eighty years; a minister about thirty years.

To show that he was not only called to believe, but also to suffer, I shall briefly recite some of his sufferings.

For his testimony against paying tithes in this gospel-day, he had taken from him by one Robert Baker, priest of Rottingdean, for one year's tithes demanded, twelve oxen, six cows, and one bull, which were sold the same day at Lewis-clift fair for one hundred and eleven pounds five shillings; but worth more.

For the worship of God, or meeting only for that end, and keeping the testimony of a good conscience, in obeying Christ's command, "Swear not at all," and abiding in his doctrine, and for not bearing arms, or sending out in the militia, and not frequenting the public worship, he was prosecuted on the statute of twenty pounds per month, and underwent imprisonment, and sustained the loss of his goods, and many other abuses. Yet it pleased the Lord to support and bless him; so that although his loss was more than one thousand pounds, and his charge of children considerable, being the father of above twenty, yet he gave them that lived good portions, being twelve; also lived to see several of them well settled in the world, leaving his youngest son in his own seat, in a much more plentiful estate than his parents left him, though he was a prisoner several years.

ELIZABETH HOPKINS, wife of Thomas Hopkins, of Glastonbury, in Somersetshire, loved truth, and those that were faithful to it, although she was but young in it; and when taken sick was not discontented, but resigned to the will of God. Being asked whether she was willing to die, she said, 'I am fitted to die, and fully satisfied. I find nothing in my way that hinders me from peace with the Lord;' and lay often praising the Lord for his great loving kindness and mercy to her, in bringing her to the knowledge of the truth. Towards her end, she said, 'Lord, make my passage out of this world easy;' which he was pleased to grant, and she passed away like a lamb, or one going to sleep. She departed in true and living faith, the 16th of the Sixth month, 1703, after several months' weakness, and was buried in Friends' burying-ground at Glastonbury.

JOHN BEERE, of Weymouth, in the county of Dorset, was born of believing parents in the year 1659, and when he grew up he embraced the same faith, and professed truth in much plainness and sincerity, and was, through the power of it, of a blameless conversation, a good example, and of great service in the church.

In the year 1693, being about thirty-four years of age, he received a gift of the ministry, in which he was a faithful labourer, though he did not travel far, but had good service in his own country, and was well beloved and esteemed by his friends and near neighbours, to whom he administered much tender and wholesome advice. In his last sickness, two days before he died, he sent for a friend and neighbour, who, when he came, asked him how he did; he replied, 'I have but one pain to encounter with, that is the pain of my body, for my mind is at ease.' And at another visit of the same friend he repeated the same. The day that he departed there were several friends and others to visit him, to whom he gave seasonable advice, desiring them to be faithful, saying, 'Although you are few in number, if you continue faithful the Lord will increase you;' and desired them to make their peace with the Lord in the time of their health, for on a death-bed they would have enough to do to struggle with the pain of the body; for he said if he had not made his peace with the Lord before he came on a dying-bed he had been miserable. Another time, his eldest daughter asking how he did, he said, 'I am waiting for my change;' and desired his children to be obedient to their mother, and keep out of all evil company. Many were the seasonable and comfortable expressions which he gave forth in the time of his weakness that cannot be remembered. He died the 5th of the Seventh month, 1703. Aged fourty-four years; a minister ten years.

SARAH SCOTT, daughter of Francis Scott, of Hambridge, in the county of Somerset, aged thirteen years, wanting four days, was educated in the way of truth professed by the people called Quakers, from the age of three years, by her uncle and aunt Whiting, who took her as their own. She was of a loving and affable temper, and sober behaviour, but of a weakly constitution, not given or addicted to any bad words or actions; yet, when she came upon a sick bed, it seemed hard sometimes for her to be reconciled to her sickness. But upon reading several places in the New Testament, concerning afflictions and chastisements, as Heb. xii., &c., she came to be reconciled to both, and afterward received great satisfaction, so that her heart was often enlarged in the love of God, and her soul did magnify the God of her salvation.

Her uncle, J. Whiting, asked her if she was willing to die; she said, 'If I had assurance of the love of God, I should.' Then he asked her if she had any thing that lay upon her mind that troubled her. She answered no, nothing in particular, but that she had lived no better, or more circumspectly; but upon his mentioning to her the mercy of God in Christ Jesus, who died for her, she said, 'If it be the will of God to take me to himself, I am content.' She frequently prayed in secret to the Lord; and once, being spoken to when still, she said, 'Let me alone, that I may meditate on my God;' and afterward said, she enjoyed the streams of the love of God, but found 'The enemy so busy, that it is hard to keep my mind staid on the Lord;' adding, she was sorry for all that did live wickedly, and lamented what many would do when they came upon a death-bed; and desired her aunt to advise one of her acquaintance to take more care of her words and actions, or she would find it hard when she came upon a death-bed.

She said, 'I have had much trouble, the enemy having been busy, when I was in meetings, so that I looked out sometimes, and neglected the inward work, for which I have known sorrow. I have gone through nights of sorrow and prayer; but now I am made willing to die. I shall go to a glorious place, where there is no temptation nor sorrow, and where all tears shall be wiped from the eyes;' adding, 'My spirit is comforted in the love of God, and if I had lived more in the fear of God, I should have been more comforted. The Lord hath been good to me,—I am willing to die; it seemed hard to me sometimes, yet now it is made easy.' And said, 'All must be humbled, and brought low, one time or other. They must bow; if they will not bow in mercy, they must in judgment.' Adding, 'It is well for me that I have been afflicted; else I might not have known the things that belong to my peace; but now I cannot say I do not know them, for I do now see them, and rejoice in them.'

Next morning she expressed a concern for a near relation, desiring that she might live in the fear of God, saying, "The fear of the Lord is the beginning of wisdom." She lamented those that live in pride, and spend much time in adorning the body, and walking wantonly. After, she magnified the Lord's goodness, saying, 'The Lord is a gracious God, and of great mercy and righteousness, and I trust in him.' She prayed very devoutly, and implored the Lord's mercy, and praised him for his goodness, and gave good advice to those present, particularly to the party afore hinted, saying, 'Be careful of thy words and carriage, especially in meetings, to keep in thy mind, for God is to be worshipped in spirit and truth, and that God had given her a measure of his grace, that she should serve him whilst she was in health, for when she came to a sick-bed, and in pain, it would be harder.' After, she said, 'Remember my love to all Friends that ask for me;' and then prayed, saying, 'O! Lord Jesus, receive my soul, if it be thy heavenly will. O! Lord, I am truly resigned to thy will. O! Lord Jesus, come quickly, if it be thy heavenly will; and O! Lord, make my passage easy. O Lord! send thy angel to conduct me to thy heavenly kingdom. O Lord! thou art beautiful. O Lord! hear my prayer, and grant me my request, if it be thy heavenly will. Give me power over the enemy; he is a cunning enemy, a subtle serpent. O Lord! keep me from his temptations, who lays his baits at every corner.'

Again she said, 'There is nothing to be compared to thy love; all the world is but as a fading flower. O! what will it avail a man, to gain the whole world, and lose his own soul. O! what need have people to go with their heads so high, when they must all be laid in the dust. O Lord! thou art sweet, thy countenance is comely. O Lord! how hast thou refreshed me many a time, after I have prayed to thee. O! that thou wouldest crown me with glory.' And said, 'O! that we may all meet again in the kingdom of heaven.' After, she said, 'O Lord Jesus! there is none like unto thee, the author and finisher of our faith, to help, and none else can.'

The day before she died, she said, 'O Lord! thou art the great physician of value, the heavenly physician, who canst do that which none else can. Thou canst raise from the dead. Speak the word, and it shall be done. Thou art a gracious God, and of great mercy, and full of righteousness. Thy mercies deserve to be had in everlasting remembrance, from the beginning of the world, to the end thereof. O! Lord Jesus, thou hast tendered my spirit, and humbled my soul. Thy works are too wonderful to be [fully] spoken of;' with many other heavenly expressions. In the evening, her relations thinking she had been departing, after some time she looked up, and said, 'Pray for me.' Her uncle Bowles being present, found a concern upon him to pray to the Lord for her. Then she said to her aunt, 'Do not grieve when I am gone;' and desired her the next time the Lord did visit her in that manner, not to disturb her. That night she took her leave of all who were about her, in a very solemn manner, taking them by the hand, and bidding them farewell; and after, said to her aunt, 'Now I am just a going,' and said, 'Come, Lord Jesus, come quickly. Into thy hands I render my soul.' Her aunt Bowles coming in, asked her how it was with her; she answered, 'Very well;' which were her last words, and in a few minutes passed away without sigh or groan, on the 27th of the Eighth month, 1703. Aged thirteen years, wanting four days. She was buried the 30th of the same, from Bull and Mouth meeting-house, at Friends' burying-ground, near Bunhill-fields, London.

WILLIAM FENNELL, aged about twelve years, son of William Fennell of Youghall in Ireland, shop-keeper, took to his bed the 24th of the 12th month, 1703, the Lord having visited him about two years before, and often followed him with the reproofs and convictions of his Holy Spirit, when he had sometimes been wild, and run to play among other children.

When he was brought on his sick bed, not many days after, he was under an inward exercise of mind, and desired his mother to read by him. Another time he desired to have the ten commandments read to him; which were, and he was asked how far he found he had kept them. He answered he had not, as he could remember, ever taken the Lord's name in vain, and that he loved and honoured his father and mother, and had been careful not to tell lies or false stories on any one, nor had he stolen any thing, except taking some plums without asking leave, and hoped the Lord would pass it by, with what else he had done amiss. Remaining very weak, he was asked if he was willing to die; he answered, 'If I thought I was fit.'

The 3d of the First month, two English friends being in town, he desired they might have a meeting in the chamber with him; which they had, and he afterwards expressed his satisfaction therein; and then he broke forth in much trembling, saying, 'O Lord! forgive all my faults that I have done, and have mercy and pity on my poor soul. Keep out the enemy that is ready to come in upon me, for none but thee, O Lord! is able to do it;' with much more. He then called for his sisters and brother, and exhorted them to love and fear God, and pray to him to fit them to die, and to love truth, and to go to meetings, and to think upon God and good things, and the Lord would love them. He bade them do what their father and mother bid them, and be obedient to them, and look in their bibles, and they would find it was God's command to children to obey their parents, for it is well pleasing to the Lord.

To one of his companions, being by, viz., Edward Lawndry, he said, 'Dost thou think thou art fit to die?' If thou thinkest thou art not, then pray to the Lord, and desire him to make thee fit, and do not mind play too much;' saying he was sorry he had so long, but he hoped the Lord would forgive him. Lying still some time, being under a concern of mind, he was asked what his concern was. After some pause he answered, 'I am desiring the Lord to bring me in with the rest of his lost sheep;' with more to that purpose, saying, 'I have cried unto him many a night, since I have been not well; for I have been a wild boy, and loved play too well, and when you have sometimes corrected me, I took it a little hard; but now I am glad you did, and I cannot express the love I now have for you, for taking that care of me. You did well; had you not done it, I might have been wilder; for,' said he, 'the Lord hath been following me, and striving with me, to bring me down these two years, and let me see when I have been running to play, if I continued running on to be wild, then weeping, wailing, and lamentation would be my portion. Sometimes I have turned back, and have gone into the garret and wept bitterly, and have desired the Lord to help me; but after, when enticed by my comrades to go, I was not able to resist the temptations, which was my great trouble, and I have got into a secret place to endeavour to retire, and often have prayed to the Lord in the night-season on my knees, when others have been asleep.' This child cried out, saying, 'Oh! the Lord loves solitariness, he doth not love laughing and joking; I never read that Christ smiled, but often prayed and wept.' Then he prayed, 'O Lord! hear me, and have pity on me; for thou knowest I am very sorely afflicted. Lord help me. Oh! it is none but thee that can do it, Lord. O Lord! be near me, and suffer not the enemy to prevail over me.'

Speaking of the Lord's prayer, this child said, 'I have much lamented how people teach their children the Lord's prayer, without minding the depth that is in it, saying, "Our Father which art in heaven;" but they that remain in wickedness are not his children, so cannot rightly call him Father. "Hallowed be thy name;" but too many dishonour it by their wicked words. "Thy kingdom come:" Oh! but too few let the Lord live and have dominion in them. "Thy will be done in earth," that is,' said he, 'in our earthen body. "As it is done in heaven;" and alas! we all know there is nothing but the will of God done there: oh! but how little of the Lord's will is done here. "Give us this day our daily bread:" O Lord,' said he, 'give me daily bread from thee. "Forgive us our trespasses, as we forgive them that trespass against us;" but oh! how unwillingly do many people forgive them that trespass against them.—How can such expect forgiveness of the Lord? "Lead us not into temptation, but deliver us from evil."' Then he said, 'Oh! leave me not in temptation, but deliver me from the tempter; for thine is the kingdom, and all power is with thee, and glory for ever. This prayer,' said he, 'people teach their children by heart, and think it is enough. I have been at play with a boy in the street, and his father hath called to him, saying, "Have you said your prayers to-day?" and he hath gone in from me, and stood behind the door, and hath said this prayer as fast as he could, for haste to go to play again. I hearkened to him all the while.'

Such careless ones he lamented; and he gave good advice to many that came to him, and advised the servant-maid against speaking bad words; and though his breath grew short, he said, 'I desire to please the Lord always;' and so continued in a wonderful manner. He was very resigned to the will of the Lord, and desired his parents to give him up freely, and then took his leave, in great tenderness, of his father, mother, sisters, and brother, and relations; desiring to have his love remembered to his grandmother, and some other relations and friends that were not present. Pausing, he said, 'Oh! what joy I feel!' praising the Lord, while strength remained, till near the minute of his departure, and resigning himself to the Lord. His last words heard were, 'O Lord!' What followed could not be understood, his breath failing, and so sweetly departed, being the 14th of the First month, 1704. Aged twelve years and a half, and two days. He kept his bed about eighteen days.

SARAH SOUNDY, wife of William Soundy, of Reading, and daughter of William Tovey, of Henley-upon-Thames, in Oxfordshire, was trained up in the fear of God, and when on her death-bed, she breathed forth in an extraordinary manner praises to the Lord; and said, 'The Lord is a merciful God. I find him so to my soul. He spreadeth a table for his children, and the dainties he sets thereon, and his children feed thereat. He honoureth me with his presence, and that is favour enough. As for this world, it is but a bubble. I would not change my condition for any of yours,' meaning those then by her bed-side, 'although I might have my health; for I can never be better satisfied to die, than now I am;' with many more heavenly expressions, which she delivered one day after another; which were not noted. She farther said, 'What have I done that the Lord should be so good to me? Many have been great sufferers; but I have done nothing; so that if I have but the least place in the kingdom, I shall be satisfied, although it be but a door-keeper.'

She died the 24th of the Twelfth month, 1703, at Ridge, and was buried in Friends' burying-ground in Henley-upon-Thames, the 28th of the Twelfth month, 1703.

MARY STUBS, daughter of Thomas Stubs, belonging to Pardshaw meeting in Cumberland, came of believing parents, by whom she was educated in the way of truth, and reached thereby in her young years, walking circumspectly, as becomes the truth. She received a public testimony seven years before her death, and visited friends in Northumberland, some part of Bishoprick, Yorkshire, and Lancashire, and friends generally in the nation of Ireland, and was well received. When visited with sickness, she was borne up in her spirit; and when her mother seemed to be troubled and sorry to part with her, she desired her to be content, for it was her great joy, and farther said, 'I see nothing that I have to do but die.' She also said, 'I am fully clear,' and so departed very sensibly the 11th of the Twelfth month, 1704, in the thirty-third year of her age, and was buried in Friends' burying-place at Eaglesfield.

AMBROSE RIGGE, late of Ryegate, in Surry, was born at Banton, in Westmoreland, and convinced of the truth about the year 1652. Being called of God to preach the gospel of peace and salvation, he was drawn to visit London, and the south and west parts of England, about the year 1655, enduring great hardships, being often imprisoned in divers jails, not for evil-doing, but preaching the truth. For refusing to swear, in obedience to Christ, who commanded, "Swear not at all," he was premunired, and made prisoner at Horsham, in Sussex, above ten years at one time. He was also whipped, and often evilly entreated and abused, which he bore with much patience, and continued faithful unto death. In the time of his sickness, wherein he died, he had great assurance of the mercy and favour of God, and said, 'I am going where the weary are at rest.' He bore his sickness with much patience; and a little before his departure, he declared, saying, 'If friends keep to the root of life in themselves, they would be the happiest people in the world.'

He departed this life the 30th of the Eleventh month, 1704, and was buried the 4th of the Twelfth month in Friends' burying-ground at Ryegate, in Surry. Aged above seventy, and a minister about forty-nine years.

GEORGE FOOKS, late of Gray's-Inn-lane, in the parish of Andrew's, Holborn, in the county of Middlesex, shoemaker, was born at Boston, in Cambridgeshire, in the year 1649, and religiously inclined from his youth. He was convinced of the blessed truth, as professed by the people called Quakers, with whom he joined in society about the age of one-and-twenty; and by believing in Christ the true light, he came to receive power to walk inoffensively; and though he could not then read, he afterwards learned to read the Holy Scriptures, and greatly delighted therein. When he came to have a family, he was careful to have them frequently read therein; and would direct those of his family to that Holy Spirit in themselves, which the Scripture testifies of, that thereby they might come to have an understanding of them, and find help in themselves to withstand evil, and to be preserved out of it. He cautioned them also against evil, and exhorted them to that which was good and well-doing.

He was a man of a tender heart and meek spirit, pitiful to the poor, and faithful to the Lord, who was pleased to give him a part in the ministry of the word of life, about the year 1691, and he travelled some time in the work thereof, and was serviceable for several years, whilst he enjoyed his health.

In the year 1704 it pleased the Lord to visit him with sore affliction of body, which he bore with much patience; and in the time of his weakness had many visits from his friends and neighbours, being well beloved by them. When some came to visit him, and said, 'The Lord comfort you,' he answered, 'The Lord is with me, and is my comfort night and day, and hath made my bed easier than I could think. Although the Lord hath been pleased to afflict my body, yet he comforteth my soul; as he hath taken away the strength of my limbs, he hath preserved my senses to praise him.'

Before he died he called his son, and bade him read the 5th, 6th, and 7th chapters of Matthew, and then observed to him the blessings mentioned therein, and said to him, 'Thou hast a privilege beyond many poor children, I would not have thee slight it; but read them often, and desire the Lord to open thy understanding in what thou readest, for it is for our help; and as thou dost so, I do believe the Lord will help thee, as he did me. My concern is for thy soul's good, which is of greater value than thy body.' Then he added, 'The Lord hath blessed my honest endeavours and labours hitherto; so that thou hast been fed and clothed with the rest of my children and family, and I have something to spare. But the greatest blessing the Lord hath blessed me with, is the knowledge of his truth; and thou hast often heard me say, [desire] that whatever the Lord should be pleased to bereave me of, he would be pleased to keep me in the sense of this blessing; and at this time I have a living sense thereof, with earnest desires to the Lord it may be so with thee. My dear child, I am going out of this world, and must leave thee, and thou wilt lose a tender father; but as thou dost mind the Lord, and think upon him, he will be a father to thee, as he was to me. Be sure thou be kind and loving to thy mother, and be ruled by her when I am gone; and remember what I have said to thee, and keep the commandments of the Lord in thy lifetime, and it will be well with thee hereafter, and then thou wilt not be afraid to die. For thy sake I could have been willing to stay longer here, but it must not be, and I am willing to submit to the will of the Lord; for it is well, it is well, or I would not have told thee so. I am not afraid to die. Once more I bid thee remember thy father's dying words.' He said also to his son, 'I never kept back the wages of any man that did any thing for me, nor ever over-reached any man in dealing, nor ever wronged any man one penny.'

Then desiring to see his daughter, she came. He said unto her, 'My child, thou wast my first-born, and the child of my love; but thou hast grieved me to the heart, and grieved the Lord, and many friends that wished thee well. I am now going out of this world, and when my trouble endeth, thine may begin. I do forgive thee, and desire the Lord to pass by and forgive thee. I do forgive thee, and I hope and believe he will; but thou must be very diligent in seeking and crying to him. Thou art now a mother of children; be sure to be a good example to them, teach them to read the Scriptures, and do thou so too; quit thyself to thy husband as a woman fearing God should. Be loving to thy mother, and she will be loving to thee and thine I know. I have seen thy condition, and considered it; the Lord bless thee, is my earnest desire. Think upon my dying words when I am gone; they may do thee good. I have been a tender father to thee: so hereafter thou mayest say. Oh! wife, how hath been and is my soul ravished with joy. I cannot express the joy my soul hath been in this night. Oh! wife, it is well; do not be troubled for me, for it is well; and as we keep close to the Lord it will be well.'

This is the account which he gave in the time of his sickness; though he sometimes met with exercises, the Lord was with him, and stood by him, for he was an honest man, and so lived and died, and no doubt is at rest in the paradise of God.

He died the 27th of the Eighth month, 1704, aged about fifty-five, convinced about thirty-four, and a minister about thirteen years. He was decently and honourably buried, being accompanied by his relations, and many friends, to their burying-place near Bunhill-fields.

ANNE TRUSS was born at Reading, where she received the truth, and suffered imprisonment for her testimony to it. She was well esteemed, being a woman who loved truth, and was zealously given up to promote its honour, and encouraged faithfulness among the professors of it, both by exhortation and example. She was often concerned in public to speak of the goodness of God, in Christ Jesus, to mankind, from a sense and taste thereof, and pressed to diligence in the worship of God, and holiness of life: and life and power attended her testimony. She often desired her last sickness might not be long; and it was indeed but about four days, and in that time she counselled her friends, neighbours, and grandchildren, who came to see her, and were with her, to prize their precious time, and to keep out of every thing that would offend the Lord, and said, 'My peace is made with the Lord.' She prayed with much sweetness for her grandchildren, and that the Lord would destroy all that in his people which was contrary to himself. A few hours before she departed, she said, 'I now hope I shall be at rest.'

She died the 17th of the First month, 1704. Aged seventy-six years.

HUMPHREY WOOLBRIDGE was convinced of truth early, and received a public testimony for it; he travelled pretty much about England in the service of truth, and wrote several books. About the year 1705, being at London, he was taken ill, and continued so some time at Friends' work-house near Clerkenwell, being troubled with a great swelling in his face and mouth, which much deprived him of his speech. But he wrote several times to Friends, that the Lord was good to him, and desired Friends to pray for him, saying, 'I see a farther weight of glory, into which I am not entered.' Another time, 'My love in the Lord is to you; my present thought is, to die is my gain, without doubt; because the love and mercy of God, that casteth out fear, is shed in my heart, to whom I bow my knee, and bless his holy name, his gracious name.'

In the Fifth month, a little before his death, he wrote to some Friends in London thus: 'The Lord is my rock, and my salvation and tower, in the time of my distress and anguish. I cried to the Lord when the billows went over my head, and the proud waves did afflict my soul. Then was my faith in God, and underneath was the everlasting arm, my salvation. So that with David I could say, "The Lord sitteth upon the floods, he reigneth as king for ever and ever."

He died the 31st of the Fifth month, 1707. Aged about seventy-four years.

WILLIAM HARRIS, of Radford-seemly, in the county of Warwick, was one who received the Truth in the love of it, in his youthful days, and being faithful, a part of the gospel ministry was given to him; in which he laboured with zeal and fervency of spirit. He was very serviceable in doctrine and discipline, serving truth and Friends in singleness of heart; seeking much the prosperity of truth, and the love and unity of Friends in it. He was fervent and frequent in admonition and exhortation to all people where his lot was cast; always having a regard to the fear of the Lord unto the last, and very honourable for his innocent life and upright conversation, wherein he walked, as a true pattern of virtue; ruling well his own house, and keeping his family in good order, wherein he was exemplary, often calling upon them to love and fear the Lord, and to wait together upon the Lord in his own family. And with much diligence, and due order to frequent their public meetings, wherein his love and faithfulness were manifest to the last.

He was taken ill in a meeting which Joseph Bains had appointed in the public meeting-house at Harbury, on the 18th of the Seventh month, 1705, but sat the meeting; and after, he was well satisfied in the will of the Lord being done, for he was not afraid to die. Being something better, he went home, and grew weaker: but the Lord enabled him, on the 23d of the Seventh month, being First-day, to go to the meeting of Friends at Harbury, and publicly declare the word of truth with much fervency, both to Friends and others; and after meeting hastened home, and grew weaker and weaker in body. On the 3d of the Eighth month, a Friend went to visit him, to whom he said, the night before had been very comfortable to him, for the Lord gave him sweet repose, so that he felt no pain. The Lord was so large in his love to him, that he showed him that the walls of salvation were about him, and that he would give him an entrance into everlasting life.

On the 6th of the same month he was taken so ill that it was thought he would scarcely live till morning. When a Friend came to see him next morning, he was a little revived, and spoke comfortably to him and those present. The next day the Friend came again to see him; and when he came into the chamber, he put forth his hand, and took him by the hand, saying, 'Thou art come to see me this once more. I am now a dying man; I wait to be dissolved; I am weary of this frail body. When the Lord pleaseth, I would be freed from it.' Several Friends coming to see him, he spoke very sensibly to them; and when they took their leave, he exhorted them to fear the Lord, and be faithful in the truth. A Friend who was related to him, taking his leave of him, seemed to be troubled; he said, 'Make no ado, neither be troubled, it is the Lord's doing.' He exhorted his elder servant to fear the Lord, and charged her to exhort her fellow-servant to fear him also, saying, 'Without it the heart will not be kept clean.'

A friend said to him, 'Thou hast been a comfort to many, I hope the Lord will remember thee in his mercy, and be a comfort to thee in this thy affliction.' He answered, 'The Lord is good to my soul. I can say, I have fought the good fight of faith, I am now finishing my course; the Lord will give me a crown of life.' A little before he departed, he signified his great love to all friends in general, and said, 'My love is to all my friends and old acquaintance.' A friend observing his exercise, said, 'Thou hast hard labour;' he said, 'The Lord will visit me in his mercy, and give me an easy passage in his own time out of this body.' And so he did, and he entered into stillness, lay the space of an hour, and quietly and peaceably departed, as a lamb going into his rest, about the 12th hour at night, the 7th of the Eighth month, 1705, aged about seventy years.

GILBERT LATEY, an ancient professor of the holy truth, was born in the parish of Issey, in the county of Cornwall, in the year 1626, and came to London in the year 1648. He was of a sober conversation and religiously inclined, and followed those that were esteemed the most religious preachers at that time. About the year 1654, he was, by the spirit of Christ and the powerful preaching of that eminent servant of the Lord, Edward Burrough, convinced of the blessed truth, as it is professed by the people called Quakers, at a meeting held at the house of Sarah Matthews, in Whitecross-street, London, in the year 1654. In the year 1659 he was concerned to bear a public testimony for truth, and against superfluity; and being by trade a tailor, would not meddle with, nor suffer his servants to put upon apparel, to set it off, any superfluities, as lace and ribbons.

He was also concerned to solicit, with other friends, the

several powers in his time, for suffering friends, and used to say friends should keep to truth, or the anointing in their solicitations, and then they might expect a blessing, and be made serviceable.

And in the year 1705, the seventy-fourth year of his age, being weak, he said he had done the work of his day faithfully, and was set down in the will of God, and there was no cloud in his way. The night before he departed, he gave counsel to those that were in the room, to fear the Lord, and not to do evil for evil, but to do good for evil; for there is, said he, no overcoming of evil, but in and by that which is good. Exhorting much to love and tenderness, saying the Lord would bless such as were found therein. A few hours before his departure, he said that there was no condemnation to them that were in Christ Jesus, 'for,' said he, 'he is the lifter up of my head, he is my strength and great salvation.'

He departed this life the 15th of the Ninth month, 1705, and was buried in Friends' burying-ground, at Kingston-upon-Thames.

WILLIAM STOVEY, late of Helperston Marsh, near Trowbridge, in the county of Wilts, was born at Aberry in the said county. He received truth as it is professed by the people called Quakers, upon its first publication in those parts, and was a very zealous encourager of faithfulness among Friends. He also received a gift of the ministry, and was often very much concerned in his travels, that truth's testimony might be kept up in its several branches, and particularly against the antichristian oppression of tithes. For bearing this testimony, as well as keeping up meetings, he was a great sufferer, being cast into several prisons, and had his cattle, and other goods, several times taken from him, even to the bed he lay on, and almost all that was thought worth removing. His last sickness was not very great in appearance, nor long; yet he signified he should never go forth of his chamber, and said, 'I can and do forgive all my enemies.' He was very cheerful in the time of his illness, and more than ordinarily glad of friends' company that came to see him, and said he was satisfied and willing, when the Lord pleased, to leave this world, in expectation of a far greater happiness in that which is to come.

He departed this life the 7th of the Eleventh month, 1705, and was buried at Cummerell, in the said county.

ELIZABETH DICKINSON, widow, was convinced in her husband's lifetime; though her husband was concerned thereat, and she met with great exercise; yet was made willing to give up, to answer the requirings of truth, and in a little time, through the grace of God bestowed upon her, being faithful to the Lord, she was made a publisher of the everlasting gospel of Christ Jesus, being well nigh the first, in Abby-holme meeting. The Lord added to her days, and the number of the church; that she lived not only to see many gathered to the Lord in her time, but many also raised to bear a public testimony for him, to the gladdening of her heart, in the thirty years she lived after she received the truth. She was of a blameless life and conversation, living answerable to the doctrine of Christ. She loved the unity of good people, and hated that which was the cause of the breach thereof. She was never tedious in her testimony. She was a mother in Israel, a terror to evil doers, and bore a faithful testimony against the workers of iniquity. She ruled well her own house; so that her advice and counsel took place with others. She was endued by the Lord with meekness and wisdom, and was freely given up to serve the truth with what she had, and the Lord blessed her. She visited Friends in Northumberland, Bishoprick, Westmoreland, Yorkshire, and Lancashire, where she had good service for the Lord. And in the year 1688 she visited Friends in Scotland, and had also good service, the Lord accompanying her with his heavenly power and presence.

In the time of her sickness, though very sharp, the Lord

preserved her in patience, and she desired friends to remember her in their near approaches to the Lord, and said, 'Lord, I am willing to die. Thou who hast made me willing, art able to make me ready. Look down upon thy afflicted handmaid, and lay no more upon me than I am able to bear.' She often desired the Lord to be near, and her last words that can be remembered before she departed, were, 'Thou Lord God of Israel, be near and "fasten my spirit;"' which it is not doubted but he was pleased to do, and received her into rest with the righteous, where no disturbance can come; but praises everlasting are sung to the Lord God and the Lamb for evermore.

She departed this life the eighth of the Eleventh month, 1705, in the sixty-sixth year of her age, and was buried at Friends' burying-place at Allonby, upon the sea-coast in Cumberland, being accompanied with many friends and relations.

SARAH BLACKHOUSE, of Yeoland-Redman, in the county of Lancaster, was convinced of the truth, by receiving the testimony of that eminent messenger and minister of the gospel of Christ, George Fox, in the year 1653, being in and about the twenty-seventh year of her age. Within a few years after, it pleased the Lord to concern her in a public testimony, to the refreshing and edifying of his churches and people, in which she faithfully laboured and travelled in the meetings whereunto she belonged, and some other adjacent meetings. She was examplary in her life and conversation, and preached truth therein to her neighbours, and those she was concerned with.

A few days before she died, her friends and relations being by her bed-side, she said, 'See that in all your meetings you wait upon the Lord, and be not sleepy. Be faithful to what he hath made known, and revealed to you: for it need not be said to you, know the Lord; you know enough, be faithful to what the Lord hath revealed, for that is the sum of all religion.' A little after she said, 'I am weak, and in much pain, I desire to be eased, when the Lord's pleasure is; through mercy he hath given me peace and rest to my soul.' She then said, 'Farewell, fare you all well in the Lord, I desire your growth and prosperity in the truth, every one for yourselves.' So in much peace and quietness of mind and spirit, she departed this life the 30th of the Fifth month, 1706, being nearly eighty years of age; had a testimony for truth about fifty years.

JOHN TOMKINS, who collected the three volumes of Dying Sayings, formerly printed, intitled, Piety Promoted, was born about the year 1663, and his honest parents were in society with the people called Quakers.

His father died when he was very young, after which his mother took care to have him religiously educated, and the Lord blessed her care, and was graciously pleased in his tender years to incline him to love and fear him. He was an obedient son, and assisting to her in her business; and as he grew in years, continued so.

When his mother married again, she had several more children by her second husband. And after she died, and her husband was reduced to a very low condition, this his son-in-law was both tender and charitable, and had a great care and regard to his children. As his love and tender compassion began to be early manifested to his relations, so did his love greatly appear to those who preached the gospel of Christ, and to the poor and afflicted in body and mind, whom he relieved, visited, and comforted. He also greatly loved and delighted in the Holy Scriptures, and diligently read and searched them. As he grew in years, he grew in grace, and in the knowledge of our Lord and Saviour Jesus Christ; and being faithful to the Lord, he was pleased to put him into the ministry, and committed to him the word of reconciliation, and made him a skilful minister for his time, in the word of life; so that he could divide it aright.

He was filled with such a holy zeal for the name and truth

of God, as was accompanied with knowledge, and was well acquainted with our Christian discipline, and careful that it might be maintained, greatly desiring where any professing truth walked not according to it, that they might be admonished and reproved; and that the works and ways of those who would not receive either, but continued loose and unfaithful, should be testified against, that friends might be clear, and the church and Sion of God might shine. He greatly delighted in her prosperity, and travailed for her welfare, and prayed that the Lord would favour her dust, and satisfy her poor with bread, and comfort all her mourners. One asking him how he did, he replied, 'Very weak, but I am willing to die, and leave this troublesome world, if the Lord sees it meet to remove me at this time.'

Lying on his bed very weak, he declared to friends then present, very fervently for some time, concerning the work of the Lord, and the prosperity of his truth in the earth; and in particular, that the Lord would have a glorious church and people, when all the dross and chaff, that did yet cleave to them, should be purged out, and blown away. That the Lord would remove that which had been the occasion of any disunion among his people, and bring them more and more into unity, and to be of one heart and mind, and that the work of the Lord should go forward in the earth, and his truth prosper over all the kingdoms of it, and many nations should be gathered to it. He also said, 'I believe the Lord will bless his people, and carry on the work he hath begun in the earth. It is my faith, that the time will come that the wicked shall be as few as the righteous are now; but there is much to be purged out of the church; there is much pride and superfluity to be done away.' Again he said, 'I have seen great things since my sickness; things which I think not lawful to be spoken.' Much good counsel and advice dropped from him, at sundry times, that was not taken down in writing, which he gave at times to his friends and relations about him, and often said to his wife, 'My dear, grieve not, thou must not grieve; I want to be where the weary are at rest, and where the wicked cease from troubling. I want to be dissolved, that I may be with the Lord Jesus Christ. The Lord will provide for thee and thy children: he hath said, 'Let the widows trust in me, and I will take care of their fatherless children.'

When he was asked if he desired to see his youngest child, he being some miles distant, he answered, 'He is young, and hath little knowledge of me. I commit him to the great God: he will take care of him.' He spoke this with more than ordinary sedateness, adding, 'I am not afraid of death. I have sought the honour of God in my day, and my reward is with him. The Lord hath been very good to me in this sickness. I can say with the Psalmist, he hath made my bed in my sickness. I have many sweet seasons from the Lord in the night when I cannot sleep. Oh! I enjoy sweet peace from him. Oh! the love of the Lord Jesus Christ is great to mankind.

'The Lord visited me in my tender years, and I have feared him from my childhood. I have delighted to wipe the shoes of those that preach the gospel, when I was a boy. Since I have been a man, I have taken more delight in serving the Lord, his church and people, than in getting worldly riches. I love the poor, and have loved to serve them, and to visit them in their afflictions. Remember my love to the poor in the quarter where I dwell.

'I love the ministry, I have a valuable esteem for the ministers, and pray God sanctify and purge them, that they may go before the flock. I pray God bless the young generation of ministers that are coming up, and make them skilful in the work, that they may divide the word aright, that like the Benjamites of old, they may shoot an arrow [or sling a stone] to an hair's breadth.'

He died the 12th of the Seventh month, 1706, aged about forty-three years; and was decently buried from the meeting-house near Devonshire-square, accompanied by a great number of friends to Bunhill burying-ground, and many living testimonies were borne to the truth, in which he lived and died.

He collected and wrote the several books following, viz.: The Harmony of the Old and New Testament; a Concordance; A

Trumpet Sounded; The Great Duty of Prayer; Piety Promoted, first, second, and third parts; which are proofs of his zeal for truth, his love to all people, and that he was well acquainted with the Holy Scriptures.

ROBERT HUBERSTIE, late of Yelland-Compers, in the county of Lancaster, was visited with the day-spring from on high, and brought to the knowledge of God's eternal truth, as professed by the people called Quakers, about the year 1653, which he received, loved, and obeyed. He was often a great sufferer by imprisonment for his faithful testimony to the truth, and by spoiling of his goods for peaceably meeting to worship Almighty God, in the spirit of his Son, according as he requires, and bearing his testimony faithfully against that cruel and anti-christian oppression of tithes. After his release out of prison, he travelled in the work of the ministry, the Lord having bestowed a good gift upon him, and committed to him the word of reconciliation. He travelled in the power of it for the good of souls, and visited the churches of Christ, through most parts of this nation, exhorting and advising friends in the love of God, to feel the life-giving presence and power of the Lord in all their meetings, that therein they might be refreshed and strengthened to wait upon God, and to worship him in his eternal spirit and truth.

Being returned, he was taken sick, and in the time thereof he had many comfortable expressions, saying, 'I have peace with God, through Jesus Christ, and am content in his heavenly will to live or die, having sought God's glory before my own interest in this world.' He often advised those present to be faithful to what God had manifested to them, and to bear a faithful testimony to the truth. After a sore fit of pain, he said, 'It is good to have the Lord near at such a pinching time as this, and to have nothing to do but to die.' A few days before he died, he called his son and the rest of his family, and said he must take his leave of them; and desired them to live in love and peace one with another, and to love the truth above all, and to bear a faithful testimony for God and his truth whilst on earth, and the Lord would bless them. He desired that his love might be remembered to faithful friends, some of whom he mentioned by name.

He bore his sickness and pain with much patience, and uttered many sweet expressions, which were not taken. He was preserved sensible to the last, having been a believer in the truth about fifty-three years, and a prisoner near five years; aged about seventy-one years.

He died the 12th, and was buried the 14th of the Eighth month, 1706.

Here followeth a Testimony of an ancient friend and acquaintance of R. Huberstie's.

'Since I have had the opportunity of reading the above-written lines, relating to my dear deceased friend and brother in the nearest and dearest relation of God's blessed truth, who was convinced thereof in the next year after I was, when we were both young in years; and remembering the glory of that day of visitation of our souls, and the comfortable fellowship of the Spirit we have since enjoyed together; and also Providence so ordering, that my lot fell to see him in his bodily weakness, and to be comforted in the beholding that sweet contented frame of spirit he lay in, together with the affecting words that then dropped from him, I felt some concern upon my mind to add in short, as followeth:

'That he was a man truly fearing God, faithful to the manifestation of truth, firm and noble in his testimony and sufferings therefor. [He was] of latter years, an able, zealous, and laborious minister of Christ Jesus, concerned for good order in the church; serving the Lord faithfully in his day, and died the death of the righteous. His latter end was like theirs, viz. full of joy in righteousness, and assurance of eternal life and glory, as he intimated to me in a divine sense thereof, a very few days before his departure, saying that he was well in mind, freely given up to the will of God, and possessed perfect peace, patiently waiting for his being delivered out of that pain and trouble of body in God's time, desiring to be remembered to all faithful friends, and desiring me, and one other friend, to be at his burial. And the Lord by providence made way, that I therein answered his desire, it being the day aforesaid, in Friends' burying-place at Yeland, where a great appearance of Friends was, and a great many of the chief and sober neighbours, yea, several that were not invited; which did demonstrate the good respect he had amongst all sorts of people. The Lord was pleased upon that solemn occasion, to bless us with his glorious presence, and to open the mouths of several of his servants in a living testimony to his truth; and also to magnify his holy and powerful name for his marvellous salvation, revealed in and through the Lord Jesus Christ our Saviour, to whom, with the Father, belong dominion, glory, and eternal praise, world without end, Amen.

'THOMAS CAMM.

'Oldworth, 26th of First Month, 1707.'

JOHN CARLILE, of the city of Carlisle, in the county of Cumberland, was born at Blackwell, three miles from the city of Carlisle, and was by trade a tanner. Through the gracious visitation of God, he was convinced of the blessed truth about the year 1673, by the ministry of John Graves, being much reached and confirmed by virtue of the power of truth. He grew and increased in faithfulness, according to his measure; and was drawn forth sometimes in a public testimony, and preached the gospel, not in the eloquence of speech, but very powerful and reaching, and in simplicity and sincerity. Although illiterate as to outward learning, yet in his doctrine and testimony he considerably opened the scriptures of truth, by the assistance of that holy Spirit that gave them forth, to the edification of the hearers, and confirmation of those gospel truths by him preached. He laboured in the work of the ministry in divers counties, as Cumberland, Westmoreland, Bishoprick, and part of Lancashire; also in Northumberland,

and in Scotland. Several were convinced by his labours of love in the gospel of Christ in many places, and remain as seals of his ministry.

He was open-hearted, and zealous for the testimony of truth, and in much love received the friends of it, who travelled in the same work, into his house. As he delighted to draw near to the well-spring of life, for divine succour and consolation, he was not unmindful often to wait upon the Lord in his family, to whom the Lord was pleased to reach, in order to their convincement, by his blessed truth. He was sometimes opened to speak a few words to them of information or exhortation; and sometimes to supplicate the Lord; and other times in silence, to wait upon the Lord in his family, to feel an increase and growth in the virtue of truth among them. Many are witnesses of the benefit and comfort they received in those his family meetings, that have been at them. Although at his first convincement in the city, and when he came to bear testimony to the truth, he was as a speckled bird among the birds of the wood, there being none who bore the same profession in the said city, and was warred against by the bitter magistrates, and severe informers, and cruel persecutors; yet such was the Lord's goodness to him, that he was preserved faithful in his testimony for the Lord through all. Some of his persecutors fell into great distress, and died miserably; and others of them fell into great poverty; so that a prison became their dwelling, and therein they died.

He was always ready to help forward and encourage every good work on truth's account, and was much given to hospitality, and was open-hearted to the poor of any society. He was of a blameless conversation, just in his dealings, and of a good report among all people, and valiant for truth and its testimony to the end. In his sickness he often exhorted Friends to be faithful to the Lord and his truth, according to their measure; saying, then the Lord would stand by them, and bring them through all the exercises they might meet with for the same, and they should have the reward of well done; with more expressions of the like nature.

Having some sight of the glory and joys of heaven, that those who are faithful and upright-hearted shall enjoy, and that evidence in himself, of his soul's everlasting peace, he signified his desire of a change, and that his wife and children might give him freely up, saying it would be well. Being sensible the time of his departure drew near, he said to his friends and neighbours present, that a little time would finish and make all things easy. In about half an hour he passed away, being the 25th of the Twelfth month, 1706; and died in the faith of Jesus, and in full unity with Friends, having borne an innocent testimony for truth in his generation, and left a good savour behind him. Aged about seventy-four years

---

JOHN ELLIS was one on whom the Lord bestowed a gift in the ministry, who laboured in the gospel of the grace of God for the good of souls, and freely preached it in the authority of divine life, to the reaching God's witness in many hearts.

He was zealous for God, and tender of the good in all; but terrible against the workers of iniquity. Grave and reverend in the exercise of his gift, his testimony full of reproof and caution; but in that meekness which made the same to be edifying. His doctrine sound, flowing from the living fountain and divine spring of life and heavenly wisdom.

He was a man of great kindness, loving, meek, and humble; a visitor of the widows and fatherless in their distress, he sympathized with them; fed the hungry, clothed the naked, according to his ability, and laboured greatly in Dorsetshire, Hampshire, Wiltshire, and Devonshire, and other places; often saying, his Father's business must not be neglected, or done negligently. As he was travelling in the service of truth, he was taken sick ten miles from his habitation. He exhorted that every one should keep close to the truth, that the Lord had made known to them, and said on his death-bed to his wife, 'It is hid from me,' speaking of his death, 'but if this is my time,

I am ready. There is nothing to be laid to my charge; there is a fountain of life that we must all come to, that runs sweetly.' His daughter standing by, he gave her a charge, that she should not mix with any in the world, and that she should not be troubled; 'for,' said he, 'I have a sure foundation.' He uttered many other sweet expressions, that could not be distinctly understood; but concluded, saying, 'I salute you all;' and departed the 31st of the First month, 1707, and was decently interred in Friends' burying-ground at Poole, the 4th of the Second month following, and several testimonies were borne to the truth on that occasion.

MARY STOUT, relict of Henry Stout, of Hartford, was an honest, ancient Friend, that was early convinced of the blessed truth, and retained her love to it, and the friends of it, unto death. Being weak and near her end, she said on her death-bed, the 31st of the First month, 1707, 'I have nothing to do but to die, if it should be this night. I have received the earnest of that inheritance that shall never fade away.' R. T. next day coming to see her, asked her how she did. She said, 'I am very weak, but very well satisfied to die, if my time be come; for the Lord is with me, and that is a precious jewel.' R. T. said, 'So it is, which the world cannot give;' she said, 'No, nor take away.' R. T. asking her if she had settled her affairs, she replied she had nothing to do but to die.

The 6th of the Second month, several Friends being come to visit her, she said, 'I take your visit very kindly, that I might see you before I die. I never was thus weak before in my life, yet I have nothing laid to my charge. The Lord hath been with me in my exercise.' Then said to G. W., 'And thou hast been a dear friend to me.'

On the 7th of the Second month, about the eighth hour in the morning, G. W. went to her, she then appearing near death, saying to her, 'The Lord make thy passage easy, and give thee rest.' And near the ninth hour the same morning, she quietly departed without sigh or groan. Aged about eighty years, and had for some years, at certain times, used to speak a few weighty and seasonable words in Friends' meetings.

FRANCES RUTT, of Hartford, was an ancient, true, and serviceable woman, to whom the Lord had given a public testimony to bear for the truth, which she had known and professed for many years, and lived therein, who was exemplary in her conversation, and a lover of her friends and all people. When near her end, and Friends stood about her, she said to them, 'You must not depend upon words, but upon the pure spring of life in your own hearts, and upon the word of the Lord that endureth for ever.'

Thus this faithful woman, who had preached the word, counselled Friends to depend upon it as that which is able to quicken and reconcile to God, sanctify and save the souls of all that are obedient thereto unto death, as no doubt she experienced it.

She departed this life the 7th of the Third month, 1707.

JOHN SAGER, of Marsden, in the county of Lancaster, was born the 3d of the Eighth month, 1627, and convinced of the truth about the beginning of the year 1653, at a meeting at Brighouse, in Yorkshire, by our dear and ancient friend, George Fox, of whom he always after retained an honourable esteem.

The said John Sager was constant and zealous in bearing a faithful testimony for truth, and against tithes, often exhorting Friends to faithfulness in their testimony against the same. He often suffered the spoiling of his goods, even in those early days; the first of which was in the year 1655. He also suffered imprisonment five times, and often under close confinement, by reason whereof his tender wife and family went through great hardships. When with his family, he was a constant attender of week-day meetings, and meetings for discipline, and very zealously concerned for the promotion thereof, being a man given up to do and suffer for the truth, of which he had received a measure, or talent, to improve, and was thereby enabled to bear all his great sufferings, and other trials, with much patience; often saying he was made willing by the power of God to give up his life as a farther seal to the testimony he had borne, if the Lord did require it. He often blessed the Lord, that he had accounted him worthy to suffer for his name's sake; desiring the Lord might forgive his adversaries what they had done against him.

In his latter days, the nearer he drew to his change, which he long waited for, he was the more raised up in living testimony in meetings, in exhortation to diligence and faithfulness in the gift received, and in praising the Lord for his mercies bestowed upon him and his people. In his last sickness, under the great weakness and distempers, which then attended his aged body, he was always cheerful and contented, praising the Lord for his merciful dealings with him. He was visited by many, both friends and others, and was often raised beyond expectation, to declare the truth, exhorting all to mind the light of Christ Jesus, wherewith they were enlightened; often saying all was well with him, he had nothing to do but to die.

The night before his departure, several Friends coming to visit him, he said, 'I believe the time of my departure is at hand, and I enjoy great peace and comfort, and desire the Lord may preserve you, when you come to lie in the condition I do, and that you may enjoy the same comfort I do now enjoy;' continuing in fervent prayer. Next morning, being very sensible to the last, he departed in great peace and quietness, being the 24th of the Fifth month, 1707. Aged seventy-nine years and nine months; a minister of Christ.

In the year 1660 he was imprisoned for not swearing, and remained a prisoner in Lancaster six weeks.

In the year 1668 he was imprisoned again for not swearing, and was a prisoner at Preston seven weeks.

In the year 1669 he was imprisoned for nonpayment of tithes at Lancaster four years and six weeks.

In the year 1687 he was a prisoner on the same account at Lancaster one year.

In the year 1691 he was a prisoner again, about tithes at Lancaster, four years and two months.

So that in all he was a prisoner nearly ten years.

SAMUEL HUNT, of Nottingham, a minister of Christ, and a faithful servant in his church, who laboured and travelled for the good of souls, was taken ill at London about the Eighth month, 1707, at the house of Thomas Huttson, in George-yard, in Lombard-street. Being apprehensive of his death, he said, 'I have laboured faithfully in the service of the Lord. I am not afraid to die, for all will be well with me.' Soon after he took his bed, he said, 'Dear Lord, thou knowest I love thee and thy truth, and have never thought much to spend and be spent for thee, and if my time be come to leave this troublesome world, I am willing.'

He said to Thomas Huttson and his wife, 'Our first acquaintance together was in the love of God, and in that let us live and abide, and in that shall we part one from another.'

About twelve hours before his departure, several friends were visiting him, and although he was very weak in body, and his distemper very sharp and strong upon him, yet he was raised in spirit, and filled with the love of Christ, insomuch that he uttered many sweet expressions, and precious sayings, and such a stream of love and life attended him, that the hearts of all friends there present were melted. He was heard to say something of the man-made ministers, but spoke so low it could not be farther understood, until he was somewhat more strengthened, and his voice raised, then he spoke audibly, and said, 'Away with this chaffy nature, it is fit for nothing but to be driven before the wind. The sound of the instrument is but empty, except the matter proceed from the pure spring of immortal life.' Then being silent, and retired in mind for some time, he broke forth, saying, 'O sweet composure of mind! Who is here? Who is here? The beloved of my soul, the chiefest of ten thousands! Dear Lord, I will not let thee go! O thy love is sweet and precious! O that we may live in thee, and dwell in thee, thou pure ocean and divine fountain of eternal sweetness! Who can withhold praising thee, thou living God! oh! we will bless thy name. Praises, honour, and glory, be given to thee, through Jesus Christ, for ever and for evermore.'

When friends were taking leave of him, he said, 'Dear friends, farewell; all is well, all is well. If we love one another, and love the Lord, and love his truth, all will be well.' When he had taken leave of his wife, and several in the family, and M. H. coming in, and his wife acquainting him thereof, he said, being sensible to the last, 'Farewell, dear Mary, farewell in Christ; we have lived in love, and in love we part;' these were his last words. He departed not long after, being the 3d of the Ninth month, 1707, aged forty-one years.

But before his departure, he dictated the following letter to his son.

'Son Samuel,

'First learn to live in the love and fear of God, and if thou meetest with any disappointment, thou mayest apply thyself to him the more freely for assistance, it being thy father's daily practice, in what exercises he hath met with in this world. Be truly honest, both towards God and man; always labouring in thy mind to contradict any thing that may be otherwise. I recommend this practice: privately to go into thy chamber twice a day, to wait upon the Lord for counsel and instruction in all things.

'And it is thy father's desire, that thou mayest be loving and dutiful unto thy mother, and loving and kind to thy wife.'

NICHOLAS GATES, late of Alton, in Hampshire, clothier, son of William Gates, of the same place, was, from the time he understood there was a God who made the world and all things therein, desirous to have the true knowledge of him. In his childhood he took great delight in reading the Holy Scriptures, and in hearing the best reformed ministers, and gave himself often to private praying to the Lord unknown, uttering words before him, until on a time in his chamber kneeling down by his bedside, in order to utter words, he was stopped, and it was said to him in his heart, as he declared and believed, by the Lord, 'Thou needest not utter words, for I know thy heart and soul's desire.' So remaining kneeling a while, he arose, but uttered no words.

About the age of twenty-one years, he came to join with those people in scorn called Quakers, and was rejected by his father, and became an alien to his father's house, and many times threatened to be cast off, yet he loved his father dearly. The Lord was more to him than his father, and fitted him for his service, and gave him a gift of the ministry, and called him forth freely to preach the gospel of the grace of God, and made him an experimental witness of the sufficiency thereof. He laboured earnestly therein in divers parts of England, to invite all to receive and come under its teachings. By the power and grace of God, he was supported under, and carried through, all the trials and exercises, stonings, stockings, reproachings, imprisonments, and spoiling of goods he met with for the truth's sake, and his testimony thereto.

He was religiously exemplary in his family, and among all where he travelled, preached sound doctrine, lived a holy life, was just in his dealing, diligent in his calling, a tender husband, a loving father, a kind friend, a good neighbour, a follower of peace, delighted in hospitality, sought unity, and laboured to preserve it in the bonds of peace. He was diligent in attending meetings, both First-days and other days, and in the service of quarterly and monthly meetings, and in taking care of the poor, and was greatly blessed of God. This servant of Christ being taken ill the 10th of the Tenth month, 1707, the first thing he expressed his care for, was the church, and to have friends preserved in unity, saying he was well satisfied with the Lord's dealing with him. 'He hath been a good God to me all along, and hath let me live to good old age, and been my support from time to time, and is so in this present exercise.' Another time he said, 'My days are expiring apace; but I have lived to see the goodness of the Lord in the land of the living.'

He then expressed his love to his wife in a very tender, affectionate manner, and prayed to the Lord that he would bless and preserve her and his children to the end, desiring they might live together in love, and watch over one another therein. He said he did not know, if he had his time to live over again, that he could die better, having the evidence in himself of well done; yet he said, if the Lord did see fit to restore him, and he could be an instrument to gain more souls to God, he could be glad; for that was his great joy, when he considered how he had spent his time in the Lord's service. This honest, zealous old man gave good advice to many that came to see him, and for their children, laying a charge upon such friends as had them, to keep their children to the plain language, and to bring them up in the fear and admonition of the Lord; and admonishing his own children to do so by their children, and to ask them questions for opening their understanding, that they might know what God is, and where he is to be found, and to do thus while they are young and tender; and said, 'Oh! that men, especially young men, did know the comfort of living a sober life.'

A neighbour coming to visit him, asked him how he did; he replied, 'Weak, and am going apace out of this troublesome world, to a place where there is neither sorrow nor trouble.' After this, he said, 'Friends were formerly known by their fewness of words, and keeping to their word in their dealings.' He very often desired Friends to keep to plainness, both in habit and speech, warning his daughter Deborah present, and his wife, to watch over her children, to keep them out of pride, saying, 'There is scarcely a worse weed than pride.' A while before he died, he said, 'The door of entrance is open into the kingdom;' into which it is not doubted but he is entered. He departed the 21st of the Tenth month, 1707, aged about seventy-four, convinced about fifty-two years; and was honourably buried on the 24th, in Friends' burying-ground at Alton, after a very solemn meeting of many Friends and others, and left his wife twenty-one children and grandchildren.

MARY MOORE, late wife of John Moore, of Eldworth, in the county of York, daughter of Thomas Camm, was seized with sickness, which continued upon her about three months, which she bore with much patience, often saying she was well content with the will of God. Her dear father being then from home in the service of truth, her husband divers times asked her if he might not write to her father, to acquaint him with her weakness, and to desire his return home. She answered she should be right glad to see him, but she would not have his service hindered upon her account, hoping when that was over he might return in due time to see her. Accordingly, upon the 30th of the Sixth month, 1707, he got to Eldworth, and found his daughter very weak; but the surprise of joy to see him had liked to overwhelm her spirits, so that for a time she could not speak to him. In a little time she got over it, and expressed her great joy and satisfaction to see him, saying, 'Now the Lord hath answered my desire; and now I leave all to his wise disposing, whether life or death.' She continued pretty easy, still, and resigned; and about a week after she grew worse; but said to her father, 'I am resigned to the will of God, and gathered out of care, touching visible things; only some fear is upon my mind touching my eldest son, that it will prove to his harm to be schooled where he now is, therefore, I desire he may be removed to some good place and school.' This was promised her should be done as speedily as well could be; at which she seemed contented and easy. She often signified her resignedness to the will of God, praying to be endued with patience to the end of her race: and the Lord was pleased to hear and answer. She bore all her long exercise with great patience. On the 12th of the Seventh month, though much weakened, she was opened and strengthened to speak very strongly, which was written down, viz.:

'Oh! what a blessing have I enjoyed in this my quarter of a year's weakness. It has been the best and most sweet, pleasant, and profitable time of all my life. I have seen the end of all worldly enjoyments. Although I have a kind father, a loving husband, and dear babes, yet I can freely, yea, heartily, with all my heart, leave all to be with Christ my Redeemer, my Saviour, and the beloved of my soul. Oh! he hath been near me, yea, with me day and night. He hath so drawn me, and won upon me, with the cords of his love, taking me by the hand, and opening his arms to receive me into his bosom, that I am overcome with his love. Very gentle has his hand been upon me; and he hath blessed me with great contentment and patience. I am freely resigned up to the will of my God. As for my poor babes, I commit them to the Lord who gave me them. They have also two good fathers, who will take care of them, where I can leave them freely; only I desire thee, father, to take care of John's schooling and education, and get him apprentice to some good Friend at Bristol, or elsewhere, as thou seest fit. All my care I have cast upon God, and upon thee, my father and my husband; so that I am easy. Blessed be the Lord for this good and precious time, wherein I am freely devoted to his will, and right glad to leave this troublesome world, having the earnest of that eternal glorious redemption, through my blessed Lord and Saviour, Jesus Christ.'

Then calling her children one by one, charged them, saying, 'Fear God, dwell in love one with another, and be sure obey your father;' then blessing them particularly in the name of the Lord, and committing them all unto him. When she parted with her youngest babe, she kissed her, and said, 'They tell me that thou, poor lamb, wilt have the greatest loss of me; yet as I have cast all my care for you upon the Lord, I am easy, and leave you to his protection and divine providence, who gave you all to me, who never fails those that trust in him, being a tender Father, both to the fatherless and motherless children.'

To her eldest son John she farther added, 'I have been a tender mother to you, and now must leave you. Therefore, dear child, observe the counsel and advice of thy dying mother, write them down, and imprint them in thy mind. First, I charge thee to fear and remember God thy Creator in the days of thy youth. Refrain all evil company; be sober and attentive to all good counsel; let not thy mind go roving after foolish toys, and do nothing but what is good and commendable; and then thou wilt not need to make any excuse or lie; for a lying tongue is an abomination to the Lord. Read, and remember what wise Solomon saith will be the portion of such as despise or neglect the good counsel of father or mother, and thereby do evil in breaking God's command, to obey father and mother. Oh! dear child, consider of these things, and be wise: God Almighty bless thee, and you all, and preserve you out of all evil. This is the one great thing that I desire for you; not to be great in the world, which hurts many; but to be great in virtue and godliness, which has the promise both of this world, and that which is to come.'

Then she lay still some little time, desiring all might leave the room except Anna, her husband's eldest daughter, betwixt whom and her there had been a great endearedness and strong bond of love. After some time her father, Thomas Camm, coming into the room again, and hearing her and her daughter Anna in discourse, sat down out of her sight, and heard her say to Anna, that she left her as a mother to her motherless children; bidding her call to mind how she and her two younger sisters, by Providence, fell under her care when very young, and how she had faithfully discharged her trust in tender care over them; and she desired no better for hers than she had done for them, when they could not do for themselves. Anna then tenderly telling her mother, she hoped that they, viz., her children, should want nothing that was in her power to do for them, she being sensible of the strong obligation of duty she was under, and so they left things. After some time, she said,

'What a comfort and joy it is, to be so near the end of this troublesome world.'

She was always very glad of friends' company in visits and little meetings, which at several times were kept in her chamber, which, she said, were to her great refreshment; the last was the evening before she died; after which, she said, 'This is likely to be the last.' Next morning she said, 'This night, and a little part of next day will finish here.' That night she had very sharp pangs, hard for her father and others to hear; so that he left the room once or twice, but could not stay easily in or out; and an exercise or concern came upon his spirit, to pray to the Lord for her; and the Lord was pleased to hear the supplication that was put up; so that she had no more such sharp pangs, and finished her course here on the 15th of the Seventh month, 1707: and it is not doubted but she is at rest with the Lord.

She was decently interred in her husband's burying-place at Eldworth, on the 17th of the same month, being her birthday, and also her marriage day, and, had she lived to that day, her age would have been thirty-eight years.

The loss of her was greatly lamented, not only by her relations and nearest friends, but neighbours, both poor and rich, her loving, innocent, and wise conduct and deportment having gained her great respect amongst persons of all sorts that knew her. Oh! that many in observing and following her pious example, may be stirred up more and more to seek after virtue and godliness, and thereby purchase to themselves a good name, as she has done, through love and obedience to the Lord Jesus Christ, is the chief design in publishing these lines.

THOMAS CAMM, late of Camsgill, in the county of Westmoreland, was born in the year 1641, of honest, religious, and godly parents, was well educated, and from his childhood inclined to be religious, and sought after the best things. He delighted in the company of the best, or most religious sort of people; and in his tender years the Lord was pleased to visit him with the light of the day springing from on high, and thereby convinced him of his blessed and unchangeable truth; even in the morning of the day, to these latter ages of the world; and after some time called him forth into the work of the ministry, for which the Lord fitted him. Being thus visited and called of God, he counted nothing too near or dear to part with for truth's sake; but left all to follow the Lord, and with his whole strength and substance was given up to serve him, and faithfully to do the work he was called to. The Lord who had called him to such a great and glorious work, as preaching the everlasting gospel, did fitly qualify him for the same, pouring forth upon him of his holy spirit, and endued him with divine wisdom, whereby he was made an able preacher of the word of life to many, and could divide it aright, according to the states of the people.

As he was thus called and qualified, so he was diligent and laborious in the work of the Lord in many parts of this nation, and was made instrumental to convince and establish many in the way of truth. His doctrine was sound, and his delivery powerful; and though his testimony was not with the enticing words of men's wisdom, yet it was in the demonstration of that divine power, which reached the witness of God in the hearts of the hearers.

Great and many were the sufferings he met with, and he very patiently bore and went through them, of many sorts and kinds, as imprisonments, spoiling of goods, mockings and scoffings from those without, and suffering among false brethren. In all which he stood firm and faithful in his testimony for truth, approving himself a true follower of Jesus Christ, suffering joyfully for his name's sake, who had counted him worthy, not only to believe, but to suffer for him. As he was a man wonderfully endued with heavenly and divine wisdom, so he was a man of great humility, very much labouring for love and unity amongst brethren, and where any thing appeared tending to a breach of it, he always used his utmost endeavours to put a stop thereto, approving himself to be a man of peace, and always laboured for it, both in the church and also amongst all sorts of people.

He was a man beloved of God, and by all good men who knew him. He was a nursing father to many, encouraging every thing that was good in the least child; but very zealous against every appearance of evil; especially against that which in any wise tended to the laying waste of that testimony which the Lord required his people to bear, being zealously concerned to keep his testimony clear in every branch of it. He was a man well qualified for discipline, and laboured very much to promote it, for the encouragement of those who were weak, and to bring to judgment those that were loose, and would let their testimony fall. He was very zealous against that antichristian yoke of tithes, and though he suffered very much on that account, yet he stood faithful to the last, and rejoiced in his sufferings upon that and all other accounts for truth's sake.

Though in the latter part of his time he was attended with much bodily weakness, which through his many hard labours, travels, and sufferings, was come upon him, yet such was his zeal for truth, and love for the friends of it, that he was willing to spend his time and strength for and in the service of truth, which he faithfully performed, to the comfort and edification of the churches of Christ.

On the 17th of the Eleventh month, 1707, having been in the love of God to visit several meetings in the upper end of Lancashire, Westmoreland, and the west of Yorkshire, he returned to his son John Moore's, at Eldworth, and that very day it pleased the Lord, by a gentle hand (as he phrased it) to bring his old distemper upon him. After some few days it grew more violent and hard upon him; he bore it with much patience, and continued in a weakly distempered state of body for five or six weeks, taking very little natural food, nor getting much sleep or rest at nights; yet could walk up and down his chamber, and was always pretty cheerful, and freely resigned to the will of God, often saying, 'I neither desire to live nor to die, but am well content, however it shall please the Lord to order it;' farther saying, 'If the Lord see meet, or have yet any farther service for me to do, it is easy with him to raise me up again; but his will be done, I am very well content, I bless the Lord.'

Near the conclusion of his days, he said, 'I have great peace and satisfaction, in that I have done the will of God. I do not know that I have much more to do, the time of my departure seems to draw nigh; but I am well satisfied. I bless the Lord, I can say with the Apostle, "I have fought a good fight; I have finished my course; I have kept the faith, henceforth there is laid up for me a crown of righteousness, which the Lord, the righteous Judge, shall give me at that day, and not to me only, but to them also that love his appearing."

One day, he being alone in his chamber, his son John Moore came and sat down by him, and asked him how he did; he answered, 'I am but weakly of body, but strong in the inner man, blessed be the Lord, who hath been my support and strength hitherto.' He then farther said, 'I have been pondering in my mind, and meditating of the wonderful and unspeakable mercies and loving-kindnesses of God, to me extended all my life long, even to this very day; that I, such a poor, weak, feeble creature, should be enabled to hold out, and go through those many trials, travails, sufferings and exercises, both inward and outward, of various kinds, that have fallen to my lot. It has indeed been the Lord's doings, who is and has been all along my buckler and my shield, he shall have the praise and the glory of all, for he alone is worthy of it, for ever and for evermore.'

His distemper continuing, and his bodily strength growing weaker, so that there was little likelihood of his recovery, he gave very plain and distinct directions concerning his burial, as one not much concerned at his approaching departure.

Being grown so weak he could not well go alone, without some little support, one evening as he was walking over his chamber floor, leaning upon his son J. Moore's arm, his legs trembled under him, which he observing, said, 'Dear John, when the pillars of the house begin to tremble, there is feeble work. But then, blessed are they who, when this earthly tabernacle is ready to be dissolved, do assuredly know that they have a habitation eternal in the heavens, whose builder and maker the Lord is; of which, for my part, I bless the Lord I am well satisfied.'

About a week before he died, several of John Moore's children being in the room with him, he said to them, 'Now I think I must leave you. If the Lord had seen meet to spare me a little longer, I might have been of service to you in counsel and advice; but the Lord, the great and wise counsellor, as you have your eye to him above all things, will not be wanting to you in counsel. I love you entirely, and the blessing of the Almighty rest upon you, if it be his will.'

He several times spoke concerning Esau; one time he said, 'Esau's mount was in part consumed and consuming, yet there were branches still remained;' and said, 'The Lord lay it waste more and more.'

Another time he said, 'Faith and patience, hope and charity, are excellent virtues; the Lord, if it be his will, endue his children and people more and more therewith.'

When he was grown so very weak that the getting his clothes on and off was somewhat difficult and troublesome, he one time said to those about him, 'Dear children, you have a great deal of trouble and exercise about me, the Lord be your reward; but you shall see a little time will put an end to all these troubles, and a happy end it will be for me, I doubt it not at all.'

Another time, being some days before he died, John Moore's eldest daughter standing by him, he took her by the hand, and said, 'Dear Anna, the Lord will reward thee for thy care and pains about me.' Seeing her affected with sorrow, as well she might be for the approaching loss of so near and dear a friend, he farther added, 'Death will not be said nay; but it will be well with me, the enemy cannot touch me. The Lord who hath been with me, and hath borne up my spirit through and over all the various exercises and trials of my time; he will be with me to the end; there is no doubt of it.'

One time lying upon his bed, in a sweet and heavenly frame

of mind and spirit, he said, 'I have served the Lord in sincerity, with all my heart, and with all my soul, and with all my strength; hallelujah, hallelujah, hallelujah.' And so went on praising and magnifying the Lord, to the melting and tendering the hearts of all present. Afterwards he said to John Moore, and some others who were with him, 'Bear me record, I die in perfect unity with the brethren; my love is as firm and true as ever in our Lord Jesus Christ, the author of our salvation.'

When grown very weak, being asked how he did, he would say, 'Weak of body, but strong in the Lord;' saying also, 'In Abraham's bosom there is sweet repose.' He divers times spoke of the efficacy and virtue of the wine of the kingdom; and about two days before he died, he seemed to be faint, and J. Moore gave him a little wine to sup, thinking it might refresh him, but his stomach could not bear it. Then looking pretty cheerfully at J. Moore, he said, 'Dear John, thou seest these things will not do; but one cup of new wine in the heavenly kingdom, with my dear and blessed Lord and Saviour Jesus Christ, will make up all.'

His strength decaying very fast, he for the most part lay very still and quiet, as one waiting for his dissolution, not saying much, unless when spoken to, and then would answer very sensibly to what he was asked.

On the day he died, he was desirous to be helped out of his bed, but seeing how very weak he was, he was put off for some time; but he still urged it. J. Moore told him, he doubted he was so weak he could scarcely bear it without fainting; but those with him told him, they were willing to help him the best they could. To which he replied very cheerfully, 'That is enough: I hope the Lord, that has been my help in many straits and difficulties, will also now help me.' So his clothes were got ready, and by degrees got most of them on; but before they had quite done, he was likely to faint: so they sat him down on the bed-side, and supported him a little. After a while he somewhat revived, and looking about him, he saw J. Moore's youngest child, betwixt two and three years old,

34*

standing before him a little way off, and he beckoned with his hand, that she might come to him, and with a little help he set her upon his knees, and affectionately kissing and embracing her, he said, 'God Almighty bless thee. The God of Abraham, of Isaac, and of Jacob, bless thee, and make thee happy, if it be his will.' Then after a little time they got his clothes something better on, and set him in his chair, where he sat a pretty while; then growing weary, he desired to lie down upon his bed, which he did, and after a little time, he was perceived to weaken very fast. He lay still and quiet, not saying any thing that could be heard or perceived; but drawing his breath sometimes quicker and sometimes slower, yet without the least disturbance, or stoppage of phlegm. He continued so for the space of about six hours; then stretching himself forth upon his bed, he departed this life without sigh or groan, as one falling into a deep sleep, on the 13th day of the First month, 1707, betwixt the hours of eleven and twelve in the night, being aged sixty-six years, nine months, and ten days.

Thus, having fought the good fight, and finished his course well, he laid down his head in peace with the Lord, and is freed from all his sufferings, sorrows, and afflictions here, and entered no doubt into the kingdom of eternal glory, for ever to live, and magnify, and praise the great God, world without end. On the 15th of the same month, his body was removed from Eldworth in Yorkshire, where he died, to his late dwelling-house at Camsgill, in Westmoreland, and on the 16th of the same month was carried in a solemn manner to Friends' burying-place at Park-end, in Preston-Patrick, being about half a mile from Camsgill. It was accompanied thither by several hundreds of people, both of the neighbourhood, and also many friends out of divers of the adjacent counties, and was there interred in a decent, Christian manner, there being a general appearance of sorrow in those present for the loss of so good and serviceable a man.

The corpse being interred, all, or most that were there, drew into the meeting-house, and had a precious edifying season together, the powerful living presence of the Lord, in an eminent manner, overshadowing the assembly, to the tendering and affecting many hearts. Divers testimonies were then borne, to the sufficiency of that universal principle of divine light and grace, which is given to be a teacher and a leader to all mankind, and is become the teacher and the leader of all those who are willing to be taught and led by it. But it is, and will be, the condemnation of all those who are disobedient to, and rebel against it, whilst they continne in that state. Also divers testimonies were borne, concerning this our dear friend, deceased, as to his faithfulness, care, and labour of love in serving God's heritage; as also with respect to the many trials, travels, and deep exercises that he had faithfully gone through in his day and time, upon truth's account; all which he was enabled to perform and go through by the power and assistance of that divine grace, and holy spirit of God, which he still accounted his buckler and his shield, his bow and his battle-axe, and by and through which, he was what he was, and to which alone, and not to him as man, the praise and glory of all was attributed.

So friends having cleared themselves of what was upon their minds, the meeting broke up, and friends parted with hearts deeply affected, and filled with the love and goodness of God, which had been plentifully shed abroad amongst them that day; praises, honour, and glory over all, be given unto God, and to the Lamb, who sits with him upon the throne, who is worthy for ever, and for evermore. Amen.

RICHARD DAVIES, of Cloddiecochion, in Montgomeryshire, by trade a felt-maker, was convinced of the blessed truth about the year 1657, and became faithful unto the Lord, through the power of it, and thereby was made a minister of the word of life, and was concerned freely to preach the gospel of salvation. He was endued with spiritual gifts, and serviceable in the exercise thereof in the churches of Christ, both with respect to his sound doctrine and exemplary conversation, and diligence to serve the widow and fatherless, and was fervent in prayer. His last sickness was but short, for he was taken ill on the Sixth-day of the week, and died on the First-day of the next following. Some Friends of Dolobran meeting came to him, and they had a meeting with him in his bed-chamber, and he desired them to pray to the Lord, that he might have an easy passage, saying, 'The fervent prayer of the righteous the Lord will have a regard to.' But his pain continuing upon him, the next day, being the 22d of the First month, 1708, about the ninth hour in the morning, he departed this life, and had an easy passage, as it were in a sleep, having often said he must sleep his long sleep. His body, on the 25th of the same month, was accompanied by a considerable number of Friends and other people, to the burying-place near his own house at Cloddiecochion, and there decently interred, and no doubt but his soul is at rest with the Lord.

Aged seventy-three; a minister about forty-five years.

SARAH GODFRY, wife of Benjamin Godfry, of Chipin, near Buntingford, in the county of Hartford, daughter of George and Sarah Robins, of Sandon, in the said county, was one who loved truth in her young years, and with a tender heart did seek the Lord often, both in and out of meetings, and was very watchful over her words, lest she should offend the Lord, or give an evil example to others. She was obedient to her parents, and tender to her brethren and sisters, and would give them good advice. After she was married, and had children, she was concerned for them, and desired a meeting at her house, for the good of her neighbours, which was had; at the conclusion of which she spoke with a loud voice, and said, 'Ever blessed and praised be the name of the Lord for this blessed opportunity;' which much affected the people, knowing her great weakness.

She also expressed her willingness to die, and leave husband and children, to go to the Lord; and then she said, 'Blessed, praised, honoured, renowned, magnified, and glorified be thy name, for thou art worthy of all blessing, praise, glory, and honour, for thou art a merciful God.' After this manner she lay praising the Lord for some time. A neighbour coming in, who was not called a Quaker, seeing her in such a heavenly frame, spoke with tears, 'She will not leave her fellow behind her: she will reap the fruit of her doings, joy unspeakable, and full of glory. What a mercy,' adds the neighbour, 'it is, the Lord lays no more upon her than he gives her patience to bear.' She answered, 'The Lord is very good to me, what a great mercy it is, that I am so willing to die; what a comfort it is, over what it would be, if I was in great distress. I feel no condemnation.' She desired her mother to hold her hands as she sat in her chair, 'for,' said she, 'I think I am going, and I feel great peace.' Her mother seeing her in such a still, comfortable condition, sat a while very still, and after she said, 'Lord, Lord, receive my soul,' and so departed like a lamb, in about a quarter of an hour.

JOHN PETERS, of the parish of Minver, in the county of Cornwall, about the 26th year of his age, received the knowledge of the blessed truth, and joined in profession with the people called Quakers. Being zealous and faithful to the Lord, he bestowed upon him a gift, and called him into the ministry of the word of life, in which he was diligently exercised for many years, and laboured in the work of the gospel of Christ freely and faithfully to the end of his days. He was a good example in his life and conversation, and careful so to walk, that the ministry might not be blamed in any thing by him, being endued with the spirit of wisdom and understanding. He travelled much, not only in the county where he lived, but frequently in the south and western counties of England, and some parts of Wales; and as he was well known, he was well received by the faithful.

When he thought he was near expiring, he got himself raised

in his bed, and said, 'It is the Lord's great mercy, who in the midst of the pains and anguish that attend our bodies, gives us resignation of mind to his divine will. This may be soon spoken of; but it is sweet to come to the living experience of it, and God hath mercifully given me this resignation and quietness of mind, in which I have peace, notwithstanding the weakness and pains I lie under.'

Then observing some young people about his bed, he counselled them to keep low in the fear of the Lord, not to seek to themselves great things, nor to post after the riches of this world; though a moderate care, within the bounds of truth, was allowable. But he spoke against extending our desires that way, to the forgetting the work of religion, and the preparation for our latter end; 'For,' said he, 'a little, with God's blessing, will suffice.' He sweetly enlarged on the benefit of his blessing, and the difference between those who enjoyed it and those who were cursed, adding, 'In my young years I had a belief raised in me, that if I lived in the fear of God, neither I nor mine should ever want: and it hath been all along confirmed to me.' He said farther, 'My heart is full of the love of God, and the sting of death is taken away. It would indeed be sad, at such a season of languishing, to have a load of sin on the soul.'

Many other seasonable counsels he then gave, that are not noted. Another day he said to Friends present, 'We have cause to be thankful to God for making known to us his truth. I am evidently satisfied that the way the Lord hath brought us into, is the way of truth.' He spoke of the necessity of living in obedience to it, that it might be a cross to our wills and bridle to our tongues, and a stay to our minds. He also said, 'Wait for wisdom and direction from the Lord, to enable for such services as he requires;' saying that the strength of man's parts was not sufficient to do the Lord's work. He counselled that love might be the principal motive in all public concerns, and therein to rebuke, to exhort, and to counsel; and if, in those labours, we meet with cross and peevish spirited people, that care might be, not to suffer the same spirit to sway us;

but to overcome the evil with good, saying, 'I have nothing in appearance but death before me; but am well satisfied, however the Lord deals with me; for,' said he, 'I am sound in mind, through the Lord's mercy, and have abundance of ease. I am not afraid to die. The sting of death is taken away;' for which he praised the Lord. Some of his relations being desirous he should try another doctor, he said, 'Be quiet, be still; if the Lord see meet to lengthen my days, he can soon heal my malady; if otherwise, I am content; for,' adds he, 'it is no small comfort to me, that I did not hearken to the persuasions of some that would have me go from one doctor to another; my confidence is in him who is alone the physician of value. If the Lord hath any further work or service for me to do, he can heal me; if not, I have done with this world.'

When near his end, he said to his wife, as he had often before, 'Mourn not for me when I am gone. I am waiting for my change, desiring to be dissolved; death is not fearful, the sting is taken away.' He often cried to the Lord for a blessing on his son, whom God had left him of ten children, and said, 'I desired, before ever God gave me a child, they might rather be taken off in the innocency of their days, than live to dishonour him. So, in the fear and favour of God, he departed this life, the 11th of the Seventh month, 1708.

Aged about sixty-three; convinced about thirty-seven; and a minister about twenty-five years.

He was also a prisoner several years for his testimony against tithes, and for refusing to swear, in obedience to Christ's command.

His body was interred the 13th of the said Seventh month, in Friends' burying-ground at Minver, being attended thither by a numerous company of Friends, relations, and neighbours; and sundry testimonies were borne to the light, life, and virtue, wherewith God had beautified our friend, while he abode amongst us; as also to the necessity of holiness and obedience, that those who succeed him might come to die the death of the righteous, and that their latter end might be like unto his.

GEORGE NEWLAND, son of George and Susannah Newland, of the city of Dublin, clothier, was an orderly and dutiful child, and sought the Lord in his young and tender years. When he was drawn or persuaded by his schoolfellows to play, or be wild, he afterwards would be under such trouble in himself, that he would weep and mourn in the night season. When about ten years of age, he desired he might be sent into the country, and retire from his companions in the city. So in a while his parents sent him into England, and boarded him at Eleanor Haycock's, widow, near Sanky, and he went to school to Gilbert Thompson, at Sanky, in Lancashire.

About the age of eleven or twelve years, the Lord concerned him to give testimony to the truth, calling him into the ministry, in which he was faithful, and travelled in the work thereof, and in the exercise of that gift the Lord had bestowed upon him, in the provinces of Leinster, Ulster, and Munster, in Ireland. Being endued with a good understanding, he was not rash to utter words, without the help or motion of God's Spirit; so that his testimony and ministry were not only instructing but edifying; and being an innocent youth, was beloved of faithful friends because thereof, and his exemplary conversation, which was according to the holy doctrine of our Lord Jesus Christ.

Between the age of eighteen and nineteen years, he was visited with lingering sickness, and his mother asked him, after some time, whether he thought he should recover; to which he then answered, he did not know, but if it was the Lord's will, he had rather die than live; but said he durst not desire it, adding, although his time had been short in the world, he had gone through a great deal of exercise and trouble, that none knew but the Lord alone. Another time he said to his mother, 'I have felt more of the Lord's love to me since I was sick, in a wonderful manner, than ever before.' Again said, 'I strove to serve the Lord in my health, and now I reap the benefit of it. I can look forward, and that is a mercy.' Being frequently comforted in spirit, and filled with the love of God, he would say, 'Oh! if the earnest be so precious, what will the fullness be!' When weak in body, he was strengthened in spirit, and enlarged to praise and magnify the Lord; and he was opened to give good counsel and advice to his brother Isaac, taking him by the hand, kissing him, saying, 'I love thee dearly; be sure thou fear and serve the Lord, and be obedient to thy parents; for though thou be young and strong now, yet thou knowest not how few thy days may be. I speak to thee in love, remember my dying words when I am gone; and that it will be enough in a dying condition, to bear the pain and affliction of body, without having a troubled conscience;' and therefore encouraged him to well-doing.

Much was spoken by him to his sister Elizabeth, whom he called also, and kissed her, and tenderly desired her to love and fear the Lord, and be dutiful to her parents; and in like manner to his sister Lydia, saying, he hoped she would be an honest woman; and said, 'In my health, when I went to bed, I did meditate and think upon the Lord, and now in my sickness I find the benefit thereof.' Then tenderly acknowledging the love and care of his parents towards him, said, 'If I live, I can never make you amends for your trouble and care over me.' A few days before his death, he said unto his mother, 'I love thee dearly;' and saluting her, said, 'I hope the Lord will reward thee for all thy trouble and care over me, and I hope we shall meet shortly, where we shall never part again.' Some hours before his departure, being overcome with the goodness of God, he was enabled to praise and celebrate his name, saying with admiration, 'How good, Lord, art thou to me! I am not worthy of the least of thy mercies and favours;' and continued to praise the Lord in such manner, that all that were in the room were reached and affected, and broken by the power of God that attended him, during that season.

His uncle John coming to take leave of him, seeing him in this condition, yet near dying, said he would not leave him till he saw him in his grave; although he had intended before to go home to his dwelling that was in the country. He was tendered to see him in such a frame of mind; though not a frequenter of the meetings of those called Quakers, but said he was satisfied this youth was going to his heavenly rest. That night he was earnest with his mother to lie down and get some rest; but after a little while called for her again, and said, 'My dear mother, take it patiently, for thou mayest rejoice that I am going.' He desired all to be quiet and still; and sent several times to see what hour it was by the clock; and being sensible his change was near, settled his head to the pillow, and quietly departed this life, like an innocent lamb, on the 24th of the Eighth month, 1708, about the 2nd hour in the morning, and was buried the 26th of the same month, in Friends' burying-place, near Dolphin's Barn, being accompanied to the grave by many friends and neighbours.

Aged near nineteen, and a minister about six years.

This testimony was given by his friends in Dublin concerning him, which I thought meet here to insert.

'It pleased the Lord to favour this youth with a gracious visitation, even in his childhood, and so to prepare him for his service, whereunto he appointed him, that there appeared deep impression of a concerned mind, for the good and eternal well-being of his soul. As he grew in years, he apparently grew in grace, and in the knowledge of God, and his son the Lord Jesus Christ; so that the Lord was pleased to put him into the ministry. Although young, he being sensible of the appearance of the Son of God in his heart, did deliver his testimony with a good understanding, not being forward or rash to utter words; but waited for that which is the fountain of all true ministry, viz., The help of the Spirit of God, that enables God's ministers to speak to the edifying, and instructing, and building up of one another in the love of God. This being the concern of this innocent youth, made him to be beloved of faithful friends who knew him; and the more, because his conversation agreed with his doctrine.

'He went abroad sometimes to visit friends in this province of Leinster, and was also in Ulster and Munster provinces, and friends had generally a love and respect for him, and there would commonly be great meetings where he was, both friends and others admiring the Lord's dealings with him, in his tender years, being but twelve years old when his mouth was first opened in meetings, in a testimony for God. We have a great loss of him, he being such a good example to our youth, both in that, and also in his conversation; too few being willing to follow him in that true nearness of walking with God, as he did; but love liberty to the flesh and will, that works not the righteousness of God, but brings trouble and grief on those who are concerned for the well-being of their immortal souls; which this youth was careful to avoid. His behaviour was more like a man of gray hairs, than one not attained to nineteen years, being not desirous of long life in this world, as he used to express sometimes; but rather that he might do his day's work, being ready and prepared, when the Lord was pleased to call him hence, to have a portion and lot in God's kingdom, of that life and peace that are everlasting. When he was visited with the sickness of which he died, which continued on him about a quarter of a year, he bore it with much patience and resignation to the will of God, and very cheerfully; which was comfortable, both to his parents and friends who visited him in the time of his illness.

'Before his departure, he was concerned to advise and counsel his brother and sister to fear and love God, and be dutiful to their parents, &c. And though it is our loss, to have such an one taken from us, we believe it is his gain to be removed from where trouble and temptations attend, to where the wicked cease from troubling, and the weary are at rest.

'From our meeting in Dublin, the 19th of the Second month 1709.

'Signed in behalf of the said meeting, by

'Amos Strettell,
'Richard Sealey,
'George Rook.'

SAMUEL WATSON, of Night Stanford, in Yorkshire, was early convinced of the blessed truth, as professed by the people called Quakers, and being faithful to the Lord, was, by his divine power and spirit, fitted for the ministry of the word of life, and called by the grace of God to preach the gospel of peace, and to labour in the service of God, for the good of souls, for many years. The Lord was with him, and he was kept in a sweet sense and feeling of the life and power of truth to the end; though in his latter time he had a long season of bodily weakness. He would very often express, not only the goodness of God to him since the time of his first convincement, but also was frequent in giving religious advice to those who visited him, saying, 'Keep in the pure fear of God, it is as a fountain of life, and from thence all our comforts come. It is that which makes people honourable, both in their youth and old age!'

He died at Chester, and was buried there the 24th of the Ninth month, 1708. Aged about eighty-eight years.

JOHN BOULTON, late of Gaunt's-Ircot, in the parish of Aldmunsbury, in the county of Gloucester, was a faithful labourer, and true minister of the gospel, who travelled freely to preach the same, and had eminent service therein, as many can witness; for a divine power attended his ministry, and many hearts were tendered, and brought into true contrition, and to sit under his doctrine with delight, and were greatly comforted, refreshed, and edified. He was very serviceable in monthly and quarterly meetings, and zealous against the antichristian yoke of tithes, and esteemed it an honourable testimony; and his faith was, that none would ever prosper in the truth, who were unfaithful therein. He was of an innocent life, and exemplary conversation, of a peaceable spirit, and made it his concern to keep love, unity, and concord, and frequently exhorted thereunto; and was an elder who deserved double honour, as a nursing father in the church of Christ, and his memory is sweet and blessed.

In his last illness he often advised friends to be faithful to what the Lord had make known to them, while they had their health; and said, 'The Lord is good to me, it is well with me. The Lord is wonderfully good to me. Again, 'If the Lord's will is to take me out of this troublesome world, I am very well content. I am in love and peace with all men; all is well. I shall go but a little before you. I have made my peace with the Lord; his will be done by me, I am contented, it is well with me.'

These words he spoke a little before his death, and growing weak, he desired the Lord to make his passage out of this life easy. A Friend then taking leave of him, who was going to the quarterly-meeting, he said, 'The salutation of my dear love, in the Lord Jesus Christ, is to all Friends;' and about an hour after, he said, 'The Lord hath been wonderfully kind to me, in making my passage easy;' and a little time after, departed in much quietness, the 29th of the Ninth month, 1709, and was honourably buried at Hossel, being accompanied by many Friends and neighbours.

Aged sixty-one years.

MARGARET DIAMON, wife of Richard Diamon, of London, merchant, was daughter of captain John Groves, late of the parish of Bermondsey, in Surry, mariner, deceased, and religiously educated by her parents in the Christian religion, among the people called Quakers, in which she continued to her end. In the latter part of her time she was visited with much sickness, and great pain; yet retained her love to the Lord, his truth, and faithful people, and her faith and hope in God, as appeared by what she declared. She said to her husband one morning, 'Oh, my dear! I have had a very wearisome night, and no rest; I have been in a bewildered state; but the Lord I believe will satisfy my poor soul, it is that I now wait for.' After this she desired her husband to call all their children, which was done; to whom, when come, she said, 'Be careful to keep near the Lord, and in plainness; that it may not be said to you, "If your mother was alive, she would not suffer you to take this liberty."'

When she had given them this charge, and tender advice on her dying-bed, worthy to be remembered, and duly observed, she desired her husband to send to her relations, which he did. When they came, she in much love spoke to them; and, although the words were not noted down, it is hoped they will be remembered by them, and her dying counsel taken; which, when she had given, she, in much sweetness took her leave of them. And after, said to her husband, 'The Lord hath been very good to us, I desire we may walk worthy; for a little time will finish here, and I am contented in the Lord's will, and hope we shall meet together in heaven, my dear and tender husband.'

Another time she said, 'The Lord hath often comforted me, and made my bed a bed of ease to me;' and then added, 'I have been wrapped up too much in outward enjoyments, now I am out of them. I have desired the Lord to search me thoroughly, that nothing may remain in me that is displeasing to him. My great care and desire to the Lord hath been, that I may hold out to the end.' Her husband answered, 'The Lord hears thy unfeigned prayers;' she replied, 'If Daniel and Moses stood by me, and said it would be well with me, it would avail nothing, unless I have the witness in myself;' adding, 'He that hath been my support to this day, I do hope and believe will be with me to the end;' and then lay still. Afterward she said, 'Lord, I beseech thee, shorten this great work for thy mercy's sake, for thy dear Son my mediator's sake, if it be thy blessed will, and support me through the valley of the shadow of death, that my faith fail not; but that an eye of faith may be kept open to look to thee. Lord, thou that commandest the winds and the raging waves of the sea to be still, and they obey thee, art able to make this sick-bed a bed of ease. Lord, be with me, I beseech thee; and then no matter what becomes of this body, nor what I go through, for there will be an end to that. Lord, be with me this night, I beseech thee, for I am a poor, weak creature; therefore, O Lord, I beseech thee, support me, receive me into thy merciful arms, and lead me into the bride-chamber, where I may for ever rest with thee.'

Then she took her husband by the hand, and earnestly entreated his heart might be to the Lord, and said, 'Leave off the cares of this life, and seek the Lord above all.' Requesting all might be still, she lay down in a sweet state, desiring to be kept humble at Christ's feet.

The day before she was taken speechless, she told her husband her speech would be taken away, saying, 'For it is the twelfth hour, and the midnight cry, that the bridegroom is come;' and said, 'I am satisfied, my lamp is ready trimmed;' and farther said, 'Oh! Jacob's God, and Israel's king, thou art able to do all things, nothing is too hard for thee. Lord, grant that my passage may be quick and short, and rather that my tongue may cleave to the roof of my mouth, than I should speak one word to dishonour thee, Lord. Lord, thou knowest what a night of sorrow and exercise this hath been to me; but thou art able to do all things, for if thou speakest the word, it is done.' Then she said to her husband, 'Oh! have thy heart to the Lord for me, and speak to them thou knowest to be honest, good Friends, to have their hearts to the Lord for me.' She then spoke her last words, viz., 'Lord, Lord, Lord, thou art Jacob's God, and Israel's king; thou art a shadow of a mighty rock in a weary land;' adding, 'Oh! Sion, Sion, the city of saints' solemnity, beauty, the beauty of holiness.' Then spoke no more, and died some time after, in peace with God, it is not doubted, and is in his paradise. She was a virtuous woman, a good wife, a tender mother, and charitable.

She was born the 16th of the Twelfth month, 1658, and died the 1st of the Tenth month, 1708, aged about fifty years; and was decently buried from the meeting-house at Horslydown, and her corpse accompanied to the burying-ground belonging to the same, by her relations and Friends, who loved her, and lamented the loss of her.

JOHN TAYLOR was born at Sillath, in Abbey-holme, in the county of Cumberland, in the year 1654, of honest parents, who educated him with the foremost in that part where he lived.

In the year 1674, the twentieth of his age, he was convinced of the blessed truth, by the testimony of John Graves, and gladly received the same in the love of it, and so continued with the people of God, waiting upon the Lord in silence the space of three years. Then it pleased the Lord to open his mouth to bear a testimony to the blessed truth, in which he was very serviceable, both among friends and others at home, and abroad in Scotland also, where he travelled three or four times; and had good service in many parts of this nation. He bore a faithful testimony for the Lord; was sound in doctrine, and of a good understanding in discipline, whereby he became very serviceable in monthly and quarterly meetings. He was a sincere-hearted man, and his deportment and behaviour such, that he had an influence upon all sorts of people, for his good deportment and meek and quiet spirit. He met with many trials of divers sorts, and yet was preserved in a meek and even temper, and he suffered much upon the account of tithes, which he bore with great patience, and was never known to murmur.

In the year 1708, in the Fourth month, he was visited with sickness, and then he gave good advice to many who came to see him, both Friends and others. Being restored to a measure of health, he visited Friends in Yorkshire, where he had good service for the Lord, and returned in great peace. About a month after he was taken with the sickness, of which he died; and in the time of his sickness he was preserved in a sweet frame of spirit, and had the evidence that he should have a mansion in the Lord's house, saying, 'I feel the spirit of the Lord coming down upon me, to change me from mortality to immortality;' and desired the Lord would make his passage easy, and he had his desire.

Aged about fifty-four, convinced thirty-four, a minister about thirty-one years.

He died the 8th of the first month, 1709, and was buried at Abbey-holme, his corpse being accompanied by many friends and others.

WILLIAM ELLIS, of Airton, in Yorkshire, was born the 5th of the Eighth month, 1658, and convinced of the living and powerful truth in the Third month, 1676. Being called and qualified by the Lord to be a minister of the gospel of peace and salvation, he was faithful to his call, and laboured and travelled in the work of the ministry in England, and Ireland, also in Maryland, Virginia, Carolina, Pennsylvania, New England, and other parts of America. A few days before his departure, he said, speaking of his convincement, 'It was a glorious day to him. And he had large tokens, that the day of his death would be so likewise.' Many sweet and edifiying expressions dropped from him, in cheerfulness of mind, which showed how ready he was to embrace death.

He died on the 4th of the Fourth month, 1709. Aged nearly fifty-one years. Convinced of truth about thirty-three years. He was buried at Friends' burying-ground, at Airton, and a large meeting there was, which was eminently attended with the presence of the Lord, and several living testimonies were there borne, to the comfort and satisfaction of many.

WILLIAM BARCRAFT, late of Bally-Britton, in King's County, in the kingdom of Ireland, aged twenty-eight years, before his departure, was taken speechless in a violent fit, but his speech returning again, he expressed himself thus to his dear wife and mother-in-law, and friends present, (being in a heavenly frame of mind, and his pain seeming to them to be taken away,) 'I am exceedingly glad to see you. The Lord's love and mercy is exceedingly great, and this is beyond my expectation, that I have mercy of the Lord to speak to you. The presence of the Lord at such a time as this, makes afflictions easy to his people, and it is an advantage friends have in feeling and enjoying the presence of the Lord. I am easy to leave this world, in hopes of a glorious time to come, in the kingdom of eternal peace. He then desired his mother-in-law to remember his dear love to his father, brother, sister, relations, and friends, and that as they had bestowed their daughter on him, now he would bestow, or commend her, and his children to the Lord, and her tender parents; 'And to my uncle,' said he, 'whom I am sure hath been tender of me.' Then desiring his wife several times, to give him freely up to the Lord, that he might be easy, he said, 'Who knoweth, but there may be a service in my going now. I desire thee, (i. e. his wife,) bring up my children in the fear of the Lord, and in plainness of habit and speech, and in lowliness, and whether they have little or much, it will be well enough.' He further said to her, 'Trust thou in the Lord, and keep near to Friends, and it will be well with thee.'

His wife being in a tender or melted frame of heart, said, 'I do trust in the Lord, and give thee up to him;' which seemed to give him much satisfaction. He called his brother-in-law James to him, and warned him to be of a savoury life, and to love the fear of the Lord, and to be careful to keep out of pride and height, and out of bad company; and added, 'Be sure to walk low and humble, and be obedient to thy parents; for I never knew any disobedient to their parents do well. Be sure to tell thy brother Joseph to walk low and humble; and if ever he expects joy and comfort, to be obedient to his mother; for when I at any time grieved my mother, I was always troubled and sorry for it. And advise thy sister Martha, to have a care of that high city, (i. e. Dublin,) and be sure to keep low and humble;' saying, 'there was great danger in that city, for youth to be led away from the Lord; but if they served the Lord carefully, it would be well with them.'

He desired a friend who was present, to tell his brother Thomas, to be of a sober life and conversation amongst people, and to be a good example in the place where he lived, and in whatever he did he should have an eye to the Lord, and not to be high-minded, but low and humble. He said, 'From a child I always loved the company of good honest friends, for which I was always the better. Though I have had weary nights and days; yet through all, I had an eye to the Lord;' adding, 'It is a brave thing to have nothing to do but to die.' To his wife, he said, 'My dear, comfort thyself, in that it will be well with me.' And to his friends that stood by, 'How many precious heavenly meetings have we had; but it hath been a great trouble to me, to see how dull and sleepy some have been, and others unconcerned, both old and young, in such a glorious day as this is, where the Lord hath appeared so eminently amongst us. Many times of late, I thought I saw a more glorious day approaching than ever. Oh! is not this (speaking of the opportunity he had with his friends) a precious comfortable thing, to have this sweet opportunity: this is what my heart desired. I care not how many young people were here, I should be glad if all the meeting, and several others were here;' adding, 'I wish all the high and lofty ones would look back, and see what they were.'

All which being spoken in a good sense of the Lord's heavenly presence, did mightily tender Friends' hearts who stood by, and ended in prayer and thanksgiving to him who lives for ever and ever, Amen. He gave good ground of hope, that the Lord showed him mercy, and called him to glory and peace for ever. And when he took leave of friends, he said, 'I am very easy;' and departed the 5th of the Sixth month, 1709.

THOMAS BARCRAFT, brother to the aforesaid William Barcraft, was taken ill of the same distemper upon the 15th of the Eleventh month following. His uncle and aunt Barcraft sitting by him, and perceiving him to be under exercise of mind for peace with the Lord, his uncle inquired of him as to his condition, and he answered as followeth: 'Sometimes I think I shall recover, and other times I think I shall not. But my desire is, if I recover, to improve my time. I find most ease in submitting myself to the will of God. I never wronged any body knowingly, nor acted any gross thing; but that which is my great trouble, is, that I did not live so savoury a life and conversation as I should have done; but gave way to lightness that was hurtful to me, of which, if I live, I hope to warn others.' He said to his uncle and aunt, 'Whenever you reproved me for such things I was always glad of it, but did not take the notice of it that I now see I ought to have done. That which seemed but little to me then, now seems a great deal; but if I should live, and not improve my time, it is best for me to go now, for I am in hopes there is mercy for me.'

He departed this life the 18th of the Eleventh month, 1709, so that he lay sick but three days. Therefore it is needful for all to improve the present time; fear God, and live soberly, and to have their conversations coupled therewith, and to take heed to reproof; not give way to lightness, nor esteem that a little thing; for it behoves young men and women, and all, to be sober, and gird up the loins of their minds, and hope to the end.

OLIVER SANSOM, late of Abingdon, formerly of Farrington, in Berkshire, was convinced of the blessed truth of God in the year 1657, received it in the love thereof, and was faithful to it. The Lord having fitted him for his service, and endued him with wisdom, understanding, and sound judgment, was pleased to call him into the ministry, to preach and labour in the gospel of Christ and love of God for the good of souls; which he did freely in this nation and Ireland, and was a valiant sufferer for the truth, and the testimony thereof, against all swearing and tithes, and what the Lord raised him up in his power to testify against. When on his death-bed, a friend came in love to see him, who said, 'We who are young in years shall greatly miss thy company amongst us;' to which Oliver Sansom replied, 'By reason of my age, it is not likely I shall continue long with you; but be you faithful, as I have been, and you will have the same reward as I am likely to have. Be you followers of Christ, as you have had me for an example, for I have been true to what the Lord hath committed to my charge.'

He was released, and taken from all his troubles and exercises here below, and received by the Lord into his paradise the 23d of the Second month, 1710, and his body was honourably buried at Abingdon. Aged about seventy-four years.

SAMUEL WRIGHT, of Wellingborough, in Northamptonshire, a faithful and honest man whom the Lord called, qualified, commissioned, and sent freely forth to preach the gospel of life and salvation by Jesus Christ, was greatly beloved and very serviceable in the country where he lived, and adorned the doctrine of God our Saviour, by a conversation becoming the gospel, and was of a good repute amongst his neighbours.

Being visited by the Lord with bodily weakness, and being at a time somewhat better, he was below stairs, but after a while he went up, when his wife asked him if he was not spent; he said, 'I feel so much comfort, and so much of the goodness of the Lord, I am come up that thou mayest partake of the same with me;' and she said she in some measure did, though under exercise, because of his weakness. He said to her often, 'Do not trouble and grieve for me, for the Lord may raise me up still, if he sees it best; if not, be contented, and put thy trust in the Lord; he can make hard things easy. Is it not better to part from thy husband in this condition, wherein thou art satisfied it will be well with him, than if not?' His wife replied, 'It will be well with thee I am well satisfied, and that is the greatest comfort I have in parting from thee. But still my loss is the greater, to part with such a good husband, with whom, if the Lord saw good, it might be as well another time, or some years hence.' He answered, 'It must not be another time; the Lord's time is the best time. I should be glad to see thee in a mind to submit to the will of the Lord in all things; for it troubles me to see thee so sorrowful. It will not be thy case alone, although I know it will be hard for thee to bear. I would not have thee cast thyself down, for then thou wilt not be able to look after me, and I shall like no body so well.'

Another time some neighbours came to see him, with whom was a great professor. They asked him how he was; he answered he was troubled with pain of body, and sick besides. They replied, he had been sick a long time. He said he never thought the time long or tedious, he had so much of the enjoyment of the presence of the Lord, and felt so much comfort, that he never thought the time long, nor his afflictions tedious, saying he was as sensible as in a time of health, and his faith the same as it had been; and his mind was stayed upon the Lord, and his life was in his hand. He farther said he had not his work to do; declaring largely his great satisfaction how happy he should be in the world to come, saying he had a taste and earnest of it.

Another time, a Friend, with several others, visiting him, he was much concerned to exhort Friends to love one another, and to strengthen one another, saying, 'It is well known what labour of love, and travail of spirit, I have had amongst you for the service of truth.' He expressed the great love of God to his soul, saying, 'What can I desire more; I am fully satisfied eternal life will be my portion; and the comfort that I feel, outbalances my pain.' He returned praises to the Lord, and was freely resigned up to his will, saying there were but two things for which he could desire to live, and they were, for the sake of his family, and upon the service of truth. He then desired his dear wife not to be too much grieved, but to be freely resigned to the will of God, saying, if she had her eye to the Lord he would bless her. And said farther, 'The Lord who hath been and is, my comfort, will be thy comfort, and that is my consolation, and will be thy consolation, for thou hadst not thy eye to beauty; thou hadst not thy eye to riches;

but thy choice was for one that feared the Lord. Therefore I do believe the Lord had a blessing for thee.'

Being concerned for his dear wife, he added, 'Seeing the Lord provided a husband for thee, according to thy desire, canst not thou say with Job, "The Lord gives, and the Lord takes away, blessed be the name of the Lord." Remember what Job said to his wife, "Shall we receive good at the hand of God, and shall we not receive evil?" For, although the Lord gave thee a husband according to thy desire, thou art not willing to give him up into his hands; for it would be better for thee, and easier for me.' She answered, 'It is too hard for me to do at present; but the Lord can make hard things easy, if I could put my trust in him.' Then he said, 'Remember how it was with Jephtha, who had but one only daughter, and when he had made a vow, that if the Lord would give him victory over his enemies, whatsoever came first forth out of his house to meet him, should surely be the Lord's; and the first that came was his daughter; so he bid her remember the nobility of the damsel; when her father wept to see her, she said, "Father, if thou hast opened thy mouth unto the Lord, do to me according to that which proceeded out of thy mouth." 'And she gave up herself, and canst not thou give me up?'

Another time some came to see him, to whom he declared he had great satisfaction to die, saying, 'I feel the Lord to be with me, and what would the great men of the earth give, to feel the same peace with God, when they come to lie upon a dying-bed.' He uttered many more sweet exhortations to his wife and friends, to the tendering and affecting of the hearts of those there present; saying, 'If I find myself weaker in body, I should be glad to have Friends in general come and see me, to wait upon God together.'

Another time he said, 'In all the afflictions I ever met with, my mind was never so stayed as in this, my mind being so much out of the encumbering things of this world, that I do believe this affliction will be for my good;' with much more.

Another time he said he did not know but death might come of a sudden, but it would be no surprisal to him. 'I am both ready and willing to die;' or if it should please the Lord to restore him, he could be willing to live, for the sake of his family, or that he might be serviceable in the gospel, for the promotion of truth; but said, 'I have such satisfaction and full assurance of my future being, that my heart is often overcome with joy;' with much more.

At another time he said, 'Lord, thou visited me in my youth, when I was but young in years, and I was given up to serve thee; as was stripling David, when he went to battle against the uncircumcised Philistine; for he went in the name of the Lord.' He also spoke concerning the brazen serpent, how the wounded were to look thereto; and of Joseph's being a fruitful bough by a well, whose branches run over the wall; saying, the archers shot at him, but the bow of faith was too strong for them. Also he said, 'It will be well with me when I am gone to another world, though I have not death very much in my view. I have been as though I was at the brink of the grave, but the Lord hath been pleased to spare me a little longer.'

Another time, friends coming to see him after a meeting, one said to him, 'Thou hast had a long time of illness;' he replied, 'I do not think the time long, by reason I have felt so much of the goodness of the Lord to me.' He testified, saying, 'According to my strength, great hath been my labour, and travail in spirit, for the prosperity of Sion, and the welfare of Jerusalem, since I was exercised with affliction;' and so bowed down, and went to prayer.

Another time he said to several friends, 'I see the wonders of the Lord in the deep, and what I now enjoy of the goodness of God, is beyond what I can express. The Lord hath been always with me in my afflictions, and is still with me;' with many more sweet expressions, that are not noted.

One asking him at another time how he did, he said, 'I am poorly, but I think I shall not die at present or suddenly, but I have not my work to do.'

At another time, about an hour before his departure, being restless as he lay in bed, his mother said, 'My poor dear child;'

to which he answered, 'I am rich;' and so he departed this life, the 29th day of the Third month, 1710.

He was buried in Friends' burying-ground, and was accompanied thither by many friends and others, and divers good testimonies were then borne unto the truth.

CHRISTOPHER RICHARDSON, late of Burton, in Yorkshire, was born at Caperby, in the same county, of honest parents, and was religiously educated.

In the time of his weakness of body, which increased so much upon him, that his recovery was somewhat questioned, his wife speaking to him, asked him how it was with him? He answered, 'It is no light matter to be concerned about our soul's salvation;' but said, 'I feel hopes to spring.' Then taking his wife by the hand, he said, 'My dear, thou hast been a loving and obedient wife to me. I desire thee to keep in patience, the Lord will be a husband to thee, and he will provide for thee, he did take care for thee before thou hadst a husband. So he that thus helped thee through many troubles and deep exercises is the same that ever he was; he will be strength to thee in time of weakness. It was the Lord's providence that brought us together; and he hath many times honoured us with his presence; but whether we be separated now or not, the Lord's will be done, for we have had a comfortable time together, and I desire we may have a comfortable parting, and things may be made easy to thee.'

Then he spoke to his father, and said, 'This I have to say to thee, thou hast been dear and tender over me, and much concerned about me, and thy care hath been to bring me up in truth's way; the Lord will reward thee for it in another world.'

His father replied, 'Child, this I have to say for thee, thou hast been a dutiful child to me.' Then his son said to him again, 'Remember my dear love [or duty] to my tender mother, and desire her to keep in patience.'

Then to his brother John, he said, 'Keep in the fear of the Lord, let it be always before thee, and it will learn thee true wisdom. Love the teachings of the Lord Jesus Christ, and that which inwardly doth check and reprove for evil; hearken to that inward voice, which tells thee when thou art turning to the right hand, or to the left; for they that disobey the teachings of it, and will have none of its reproofs, a day of desolation will overtake them, before they be aware, and such will be ruined for ever.' Then taking a brother of his by the hand, he said, 'Farewell, I do wish thy eternal welfare, and desire thee to be faithful to what God hath made known to thee. I believe thou knowest enough, give up to the manifestation of the spirit of truth, and bring thy children up in the nurture of it.' The brother answered, 'We can do nothing of ourselves, without God Almighty's assistance;' his reply was, 'God hath extended a measure of his grace to every one to profit withal; so there will be no pleading of excuse. I desire thee to have a care of giving way to that which will draw thy mind away from the Lord, for if thou dost, thou wilt be undone for ever, as sure as I hold thee by the hand.'

He also declared he was willing to leave the world, and all that might be enjoyed in it, if it should please the Lord to take him away at that time, that he might leave a good savour behind him; signifying the troubles that are here, and the peace that is with the Lord, and his satisfaction he had in his own particular. One who was by, said, 'It is well it is so with thee; I am glad to hear such expressions from thee.' He then said to them about him, 'There are many, when they are brought low in sickness, begin to consider how they have spent their time, and see their lamps untrimmed, and want oil, like the foolish virgins, that are ready to say, Oh! that it would please the Lord to lengthen their days, so as to raise them up again; then they would be better prepared for their final change.'

Then he said, 'I see a portion in the kingdom of heaven, a place among the sanctified is better than a thousand worlds. So,' said he, 'let not the things of this world hinder you; for the cares of this life, and cumbering things, do but gender to bondage.'

Then he said, 'My dear love to all my brothers and sisters. I desire they may be careful to bring up their children in the nurture of truth.' Adding, 'Tell my sister Jane from me, that she be not unmindful of her first love; but that she bow to truth, and stand in the dominion of it, and learn humility, and prize truth above all.'

He then remembered his love to some particular friends; and added, 'My love is to all faithful Friends.' His wife asking him how it was with him, he said, 'I am very easy, the Lord's will be done:' then he ceased to speak any more for a while, till about three or four hours before he departed; and then he said, though with a very low voice, 'Seek Christ Jesus our Saviour;' these were the last words those present could remember. He was patient in his sickness, and freely resigned to the will of the Lord, and concerned in love to give advice, as aforesaid, and declare his sense and experienee of the Lord's goodness, and salvation by him; and no doubt is entered into that which, as he declared to his wife in the early part of his sickness, is better than outward rest, the paradise of God, or holy kingdom of eternal life and glory, where his soul will rest in peace for ever.

He departed this life the 7th of the Sixth month, 1706, and was buried the 9th, at Caperby, in Friends' burying-ground; being accompanied thither by many Friends and neighbours.

ELIZABETH HAYDOCK, daughter of Henry and Martha Haydock, was born at Warrington, in Lancashire, the 17th of the Sixth month, 1686. Her father died before she was two years old, and she was educated amongst the people of God called Quakers, by her mother, and was loving and obedient to her till death, and lived in love and peace with her brother and sister, and was very affectionate to them, never being known to jar or contend with them. She was of a kind and courteous behaviour to all, by which she gained abundance of love, both with great and small. Some time before her death, she laboured with her mother, for her consent that she might go and live with some honest Friend, to which her mother at last complied, and she went to her beloved uncle, Robert Haydock. But in a short time, being taken ill, she returned to her mother, and soon after she came home, said, 'I fully believe I must not recover, and I am content in the will of God.'

Her sickness continuing, her mother, brother and sister were desirous a doctor might be had, which was proposed to her, and she said, 'To make you easy, I am willing, but I believe he will do me no good, for I must not recover, I believe.' Her mother seeing she grew very weak, asked her how things were with her, as to her future state in the world to come; she, after some due deliberation, said, 'My dear mother, I am no ways afraid to die, for things are now well. I have a very easy mind upon all accounts, and towards every body. I find nothing stands in my way but thee, my tender mother. I fear it will be hard for thee; but be thou easy, for I am well; and if I live to old age, I can but be well. I am given up to die, or to live, as the Lord pleaseth, since I came to thee; but before I came, I had a hard time. The enemy would needs have persuaded me that there was little hope for me, and that I should not find peace, under which I wept, and laboured, none knowing my sorrow I was in, neither did I make it known to any till now. But I bless God I am now satisfied, and free from any fear, and believe all will be well, and I shall go to rest; for, dear mother, I see nothing but trouble in the world, and I do not desire to live in it; we must leave it.'

Though her weakness continued, and her pain was sharp, she was preserved still and quiet, and in abundance of patience, and was not heard to murmur in the least, but said, 'Lord afflict me how thou pleasest, so thou wilt but be pleased to give me patience and an easy passage at last.' Then she lay still some time, and after said to her mother, being then under a deep travail of spirit, because of her sore affliction, 'Let us pray to the Lord.' Soon after, her mother knelt down, and prayed to the Lord for her, and freely resigned her up to him, that his will might be done in and with her; after which she was pretty easy in herself, and said, 'Oh! dear mother, I once thought I never should have come to that experience I now have. I now know a stay to my mind, and silence to my own thoughts. I am at times quit of all thoughts of the things of this world.' Her mother being weeping by her, she said, 'Weep not, my tender mother, it is better for me to die, than to live;' her mother said, 'If it be the will of the Lord, I desire none of mine might die of such a lingering distemper, as now thou art under, thy pain is so great.' She replied, 'Do not desire so, for it is sad for youth to be quickly snapped away, and not have time to remember their latter end; it hath been good to me.'

About two weeks before she died, she took her bed, for the most of which time she uttered many sweet and sensible expressions. One time her mother withdrew from her into another room, yet in her hearing, and heard her say unto the Lord, 'All might, power and glory is with thee;' and continued pouring forth her spirit unto God, saying, 'Lord, I am ready. Oh! tarry not sweet Lord. Oh! deliverance, deliverance, I cry to thee for. Oh! God, deliver my soul. I feel nothing to hinder; but, oh! Lord, if any thing be in my way, remove it, oh! my God.' Afterward said to her mother, 'I fear thou holdest me, oh! do not so; neither weep for me, for my tears are dried up. I feel no cause for any; neither mourn for me, for I shall go to rest. I had rather be with Almighty God, than enjoy all this world, it is nothing to me.'

At another time, when her mother and relations thought her near going, recovering a little strength, she kissed her mother, father, brother, and sisters, and said, 'Lord Jesus, receive my spirit. I am ready, tarry not, but deliver me out of my pain.' Her mother said, 'The Lord is supplicated for thee, and thy deliverance draws near, I do believe, and thy time will not be long; my spirit is earnest with thine, that he may ease thee; but it is the Lord, he must do what he pleaseth; breathe thou to him, my dear child, for patience.' She replied, 'Poor Job had it, and the Lord hath given it me all along, and I hope he will give it me still.' She desired that her ever dear friend, Benjamin Bangs, might be sent for; and he was, and came. After he had been some time with her, she fixed her eyes upon him steadfastly, and said, 'My pain is very great, pray thou to the Lord for me;' and was very still a while, in which time the spirit of prayer from God came upon him, and he prayed both powerfully and with much fervency of spirit to the Almighty for her, that it might please him to ease her of her pain. And the Lord was entreated for her, and in a little time her pain was wholly taken away; and she said, 'I bless the Lord, I am easy, both in body and mind. I have nothing to do, but wait the Lord's time.'

That night she had some rest, and lay very still, and free from pain; and in the night said to her mother, 'My dear love is with thee. I love thee above all the world; and my love to all my dear relations, I shall see them no more, and to my weak aunt at Penketh, who was kind to me when I was there.' Next day she said to her mother, with a cheerful countenance, 'Dear mother, I have now done, four or twelve of the clock, I think I shall not pass that time. Be thou easy and content, or else thy time will be but short. There is nothing in all this world hath been so dear to me as thou; but I hope thou canst not desire my stay.' Her mother asked her if she was sensible of her coldness; she replied, 'Yea, and of my sweating too, and if it is death's sweat, it is welcome to me. Let it be so to thee, dear mother. The Lord Jesus is my Saviour, I can embrace death with open arms, it is welcome, I fear nothing. I have sometimes heard thee, and some other Friends say in meetings, that the dead, though ever so lovely when alive, were in no wise pleasant to the living, when dead. I am partly dead, and must be buried out of thy sight. The Lord be with our spirits, and bless you all.' She went away like a lamb, innocently, the 8th of the Sixth month, 1710, and was buried the 13th of the same, being attended to her grave by many Friends and others. Aged twenty-four years wanting eight days.

JOHN BANKS was born in the year 1637, in Sunderland, in the parish of Issell, in the county of Cumberland, of honest parents, his father a fell-monger and glove-maker. At sixteen years of age, he was, by the great power and pure spirit of God, and the revelation thereof, in and through the Lord Jesus Christ, in his heart, brought to the knowledge of God, and the way of his blessed truth, before ever he heard any one called Quaker preach; and in himself was directed to go to the meeting of the said people, it being shown him, and signified to him they were the Lord's people. So he went the next First-day to a meeting of the aforesaid people at Pardshaw, where very few words were spoken; but a paper was therein read, which was suitable to his condition; and through waiting diligently in the light of Christ, and keeping to the power of God, he came to experience the work thereof, and freedom from bondage, through faithfulness to the Lord.

In the year 1663, being qualified by the Lord, he was drawn in his spirit to visit some neighbouring counties, and laboured in the work of the ministry.

In the year 1668, being farther grown in the truth, he was made willing to forsake all, to answer the Lord's requirings, and he travelled into the south and west of England in the Lord's service. After that, from year to year he laboured zealously to preach the gospel of peace, not only in England, but Scotland and Ireland; he crossed the sea twelve times, and often with great difficulty and danger of life by sea, in great tempests and storms, and by robbers on land. He was made instrumental to turn many by his zealous labours in the gospel of God, to righteousness, who remain witnesses of the same, and seals of his ministry. He had much suffering by loss of goods, imprisonment, and hardships therein; which he was enabled to go through, for the Lord was with him, and supported him, and blessed his labours; so that many, both men and women, were convinced and confirmed in the truth by him, and became faithful and able ministers, and so continued until death, and others yet remain.

In the year 1696 he married his second wife at Glastonbury

in Somersetshire, settled at Mear, until about two years before his death he removed to Street, in the said county.

He likewise was concerned, in the love of God, a month or two before his death, notwithstanding his age and weakness, to visit Friends at divers of their meetings, and had comfortable seasons with them, both at their meetings of public worship, and at their monthly meetings, held to take care of the poor and fatherless children and widows; for he was zealous for good order and Christian discipline in the church, and that those things that were honest, just, pure, and of good report, and that had any praise in them, should be followed. Indeed, it was admirable to those who knew him, and the weak condition he was in, how in his last journey at Somerton, he was in the meeting, which was very large, enabled to preach nearly an hour and a half, and bore a sound testimony to truth, and against outside shows, that wanted substance, with much presence of mind, and with good distinction in his doctrine; the which gave demonstration, not only of the strength of his memory and quick understanding, but sound judgment in things spiritual. His preaching was comfortable, refreshing, and edifying to the meeting; and he earnestly pressed Friends to be faithful to the small appearance of truth, encouraging such as were weak, on whom Amalek chooseth to vent his malice, to a holy zeal.

After meeting, it was sufficient task for two men to lead him to his quarters, though he was very cheerful, and signified his great satisfaction in his service and travail, and next went to Friends' meeting at Puddimore, and after to a meeting at Yeovill, where many Friends were. In his public service there, he was very lively and quick in discerning the states of several, and afterward returned home, where, in the Seventh month, 1710, he was taken with great pain in his back; yet he often said, 'Though my pain is great, my soul doth magnify the Lord for his goodness towards me;' adding, 'He hath provided a good place for me in heaven.'

On the 22d of the Seventh month 1710, several Friends

being present, after some time of waiting in silence upon the Lord, he said these words, or to this effect:

'Dear friends, I counsel you in the love and fear of God, to keep your meetings for the worship and service of God, both First-days and week-days, (mind that), and also monthly and quarterly meetings, which were set up by the power of God, to keep things in good order amongst us.' Farther he said, 'My love hath been so great to Friends at Glastonbury and Street, that I have ventured my life in riding through deep waters to visit them, when I have had a concern from God upon my mind: so that you can say, I have been a good example to you in keeping to meetings, as well as in other things.'

Then he said, 'Although I am weak in body, and do not know whether I may live much longer or not, yet I do not see death at present. However, I am strong in the Lord, and in the power of his might, and have nothing to do but to die, for I am rich in faith and good works towards God, and my cup is full of the love of God. Whether I live or die, it will be well with my soul; for, blessed be the Lord, I can say, with the wise and holy Apostle Paul, that I have fought a good fight, I have kept the faith, henceforth there is laid up for me a crown of righteousness. And did the apostle say for himself only? no, he was wiser than so, but to all them that love his appearing.'

Some Friends of Somerton taking their leave of him, he said to them, 'Give my dear love to Friends at Somerton, and tell them that my soul is alive unto God.' To a young man of that place, lately convinced, dear John Banks said, 'Art thou the young man that lives at Somerton, lately convinced of the blessed truth?' he answered, Yes. 'The Lord,' said John Banks, 'be with thee; and I desire thee, in his love, to give up in obedience to the working of the spirit of God in thy heart, and then he will do great and glorious things for thee. And do not thou stumble at the cross; for the more thou lookest at it, and puttest it off, the harder it will be for thee to take it up.'

To another Friend, when he took him by the hand at parting, he said, 'My dear love to thee, and all that are faithful unto God.'

To another that bade him farewell, he answered, 'I do fare well in the Lord; my love is to thee, and all the faithful in Christ;' adding, 'Joseph is yet alive, and that is enough.' Then he earnestly desired Friends to keep in the unity of the spirit, which is the bond of peace.

A great deal more good advice, in the living and eternal power of the great eternal God that attended him, he gave, which is not noted; but at the delivery thereof, the hearts of many were tendered, and tears ran down from their eyes.

On the 24th of the Seventh month, a Friend, visiting him, asked him how it was with him; he answered, 'Very sick, and full of pain in my feet and legs, thighs and bowels; but the Lord helps me, else I should cry out aloud; truth helps me, and ever hath, since I believed in it.'

The day he died, being the 6th of the Eighth month, 1710, and Sixth day of the week, he said to a Friend, 'It is well with me, and I have nothing to do but to die;' and said, 'I shall end in truth as I began.' So had an easy passage hence, and after all his labours, sufferings, and travels, is entered into rest; and there is no doubt of his portion in the everlasting kingdom of eternal glory for ever, to sound forth praises and hallelujahs unto the Lord God, and the Lamb that sits upon the throne, who is worthy.

He was honourably buried in Friends' burying-ground at Street, in Somersetshire, the 12th of the Eighth month, 1710.

Aged seventy-three, convinced fifty-seven, and a minister forty-seven years.

END OF THE FIRST VOLUME.

www.ingramcontent.com/pod-product-compliance
Lightning Source LLC
LaVergne TN
LVHW021138110826
845150LV00005B/1063

* 9 7 8 1 4 2 5 5 4 9 0 9 1 *